MUSEUM OF ART

BRIGHAM YOUNG UNIVERSITY

M. SETH AND MAURINE D. HORNE CENTER

FOR THE STUDY OF ART

SCHOLARLY SERIES

ETRUSCAN
ITALY

ETRUSCAN ITALY

*Etruscan Influences on the Civilizations of Italy
from Antiquity to the Modern Era*

Edited by John F. Hall

MUSEUM OF ART — BRIGHAM YOU

TITLE PAGE: Sarcofago degli sposi ("Sarcophagus of the Married Couple"), terracotta, Banditaccia Cemetery, Cerveteri, late sixth century B.C., Rome, Museo di Villa Giulia. *Photo courtesy of Soprintendenza archeologica per l'Etruria meridionale.*

Brigham Young University and Museum of Art, Provo, Utah 84602
©1996 by Brigham Young University. All rights reserved.

LIBRARY OF CONGRESS CATALOGING-IN-PUBLICATION DATA

Etruscan Italy : Etruscan influences on the civilizations of Italy from antiquity to the modern era / edited by John F. Hall.
    p.   cm.   — (M. Seth and Maurine D. Horne Center for the Study of Art scholarly series)
    Includes bibliographical references and index.
    ISBN 0-8425-2334-0
    1. Etruscans. 2. Italy—Civilization—Etruscan influences.
I. Hall, John Franklin. II. Series.
DG223.3.E88 1995
945—dc20   96-4500
                                                                CIP

PRINTED IN THE UNITED STATES OF AMERICA.

Contents

The Mausoleum of Augustus: Etruscan and Other Influences

Tyrrhena Regum Progenies: Etruscan Literary Figures

Quia Ister Tusco Verbo Ludio Vocabatur: The Etruscan

Contribution to the Development of Roman Theater

POST-ROMAN ITALY

List of Abbreviations

BPI	Bollettino di paletnologia italiana
ClAnt	Classical Antiquity
CPh	Classical Philology
CQ	Classical Quarterly
DArch	Dialoghi di archeologia
EClás	Estudios clásicos: Organ de la Sociedad española de estudios clásicos
EMC	Echos du monde classique (Classical Views)
GMusJ	The J. Paul Getty Museum Journal
Gymnasium	Gymnasium: Zeitschrift für Kultur der Antike und humanistiche Bildung
HASB	Hefte des Archäologischen Seminars der Universität Bern
Historia	Historia: Revue d'histoire ancienne
HSCP	Harvard Studies in Classical Philology
IL	L'Information littéraire
JHS	Journal of Hellenic Studies
JRGZ	Jahrbuch des Römisch-Germanisch Zentralmuseums
JRGZ (M)	Jahrbuch des Römisch-Germanisch Zentralmuseums (Mainz)
JRS	Journal of Roman Studies
Klio	Klio: Beiträge zur alten Geschichte
Latomus	Latomus: Revue d'études latines
MDAI(A)	Mitteilungen des Deutschen Archäologischen Instituts, Athenische Abteilung
MDAI(R)	Mitteilungen des Deutschen Archäologischen Instituts, Römische Abteilung
MH	Museum Helveticum: Revue suisse pour l'étude de l'antiquité classique
MMAI	Monuments et mémoires publiés par l'Académie des inscriptions et belles-lettres (Fondation Piot)
MonAL	Monumenti antichi: Pubblicati dall'Accademia dei Lincei
NSA	Notizie degli scavi di antichità
OAth	Opuscula Atheniensia: Acta Instituti Atheniensi Regni Sueciae

ORom	*Opuscula Romana: Acta Instituti Romani Regni Sueciae*
Padusa	*Padusa: Bollettino del Centro polesano di storici archeologici ed etnografici (Rovigno)*
PBSR	*Papers of the British School at Rome*
Phoenix	*The Phoenix: The Journal of the Classical Association of Canada*
PP	*La parola del passato: Rivisti di studi antichi*
PPS	*Proceedings of the Prehistoric Society*
RA	*Revue archéologique*
RhM	*Rheinisches Museum*
RHR	*Revue de l'histoire des religions*
RIL	*Rendiconti dell'Istituto Lombardo: Classe di lettere, scienze morali, e storiche*
RPAA	*Rendiconti della Pontificia accademia romana di archeologia*
RSA	*Rivista storica dell'antichità*
RSP	*Rivista di studi pompeiani*
SE	*Studi etruschi*
SMSR	*Studi e materiali di storia delle religioni*
StudRom	*Studi romani: Rivista bimestrale dell'Istituto di studi romani*
TAPhA	*Transactions and Proceedings of the American Philological Association*

STANDARD REFERENCE WORKS

ABV	J. D. Beazley, *Attic Black-figure Vase-painters* (Oxford, 1956)
ANRW	W. Haase and H. Temporini, eds., *Aufstieg und Niedergang der römischen Welt: Geschichte und Kultur Roms im Spiegel der neueren Forschung*, 2 vols. in numerous parts to date (Berlin, 1972–)
ARV²	J. D. Beazley, *Attic Red-figure Vase-painters*, 2d ed. (Oxford, 1963)

CIE	C. Pauli et al., eds., *Corpus Inscriptionum Etruscarum*, 2 vols. (vol. 1: Leipzig, 1893–1902; vol. 2: Leipzig, 1936)
CII	A. Fabretti et al., eds., *Corpus Inscriptionum Italicarum* . . . (Turin, 1867)
CIL	Th. Mommsen et al., eds., *Corpus Inscriptionum Latinarum*, 17 vols. in numerous parts to date (Berlin, 1863–)
CSE	*Corpus Speculorum Etruscorum*, 17 vols. to date, with varying editors and places and dates of publication
CVA	*Corpus Vasorum Antiquorum*, numerous fascicles to date, with varying editors and places and dates of publication
ES	E. Gerhard, *Etruskiche Spiegel*, 4 vols. (Berlin, 1840–67)
ES 5	A. Klügemann and G. Körte, *Etruskiche Spiegel*, vol. 5 (Berlin, 1897)
FGrHist	F. Jacoby, *Die Fragmente der griechischen Historiker*, 3 vols. (vols. 1 and 2: Berlin, 1923–30; vol. 3: Leiden, Neth., 1940–58; reprint of all vols., Leiden, Neth., 1954–)
InscrIt	A. Degrassi, ed., *Inscriptiones Italiae*, vol. 13, fasc. 1–2 (Rome, 1947, 1963)
ILLRP	A. Degrassi, ed., *Inscriptiones Latinae Liberae Rei Publicae*, 2 vols. (vol. 1, 2d ed.: Florence, 1965; vol. 2: Florence, 1963)
ILS	H. Dessau, ed., *Inscriptiones Latinae Selectae*, 3 vols. (Berlin, 1892–1916)
LE	W. Schulze, *Zur Geschichte lateinischer Eigennamen*, Abhandlungen der Kgl. Gesellschaft der Wissenschaften zu Göttingen, Philologisch-Historische Klasse v (Berlin, 1904)
LEW³	A. Walde and J. B. Hoffman, *Lateinisches Etymologisches Wörterbuch*, 3d ed. (Heidelberg, 1954)

LIMC	H. C. Ackermann and J.-R. Gisler, eds., *Lexicon Iconographicum Mythologiae Classicae*, 7 vols. to date (Zürich, 1981–)
MRR	T. R. S. Broughton, *The Magistrates of the Roman Republic*, 2 vols. (1951; reprint, Cleveland, Ohio, 1968)
OCD	N. G. L. Hammond and H. H. Scullard, eds., *Oxford Classical Dictionary*, 2d ed. (Oxford, 1970)
OLD	P. G. W. Glare, ed., *Oxford Latin Dictionary* (Oxford, 1982)
ORF⁴	H. Malcovati, ed., *Oratorum Romanorum Fragmenta Liberae Rei Publicae*, 4th ed., 2 vols. (Turin, 1976–79)
PIR	E. Klebs, H. Dessau, and P. de Rohden, *Prosopographia Imperii Romani, Saec. I, II, III*, 3 vols. (Berlin, 1897–98)
PIR²	E. Groag and A. Stein, *Prosopographia Imperii Romani, Saec. I, II, III*, 2d ed., 5 vols. to date (Berlin, 1923–)
PLRE	A. H. M. Jones, J. R. Martindale, and J. Morris, *The Prosopography of the Later Roman Empire*, 3 vols. (Cambridge, 1971)
RE	G. Wissowa et al., eds., *Paulys Realencyclopädie der classischen Altertumswissenschaft, Neue Bearbeitung*, 2 series of 23 and 10 vols. respectively plus 15 vols. of supplement to date (Stuttgart and Munich, 1893–)
Roman Papers	R. Syme, *Roman Papers*, ed. E. Badian and A. R. Birley, 5 vols. (Oxford, 1979–88)
RRC	M. H. Crawford, *Roman Republican Coinage* (Cambridge, 1974)
TLE	M. Pallottino, *Testimonia Linguae Etruscae* (Florence, 1954)

Preface

During the past decade a slow but steady increase of interest in the Etruscans has occurred among American classicists and archaeologists. A better understanding of many of the past findings of Etruscan studies, as well as important new discoveries and their prompt dissemination, may—at least in part—account for this growing recognition that Etruscan civilization, both in and of itself and as the cultural predecessor of Rome, demands greater attention. Fortunately, works are available for classicists who wish to expand their familiarity with the Etruscans. Among those L. Bonfante suggests in the preface of the collaborative work *Etruscan Life and Afterlife*—itself an important contribution to the field—are two that seem to me particularly important: M. Pallottino's *The Etruscans*, edited in English by D. Ridgway, and O. Brendel's *Etruscan Art*. For the student of early Rome, R. M. Ogilvie's *Early Rome and the Etruscans* and A. Alföldi's *Early Rome and the Latins* effectively highlight Etruscan involvement in archaic Rome and the borrowings of Roman culture and society from Etruscan antecedents. And in the midst of this revival of scholarly attention came the 1992–94 Vatican Etruscan exhibit in the United States, which has heightened the interest of professional and layman alike in matters Etruscan.

When Brigham Young University concluded an arrangement with the Vatican to engage the traveling exhibition "The Etruscans: Legacy of a Lost Civilization" as the inaugural exhibit of its new Museum of Art, plans for the six months of activities associated with the exhibition gave high priority to the organization of a scholarly symposium. The theme of the symposium was announced as Etruscan Italy, and an invitation was issued for papers which pertained to Etruscan civilization

FIGURE 1. *L'arringatore* ("The Orator"), bronze, poss. Sanguineto, ca. 90–50 B.C., Florence, Museo Archeologico. *Photo courtesy of Museo Archeologico.*

and, in particular, to the influence of Etruscans on the civilizations of Italy. The symposium was much enjoyed by participants from throughout the United States and Canada, as well as the Brigham Young University community, and funding was obtained from the university and museum to permit the publication of a number of the papers presented at it, resulting in the present offering. *Etruscan Italy: Etruscan Influences on the Civilizations of Italy from Antiquity to the Modern Era* constitutes the first in a series of publications which will be issued by the Museum of Art in conjunction with those major exhibits which include academic symposia.

The volume is structured in loose chronological fashion, with groupings of papers that pertain to aspects of Etruscan culture and influence in the pre-Roman, Roman, and post-Roman periods of Italy. Although some revision of the original presentations has occurred in preparing the papers for publication, a few of them retain by design certain elements of the oral format. In particular, Robert E. A. Palmer's "Locket Gold, Lizard Green," one of the keynote presentations of the symposium and BYU's 1994 J. Reuben Clark III Lecture in Classics and the Classical Tradition, was so thoroughly enjoyed by participants that Professor Palmer acceded to requests that it be published as delivered, preserving the flavor of the oral presentation.

The intent has been to prepare an anthology which would be directed not only to a scholarly audience of Etruscologists, classicists, classical archaeologists, and art historians, but also to students, both graduate and undergraduate. For the purpose of widest reader understanding, two appendices have been included, one a chronological table and the other a list of technical terms.

Regarding editorial preparation, since the volume includes articles from separate, if related, disciplines, the volume accords in most matters with *The Chicago Manual of Style* rather than following the style requirements of any single discipline, with a few exceptions to accommodate disciplinary expectation. In matters of abbreviation, primary sources are cited consistent with the abbreviation format of the *Oxford Latin Dictionary* and the *Greek-English Lexicon* of Liddell, Scott, Jones, and McKenzie. Abbreviations not appearing in these works are entered in the style of *The Oxford Classical Dictionary.* Modern works are cited in full, either in the endnotes or in the volume's list of abbreviations. Titles of periodicals, also included in the list, are abbreviated according to the form standardized in *L'Année philologique*. Finally, foreign titles have been capitalized according to the formats customary in the respective languages. In the case of Latin, titles have consistently been capitalized according to principles of English customarily employed in the United States.

It remains to thank those individuals without whose assistance this volume could not have been issued. Dr. James Mason, director of Brigham Young University's Museum of Art, and Virgie Day, associate director, helped to sponsor the symposium and to supply funding for the publication of the volume. Associate Academic Vice President J. Bevan Ott approved the project and secured further funding to make publication possible. Special acknowledgment is due Elizabeth W. Watkins, associate editor of Scholarly Publications, whose untiring efforts in editing the submissions of contributors and whose patience in learning the conventions of an unconventional discipline have made possible the preparation of the volume. Similarly, thanks must be rendered to Howard A. Christy and Jennifer S. Harrison, also of the university's office of Scholarly Publications, for their efforts in behalf of the volume and for the sharing of their considerable editorial skills. The design and typographic talents of Bruce Patrick and Jonathan Saltzman have made this volume highly readable and pleasing to the eye. The work of research assistants Sally Turner Johnson, Emily Sewell, and Trevor Luke was most helpful in preparation of the bibliography. Holly Wettstein has assisted immeasurably in many different ways in the success of the venture. I also acknowledge the cooperation and accommodating efforts of all the contributing scholars. Finally, I cannot omit an expression of appreciation to Pam, John, James, and Jefferson, who patiently bore the distraction of a husband and father whose time for almost three years has been hopelessly diverted by the planning, transpirance, and aftermath of the Etruscans' visit to Utah.

—John F. Hall
Provo, Utah
June 1995

ETRUSCAN
ITALY

ETRURIA

MARE ADRIATICUM

MARE TYRRHENUM

[FELSINA, FELSNA]
BONONIA
(Bologna)

[RAVENA]
RAVENNA
(Ravenna)

MARZABOTTO
(Marzabotto)

VIA AEMILIA

F. Rhenus (Reno)

A P E N N I N I   M O N T E S

[ARIMNA]
ARIMINUM
(Rimini)

LUCA
(Lucca)

[VISUL]
FAESULAE
(Fiesole)

(Quinto
Fiorentino)

FLORENTIA
(Firenze, Florence)

PISAE
(Pisa)

F. Arnus (Arno)

(Cetamura)   (Gaiole-in-Chianti)

ARRETIUM
(Arezzo)

(Castellina)

[VELATHRI, VELAURI]
VOLATERRAE
(Volterra)

[SAENA]
SAENA
(Siena)

[CURTUN]
CORTONA
(Cortona)

F. Chiana

F. Tevere (Tiber)

IGUVIUM

MURLO
POGGIO CIVITATE

F. Umbro (Ombrone)

SANGUINETO
(Sanguineto)

L. Trasimenus
(Trasimeno)

FUFLUNA
POPULONIA
(Populonia)

VIA AURELIA

CLEVSIN
CLUSIUM
(Chiusi)

[PHERSNA, PERUSNA]
PERUSIA
(Perugia)

VETLUNA
VETULONIA
(Vetulonia)

L. Prilius

VIA CASSIA

VIA CASSIA

RUSELLAE
(Roselle)

F. Fiora

ORVIETO
(Orvieto)

F. Albinia (Albegna)

L. Volsiniensis
(di Bolsena)

[VELSNA, VELZNA]
VOLSINII
(Bolsena)

ACQUAROSSA
FERENTUM, FERENTIUM

ORBATELLO
(Orbatello)

TUSCANIA
(Tuscania)

[SURINA]
SURRINA
(Viterbo)

CUSA
COSA
(Cosa)

[VELECHA]
VULCI
(Vulci)

TARCHNA
TARQUINII
(Tarquinia)

BLERA
(Blera)

L. di Vico

FESCENNIUM

SAN GIOVENALE

[SUTHRI]
SUTRIUM
(Sutri)

L. di Bracciano

F. Tevere (Tiber)

PYRGI
(Santa Severa)

CISRA
CAERE
(Cerveteri)

VEIA
VEII
(Veio)

[RUMA]
ROMA
(Rome)

LEGEND

Etruscan place names   CLEVSIN
(Where known; uncertain names in brackets)

Roman place names   CLUSIUM

Present Italian place names   (Chiusi)

Primary Roman roads   VIA CASSIA

Rivers: *F. Fiora* Lakes: *L. Trasimenus*
(Alternative names in parentheses)

Hilly areas   Mountainous areas

N

SCALE

0   50
km

Etruscan Italy:
A Rediscoverable History?

JOHN F. HALL

> So great was the might of Etruria that it filled with the fame of its name not only the land but also the sea, throughout the whole length of Italy from the Alps to the Straits of Sicily.
>
> —LIVY[1]

In A.D. 46 the municipal council of Alexandria, then the center of higher learning in the Graeco-Roman world and the largest and wealthiest city in Rome's provinces, enacted a measure designed to honor Ti. Claudius Caesar Augustus Germanicus, emperor at Rome and benefactor of Alexandria. Statues were not erected, nor were monuments constructed. Rather, yearly recitals were arranged in Alexandria in honor of Claudius—a fitting way to do homage to the savant who seems to have preferred his books and researches to the governance of empire. The subject matter for these academic readings was significant: a complete recitation of the twenty books of the emperor's own *Tyrrhenica*, a comprehensive history of Etruria published before his accession.[2] A work about Etruscans is hardly surprising for Claudius, whose closest associates were leading senators of Etruscan ancestry and two of whose four wives had likewise been drawn from Etruria's nobility.[3] Amazement arises only when considering how even an Etruscophile like Claudius could find sufficient material

---

FIGURE 1. Map of central Italy showing area of Etruscan influence and many of the sites named in this volume.

to fill a twenty-book treatise about a people that in the present day is so little known and so widely mischaracterized.

Claudius was by no means the only Roman to compose Etruscan history. Rome's own Etruscan period and consequent cultural inheritance, if not her proximity to and long relations with Etruscan states, had guaranteed the attention of Roman authors to Etruria and its people. The earliest Roman annalists dealt extensively with the Etruscans: Fabius Pictor, in a manner lately claimed to be marked with an ill will motivated by patriotic fervor;[4] and Cato, apparently in more judicious fashion, as he acknowledged a period of Etruscan domination over Italy.[5] Etruscans appeared plentifully in the Roman chronicles as their history intersected that of Rome. By the last century B.C., however, Roman authors concerned themselves with matters Etruscan in and of themselves. Topics of Etruscan culture, society, and religion, learned perhaps from Etruscan sources then still extant, appear in the writings of Romans of Etruscan ancestry such as Nigidius Figulus, Caecina, and Tarquitius Priscus.[6] Similarly, Roman antiquarians of the period, most notably Varro, included in their work information pertaining to Etruria and its inhabitants. Since the fragmentary remains of early Roman historical writing have survived only marginally better than Etruscan literature, it is to Varro, the elder Pliny, or other writers of antiquarian lore that the modern scholar is indebted; their occasional comments about things Etruscan provide much of the scant literary testimony about Etruscan Italy.[7]

In the early imperial period we find the first proper history of Etruria written by a Roman author: Verrius Flaccus, tutor to the grandsons of Augustus, composed a *Res Etruscae*. A generation later, the *Tyrrhenica* of Claudius satisfied the Roman interest in Etruscan history. Not only did Claudius have the works of the above-mentioned authors to draw upon for source material, but also the sources, both Etruscan and Greek, used by his predecessors—presumably still in existence at that time. Granted, none of the Etruscan works survive; but it can be ventured that there were more than a few of the *Tuscae historiae*, to which Varro refers, and that the *fabulae Etruscae* cited by Varro and Servius may have been historical in theme, perhaps comprising much the same topical matter as the *elogia*, whose subjects have recently been confirmed as actual characters of Etruscan history.[8]

The Romans were sufficiently well acquainted with their Etruscan neighbors to provide generally sound information about them. On the other hand, certain Etruscan customs that struck travelers and traders from abroad as strange account for the sorts of information preserved about Etruscan Italy in, for example, Greek sources. Harris explains that

> Greek writers had, of course, possessed fragments of information and misinformation about the Etruscans before the fourth century; but it was then that the ethnographical writers formed a general view of the Etruscans, and it was one that influenced most later writing about them. What we know of fourth-century writing depends on Athenaeus' interest in wantonness. The wantonness of the Etruscans was in fact a *topos*, a literary theme for these Greek ethnographers.[9]

The literary excesses of certain Greek authors are such that the value of their writings as sources for legitimate history is dubious. Hellenistic authors did, fortunately, treat other aspects of Etruscan civilization, and still later Greek authors of the Roman era made occasional reference to Etruscans. One of these was Dionysius, who not only dealt with Etruscan involvement in Roman history but announced that a work on Etruscan Italy would follow his *Roman Antiquities*.[10]

In ancient times, then, an extensive corpus of written material about the Etruscans—not only from Greek or Roman authors, but presumably also from Etruscans themselves—appears to have been readily at hand. Today, however, although considerable material from several Roman historians and antiquarians is still extant, the works of most of the above-noted authors survive not at all or only in fragmentary form. Compounding this lack of existing primary sources is the unreliability of what sources remain available, since some Roman narratives (possibly for reasons of patriotism) and certain Greek writings (whose authors held negative views concerning Etruscans in general) sometimes provide erroneous information. Consequently, great difficulty confronts efforts to reconstruct Etruscan civilization and write Etruscan history. In view of this predicament, Pallottino's assessment deserves attention:

In many of its aspects, we are forced to regard and study the civilization of Etruria as if it were a prehistoric civilization although it belongs fully to historical times; for we are often almost wholly limited to its external and material manifestations. We have not, in fact, the direct light thrown by a great literary tradition to help us penetrate into the thought, feelings, and way of life of its creators as it is possible to do with the other great peoples of the classical world.[11]

In the absence of an adequate literary record of or about Etruscan culture and history, it is necessary to rely upon epigraphical records and the methodologies of archaeology and anthropology. A written record that is comparatively abundant, if limited in scope, is constituted in Etruscan inscriptions, not only from Etruria proper but from other parts of the peninsula where Etruscan presence was strong. Two specialized fields of Etruscan language studies utilize inscriptions less for linguistic interpretation than to determine Etruscan presence throughout Italy. These fields are onomastics and toponymics—the study of proper names and place names. The work of Schulze and, much more recently, of Rix provides sound basis to indicate which gentilicial names of the Roman era derive from Etruscan proper names.[12] With this information it is possible to utilize Latin epigraphic evidence—more abundant than the Etruscan inscriptions—to determine the presence of Etruscans or their descendants in various regions of Italy. Outside of Etruria, Etruscan-derived names are most prevalent in Rome itself but are also common in areas where Etruscan colonization or overlordship is historically known: Campania, certain locales in the Po region, and several municipalities in Umbria and Latium. The distribution accords well with ancient testimony pertaining to the expansion of Etruscans throughout the peninsula. This kind of information, when combined with other products of the archaeological record, permits a comprehensive treatment of the sort performed by M. Frederiksen to demonstrate the extent of the Etruscan presence and local influence in Campania.[13]

Other products of archaeological investigation provide additional information relating to Etruscan social and economic history. The excavation of structures and foundations discloses the nature of Etruscan architecture, building and engineering, and urbanization and town planning. Analysis of tombs and graves provides information useful in reconstructing the sociology of the Etruscan world: class division, family organization, and occupation differentiation. Tomb paintings and art objects found in tombs permit the identification of Etruscan physical characteristics, dress, social customs, and, to a degree, religious beliefs. In particular, bronze mirrors, which attest to the high level of technical skill attained in Etruscan metallurgy and engraving, afford glimpses into Etruscan religion and myth through their representations of gods and heroes. Artifacts and utensils indicate the nature of Etruscan technology, while armor and weaponry reveal aspects of that Etruscan military prowess so long effective in dominating the other peoples of Italy. The presence in Etruria of foreign artifacts— Greek, Phoenician, and Carthaginian—suggests the widespread trade contacts of the Etruscans, as does the discovery of Etruscan goods in other areas of the Mediterranean.

Despite the contributions archaeology can make to understanding Etruscan civilization, the field's very nature limits its ability to rediscover Etruscan history in that it produces only a random sampling of evidence, a partial depiction of society. While definite conclusions can be drawn about particular topics of art history or the history of technology, broader questions of political, social, and economic history remain largely unanswered. Archaeological and, for that matter, epigraphical evidences are most reliable when used in tandem with the historical tradition of a culture as contained in its literary sources, of which essentially none remain for Etruria. In the absence of Etruscan literature, the techniques of comparative history become important for drawing conclusions concerning Etruscan society from the study of Rome during its monarchical and early Republican period when, as an *urbs Etrusca*, Rome was not only governed by Etruscan rulers but in many other respects was firmly set in the Etruscan cultural sphere.[14]

Surely, rediscovering Etruscan Italy requires an interdisciplinary approach. The convergence of specialized disciplines and methods is a requisite instrument for providing the evidence and documentation necessary to examine Etruscan Italy and its influence on later eras, whether as a whole or in its various separate aspects. Several of the essays in this volume address their topics using multiple methodologies, in what K. A. Raaflaub has described as

> the "comprehensive approach," meaning that all available sources must be used adequately and to their full extent. "All" means not only the historiographical, epigraphical, and archaeological sources, but also information scattered in the works of antiquarians and lexicographers, . . . and the evidence provided by linguistic analysis and social, political, military, religious, and legal institutions.[15]

Other essays in the volume apply the more traditional methodological approaches appropriate to the fields being investigated. While the former kinds of papers entail a degree of synthesis, the latter require the reader's consideration of them in combination with all the essays of the volume to make a synthesis which informs about the Etruscan presence in Italy.

The volume is by no means comprehensive; but its chapters, when considered together, delineate several enduring themes of Etruscan Italy. First, Etruscan contributions to the technical advances of civilization, to arts and letters, and to religion were sufficiently appreciated to influence neighboring peoples of Italy, as well as peoples with whom trade rendered contact possible. Second, elements of the life and culture of other peoples of Italy, particularly the Romans, were in many instances derived from Etruscan civilization. Third, just as Etruscans themselves did not disappear but continued as contributing members of Roman society, so too the continuation of Etruscan culture is demonstrable in Roman civilization. Fourth, the influence of the Etruscans in the life and culture of the Italian peninsula lingers even into the modern era. At least to this degree, the history of Etruscan Italy is rediscoverable.

The essays are arranged in three groups in loose chronological fashion: those which address an aspect of Etruscan Italy most associated with the Etruscan or pre-Roman period appear first, followed by those which emphasize matters Etruscan in the Roman era, and finally those which pertain primarily to post-Roman Italy. Of the first group, most essays treat archaeological or art history topics, except for Robert E. A. Palmer's, the keynote presentation of the symposium, which considers aspects of Etruscan religion. The second group of essays includes historical, archaeological, literary, and fine arts topics. The final group depicts physical representations of continued Etruscan influence in both Renaissance and modern Italy. Topics are sometimes related and sometimes not. Among the offerings of contributors, both differences of opinion and agreement present themselves without editorial intervention.

Robert E. A. Palmer uncovers an important component of Etruscan religion in his examination of the Vatican exhibit's bronze statuette of the boy with the *bulla* and its votive inscription to the god Tec Sans. Only the famous *Arringatore* statue preserves a similar inscription. In almost "Holmesian" fashion, this excursus through the hidden places of Roman religion associates Tec Sans with the god Sancus; the *Lares* and their enemies, the *laruae;* the wearing of the bulla; the coming to manhood of Roman youth; and the warding off of evil through the potency of the green lizard. A facet of Etruscan religion is in this manner rediscoverable through investigation of aspects of Roman religion whose origin is, thus, demonstrably Etruscan.

Mary E. Moser provides new evidence for the old question of the beginnings of Etruscan Italy by examination of recent archaeological finds in the vicinity of Vulci. These Protovillanovan sites provide evidence for extensive habitation of the region at an early period. Comparison to continuous settlement patterns at Tarquinii from Protovillanovan into Villanovan times suggests constant inhabitation of Vulci and other major Etruscan sites dating back to 1200 B.C.

The next three essays consider Etruscan art objects and the information they furnish about Etruscan culture. Helen Nagy offers a thorough analysis of an engraved mirror which purportedly depicts the mythical judgment of Paris. The variations of iconography between it and other mirrors of similar design are sufficiently extensive to call into question the identification and require explanation for their cause, which may be more related to marketing than mythological revision.

Alexandra Carpino examines three Etruscan relief mirrors to illustrate that, despite the Greek mythological foundation of the scenes depicted, Etruscan reinterpretations are indicated in changed elements of the myths. Such alteration seems to occur as the myths are adapted to Etruscan religious beliefs or historical circumstances, revealing the strength and versatility of the culture in Etruscan Italy.

Lisa Pieraccini proposes the *dolio* as an elegant yet functional example of the contribution to Italy of Caeretane pottery manufacture. *Dolii* are discussed in many respects, including their manufacture and production, use, and extent of distribution. Several of the prevalent decorative elements are examined in terms of art history to illustrate the influence of external cultures on Etruscan decoration during the Orientalizing period.

Dorothy Dvorsky Rohner utilizes the methodologies of ethno-archaeology to investigate Etruscan domestic architecture, its relation to Etruscan cultural identity, and its function as a paradigm for Roman domestic architecture. Architectural patterns in the foundation footprints of domestic structures at Etruscan cities such as Veii and Vetulonia, as well as Etruscan ruins at Acquarossa, San Giovenale, and Marzabotto, constitute the source material for the study. Comparison to Greek domestic forms highlights the extensive differences between Etruscan and Greek domestic forms, while comparison to Roman domestic architecture accentuates the many similarities.

In the first group of essays, those of Palmer and Rohner reveal Rome's cultural borrowings from Etruria. The influence exerted by Etruscans on the developing civilization of Rome is further illuminated by the offerings of the second group of essays, which treat topics of Etruscan governance at Rome; assimilation of Etruscans into Roman society; and Etruscan ties to Roman architecture, literature, and the arts.

John F. Hall's essay examines Etruscan Rome, analyzing both government and religious institutions in monarchical Rome and exploring the continuation of Etruscan rule at Rome during the early Republic by powerful Etruscan aristocratic families who maintained their Etrusco-Roman identity and held high magisterial office in the state. A second period of extensive Etruscan influence in Roman government developed during the civil wars at the end of the Republic and was consolidated under Augustus, explaining the prevalent interest in *res Etrusca* during the Augustan era which is noted in succeeding essays.

Helena Fracchia surveys the excavations of Etruscan and Roman Cortona in terms of settlement patterns and the use and reuse of sites and monuments, demonstrating the continuity of influence on Cortona through its development from an Etruscan town to an Etruscan town under Roman domination to a Roman town inspired by its Etruscan past and cultural heritage. She gives particular attention to recent finds in the Ossaia region of Cortona, uncovered through the joint excavations of the University of Alberta and the Università di Perugia, including principally the villa of the Vibii Pansae, prominent at Rome under Caesar and Augustus.

Mark J. Johnson reviews Etruscan architectural influences on the design of the mausoleum of Augustus. The tradition of Etruscan architectural influence at Rome is assessed, specifically as regards funerary architecture. Reasons for the interest Augustus showed in Etruscan and related Trojan themes are considered in connection with his selection of an Etruscan model for his mausoleum.

Roger T. Macfarlane provides an excursus through Latin literature of the Augustan age, both to review the work of Etruscan literary figures and to consider the treatment of Etruscans and Etruscan themes in the literature of the era. From the little-known Cassius Etruscus to Maecenas and Vergil, Etruscan contributions to Roman literature are noted. Horace, Ovid, and other poets of the time are examined in relation to their praise or condemnation of persons and things Etruscan.

Robert L. Maxwell undertakes an examination of Etruscan theater arts and Livy's claim that from that provenience Roman theater originated. Literary and art history evidence is adduced, along with information provided from recently discovered papyri to link Roman theater, and especially Roman comedy, with mime and other kinds of performances from Etruria which may have been celebrated as part of religious and funerary ritual.

Harrison Powley's essay on Etruscan musical legacy collects what information is available through reference to Etruscan tomb paintings, examination of comments about Etruscan music in primarily Roman literary and historical sources, and comparison to what is known of Greek and Roman music, the latter of which may have been much influenced by Etruscan music and certainly employed several musical instruments of known Etruscan origin. Even so, because no written transcriptions of Etruscan music survive, little is knowable about an area which appears to have comprised a very important component of Etruscan life.

The final essays of the volume belong to the post-Roman era. Steven Bule ranges through numerous examples of Renaissance art to illustrate the effect wrought on it by Etruscan art. This broad topic is made quite manageable by selectivity of works treated and by comparison of the art of Renaissance Tuscany to that of other regions of Italy. The conclusion is apparent: a different quality inherent in Tuscan art may derive from both the historical influence of Etruscan art and the recognition by Tuscan notables of certain aspects of their own Etruscan descent and heritage.

Nancy Thomson de Grummond commences her discussion of Etruscan Italy today with reference to recent studies in Etruscan anthropology, designed in part to determine the possibility of surviving Etruscan ethnic characteristics in the present population of certain areas of Tuscany. She proceeds to considerations of terrain, land use, crop production, architectural elements and building materials, and customs of daily life, including religious practices and attitudes toward the supernatural.

Thus, in a fitting end to a volume designed to print papers from a symposium about Etruscan Italy and its continuation into Roman and later eras, de Grummond returns the reader to Palmer's initial topic of Etruscan religion. For religion, expressing as it does the most deeply held beliefs of a people, molds that people's culture and world view to an extent that centuries of time and change cannot completely efface. Just so, Etruscan Italy, at least in certain respects, may be with us still, not only as manifested in Italy today but also through the effects that Etruscan life and culture—even if in part through a Roman intermediary—exert on our own civilization and individual lives each day. Although that influence is not commonly known or easily recognizable, it nevertheless still remains.

NOTES

Throughout this volume, for the convenience of the reader, the customary method of referring to a previously cited work by a shortened title has been supplemented by a cross-reference to the note in which the work first appeared. Thus, in note 5 below, "supra n. 2" refers the reader to the note in which Harris's *Rome in Etruria* is cited in full.

1. Liv. 1.2.5: . . . *tanta opibus Etruria erat ut iam non terras solum sed mare etiam per totum Italiae longitudinem ab Alpibus ad fretum Siculum fama nominis sui implesset . . .* (my translation).

2. For a brief summary of the contributions of Claudius to Etruscan studies, see W. V. Harris, *Rome in Etruria and Umbria* (Oxford, 1971), 4, 14, 27–28; J. Heurgon, "La Vocation étruscologique de l'empereur Claude," *CRAI* (1953): 92–97.

3. J. F. Hall, "The Municipal Aristocracy of Etruria and Their Participation in Politics at Rome, B.C. 91–A.D. 14," (Ph.D. diss., University of Pennsylvania, 1984), 156–58, 183–84, 398.

4. See, in this volume, the essay by John F. Hall, 150–51 and n. 5.

5. Harris, *Rome in Etruria*, 19 (supra n. 2).

6. The contributions of these writers is reviewed in ibid., 6–7. See also Hall, "Municipal Aristocracy," 208–9, 248, 317, 387–88 (supra n. 3).

7. Harris, *Rome in Etruria*, 10–14 (supra n. 2).

8. A review of the authors of Roman works about Etruscans and their probable sources is provided in ibid., 10–14, 26–27. The elogia of Tarquinii constitute the subject of M. Torelli, *Elogia Tarquiniensia*, Studi e materiali di etruscologia e antichità italiche, 15 (Florence, 1975).

9. Harris, *Rome in Etruria*, 14 (supra n. 2).

10. A discussion of the treatment of Etruscans in Greek sources is found in ibid., 14–17.

11. M. Pallottino, *The Etruscans*, ed. D. Ridgway, trans. J. Cremona (London, 1975), 153.

12. W. Schulze, *Zur Geschichte lateinischer Eigennamen* (see *LE* in list of abbreviations for full bibliographic information); H. Rix, *Das etruskische Cognomen . . .* (Wiesbaden, Ger., 1963).

13. M. Frederiksen, "The Etruscans in Campania," in *Italy before the Romans: The Iron Age, Orientalizing, and Etruscan Periods*, ed. D. and F. R. Ridgway (London, 1979), 277–312.

14. See, for example, M. Pallottino, "The Origins of Rome: A Survey of Recent Discoveries and Discussions," in *Italy before the Romans*, 198 (vol. supra n. 13).

15. K. A. Raaflaub, ed., *Social Struggles in Archaic Rome: New Perspectives on the Conflict of Orders* (Berkeley, Calif., 1986), 9. While Raaflaub's observations are intended as a means of considering problems of the early Roman Republic, they seem by no means inappropriate to the present study.

PRE-ROMAN
ITALY

Locket Gold, Lizard Green

ROBERT E. A. PALMER

This essay examines an aspect of boyhood: the means of the protection of boys. The Vatican exhibit displays two objects that illustrate this subject.[1] First, we have the bronze figure of a boy (figure 1) naked and holding two playthings: a bird and a ball. He wears ankle-rings, wrist-rings, and around his neck a twisted chain from which hangs a locket the Romans called *bulla,* or bubble.[2] Its Etruscan name we do not know. On his right leg are cut the four words of a dedication: *fleres tec sansl cver* ("offering to so-and-so god as a gift").[3] Also in the exhibit is displayed a gold bubble locket, with gold chain, that comes from the Roman port of Ostia.[4] It had been put with the ashes of the dead boy, for whom it had done no good.

The gold locket was worn by Etruscan and Roman boys as a means of protection. This is a usage that is clear in its intent, but it is unclear in the property and power of the locket and of a garment I will mention in a moment. The Etruscan bronze boy was found in a village called Sanguineto on the shores of Lago Trasimene in the territory of the Etruscan city of Cortona. (The name of modern Sanguineto will recur.)

The god who received the bronze boy is said, on inference, to have been a possible protector of children. First, however, we must note the absence of the bubble locket for the protection of both Etruscan and

Roman girls, whereas boys were supposed to wear them. Secondly, neither a child nor a locket assures the inference that the god to whom this small statue was dedicated functioned in protection of children or, specifically, of boys.

The god whose name is inscribed has two names, *tec* and *sans*. The second name, which will immediately concern us, is a divine epithet identifying the deity's function. Tec Sans is recorded on only one other object: a dedication, also inscribed on a bronze statue. Its text is longer and therefore less comprehensible. The statue is very, very famous. Here we have *Arringatore*, the public speaker, a full-grown man—a full-grown man, of course, *not* wearing a locket (see figure 1 on p. xiv). We infer from the inscription his personal name.[5] The purpose of his inscription is clearly stated: *fleres tece sansl* ("offering to Tec Sans").[6] The inference from the boy with locket that the god Tec Sans protected boys is now suspect. We might also infer protection of a public speaker. Indeed, we can show how wrong it is.

There are other bronze boys wearing bullae that were given to other gods in Etruria. In the Vatican, beside the boy from Sanguineto, is displayed a bronze boy with locket. He was found at Tarquinii. His dedicatory inscription tells us that he was given to a god of Latin, not Etruscan, origin: namely, the god Silvanus.[7] Indeed, in our exhibit we may have a headless Silvanus, who normally held a pruning hook as part of his paraphernalia.[8] As his name speaks his place, so Silvanus belonged and functioned in woods. Better, let us return to Cortona, in whose territory lay the place from which the boy given to Tec Sans comes.

This male child was found on a different site (Montecchio). Here is another naked boy, this one holding a goose. His bubble locket hangs from a ribbon—or more likely a leather thong—which is fringed at the end. You can see that the goose-boy was also inscribed on his right leg and up his hip with an inscription that permits us to assume he was given to one or both of two gods named Thuflthas or Tlenacheis. Of them we know nothing. But, to our advantage, three other bronze objects were uncovered with the locketed boy with the goose: firstly, a candelabrum inscribed as a gift to one of the just-mentioned gods, whose nature is not known to us; secondly, a bronze statuette of a woman also holding a bird; and lastly, a bronze scoop shovel.[9] We now have little reason to articulate shrines construable as religious centers for the protection of boys or, for that matter, of girls, too.

These Etruscan bronze boys wearing bubble lockets were dedicated to several gods. To pursue the Etruscan god Tec Sans, we shall have to take a path diverse from the path of inference from the locket that protects.

Let us recall that the boy for Tec Sans was found at the village of Sanguineto. Of Tec we can say little; of Sans, much. Sans, the epithet, is well known but not recognized. First, we shall travel by flying crow over the hills some thirty Roman miles to Iguvium. There we can read bronze tablets recording many elaborate religious rituals. Some of these rituals, written in a language related to Latin and quite unrelated to incomprehensible Etruscan, contain the same epithet both as epithet of gods and as an independent deity—*sansi,* or *sace.*[10] Among offerings appropriate to this god or to a god bearing the epithet at Iguvium were wheels or discs. At last we are on firm ground, for we know the word *sans* of Iguvium, and thereby the Sans of Sanguineto, in three other dialects of central Italy, including Latin. He is the Latin Sancus, god of oaths. He is also sometimes called, in Latin, Sangus, with a *g.* Doubtless, we have in his name the root word of the name of the village Sanguineto.

Now we shall turn our eyes from Etruria to Latium, from Cortona to Rome. The Romans worshipped Sancus/Sangus, a name which was normally but not always found as functional epithet of a seed-god, Semo.[11] Perhaps Etruscan Tec Sans of Sanguineto may be identified with the Romans' (Semo) Sancus, god of oaths.

In the latter half of the fourth century B.C., well before the bronze boy and bronze man were dedicated to Tec Sans, the Romans captured a rebel leader who had broken his treaty oaths. His property was confiscated and sold; the proceeds were converted to bronze wheels or discs. The very same offerings given *sansi* at Iguvium we know to have been put in the Roman temple of Sancus/Sangus in circumstances of treaty violation.[12] The name *Sancus,* perhaps once an adjective, yielded a very important verb for Latin speakers: *sancire,* "to render something *sancus.*" One swore an oath in early Rome *sancte.* The word has yielded, in English, "sanction" and the far more common word "saint." The bronze boy and the bronze public speaker were religious gifts to an Etruscan god who was probably associated with oaths, as his namesake in Iguvium and at Rome were.

Now we turn back to our golden lockets worn by Etruscan and by Roman boys. Latin authors make clear that the badges of boyhood, the bubble locket and the embroidered toga, were culturally borrowed by Romans from Etruria. We have no such representations of Roman boys so early. According to legend, the Etruscan king of Rome, Tarquinius Priscus, awarded his fourteen-year-old son the gold locket and the embroidered toga for bravery on a battlefield.[13] Centuries later, according to an incomplete historical account, a noble Roman boy wore only the locket and embroidered toga when he rode into battle and killed an enemy. The occasion is thought to have fallen in the very dark days after Roman defeats in the second Punic War. The boy ultimately became consul at Rome and chief pontiff, presiding over all of Roman religion.[14]

Other explanations of the badges, locket and toga, offer other occasions. For one, they were accorded only the sons of cavalrymen—that is, of men with the highest census ratings but not necessarily nobles.[15] However, in the days for which we are best informed, locket and embroidered toga merely designated boys of free birth.[16] On the relief from the Altar of August Peace two small members of the first Roman emperor's family are shown with the locket. They hang from boyish necks by leather thongs. The female in the foreground on the left is Antonia the Younger, and to the right stands her husband, Nero Tiberius Drusus. Behind him to the fore marches Antonia the Elder. To the left is Germanicus, to the right Domitius Ahenobarbus, with a modern head—the sons of the two Antonias.[17] The emperor Nero was descended directly from these boys: Germanicus, a grandfather; Domitius, the other grandfather. Although these lockets are worn by boys of the highest families, at the time of this relief any freeborn Roman boy was expected to wear a locket on a thong.

Indeed, after the same Punic War I mentioned earlier—that is, about 200 B.C.—the sons of freedmen were allowed by law to adopt the embroidered toga and the thong, but not the locket, which was reserved to the freeborn boys.[18] In my view, the thong, too, had protective virtues. Otherwise, why wear it? That is, the leather of the thongs will have had the same quality as the locket because it was cut from the hides of sacrificial animals.[19] Unlike early Roman society, Etruscan society was overlaid like a solid paramount stratum upon a working or serf class of non-Etruscan natives. Very probably, no non-Etruscan boy was allowed to wear the locket. The locket perhaps in part protected Etruscan boys from the non-Etruscan evils among which they grew up. Romans permitted the freeborn Roman boy to wear the locket and the embroidered toga.

At the end of boyhood—that is, at about age fourteen or fifteen—the Roman boy doffed the embroidered toga and the locket and donned a man's plain toga unless and until he was elected to a Roman magistracy, when he again wore the embroidered toga—a man-sized one, we hope. In the distant past, the embroidered toga may have been thought to protect those who especially needed protection: namely, boys and politicians. But the gold locket a Roman boy gave up forever and bestowed on gods called *Lares*.[20]

There are several representational examples of this practice. An altar, also in the Vatican collection, comes from the Roman, formerly Etruscan, city of Caere. The Lares at either side are almost tradition-ally shown. They stand on a ledge of rock outcrop. You notice in detail that each Lar wears the locket that had once been worn by some boy grown to adulthood. Only the Lares of this altar are shown wear-ing a dedicated locket.[21] Like many other Lares, these from Caere seem quite jolly and representative of their divine breed, except that they wear what was given them as dedication: the locket. At all events, Lares were too old to need the locket.

On a fragment of an altar from Rome itself we see the abbreviated name of the Lares whose altar it was. On the back of the same piece were shown—within an oak-leaf wreath—the wine bucket, an object sometimes carried by a Lar instead of a second drinking horn, and a pair of bubble lockets on their thongs. This fragment belonged to a peculiar kind of altar dedicated to Lares at the many intersections of streets in the city.[22]

In town and country Lares were expected to watch over boundaries, property lines, country crossroads, and urban intersections. If we match the Roman boys' lockets to the circumstances of places of worship of Lares, we can assume that Lares oversaw boys so long as they stayed within their bounds and that otherwise the lockets protected boys wherever they went. Being gold, the lockets were suitably given to local protective Lares when boys survived into manhood. Otherwise they went to their graves with the locket—as we have previously observed as having happened at Ostia.

Against whom did Lares protect the Roman boys? The Romans had a notion of evil Lares called *laruae*—not really Lares, but the enemy of Lares. The *laruae*—in English our "larvae"—resembled in a sense our bogeymen or hobgoblins when Roman nannies spoke of them. But, indeed, they had a more serious character, for they could drive mad or do other harm. They were spooks or haunts. They probably haunted that most hauntable of hauntable places, the crossing of roads and of boundaries, notorious in antiquity for their evil spirits.[23]

So far, I have talked about the god to whom the bronze boy of Sanguineto was dedicated, about Etruscan and Roman boys wearing gold lockets, and about the Roman gods called Lares to whom Roman boys surrendered them at manhood. If I do not soon reach green lizards, the reader's patience will be tired, for I am sure that most know something about gold lockets but few have learned the worth of a green lizard.

So far I have said nothing of the contents of the locket. My silence has been up to now a sign of wisdom because no author in antiquity has so much as obliquely hinted at what a bubble locket on a boy's neck contained. Only one author, and he writing in about A.D. 400, expresses the notion underlying the locket when speaking of it as worn in front by a triumphant general. It enclosed curatives (*remedia*) that were believed very strong against what has no appropriate English rendition.[24] The Latin is *invidia*, the origin of our word "envy," but also meaning jealousy, hatred, and literally the act of looking askance. We now enter the world of superstition and of uncontrolled irrationality. Invidia also is the evil eye.[25] It and other sorts of evil had no clear, let alone rational, source. The *laruae* against whom stood Lares belonged to that world of nonreason. No one saw a *larua;* only their harm was sensed.

Let us return to the Roman temple of Sancus/Sangus, but just for a moment. In it stood a bronze statue of Tanaquil, which some Romans thought went back to the days of her husband, the Roman king Tarquinius Priscus. Romans also believed that the Etruscan Tarquin gave his son the first locket and embroidered toga. The statue of Tanaquil in Sancus/Sangus' temple showed her to be spinning wool. But let us turn our attention to the sash of this bronze lady. According to legend, Tanaquil herself had discovered curatives and put them in her sash. In the days of our reporting source, people in danger took scrapings from her sash and called these *praebia* for warding off evils.[26] Now this word *praebia*, standing for a current Latin word *remedia*, was obsolete. Another author has to go back two centuries—to about 200 B.C.—in order to cite the word.[27] He says that *praebia*, from a Latin verb meaning "to hold in front," are the remedia that boys wear on their necks. This manner of wearing, too, was required of triumphant generals. They had to wear the locket in front; otherwise the locket did no good against a hateful glance. Bronze scrapings from Tanaquil's sash would have qualified as praebia for a boy's neck.

The boy's locket probably held a physical object, even though we are once told that gold by itself was applied to babies so that the "poisoning" they met would be less harmful.[28] For instance, amber had curative powers and would be attached to babies as an *amuletum*, the word giving us "amulet" in English.[29] And in another recipe of folk medicine, amber at the throat warded off tonsillitis.[30] Attached to the neck, one variety of amber rubbed with honey cured fever and earache, and rubbed with Athenian honey cured blurred vision.[31] Sometimes neither the locket nor the amuletum sufficed. Here is an inconsistent recipe: if a dreaming baby should see a snake or a poisonous toad his nursemaid should spit three times—in his mouth.[32]

And now for the *pièce de résistance* that comes from a medical treatise written about A.D. 400 by a man who was not only Christian but a high imperial official and so presumably intelligent:

> On Jupiter's day [i.e., our Thursday] at the time of the old moon
> in September, or even on any other day, take a green lizard, dig out
> his eyes with a copper needle, and put them in a locket . . . and hang
> it from your neck. So long as you wear this cure [*remedium*] you will
> not have eye pain.[33]

This passage is the only one in all Latin letters that gives the curative contents of a bubble locket.

Over three centuries before our Christian official wrote, another author tells of many medicinal uses of a green lizard, whole or in part or reduced to ash. Of thirteen prescriptions, two were for eye disease; but there are green lizard recipes for swelling of lymph glands, pleurisy, foot lesions, paralysis and apoplexy, tertian fever, reduction of scar tissue, and infantile teething.[34] Only one medicinal instruction calls for lizard eye—the right eye is specified—to cure quartan fever (i.e., malaria or ague).[35]

Bronze scrapings from Tanaquil's sash seem quite mild if less advanced medicine. The wool-spinning Tanaquil embodied the notion of the dutiful wife and mother, at least in an Etruscan way. And so I will conclude with the strange report of cash transactions after Roman weddings. According to law already old in the first century B.C., when the bride entered her husband's house she carried in her hand one bronze ace to give to her husband, another in her foot to put on the hearth for house Lares, and a third ace that she laid aside in a purse to bestow on the neighborhood crossroads.[36] I venture to explain that she held back her last ace until her son(s) had reached manhood and then bestowed it on Lares of her neighborhood crossroads on the occasion when her last son attained manhood and gave them his locket gold.

Between the earliest appearances of lockets hanging from a boy's neck on Etruscan sculptures and from the legendary award of a locket by king Tarquin to his son and from Tanaquil's legendary discovery of praebia down to the medicinal prescription of lizard eyes written by a late antique official, at least a millennium passed. Today one millennium and six centuries have elapsed since readers learned the recipe for eyes of lizard green taken on Thursday of September's old moon and kept at the neck in a locket gold to prevent eye pain.

Today, in 1994, we hear talk of universal medical insurance. What is more, we hear talk of the efficacy of what is called alternative medicine. A latter-day Tanaquil has left her spinning to promote our general welfare. But can we wait for truly universal medical insurance with coverage for alternative medicine? Of course not! My advice to this audience is: wear one bubble locket, gold. If that is not efficacious, according to the timetable hunt for one lizard, green, and prepare according to recipe.

And if that, too, is not efficacious? Put a vitamin C in your locket.

NOTES

1. I refer to the exhibition catalogue, F. Buranelli, *The Etruscans: Legacy of a Lost Civilization: From the Vatican Museums*, trans. N. T. de Grummond (Memphis, Tenn., 1992). Although prepared for the exhibition at the Memphis Pink Palace Museum, Memphis, Tennessee, the catalogue also served for the exhibition at the Museum of Art, Brigham Young University, Provo, Utah, where I saw it. I take the opportunity to express many thanks to John F. Hall, who organized our conference, and to James Mason, who organized the exhibition in the new Museum of Art, and to their colleagues and associates for admirable hospitality.

2. For Roman *bullae* in art, see H. R. Goette, "Die Bulla," *BJ* 186 (1986): 133–64. For more on the bronze boy, see Buranelli, *Etruscans: Legacy*, no. 44 (supra n. 1); M. Cristofani, *I bronzi degli Etruschi* (Novara, It., 1985), 299 no. 127.

3. *CIE* 4561 = *TLE* 624 = H. R. W. Rix, *Das etruskische Cognomen: Untersuchungen zu System, Morphologie, und Verwendung der Personnamen auf den jüngeren Inschriften Nordetruriens* (Wiesbaden, Ger., 1963), Co. 3.8.

4. Buranelli, *Etruscans: Legacy*, no. 45 (supra n. 1); W. Helbig, *Führer durch die öffentlichen Sammlungen Klassischer Altertümer in Rom: Die Päpstlichen Sammlungen im Vatikan und Lateran*, vol. 1, 4th ed. (Tübingen, Ger., 1963), no. 767.

5. Cristofani, *I bronzi degli Etruschi*, 67–70, 300 no. 129 (supra n. 2). See also, in this volume, the essay by Helena Fracchia, 198.

6. *CIE* 4196 = *TLE* 651 = Rix, *Cognomen*, Pe. 3.3 (supra n. 3).

7. Cristofani, *I bronzi degli Etruschi*, 299 no. 126 (supra n. 2). *CIE* 5549 = *TLE* 148 = Rix, *Cognomen*, Ta. 3.7 (supra n. 3).

8. Buranelli, *Etruscans: Legacy*, no. 131 (supra n. 1); Helbig, *Führer*, no. 684 (supra n. 4).

9. For the goose boy, see Cristofani, *I bronzi degli Etruschi*, 299–300 no. 128 (supra n. 2). All four objects are now in the Rijks Museum, Leiden. See A. Neppi Modona, *Cortona etrusca e romana nella storia e nell'arte*, 2d ed. (Florence, 1977),

142–44; *CIE* 446 = *TLE* 652 = Rix, *Cognomen*, Co. 3.6 (supra n. 3). All four bronze objects are shown in one photograph in L. B. Van Der Meer, *The Bronze Liver of Piacenza* (Amsterdam, 1987), 97, cf. 98.

10. *Tab. Iguv.*, esp. IIa 4, IIb 10, VIb 3; J. W. Poultney, *The Bronze Tables of Iguvium*, American Philological Association Monograph (Baltimore, 1959), has a good commentary and index.

11. G. Wissowa, *Religion und Kultus der Römer*, 2d ed. (Munich, 1912), 129–31.

12. Liv. 8.19–21; *Tab. Iguv.* IIb 23.

13. Plin., *Nat. Hist.* 33.10; Plu., *QR* 101; Anon., *Vir. Ill.* 6.9; Macr. 1.6.8–14.

14. V.Max. 3.1.1; *RRC*, no. 419/1.

15. Plin., *Nat. Hist.* 33.10; Macr. 1.6.8–14.

16. Scip.Min. fr. 30 *ORF*⁴, 133; Cic., *2 Ver.* 1.152; V.Max. 5.6.8; Suet., *Rhet.* 25 (p. 30 Brugnoli); Anon., *Vir. Ill.* 6.9.

17. Ara Pacis, long rt. wall: e.g., E. Simon, *Ara Pacis Augustae* (New York, n.d.), pl. 15.

18. Plin., *Nat. Hist.* 33.10; Juv. 5.164–65; Macr. 1.6.13–14.

19. *ILLRP* 509; Plin., *Nat. Hist.* 36.151.

20. Prop. 4.1.131–32 (cf. Hor., *S.* 1.4.65–66; Porph. ad loc.); Juv. 5.30–31.

21. Vatican Museums, inv. 9964; Helbig, *Führer*, 14 no. 1058 (supra n. 4).

22. Musei Capitolini, inv. 1276; see H. S. Jones, *A Catalogue . . . Sculptures of the Palazzi dei Conservatori* (Oxford, 1926), 243–44; Goette, "Die Bulla," 138–39 (supra n. 2).

23. Plaut., *Am.* 777 and frs. 6–8 (Non. p. 64L), *Aul.* 642, *Capt.* 598, *Cas.* 592, *Men.* 890, *Mer.* 981; Fest. 114L; Var. in Arn., *Adv. Nat.* 3.41 = *ARD* 15.8 (p. 189 Agahd); Aug., *CD* 9.11 (p. 382 Dombart). See *LEW*³, s.v. "*larua.*" On Lares, see Wissowa, *Religion und Kultus der Römer*, 166–75 (supra n. 11).

24. Macr. 1.6.9–10.

25. Cf. Cic., *Tusc.* 3.9.20 (cf. Plin., *Nat. Hist.* 7.18); Catul. 5.12; Ov., *Met.* 7.366; Apul., *Met.* 4.14.

26. Ver.Fl. in Fest. 345L. (cf. Fest.-Paul. 215L); Var. in Plin., *Nat. Hist.* 8.194; Plu., *QR* 30.

27. Var., *L.* 7.107, quoting Naevius.

28. Plin., *Nat. Hist.* 33.84.

29. Ibid., 37.50.

30. Ibid., 37.44.

31. Ibid., 37.51.

32. Ibid., 28.39.

33. Marcel., *De Medicamentis* 8.50; see *PLRE* 1, Marcellus 7.

34. Plin., *Nat. Hist.* 29.118, 129–30 (cf. 116); 30.36, 53, 80, 86, 90, 104, 120, 135 (cf. 52, 71).

35. Ibid., 30.99.

36. Var., *VPR* fr. 25 Riposati (Non. p. 852L).

The Origins of the Etruscans:
New Evidence for an Old Question

MARY E. MOSER

The question of Etruscan origins has been debated since classical times, when the argument was couched in terms of ethnicity: for Herodotus, the Etruscans were immigrants to Italy from Asia Minor;[1] Dionysius of Halicarnassus, on the other hand, found them to be descendants of ancient, autochthonous peoples of Italy.[2] However, the premise of Herodotus' assertion of Lydian origins for the Etruscans has perhaps been more influential to the subsequent debate of this question than the assertion itself: that is, the premise that Etruscan culture, or at least its roots, might be found fully formed outside ancient Etruria. Indeed, modern authorities, especially those writing in the first half of this century, took up the argument along the lines handed down by their classical counterparts:[3] some maintained theories of eastern or northern origin, essentially repeating the Herodotean model of bearers of Etruscan culture immigrating to Italy en bloc. Although the supporters of an autochthonous, Italic origin did not have to contend with issues of immigration, they were constrained to explain how such a rich and sophisticated culture as the Etruscans possessed could have been born from what appeared to be impoverished and rather backward prehistoric cultures of Italy.

M. Pallottino's magisterial critique of scholarship on the origins of the Etruscans, published in 1947,[4] pointed out the flaw inherent in Herodotus' premise. Pallottino argued that Etruscan culture cannot be

FIGURE 1. Fiora River at Ponte San Pietro, looking south. *Photo by author.*

viewed as a monolithic entity, fully formed in all its elements at any given moment, and therefore capable of being detached from its setting in ancient Etruria, to be relocated elsewhere in some putative foreign homeland. Pallottino's admonishment of his colleagues to abandon the search for origins in favor of reconstructing the development of Etruscan culture in situ, in Etruria, led to a redirection of Etruscan scholarship.

In the decades following Pallottino's comments, prehistoric Italic archaeology has experienced virtually a new birth, both in terms of the excavation of new sites and interpretative research. Noteworthy progress has been made in clarifying the cultural developments of two successive periods, the Final Bronze Age[5] and the early Iron Age.[6] The Final Bronze Age, dated between circa 1200 and 900 B.C., is characterized in Etruria, as elsewhere in Italy, by the Protovillanovan culture,[7] best known perhaps for its practice of cremation and deposition of cremated remains in biconical urns. Following on the heels of the Final Bronze Age period, the early Iron Age, dated between about 900 and 700 B.C., has been thought to witness the foundation of Etruscan sites by peoples of the so-called Villanovan culture.[8] This culture, too, is characterized by the use of cremation in biconical urns; indeed, it has been the evidence from extensive cremation cemeteries at sites such as Tarquinia and Cerveteri which allowed archaeologists to date the founding of Etruscan sites to around 900 B.C.[9] Despite the similarities between the Protovillanovan folk of the Final Bronze Age and the Villanovan peoples of the early Iron Age—the practice of cremation and the use of biconical ash urns spring immediately to mind—the broader cultural relationship between them has not been well understood.[10] However, recent finds from southern Etruria provide evidence to clarify their relationship, suggesting, first, that the choice of Etruscan sites such as Tarquinia or Vulci follows a pattern developed in the final centuries of the Bronze Age and, secondly, that the foundation of Etruscan sites may well date to the Final Bronze Age rather than the early Iron Age, as previously thought. In simple terms, the founders of Etruscan cities may have been Protovillanovans, not Villanovans. This evidence has naturally returned the question of Etruscan origins to the forefront of scholarly discussion, for its interpretation proposes to alter significantly our present understanding of the roots of Etruscan culture. After sketching an outline of Protovillanovan culture as found in southern Etruria, I shall review some of the evidence which suggests that Etruscan sites were first occupied in the Final Bronze Age period, and finish with a discussion of possible reasons for the foundation of Etruscan cities.

A region of southern Etruria especially rich in finds of the Protovillanovan culture is the Fiora River valley (figure 1),[11] where the Etruscan city of Vulci would rise in a later period. Evidence from both settlements and cemeteries suggests that the middle course of the valley was an epicenter of Protovillanovan occupation; to date, evidence exists for as many as fifteen settlements and six cemeteries in the zone during the Final Bronze Age.[12] The coastal area, too, was occupied—although less densely, according to present research.[13] What physical resources does the middle zone of the valley offer which attracted such a concentration of habitation? First, topography characterized by steep-sided plateaus, naturally defensible on three sides (figure 2);[14] a striking feature of many Protovillanovan settlements is their location on

FIGURE 2. Fiora River at Poggio Buco, looking north. *Photo by author.*

the tops of prominent hills or plateaus.[15] Second, easy access to water, pasturage, and farmland (figure 1); the Protovillanovan economy was a mixed one, based principally on agriculture and stock-keeping.[16] Third, the Fiora River valley itself was an important communication route between the coast and inland; G. Barker suggests that the valley was used as a transhumance route perhaps as early as the Neolithic period.[17] Finally, copper ores, a vital resource to Protovillanovan bronzesmiths, exist in the middle zone of the valley, on the right bank of the river.[18] These features—a preference for easily defensible sites on the tops of plateaus with the means to support a mixed economy nearby, access to the natural communication routes provided by river valleys, and proximity to native mineral ores—typify the occupation pattern of coastal Etruria during the Final Bronze Age period.[19]

Protovillanovan settlements are typically small hut villages of about 4.5 hectares in extent, with a population estimated in the low hundreds.[20] In the Fiora River valley, our best evidence comes from Sorgenti della Nova, a plateau site occupied throughout the Final Bronze Age period.[21] Although this settlement is atypical in its size— it is one of the largest Protovillanovan villages excavated to date in southern Etruria[22]—the domestic architecture parallels that found at contemporary sites. Bedrock cuttings for over one hundred huts spread densely over the summit of the plateau and on artificial terraces cut into its steep sides.[23] The huts vary in shape and size: oval or sub-circular plans seem to predominate, but rectangular examples are also found. Their dimensions range from about three by three meters to about five by three meters.[24] Sorgenti della Nova also provides unusual evidence for the use of artificially cut grottoes as dwellings and storage spaces: a series of large chambers were cut into the northern flank of the plateau, in close association with huts on the adjacent terrace.[25] Interspaced between the doorways of the grottoes are the remains of several communal ovens.[26] To date, the excavations at Sorgenti della Nova have not yielded evidence of craft production on the site.[27] However, discoveries at Scarceta, a contemporary site on the opposite side of the valley, demonstrate that at least some Proto-villanovan settlements included areas set aside for bronze foundries and the working of bone tools and implements.[28]

Although Protovillanovan cemeteries are well attested in the Fiora River valley, rarely are they associated with contemporary settlements;[29] for example, the cemeteries belonging to the villages at Sorgenti della Nova and Scarceta have not been located. Rather, there is evidence for a scattering of small-sized cemeteries in the middle zone of the valley; thirteen burials is the maximum found in any one of them.[30] Cremation is the exclusive rite. The ashes and personal ornaments of the deceased are found inside a biconical urn covered by an overturned bowl. Often, the urn and bowl are placed inside a large oval container made of tufa, which is interred in a circular hole dug into the ground.[31] Sometimes the hole itself is lined with stone slabs.[32] Protovillanovan burials are generally characterized by a scarcity of grave gifts;[33] most often, no gifts accompany the urn and bowl. Sometimes a simple bronze *fibula* is found inside the urn, from time to time accompanied by paste or amber beads.

One of the most remarkable settlements in the Fiora River valley during the Final Bronze Age period is Crostoletto di Lamone, a plateau site found at the edge of the Selva di Lamone.[34] Explorations made before the site was ploughed under by the owner in possession of the land documented a series of very substantial megalithic walls,[35] made of local limestone boulders; as found, the walls were between one and two meters thick and about two meters in height. No pattern in their placement is recognizable, and their purpose is unknown; it has been variously suggested that they were intended for defense of the site, for the division of the site into zones, or for terracing.[36] Hut foundations were identified nearby but could not be excavated before the site was destroyed.[37] In the same area, eight tumulus tombs were explored;[38] several more were recognized but not excavated. The tumuli range in diameter from five to fourteen meters; they were up to 1.5 meters in height when found. Within one of the mounds, Tumulus I,[39] a dolmen-like burial chamber was discovered—that is, a long corridor lined with standing stone slabs. This mound, and several others on the site, produced evidence of both cremation and inhumation burials. It is believed that the construction of some of the tumuli may date back to the Late Bronze Age, when inhumation was the preferred burial rite; during the Final Bronze Age, these tumuli were reused for cremation burials.[40] The megalithic walls and burial tumuli at Crostoletto have been used by some archaeologists as evidence of a burgeoning stratification of Protovillanovan society,[41] an issue which has long vexed archaeologists, given the apparent "egalitarian" quality of Protovillanovan burials in general. Moreover, it has been suggested that the site of Crostoletto can be used to infer a "hierarchical" organization of settlements in the most populous zones of the Protovillanovan culture, such as the middle course of the Fiora River valley.[42] According to this interpretation, sites such as Crostoletto, with its massive stone walls and atypical tumulus burials, and Sorgenti della Nova, due to its large size and population, would have served as leading communities in their zones and sources of likely social and cultural influence for smaller settlements, but without direct political domination.

The quickening of cultural development which takes place during the Final Bronze Age is perhaps most unequivocally documented in the production of metal goods.[43] It is significant that the greatest concentrations of Protovillanovan settlement in Etruria occur in the zones where mineral resources are available—the Tolfa Hills, located between Cerveteri and Tarquinia; the Fiora River valley; and, further north, the Colline Metallifere. And although bronzes are not found in great number in either settlements or burials,[44] bronze hoards[45] dated to the Final Bronze Age period have been found throughout coastal Etruria, including two in the Fiora River valley.[46] Most include ingots and broken tools, in addition to finished goods, and so were probably the stock-in-trade of itinerant bronzesmiths.[47] The finished products demonstrate, generally, a rise in the rate of bronze production relative to earlier periods and, by the end of the Final Bronze Age, the emergence of local or regional schools of bronzeworking tied to preferences for particular types and styles of objects.[48] Moreover, the number and variety of tools—such as axes, chisels, and harpoons—increase during the period, evidence of the growing importance of bronze production to Protovillanovan economy.[49] Finally, Protovillanovan bronzes suggest that an extensive range of contacts, within Italy and abroad, was involved in the exchange of metal ores and finished objects.[50] N. Negroni Catacchio has found evidence of such contact between the Po River valley and the Fiora River valley in a particular type of bronze spade found at Sorgenti della Nova[51] and Frattesina di Polesina,[52] a large Protovillanovan village in the Veneto region of northern Italy. She suggests that some of the sites in the Fiora River valley acted as suppliers of metal ores to contemporary settlements in the Po River valley and that the circulation of prestige items such as amber and vitreous paste beads was linked to the exchange of metals.[53]

The Final Bronze Age period, then, witnessed a dense occupation of coastal southern Etruria; present evidence indicates that this is a time of significant demographic increase.[54] The choice of settlement sites was influenced by the needs for particular types of natural resources—grazing and farmland, metal ores—and a preference for easily defended places close to communication routes furnished by river valleys. Large-sized settlements, some with monumental architecture, may have acted as trend-setting centers. While the construction of the massive walls found at Crostoletto di Lamone probably implies a centrally organized division of labor,[55] other aspects of the socioeconomic organization of Protovillanovan villages can only be guessed at. R. Peroni reconstructs an elaborate "noble-client" system, in which an aristocratic class controls the use of land which is still communally owned;[56] other scholars accept a tribal organization headed by elite families.[57] Protovillanovan centers such as Sorgenti della Nova and Crostoletto are often deemed "protourban"[58]—that is, possessed of some features which characterize true cities[59]—although theoretical studies which might support such an assertion have yet to be carried out. Perhaps relevant to this issue is evidence which suggests that, by the end of the Final Bronze Age, metalsmiths are probably no longer to be considered itinerant—that is, serving numerous communities throughout a given zone; rather, they were tied to individual villages due to an increased demand for their products.[60]

Fieldwork of the last two decades has documented that the sites of the historical Etruscan cities were frequented as early as the Final Bronze Age period.[61] Sherd scatters attributed to the Protovillanovan period have been found on the plateaus of several of the southern coastal cities, such as Tarquinia[62] and Veio.[63] Additionally, in cemeteries of early Iron Age date, an occasional Protovillanovan burial has been found,[64] or objects which perhaps indicate that the area had been used as a cemetery during the Final Bronze Age period as well.[65] At Vulci, although no material associated with the Protovillanovan period has been found on the plateau itself, potsherds and a bronze fibula of Protovillanovan type have been retrieved from areas to the east and north of the city—areas subsequently occupied by cemeteries during the Villanovan period.[66] Despite the consistency of such finds in and around Etruscan cities, unequivocal proof of permanent settlement on these sites during the Final Bronze Age period—that is to say, the sort of proof which might be produced through the excavation of a stratified sequence of habitation—has been lacking.

However, the recent excavation of a habitation and ritual area on the Civita plateau at Tarquinia has provided evidence that the earliest settlement of this site in fact dates to the Protovillanovan period.[67] The excavated area lies about seven hundred meters west of the Ara della Regina, at the center of the Etruscan city. Here, a stratified sequence offers the first secure evidence of the close relationship between Protovillanovan and Villanovan habitation. Beneath remains of a settlement and ritual zone dated to the tenth and ninth centuries B.C.[68]— the early Iron Age period—lies a stratum associated with typical Protovillanovan sherds.[69] The conformation of the structures at this level remains unclear, due to the continuous occupation of the spot through the Hellenistic period. However, the excavator reports the discovery of several floors of crushed stone, a series of postholes carved in the bedrock perhaps attributable to hut foundations, a number of refuse pits, and remains of an oven made of baked clay which had been embedded in one of the floors—elements typical of Protovillanovan villages. Although the full excavation of the site is not complete and many questions remain concerning the Protovillanovan level and its relationship to structures in the overlying stratum,[70] it is nevertheless our first direct evidence for the settlement of an Etruscan city prior to the early Iron Age period.

Perhaps there is a wider context for the finds from Tarquinia. First, the occupation level excavated there demonstrates that at least one major Etruscan center was established in the Final Bronze Age period by members of the Protovillanovan culture. This finding should be understood within the context of evidence from other centers, such as Vulci, which suggests a pattern of frequentation of many Etruscan sites in the Protovillanovan period.[71] That is to say, Villanovan settlements of around 900 B.C. were not made on virgin soil, as has been supposed,[72] but developed on already established sites.[73]

Secondly, it has long been recognized that almost all Protovillanovan sites in southern Etruria were abandoned around 900 B.C., at the time when Villanovan centers with their large cremation cemeteries were established.[74] Whether there was a connection between these two circumstances and what the nature of that connection might have been were unclear.[75] The fact that the Protovillanovan center at Tarquinia was not abandoned at this time might provide some explanation for this radical change in settlement patterns, which coincides with the end of the Bronze Age and beginning of the early Iron Age. Tarquinia and the other principal Villanovan centers of southern coastal Etruria—Cerveteri and Vulci—are sites remarkably similar to those typically occupied by Protovillanovan folk.[76] They are plateau sites, steeply flanked on three sides, naturally well fortified; water, pasturage, and farmland are easily accessible; they lie on or near communication routes provided by river valleys; and mineral resources are nearby. In fact, the physical environment of these sites differs from those occupied in the Protovillanovan period in only two features: the plateaus are much larger in extent (between 90 and 160 hectares,[77] as opposed to 4.5 on average for Protovillanovan sites), and they are located near the coast. Perhaps, then, one reason for the abandonment of Protovillanovan sites around 900 B.C. was overpopulation;[78] the old plateaus had become too small and their agricultural resources too meager to support the increase of population witnessed during the Final Bronze Age period. This is not to discount the importance of maritime trade, so often evoked as a determining factor in the siting of Etruscan cities near the sea;[79] by 800 B.C. the coastal centers were engaged in a vigorous trade in metals among themselves[80] and with overseas partners, especially Sardinia.[81] However, I do wonder what Herodotus might have made of Protovillanovan land-hunger as a cause for the foundation of Etruscan cities.

NOTES

1. Hdt. 1.94.

2. D.H. 1.28.

3. For a review of scholarship on the origins question, see M. Pallottino, *The Etruscans*, rev. ed., ed. D. Ridgway, trans. J. Cremona (Harmondsworth, Engl., 1978), 64–81.

4. M. Pallottino, *L'origine degli Etruschi* (Rome, 1947), 113 ff.

5. See, for example, R. Peroni, ed., *Il bronzo finale in Italia: Archeologia, materiali, e problemi 1* (Bari, It., 1980); also *Il bronzo finale in Italia: Atti della XXI riunione scientifica dell'Istituto italiano di preistoria e protostoria . . .* (Florence, 1979), hereinafter cited as *Atti XXI*.

6. For central Tyrrhenian Italy, see A. M. Bietti Sestieri, *The Iron Age Community of Osteria dell'Osa: A Study of Sociopolitical Development in Central Tyrrhenian Italy* (Cambridge, 1992), with bibliography; also, A. M. Bietti Sestieri et al., *Roma e il Lazio dall'età della pietra alla formazione della città* (Rome, 1985), 149–94.

7. Surveys of the history of scholarship and of the material evidence pertinent to the Protovillanovan culture may be found in F. Rittatore Vonwiller, "La cultura protovillanoviana," *Popoli e civiltà dell'Italia antica* 4 (1975): 11–60; M. A. Fugazzola Delpino, "Problematica protovillanoviana," *Origini* 10 (1976): 245–332; M. A. Fugazzola Delpino, "The Proto-Villanovan: A Survey," in *Italy before the Romans: The Iron Age, Orientalizing, and Etruscan Periods*, ed. D. Ridgway and F. R. Ridgway (London, 1979), 31–51.

8. An excellent overview is provided by G. Bartoloni, *La cultura villanoviana: All'inzio della storia etrusca* (Rome, 1989).

9. Bartoloni (ibid., 98–102, with bibliography, 104) summarizes the extensive scholarship on early Iron Age chronology.

10. M. Pallottino reviews the present state of this issue in "Prospettive attuali del problema delle origini etrusche," in *Atti del Secondo congresso internazionale etrusco . . .* (Supplemento di *SE*) (Rome, 1989), 1:57–58, hereinafter cited as *Secondo congresso*.

11. Summarizing treatments can be found in N. Negroni Catacchio, "Il bronzo finale nella valle del fiume Fiora," in *Atti XXI*, 321–27 (vol. supra n. 5); Rittatore Vonwiller, "La cultura protovillanoviana," 30–35 (supra n. 7).

12. For a list of sites, see F. Rittatore Vonwiller et al., "Preistoria e protostoria della valle del fiume Fiora," in *La civiltà arcaica di Vulci e la sua espansione: Atti del X convegno di Studi etruschi e italici* (Florence, 1977), 99–165 (vol. hereinafter cited as *Atti X*), esp. section written by N. Negroni Catacchio, 132–49; also M. A. Fugazzola Delpino and F. Delpino, "Il bronzo finale nel Lazio settentrionale," in *Atti XXI*, sites 3–18, 277–84 (vol. supra n. 5); F. di Gennaro, *Forme di insediamento tra Tevere e Fiora dal bronzo finale al principio dell'età del ferro . . .*, 14 (Florence, 1986), 32–56 pass.

13. M. Cristofani, "Il popolamento," in M. Cristofani, ed., *Gli Etruschi in Maremma* (Milan, 1981), 33. Two coastal sites of some importance in the Final

Bronze Age are Grotta "Sassi Neri," a cave frequented from the Early Bronze Age through the Etruscan period, perhaps with ritual function (Negroni Catacchio in Rittatore Vonwiller, "Valle del fiume Fiora," 149 [supra n. 12]; N. Negroni Catacchio, "Ritrovamenti dell'età del bronzo sul colle di Talamonaccio [Orbetello-Grosseto]," *RSP* 34 [1979]: 261); and Archi di Pontecchio, a hill settlement found about 5 km south of Vulci, apparently occupied throughout the Bronze Age (di Gennaro, *Forme di insediamento*, 55–56, with bibliography and fig. 9A [supra n. 12]).

14. For the physical environment of the Fiora River valley, the best treatment remains that by Rittatore Vonwiller, "Valle del fiume Fiora," 99–103 (supra n. 12).

15. F. di Gennaro, "Organizzazione del territorio nell'Etruria meridionale protostorica: Applicazione di un modello grafico," *DArch*, 2d ser., 4 (1982): 103, with bibliography. See also R. Peroni and F. di Gennaro, "Aspetti regionali dello sviluppo dell'insediamento protostorico nell'Italia centro-meridionale alla luce dei dati archeologici e ambientali," *DArch*, 3d ser., 4 (1986): 194–98, where di Gennaro suggests that the pattern of hilltop settlement in southern Etruria was already developed in the Middle Bronze Age. For a critical appraisal of the evidence, see Bietti Sestieri, *Iron Age Community*, 30–31 (supra n. 6).

16. See A. M. Bietti Sestieri, "Produzione e scambio nell'Italia protostorica: Alcune ipotesi sul ruolo dell'industria metallurgica nell'Etruria mineraria alla fine dell'età del bronzo," in *L'Etruria mineraria: Atti dei XII convegno di Studi etruschi e italici* (Florence, 1981), 243–44, with bibliography; also Bietti Sestieri, *Iron Age Community*, 34–35 (supra n. 6).

17. G. Barker, "The Conditions of Cultural and Economic Growth in the Bronze Age of Central Italy," *PPS* 38 (1972): 189–93 and fig. 8.

18. D. De Rita and L. Versino, "Geologia e geomorfologia," in N. Negroni Catacchio et al., *Sorgenti della Nova: Una comunità protostorica e il suo territorio nell'Etruria meridionale* . . . (Rome, 1981), 72 and pl. 12; G. Tanelli, "I depositi metalliferi dell'Etruria e le attività estrattive degli Etruschi," in *Secondo congresso*, 3:1413 (vol. supra n. 10).

19. See n. 15 above.

20. Peroni and di Gennaro, "Aspetti regionali," 195 (supra n. 15); F. di Gennaro, "Il popolamento dell'Etruria meridionale e le caratteristiche degli insediamenti tra l'età del bronzo e l'età del ferro," in *Etruria meridionale: Conoscenza, conservazione, fruizione* . . . (Rome, 1988), 69, 76.

21. N. Negroni Catacchio et al., *Sorgenti della Nova: Una comunità protostorica e il suo territorio nell'Etruria meridionale* . . . (Rome, 1982), the latest of the two exhibition catalogues of the same title (1981 work supra n. 18); hereinafter cited as Negroni Catacchio, *Sorgenti della Nova* (1982); also excavation reports by the same author in the "Notiziario" section of *RSP* 39 (1984): 362–63; 40 (1985–86): 407; 41 (1987–88): 402.

22. N. Negroni Catacchio, "L'abitato del bronzo finale di Sorgenti della Nova: Possibilità di confronti con i modelli abitativi dei centri villanoviani," in *Secondo congresso*, 1:273 n. 5, and 276 (vol. supra n. 10); N. Negroni Catacchio, "La fase di transizione bronzo-ferro in Etruria alla luce degli scavi di Tarquinia," in *Tarquinia:*

Ricerche, scavi, e prospettive ... , ed. M. Bonghi Jovino and C. Chiaramonte Trère (Milan, 1987), 220, n. 2.

23. For an excellent summary of the domestic architecture, see Negroni Catacchio, "L'abitato del bronzo finale," 275–76 (supra n. 22).

24. P. Ucelli Gnesutta, "L'abitato delle Sorgenti della Nova," in *Atti XXI*, 329–37 (vol. supra n. 5).

25. Ibid.

26. Negroni Catacchio, *Sorgenti della Nova* (1982), 49 (supra n. 21).

27. See A. M. Bietti Sestieri, "La cultura di villaggio," in *Civiltà degli Etruschi*, ed. M. Cristofani (Milan, 1985), 29, for a discussion of likely village-based artisan activities.

28. A. Soffredi, "L'abitato all'aperto dell'età del bronzo di Scarceta (Manciano-Grosseto)," in *Atti X*, 167–72, with bibliography (vol. supra n. 12); R. Poggiani Keller in "Notiziario" section, *RSP* 40 (1985–86): 402–4; Bietti Sestieri, *Iron Age Community*, 35 (supra n. 6).

29. For an excellent summary of Protovillanovan cemeteries and grave goods, see Bietti Sestieri, "La cultura di villaggio," 27–29 (supra n. 27).

30. See Bietti Sestieri's proposal that the low number of burials found in Protovillanovan cemeteries (i.e., the scarcity of Protovillanovan tombs in general) might be a result of burial customs which have left no archaeological trace: ibid., 27–28.

31. E.g., at Castelfranco Lamoncello; see Negroni Catacchio in Rittatore Vonwiller, "Valle del fiume Fiora," 139–41 (supra n. 12).

32. As at Cavallin del Bufalo; see M. Ceccanti, "Notiziario" section of *RSP* 35 (1980): 385–86.

33. Bietti Sestieri, "La cultura di villaggio," 28–29 (supra n. 27).

34. R. Poggiani Keller and P. Figura, "I tumuli e l'abitato di Crostoletto di Lamone (prov. di Viterbo): Nuovi risultati e precisazioni," in *Atti XXI*, 346–81, with preceding bibliography (vol. supra n. 5).

35. Ibid., 347, 349, and fig. 1.

36. R. Peroni, "Interventi," in *Atti X*, 284 (vol. supra n. 12); see also Poggiani Keller and Figura, "Crostoletto di Lamone," 377–79 (supra n. 34).

37. Poggiani Keller and Figura, "Crostoletto di Lamone," 348–49 (supra n. 34).

38. Ibid., 355–70.

39. Ibid., 355–58 and fig. 4.

40. Ibid., 373–77.

41. See, for example, Rittatore Vonwiller, "Valle del fiume Fiora," 109, 156–57 (supra n. 12); R. Peroni and N. Negroni Catacchio, "Ultime pagine di Ferrante Rittatore Vonwiller sul 'protovillanoviano,'" in *Atti XXI*, 38, with comments by M. Pallottino, 46 (vol. supra n. 5); Bietti Sestieri, "La cultura di villaggio," 28 (supra n. 27), offers a critical view.

42. Bietti Sestieri, *Iron Age Community*, 31 (supra n. 6); Bietti Sestieri, "La cultura di villaggio," 27 (supra n. 27); Negroni Catacchio, "La fase di transizione," 219–20 n. 2 (supra n. 22); di Gennaro is more cautious in "Organizzazione del territorio," 105 (supra n. 15), and in Peroni and di Gennaro, "Aspetti regionali dello sviluppo," 193–94 (supra n. 15).

43. A. M. Bietti Sestieri's contributions to the study of Bronze Age metal production are particularly important; see "The Metal Industry of Continental Italy (13th–11th Century B.C.) and Its Connections with the Aegean," *PPS* 39 (1973): 383–424; also n. 16 above. For summary treatments, see Bietti Sestieri, "La cultura di villaggio," 29–30 (supra n. 27); Bietti Sestieri, *Iron Age Community*, 35–36 (supra n. 6).

44. See, for example, the comprehensive list of bronzes from the Fiora River valley discussed by Negroni Catacchio in "Il bronzo finale nella valle del fiume Fiora," 321–27 (supra n. 11).

45. Fundamental studies by R. Peroni include: . . . *Ripostigli del massiccio della Tolfa*, Inventaria archeologica, Italia, 1 (Florence, 1960); . . . *Ripostigli del grossetano*, Inventaria archeologica, Italia, 2 (Florence, 1961). G. L. Carancini, "I ripostigli dell'età del bronzo finale," in *Atti XXI*, 631–41, with bibliography (vol. supra n. 5), proposes a three-phased chronological subdivision of Final Bronze Age hoards.

46. The Piano del Tallone and "tra Manciano e Samprugnano" hoards, both found near Manciano on the right bank of the river; see, most recently, E. Pellegrini, "Nuovi dati su due ripostigli dell'età del bronzo finale del Grossetano: Piano del Tallone e 'tra Manciano e Samprugnano,'" *BPI* 83 (1991–92): 341–60, with preceding bibliography.

47. Bietti Sestieri, "La cultura di villaggio," 29 (supra n. 27).

48. Ibid.

49. Ibid., 29, 30.

50. Ibid., 30.

51. Negroni Catacchio, "Il bronzo finale nella valle del fiume Fiora," 325 and fig. 1, item 8 (supra n. 11).

52. N. Negroni Catacchio, "Rapporto tra l'area alto-adriatica e quella medio-tirrenica durante il bronzo finale," *Padusa* 20 (1984): 515–17.

53. Ibid.; Pellegrini, "Nuovi dati su due ripostigli," 348 (supra n. 46), however, does not discount the possibility of an extra-Italian origin for some types of bronze objects found at Frattesina. See also the report of a bone object linked to types from the Veneto found in the Final Bronze Age settlement at Le Sparne: A. Zanini, "Notiziario," *RSP* 42 (1989–90): 370–72.

54. Peroni and di Gennaro, "Aspetti regionali dello sviluppo," 194–95 and figs. 1–2 (supra n. 15).

55. Bietti Sestieri, "La cultura di villaggio," 29 (supra n. 27).

56. Peroni and Negroni Catacchio, "Ultime pagine," 33–43 (supra n. 41); R. Peroni, "Presenze micenee e forme socioeconomiche nell'Italia protostorica," in

Magna Grecia e mondo miceneo: Atti del XXII convegno di studi sulla Magna Grecia, ed. G. Pugliese Caratelli (Taranto, It., 1983), 269–70, 280–81.

57. See contributions by G. Colonna and M. Pallottino in discussion of Peroni's remarks, "Ultime pagine," 44–46 (supra n. 41). Bietti Sestieri opts for a simpler structure, based on the family, in "La cultura di villaggio," 29 (supra n. 27).

58. For example, M. Pallottino, in remarks following "Ultime pagine," 45 (remarks supra n. 57), argues against G. Colonna's objection to the use of this term to describe Protovillanovan settlements. Peroni finds them to be "preurban" in "Presenze micenee," 280–81 (supra n. 56).

59. Negroni Catacchio attempts to differentiate between characteristics of a "village" and a "city" in "L'abitato del bronzo finale di Sorgenti della Nova," 272–73 (supra n. 22).

60. Bietti Sestieri, "La cultura di villaggio," 29–30 (supra n. 27).

61. Negroni Catacchio, "La fase di transizione," 221–26, with bibliography (supra n. 22), discusses the relevant evidence for all Etruscan cities in Etruria.

62. For sherds at Castellina and Pian di Civita, see di Gennaro, *Forme di insediamento,* 63, 65, and fig. 11C (supra n. 12).

63. Porta nordovest; see ibid., 103–4, fig. 24B, with discussion, 65.

64. From Veio, on Tomb 838, Casale del Fosso cemetery, see A. P. Vianello Cordova, "Una tomba 'protovillanoviana' a Veio," *SE* 35 (1967): 295–306, pls. LIV–LVI; from Cerveteri, Sorbo cemetery, Fondo Chiana zone, on Tomb 163, see R. Vighi, "Il sepolcreto arcaico del Sorbo," *MonAL* 42 (1955): 75, fig. 10, pl. III.

65. On unpublished sherds from the Poggio Selciatello di Sopra cemetery at Tarquinia, see M. A. Fugazzola Delpino in M. Bonghi Jovino, ed., *Gli Etruschi di Tarquinia* (Modena, It., 1986), 56–57, with bibliography; see also di Gennaro, "Il popolamento dell'Etruria meridionale," 79, n. 27 (supra n. 20). This is also the case at Vulci.

66. The early notices of Protovillanovan material at Vulci in Fugazzola Delpino and Delpino, "Il bronzo finale nel Lazio settentrionale," 282 and 284, sites 15–18 (supra n. 12), and di Gennaro, *Forme di insediamento,* 32–36, figs. 1D and 2A (supra n. 12), have proven to be too optimistic: see corrections in di Gennaro, "Il popolamento dell'Etruria meridionale," 69 n. 19 (supra n. 20). Of secure attribution remain the fibula from the Ponte Rotto necropolis area to the east of the plateau, a vase fragment from Poggio Maremma, northwest of the Ponte dell'Abbadia (see di Gennaro, *Forme di insediamento,* pl. 4, site "B" [supra n. 12]), and the remains of a cremation burial (fragmentary urn, bowl, and terracotta spool), probably of Proto-villanovan date, from the Osteria cemetery, to the north of the plateau, published by K. Raddatz, "Eisenzeitliche Fundstellen von Vulci," *Praehistorische Zeitschrift* 58 (1983): 227–28, 244, and items 11–13 in fig. 8 (Fundstelle 5).

67. Bonghi Jovino, *Gli Etruschi di Tarquinia* (supra n. 65); M. Bonghi Jovino, "Gli scavi nell'abitato di Tarquinia e la scoperta dei 'bronzi' in un preliminare

inquadramento," in Bonghi Jovino and Chiaramonte Trère, *Tarquinia*, 59–77 (vol. supra n. 22).

68. See Bonghi Jovino, *Gli Etruschi di Tarquinia*, 89–92 (supra n. 65); Bonghi Jovino, "Gli scavi nell'abitato di Tarquinia," 62–63 and pl. XVII (supra n. 67).

69. Bonghi Jovino, *Gli Etruschi di Tarquinia*, 83–89 (supra n. 65); Bonghi Jovino, "Gli scavi nell'abitato di Tarquinia," 61–62 (supra n. 67).

70. For example, the use of a "natural cavity" (feature 263) as a ritual zone during the Final Bronze Age and successive periods: Bonghi Jovino, *Gli Etruschi di Tarquinia*, 84–85 (supra n. 65); Bonghi Jovino, "Gli scavi nell'abitato di Tarquinia," 62 (supra n. 67).

71. See Negroni Catacchio, "La fase di transizione," 226 (supra n. 22), for a summary of the evidence.

72. E.g., B. d'Agostino, "La formazione dei centri urbani," in Cristofani, *Civiltà degli Etruschi*, 44 (vol. supra n. 27).

73. Negroni Catacchio, "La fase di transizione," 220–21 (supra n. 22).

74. Di Gennaro, "Organizzazione del territorio," 108, 110 (supra n. 15); Peroni and di Gennaro, "Aspetti regionali dello sviluppo," 196 (supra n. 15); for Vulci and its territory, see Rittatore Vonwiller, "Valle del fiume Fiora," 109–10 (supra n. 12); G. Colonna, "La presenza di Vulci nelle valli del Fiora e dell'Albegna prima del IV secolo a.C.," in *Atti X*, 193 (vol. supra n. 12).

75. The deliberations on this issue have been innumerable. For an economic viewpoint, see Negroni Catacchio in Rittatore Vonwiller, "Valle del fiume Fiora," 162–63 (supra n. 12), and contributions by M. Torelli and R. Peroni in "Interventi," in *Atti X*, 281–87 (vol. supra n. 12). Colonna's remarks in "La presenza di Vulci" (supra n. 74) about the continuity of settlement patterns between the Final Bronze Age and the early Iron Age seem prescient. Fugazzola Delpino and Delpino ("Il bronzo finale nel Lazio settentrionale," 312–13 [supra n. 12]) opt for a violent "crisis" caused by social upheavals.

76. See Negroni Catacchio, "La fase di transizione," 221, 226 (supra n. 22), where she cautions against overestimating the significance of changes in the settlement patterns at the end of the Bronze Age.

77. Di Gennaro, *Forme di insediamento*, 135 (Vulci, 90 hectares), 136 (Tarquinia, 120 hectares), 139 (Cerveteri, 160 hectares) (supra n. 12).

78. Suggested by Negroni Catacchio, "L'abitato del bronzo finale di Sorgenti della Nova," 282–83 (supra n. 22).

79. Cf. Bartoloni, *La cultura villanoviana*, 107 (supra n. 8).

80. Ibid., 152–58, with bibliography, 171–72.

81. Ibid., 165–70, with bibliography, 173. Vulci's contacts with Sardinia are documented by a set of bronze objects (a chieftain-priest figurine, and a miniature basket and stool) found in a cremation tomb from the Cavalupo cemetery, dated ca. 800 B.C.; see M. T. Falconi Amorelli, "Tomba villanoviana con bronzetto nuragico," *AC* 18 (1966): 1–15.

The Judgment of Paris?
An Etruscan Mirror in Seattle

HELEN NAGY

Etruscan mirrors have long been the focus of scholarly attention.[1] E. Gerhard's monumental volumes could not help but raise the browser's wonder at the rich range of types and subjects found in these relatively humble objects. For a century Gerhard's tomes have provided the most practical source, especially for iconographic research, on Etruscan mirrors. Today the multiplying volumes of the *Corpus Speculorum Etruscorum*,[2] an international project devoted to the publication of descriptions of all known Etruscan mirrors, allow for an ever wider scope of studies on these objects. Thanks to the scientific nature of these fascicles, scholars are in a better position to assign dates, to identify workshops, and to speculate on economic factors affecting the production and patronage of the mirrors. Described in these sources is the focus of the present study, an object that provides some insight into production practices and raises questions regarding iconographic variations and the sources for them.

Seattle Art Museum inventory number 48.36 is a typical circular tang mirror with an extension between the disc and the tang.[3] The mirror is 26.4 centimeters long and has a diameter of 17.8 centimeters; its weight is approximately 400 grams. The tang was made to be inserted into a separate handle; these were typically of bone or ivory,

FIGURE 1. Engraved Etruscan mirror, third century B.C., Seattle Art Museum, inv. 48.36. *Photo courtesy of the Seattle Art Museum, Eugene Fuller Memorial Collection.*

although a few independent bronze handles also survive.[4] The tang of this mirror has a tapering shape, classified by R. D. De Puma as type TI, with a squared base.[5]

The mirror is well preserved with a lovely green patina and occasional patches of brownish speckles and encrustation (figure 1). On both sides the incised lines have subsequently been filled with a white substance. The obverse, or reflecting side, is slightly convex (figure 2). A palmette ornament emerging from two volutes decorates the extension; this is a common motif which occurs in a number of variations on mirrors of a wide chronological range.[6] The reverse has a gently concave profile. A narrow rim protects the disc, and the extension on this side is decorated with a simple three-petal lotus bud, a ubiquitous element on Etruscan mirrors of many types.[7] The entire field of the disc is filled with a scene composed of four large figures

FIGURE 2.
Seattle Etruscan mirror, obverse. *Photo courtesy of the Seattle Art Museum, Eugene Fuller Memorial Collection.*

arranged to complement the circular shape (figure 3; see also figures 1 and 6). Behind this group is a reduced pedimental façade that neatly fills in the circle. The lines of incision are fine and even and suggest a confident hand.

The figure on the left, a woman nude except for a Phrygian cap, necklace, and fancy shoes, stands with her right leg forward and turned out so that her foot appears foreshortened. Her left hand is raised up to her chin and seems to grasp the edge of a mysteriously draped mantle; the folds are visible behind her on both sides, but there is no means for its attachment on her shoulders. Her right arm hangs slightly behind, as if pushing back the mantle. Shoulder-length curls in concentric circles escape from the cap. The mouth is a gentle arc; the eye is open in profile but with the iris a full circle. Eyelid and eyebrow are indicated.

FIGURE 3.
Seattle Etruscan mirror, reverse. *Photo courtesy of the Seattle Art Museum, Eugene Fuller Memorial Collection.*

The next figure, a woman, occupies virtually the full center of the composition. She wears a long sleeveless *peplos* pinned on the shoulders;[8] it has a long overfold and is belted loosely at the waist with a resulting *kolpos*. She, too, wears shoes; her right foot is turned out in profile, while the left steps forward and is foreshortened in a position parallel to the right foot of the nude figure. The woman also wears a simple torque. Her head is turned somewhat to her right; the face is in three-quarter view. The mouth is a bow with a line below (figure 4). This figure has her left arm akimbo, hand turned out above the knee. Her right hand is raised to her face, fingers apart. Her hair is arranged in concentric curls with a double topknot.

The third figure is virtually hidden behind the woman in the center and the figure on the right. His head (it is probably a male because of the mantle he wears) is seen in profile. He wears a Phrygian cap and with his right hand pulls a tip of his mantle up to his chin. Curved broken lines hastily indicate short hair below the cap.

The figure on the far right, again a woman, appears to be seated, although we see no seat. She also wears a Phrygian cap decorated with dots, a bead necklace, and a peplos belted below the breasts to form a gentle kolpos. A mantle draped across her legs and lap hides the edge of the overfold. Her left leg is stretched out, the foot foreshortened; the right foot peeks out in profile amidst the confusion of hems and feet. The woman's left arm hangs by her side; the right hand is raised to her face in a gesture that parallels that of the central figure.

The mirror, of unknown provenience, may be dated early in the third century B.C. This date, however, is necessarily approximate, since it is based on typological and stylistic affinities with comparable objects, most of which are also dated the same way. As more volumes of the *CSE* appear, scholars will be in a better position to assess the chronology of mirrors based on the results of chemical analysis and on the archaeological context of comparable objects.[9]

The stylistic features of Seattle 48.36 are somewhat eclectic. The two figures on the right have very large heads in proportion to their bodies. The left two are somewhat more "normal." The nude figure's torso is elongated; the central figure's garments also emphasize the vertical. The artist relies on double parallel lines (figure 5), but except for the stippling used to "model" the anatomy of the nude figure there is no attempt at shading, although foreshortening and overlapping of the figures and the diagonals of the architecture do suggest some depth.

Four-figure compositions of the sort represented on the Seattle mirror are very common on Etruscan mirrors of all varieties. They occur with a remarkable assortment of protagonists who are often difficult to identify.[10] Two mirrors that may appear nearly identical at first glance could well represent widely different subjects with the simple variation of a single figure.[11] A frequent category shows the Dioskouroi in the company of other divinities; these compositions occur with seemingly endless variations.[12] Often the protagonists defy identification without the aid of inscriptions.[13] Such compositions are the most characteristic subjects on the so-called *Kranzspiegel* (or "spiky-garland") group of hand mirrors.[14] The subject matter of the mirror in Seattle has been interpreted as the "judgment of Paris," a common theme of such four-figure compositions.[15] On closer

FIGURE 4 *(above left).* Detail of reverse of Seattle mirror showing face of central figure. *Photo courtesy of the Seattle Art Museum, Eugene Fuller Memorial Collection.* FIGURE 5 *(above right).* Detail of reverse of Seattle mirror showing drapery of central figure. *Photo courtesy of the Seattle Art Museum, Eugene Fuller Memorial Collection.*

examination, however, we can accept this identification only if we agree that the hidden figure is male and therefore represents Paris. Even assuming the male gender of this figure, such an interpretation is problematical.

The theme of the judgment of Paris occurs in Greek art from the seventh century B.C. on.[16] The famous Chigi vase in the Museo di Villa Giulia[17] provides one of the earliest examples. On this small Protocorinthian *olpe* the scene in question takes place just below the handle. The three goddesses, preceded by Hermes, move in a line from the right and approach Paris, who faces them. Two of the goddesses—Athena and Aphrodite—are indicated by inscriptions. Another early instance of this subject is on an ivory comb from Sparta[18] dated approximately 600 B.C., where a comfortably enthroned Paris calmly greets the arrival of the goddesses, whose extended hands imply as much their pleas as their gifts. In both of these early works Aphrodite, the eventual winner of the contest, arrives last. On the Chigi vase she is identified by the inscription, as mentioned; on the Spartan comb her identity is indicated by the enormous bird (her goose) that stands behind her.

Over several centuries the theme continued to occupy Greek artists, occurring on black- and red-figure vases with some frequency and with ever richer iconographic variation.[19] In addition to Paris and the three goddesses, Hermes is an important figure in these representations. He is usually shown conducting the three contestants to a (frequently) seated Paris,[20] who is often accompanied by a dog or some other animal or is shown seated on a rock to emphasize his pastoral occupation.[21] At times, understandably reluctant to assume his role as beauty contest judge, he flees the approaching Hermes, who in some instances restrains Paris physically.[22]

The variations in the representation of this subject in Greek art are numerous. Sometimes extra protagonists are added;[23] in other instances the number is notably reduced.[24] Similar variations on the theme occur in Magna Graecia as well, where it assumes a significance and iconography of its own, as J.-M. Moret points out in a study of a number of southern Italian vases representing the judgment of Paris.[25] Moret found that the role of Hera receives special emphasis, especially on Paestan vases, thus underlying her important position and gift to Paris.[26] The significance of the gifts of the goddesses, rather than the selection of Aphrodite as winner, seems also to be the primary concern in the early Greek works. As already pointed out, both on the Chigi vase and on the Spartan comb Aphrodite is last in line and has no visibly favored status. Aphrodite's significant position is made explicitly evident by her nudity only after the middle of the fifth century, although earlier she is sometimes shown set apart or in fancier clothes than the other divine women.[27]

The theme of the judgment of Paris appears early in Etruscan art. On the "Boccanera plaques" from Cerveteri, now in the British Museum, an energetic Hermes, identified by his hat and traveling mantle and followed by the goddesses, urges a bearded Paris to his task.[28] Aphrodite is again last, but not without a certain advantage, as she displays her ample thighs and fancy shoes below the short hem of her garment. The subject is also represented by the Paris Painter on the shoulder of a Pontic *amphora* from Vulci of the mid–sixth century B.C., now housed in Munich.[29] Hermes is leading the goddesses (Aphrodite last) to Paris, who is shown on the other side of the neck tending his flock. Hermes is preceded by a bearded, white-haired man whose identity has been disputed but who certainly cannot be Paris.[30]

The processional or linear approach used for the most part in vase painting or on wall plaques, or to fill other rectangular or broad fields, obviously had to be adapted to suit the circular format of the mirrors. Most of these, therefore, show densely grouped protagonists. Hermes is present on a number of mirrors, especially those with five figures;[31] but the general preference for four-figure compositions usually results in his elimination. Furthermore, the mirrors seldom represent the rustic terrain or dog indicated on many of the Greek and southern Italian vases. Instead, the figures are regrouped to fit the circular frame, often in front of an architectural façade which is quite wrong for the story but instead suggests a theatrical setting.

Unmistakably identifiable examples of the judgment of Paris on Etruscan mirrors usually emphasize the connection between Aphrodite and Paris by means of gestures, glances, or the placement of the principal figures. Frequently Aphrodite and Paris are placed on opposite sides of the field in similar positions, their glances echoing one another.[32] On other examples, either Paris or Aphrodite occupies center stage.[33] On the Seattle mirror the two women on the outside are engaged in a hypnotic exchange, as the other two figures stare at the nude Aphrodite. The connection between Aphrodite and the hidden male figure (if Paris) by means of an appraising glance is not made here. Instead, everyone stares at the nude goddess as if wondering if she had forgotten to dress.

The Seattle mirror is not a unique example of such garbled iconography on Etruscan mirrors. Gods, goddesses, and heroes are often combined in seemingly haphazard groups. An example of such a case, a hand mirror of the spiky-garland variety in the J. Paul Getty Museum, was published by L. Bonfante.[34] This mirror shows four figures: two identical youths, wearing little beyond Phrygian caps, who frame the two other figures, Athena on the left and a mostly nude youth. Were it not for the accompanying inscription on the border of the mirror, one would assume that the flanking youths represent the Dioskouroi. Indeed, in numerous similar compositions they are, or have been assumed to be, the Dioskouroi.[35] But on the Getty mirror, as well as on a number of others, their identities have been changed into totally different characters simply by means of the inscriptions.[36] On the Getty mirror the figures are indicated as *Menle* (Menelaos) on the right and *Pru   the* (Prometheus?) on the far left. The characters in the center are *Talmithe* (Palamedes?) on the right and *Mer   a* (Minerva), partly hidden. On a similar mirror in Paris (Cabinet des Médailles, inv. 1291) *Laran, Turan, Menerva*, and *Aplu* are indicated.[37] Bonfante remarked that "such a light-hearted approximation of any figure and name is typical of this group of Hellenistic mirrors."[38] However, the occurrence of certain pairs of names and not necessarily of the figures they "signify" suggests, according to Bonfante, that they were added by the workshop to satisfy a literate clientele who knew the various protagonists from the stage.[39] It seems that it was the written names, not the configuration of the protagonists, that called to mind a particular drama. This connection with theater would also explain the omnipresent architectural background.

The Seattle mirror can be assigned to a small group of large tang mirrors of similar dimensions that show like compositions and provide close stylistic parallels. The group is vaguely related to a larger category assigned by G. Mansuelli to the "Menelaos master."[40] The similarities characterizing this larger group, however, are limited to a few details, such as the peculiar treatment of the hair. The subcategory of the Seattle mirror is distinguished by the size and form and by the simple lines, which are generally sure but in some instances deteriorate into downright clumsiness. Even in such a small group we can ascertain a significant iconographic variety. The Seattle mirror (figure 6) and three others form a particularly tight unit within the subcategory, with a few closely related pieces which result in a distinct subcategory.

The first of the three, now in Frankfurt (Museum für Vor- und Frühgeschichte, inv. 1984.6), is of uncertain provenience but may come from Città delle Pieve. U. Höckmann dates this mirror to the late third or early second century B.C.[41] Its height is 31 centimeters, including the handle, and its diameter is 17.7 centimeters (figure 7).[42] This mirror retains its ivory handle, or has been joined with one since its recovery. At first glance, the composition of its engraved scene appears virtually identical to that of the Seattle mirror. However, closer examination of the differences between the two reveals that the nude woman on the left wears a *stephane* and a bracelet but has no necklace. The second figure has no pins on her shoulders, nor does she appear to wear a necklace. The hidden figure is similar to his counterpart, but he has *two* right hands! The artist apparently took details from two models and somehow mixed them together. Finally, the figure on the right is definitely male. But, judging from the mantle, so is the hidden one. This scene, therefore, cannot represent the judgment of Paris. Höckmann considers the hidden figure on the Frankfurt mirror to represent Athena.[43] As this character is almost identical to the corresponding figure on the Seattle mirror, would that mean that four women are being depicted? According to Höckmann, yes.[44] It is probably best to avoid specific identifications, while recognizing the close reliance on identical workshop prototypes for the individual figures.

The Frankfurt mirror is somewhat sloppier in execution than the one in Seattle. The drapery behind the nude female makes no sense

FIGURE 6. Reverse of Seattle Etruscan mirror in line rendering for comparison purposes. *Drawing by author.*

FIGURE 7. Engraved Etruscan mirror, possibly from Città delle Pieve, late third or early second century B.C., Frankfurt, Museum für Vor- und Frühgeschichte, inv. 1984.6. *Drawing from U. Höckmann,* CSE *BRD 1 (Munich 1987), no. 16.*

FIGURE 8. Engraved Etruscan mirror, probably from Castanetta, third century B.C., Braunschweig, Herzog Anton Ulrichs Museum, inv. AB 234. *Drawing from U. Liepmann,* CSE *BRD 2 (Munich 1988), no. 3.*

FIGURE 9. Engraved Etruscan mirror, third century B.C., Paris, Bibliothèque Nationale, Cabinet des Médailles, inv. 1295. *Drawing from Gerhard,* ES *1, pl. 194.*

and her form is more awkward; the second figure's drapery lacks the double lines and the hem to the overfold; the architecture is more hurriedly executed. Overall, the lines are less secure and clumsier.

The second mirror, at Braunschweig's Herzog Anton Ulrichs Museum (inv. AB 234), is 17.6 centimeters in diameter. Its exact provenience is unknown, but it is probably from Castanetta; the object was a gift of Theodore Stützel in 1899, and most of his collection came from Castanetta.[45] This work (figure 8) is also clumsier in execution than the Seattle mirror but is clearly related. The nude figure on the left is now male but wears the Phrygian cap, like the Seattle Aphrodite. The female figure by his side wears a torque, bracelet, and earrings and holds up an edge of an otherwise invisible mantle, evidence again that the artist was probably working from prototypes and combining parts—a hand, head, body, and so forth—to make a whole that at times resulted in illogical or confusing figures, such as the one with the extra hand on the Frankfurt mirror. The figure on the right is also male, similar to the corresponding figure on the Frankfurt mirror. The hidden figure's one visible hand parallels the gesture of the lower of the two right hands of his counterpart on the Frankfurt mirror. The use of double lines is abandoned; the faces are so crudely rendered as to be almost idiotic in their expressions.

The mirror completing the Seattle subcategory is in Paris (Cabinet des Médailles, inv. 1295). Measuring 17.3 centimeters in diameter, it has no specific provenience and was once part of the Durand collection (figure 9).[46] Of the four, this one is the most complex in details. The pediment is supported by columns, and the drapery folds have a certain flourish in addition to the double lines. On the left is again a male figure in a pose that combines elements of the corresponding Seattle Aphrodite (right arm hanging and right leg with foreshortened shod foot) and the Braunschweig figure (left leg and gender). This figure wears a helmetlike hat that probably identifies him as Hermes, who is frequently shown on mirrors wearing a similar hat.[47] His hair is completely different from that of the other figures in the grouping: it hangs in a series of thick, wavy locks. The cape now makes a little more sense, but his left leg hovers in the air, suggesting that the prototype had a support for the foot that was suppressed by the artist of this mirror.[48] The second figure from the left is similar to her counterpart on the Seattle mirror but wears a wreath and has fancier shoulder pins and earrings. Her left arm is raised, and with the right she holds up the edge of an otherwise nonexistent mantle.[49] Her lower body does not join logically with the upper part; the folds of her garment begin by her side and show no modeling. The hidden figure is a woman, and she now turns toward the viewer. Her hair is arranged in a fashion similar to that of the second figure on the Seattle mirror, with two top curls. The male figure on the right is virtually identical to his counterparts on the Frankfurt and Braunschweig mirrors. Again, the subject cannot be the judgment of Paris; but on a hand mirror in the Chigi collection in Siena is an almost identical Hermes (in hair, helmet, pose, and so on, although the right arm is differently placed) in the company of the three goddesses Aphrodite, Hera, and Athena.[50] This same Hermes appears on a mirror in the Vatican Museum (inv. 12665), with Achilles and two goddesses, in a scene perhaps representing the arming of Achilles, with the hero having just assumed his weapons.[51]

A number of additional mirrors of the same type and like dimensions exhibit similarities to the Seattle group and may probably be associated with the same workshop.[52] These objects, all tang mirrors, show similarly crowded compositions of seemingly monumental figures and like decoration of the extension. However, while each includes some details similar to those characterizing the Seattle group, none can be firmly inserted as a member. They must therefore be regarded separately for now.

The four mirrors of the Seattle group share type, shape, dimensions, extension ornament, like grouping of similar figures with heavy proportions and large heads, the gabled architectural backgrounds, and such details as the treatment of the hair, gestures, poses, and the excessive use of the Phrygian cap. Yet no two are the same. This suggests that, while they may have been produced in the same workshop (at Chiusi or in its vicinity) using identical models, the identities of the figures were varied, perhaps to provide each piece with a separate subject and thus add variety to the workshop's offerings or to meet the needs of diverse patrons, who in these cases unfortunately seem not to have wanted to display their erudition by means of identifying inscriptions.

In the end, examination of the scene on the Seattle mirror in the context of its companion pieces does little to identify the subject being represented. Is it the judgment of Paris? We may never know for certain. Nevertheless, this comparative study does shed some light on the commerce evident behind the mirrors—the demand that led to their production and the techniques that determined their final form. Although the engraver who produced the Seattle mirror must remain anonymous, by placing his work in the context of similar objects, researchers can come closer to understanding the factors that led to the products of his workshop.

NOTES

1. See esp. *ES* 1–4; *ES* 5; N. T. de Grummond, ed., *A Guide to Etruscan Mirrors* (Tallahassee, Fla., 1982). For additional sources consult the bibliography of any recent fascicle of the *CSE*, such as R. D. De Puma, *CSE* USA 2: Boston and Cambridge (Ames, Iowa, 1993).

2. At the time of this writing seventeen volumes of *CSE* have been published, including collections in former East and West Germany (DDR and BRD, respectively); France (the Louvre); Italy (Bologna); Denmark; the Netherlands; Hungary and Czechoslovakia; Great Britain (Cambridge); and two USA fascicles. The publication of the *CSE* volumes of the great Italian collections is anxiously awaited.

3. The mirror is a gift of the Eugene Fuller Memorial Collection, purchased on 28 January 1948 from the Heeramaneck Galleries. For bibliography on it, see *Seattle Art Museum Handbook* (Seattle, 1951), 107; *The Nude in Art: Vancouver Art Gallery, November 3–29, 1964* (Vancouver, B.C., 1964), no. 1; M. del Chiaro, *Etruscan Art from West Coast Collections* (Santa Barbara, Calif., 1967), 44 no. 60; L. E. Lord, "The Judgment of Paris on Etruscan Mirrors," *AJA* 41 (1937): 602–6.

I wish to thank Dr. Gail E. Joyce, registrar of the Seattle Art Museum, for her generous assistance with my research, and Susan Dirk for the excellent photographs and slides of the mirror.

4. De Grummond, *Guide to Etruscan Mirrors*, 11 (supra n. 1); De Puma, *CSE* USA 2, 14–15, and fig. 3, which shows an independent bronze handle (supra n. 1). For additional examples of bone handles, see U. Höckmann, *CSE* BRD 1 (Munich, 1987), no. 16 (round bone handle); U. Liepmann, *CSE* BRD 2 (Munich, 1988), nos. 16 (mirror with bone handle), 20, 22, 23 (fancy carved bone handles);

B. von Freytag gen. Löringhoff, *CSE* BRD 3 (Munich, 1990), no. 19 (mirror with simple bone handle).

5. For terminology, see De Puma, *CSE* USA 2, 13–20 (supra n. 1); specifically on tang types, see ibid., 16.

6. For a few examples, see Höckmann, *CSE* BRD 1, nos. 23, 38 (supra n. 4); Liepmann, *CSE* BRD 2, no. 29 (supra n. 4); Freytag Löringhoff, *CSE* BRD 3, nos. 5, 19 (supra n. 4).

7. For hand mirrors, see Liepmann, *CSE* BRD 2, no. 14 (supra n. 4); for a tang mirror, see Freytag Löringhoff, *CSE* BRD 3, no. 19 (supra n. 4), among the many other examples.

8. For descriptions and definitions of Etruscan garments, see L. Bonfante, *Etruscan Dress* (Baltimore, 1975).

9. For some recent studies on dating hand mirrors, see U. Höckmann, "Die Datierung der hellenistisch-etruskischen Griffspiegel des 2. Jahrhunderts v. Chr.," *JDAI* 102 (1987): 247–89. Another discussion of the problems of dating and an example of the significance of context is offered by H. Salskov Roberts, "Later Etruscan Mirrors: Evidence for Dating from Recent Excavations," *ARID* 12 (1983): 31–54. For specific examples of the problems raised in dating, see Freytag Löring-hoff, *CSE* BRD 3, 42 no. 19 (supra n. 4). In this case, vaguely dated parallels are used as well as stylistic parallels and other art forms. I. B. Weinman's significant study, *Malstria-Malena: Metals and Motifs in Etruscan Mirror Craft* (Göteborg, Swed., 1990), esp. chap. 15 (230–42), raises the importance of metal analysis as a tool for dating or for confirming approximate dates.

10. A glance through any volume of the *CSE* or of *ES* 1–4 will yield numerous examples of four-figure compositions, many of which look identical or nearly so. In most instances the individual figures defy precise identification. On this see also L. Bonfante, "An Etruscan Mirror with 'Spiky Garland' in the Getty Museum," *GMusJ* 8 (1980): 147–50.

11. For example, in Paris (D. Rebuffat-Emmanuel, *CSE* France 1, Louvre 1 [Rome, 1988], no. 23) and Hamburg (Liepmann, *CSE* BRD 2, no. 19 [supra n. 4]) are typologically identical hand mirrors with nearly identical four-figure compositions. The third figure on the left is female on the Paris mirror but male on the one in Hamburg. This must result in a completely different interpretation of the scene.

12. For a discussion of the Dioskouroi on Etruscan mirrors, see R. D. De Puma, "The Dioskouroi on Four Etruscan Mirrors in Midwestern Collections," *SE* 41 (1973): 159–70. The mirror pictured in Liepmann, *CSE* BRD 2, 32 no. 10 (supra n. 4) is identified as the Dioskouroi in conversation with two female divinities; 36 no. 12 in the same work represents a scene virtually identical to no. 10. See entry for no. 12 for a discussion of problems of identifying such seemingly identical groups. An inscribed mirror in Frankfurt (Höckmann, *CSE* BRD 1, no. 15 [supra n. 4]) shows the same composition (the background is somewhat different). The figures here are identified from right to left as Paris (*Elax*), Hera (*Un/i/*), and Athena (*Me/ra/*); the fourth inscription is missing. For a recent treatment of these types and

an attempt to attribute them, see J. Gy. Szilágyi, *CSE* Hongrie, Tchécoslovaquie (Rome, 1992), 63–64 no. 21. The short garments and Phrygian caps of the flanking figures in these examples most closely resemble the numerous representations of the Dioskouroi alone (de Grummond, *Guide to Etruscan Mirrors*, 158 [supra n. 1]; D. Rebuffat-Emmanuel, *Le Miroir étrusque: D'après la collection du Cabinet des Médailles*, Collection de l'Ecole française de Rome, 20 [Rome, 1973], 464–74).

13. Höckmann, *CSE* BRD 1, no. 15 (supra n. 4); for the mirror in the J. Paul Getty Museum, see Bonfante, "Etruscan Mirror with 'Spiky Garland,'" 147–54 figs. 1–3 (supra n. 10); de Grummond, *Guide to Etruscan Mirrors* (supra n. 1); for a discussion regarding the interpretation of such a four-figure composition, see M. Renard, "Miroir étrusque inédit de la Collection P. Desneux," in *Hommages à Waldemar Deonna*, Collection Latomus, 28 (Brussels, 1957), 411–17. See also Rebuffat-Emmanuel, *Le Miroir étrusque*, esp. 462–63 (supra n. 12), for a discussion of four- and five-figure "stereotyped" compositions.

14. For this category in general, see R. Herbig, "Die Kranzspiegelgruppe," *SE* 24 (1955–56): 183–205. More recently, see U. Höckmann, "Zur Datierung der sogennanten Kranzspiegel," in *Atti del Secondo congresso internazionale etrusco . . .* (Supplemento di *SE*) (Rome, 1989), 2:713–20.

15. F. Brommer, *Denkmalerlisten zur griechischen Heldensage* (Marburg, Ger., 1976), 3:353–55; *ES* 5:112–31, pls. 98–105. C. Clairmont, *Das Parisurteil in der antiken Kunst* (Zurich, 1951), 65–76, lists Etruscan mirrors representing the judgment of Paris; many are four-figured compositions. Lord, "Judgment of Paris on Etruscan Mirrors" (supra n. 3), provides a list of possible variations in figural arrangements for this theme. See also E. Simon, "Etruskischer Griffspiegel mit dem Urteil des Paris," *AA* (1985): 299–306.

16. For the representation of this theme in Greek art, see Clairmont, *Das Parisurteil in der antiken Kunst* (supra n. 15); J. Harrison, "The Judgment of Paris: Two Unpublished Vases in the Graeco-Etruscan Museum at Florence," *JHS* 7 (1886): 196–219. Pausanias (3.18.12, 5.17.5) describes two famous early works (now lost) representing this theme: the chest of Kypselos and the throne at Amyklai, both probably of the seventh century B.C. For a hypothetical reconstruction of the chest of Kypselos, see K. Schefold, *Myth and Legend in Early Greek Art* (New York, 1966), 72–73, fig. 26.

17. From a grave at Formello near Veio; attributed to the Macmillan Painter. K. Fittschen, *Untersuchungen zum Beginn der Sagendarstellungen bei den Griechen* (Berlin, 1969), 169, sb69; D. Amyx, *Corinthian Vase-Painting in the Archaic Period* (Berkeley, Calif., 1988), 32 no. 3; 369–70 ("Chigi Painter"). For a discussion of the Chigi vase and illustration of the judgment of Paris, see T. Rasmussen, "Corinth and the Orientalising Phenomenon," in *Looking at Greek Vases*, ed. T. Rasmussen and N. Spivey (Cambridge, 1991), 57–62.

18. Athens, National Museum, inv. 15368, from the Sanctuary of Artemis Orthia; R. M. Dawkins, ed., *The Sanctuary of Artemis Orthia at Sparta . . .*, Society for the Promotion of Hellenic Studies Supplementary Papers, 5 (London, 1929), 223

pl. 127; *LIMC* 11:499 no. 6 pl. 376, s.v. "Alexandros"; K. Reinhardt, *Das Parisurteil* (Frankfurt, 1938), pass., pl. 1.

19. Clairmont, *Das Parisurteil in der antiken Kunst*, pass. (supra n. 15); Harrison ("The Judgment of Paris," pass. [supra n. 16]) noted an iconographic development from the processional format to a more free arrangement of the figures in landscape with accessory figures and objects by the late fifth to early fourth century B.C. This is especially true in southern Italy. For some early examples of vases, see J. de la Genière, "A propos d'un vase grec," *MMAI* 63 (1908): 31–56 regarding a tripod *kothon* in Lille (fig. 4) and a similar representation, also on a tripod kothon (fig. 5) by the C Painter (Louvre, inv. CA 616); see also *ABV* 58 no. 122. De la Genière also illustrates a late example by the Meidias Painter (fig. 17) in Karlsruhe (Badischen Landesmuseum, inv. 259) in which a lavishly clad Paris performs the judgment in a rocky landscape surrounded by the principal protagonists, as well as some attendant figures (*ARV²* 1315).

20. For the significance of Hermes, see J.-M. Moret, "Le Jugement de Paris en Grande-Grèce: Mythe et actualité politique: A propos du lébès paestan d'une collection privée," *AK* 21.2 (1978): 88; pl. 22.4 shows Hermes approaching a seated Paris.

21. See Clairmont, *Das Parisurteil in der antiken Kunst* (supra n. 15); this configuration is found mostly on red-figure vases. See also references in I. Jucker, "Ein etruskischer Spiegel mit Parisurteil," *MH* 39 (1982): 7–9. Louvre, inv. A.478, a black-figure *kylix*, shows a fleeing Paris accompanied by a huge dog and pursued by a winged Eris, then Hermes (de la Genière, "A propos d'un vase grec," figs. 11, 12 [supra n. 19]).

22. Lydos in British Museum, inv. 1948.10–15.1 (*ABV* 108 no. 8); also a neck amphora in Florence, Museo Archeologico, inv. 70995 (*ABV* 110 no. 32), on which Hermes exerts himself to catch the fleeing Paris. For illustrations of these, see J. D. Beazley, *The Development of Attic Black-Figure* (Berkeley, Calif., 1986), 40–41 pl. 35 nos. 3–5. See de la Genière, "A propos d'un vase grec" (supra n. 19), which provides several additional examples.

23. These are especially common during the fifth century B.C. and later, although some early examples include the figure of Eris (see de la Genière, "A propos d'un vase grec," figs. 5, 11, 12 [supra n. 19]).

24. Moret, "Le Jugement de Paris en Grande-Grèce," 80 pl. 22.4 (with Aphrodite and Athena omitted), 82 nos. 3, 4 (with Paris omitted), 83 pl. 25.2–4 (Berlin), 83 pl. 27 (Naples) (supra n. 20).

25. An interesting study of the theme in southern Italian vase painting appears in ibid.

26. Ibid., 80, 82 nos. 3, 4. Moret also discusses at some length the significance of the promises of the goddesses, and particularly that of Hera. Helen in Euripides' *Trojan Women* (919–34) lists the gifts of the goddesses.

27. For an overview of Aphrodite's attributes and their changes with time, see Clairmont, *Das Parisurteil in der antiken Kunst*, 108–10 (supra n. 15).

28. From the Banditaccia cemetery, second quarter of the sixth century B.C.; see F. Roncalli, *Le lastre dipinte da Cerveteri* (Florence, 1905), 28–33, 69–77, pls. XII–XV; S. Haynes, "Ein etruskisches Parisurteil," *RhM* 83 (1976): 227–31.

29. J. D. Beazley, *Etruscan Vase Painting* (New York, 1976), 1, 12 pl. 1 nos. 3–4; L. Hannestad, *The Paris Painter: An Etruscan Vasepainter*, trans. M. Moltesen, Historisk-filosofiske meddelelser, 47.2 (Copenhagen, 1974), 5 no. 1 pls. 1–2.

30. See Clairmont, *Das Parisurteil in der antiken Kunst*, 18 (supra n. 15), for some suggestions. A similar bearded old man is shown on a mirror from Todi in the Museo di Villa Giulia (de Grummond, *Guide to Etruscan Mirrors*, fig. 101 [supra n. 1]); he is identified by an inscription as *Tecrs*.

31. Clairmont, *Das Parisurteil in der antiken Kunst*, 65–66 nos. K203–K206 (supra n. 15) (K203: Villa Giulia; K204: Orvieto; K205: Villa Giulia; K206: Louvre [see also Rebuffat-Emmanuel, *CSE* France 1, no. 4 (supra n. 11)]); Jucker, "Ein etruskischer Spiegel mit Parisurteil," 6 (supra n. 21), to give just a few examples. For a discussion of the general representation of Hermes in the context of the "Judgment," see Clairmont, *Das Parisurteil in der antiken Kunst*, 106 (supra n. 15).

32. For example, the lovely mirror in the Museo di Villa Giulia from Todi (M. Sprenger and G. Bartoloni, *The Etruscans: Their History, Art, and Architecture* [New York, 1983], fig. 238) that includes extra figures shows Paris very much in "contact" with an unabashedly nude Aphrodite. The other figures are left outside their sphere of contact. On a mirror from Orvieto (*ES* 5:184), the connection between Aphrodite and Paris is further emphasized by their gestures. A mirror in Oberlin (R. D. De Puma, *CSE* USA 1: Midwestern Collections [Ames, Ia., 1987], no. 28, discussion of type on 48) shows both Aphrodite and Hera nude; but Aphrodite turns to Paris, thereby excluding the other two figures. Paris and Hera face one another on a mirror in Houston (de Grummond, *Guide to Etruscan Mirrors*, fig. 6 [supra n. 1]), but Aphrodite stands possessively close by Paris and gazes at him.

33. For Paris in the center, see Brussels, Musées Royaux, inv. R 1253 (R. Lambrechts, *Les Miroirs étrusques et prénestins des Musées Royaux d'Art et d'Histoire à Bruxelles* [Brussels, 1978], no. 3).

34. Bonfante, "Etruscan Mirror with 'Spiky Garland,'" 147–54 (supra n. 10).

35. Ibid.; see also n. 12. On the Dioskouroi, see also, in this volume, the essay by Alexandra Carpino, 69, 74ff.

36. Ibid., 147–48.

37. Rebuffat-Emmanuel, *Le Miroir étrusque*, no. 9 pl. 9 (supra n. 12).

38. Bonfante, "Etruscan Mirror with 'Spiky Garland,'" 148 (supra n. 10). She cites J. D. Beazley's remarks in a similar vein ("The World of the Etruscan Mirror," *JHS* 69 [1949]: 16).

39. Bonfante ("Etruscan Mirror with 'Spiky Garland,'" 152–54 [supra n. 10]), comments that on a variety of Etruscan objects representations of "themes from the tragedies of Euripides were favorites, though the Etruscan public may have known these only indirectly, by way of adaptations by local Etruscan, or Roman playwrights."

On representations of comic theater in Etruria, see V. Jolivet, "Aspects du théâtre comique en Etrurie préromaine et romaine: A propos d'un vase étrusque à figures rouges du Musée du Louvre," *RA* (1983): 13–50. See also, in this volume, the essay by Robert L. Maxwell, 267–85.

40. *SE* 19 (1946–47): 59–62.

41. Höckmann, *CSE* BRD 1, 39–40 (supra n. 4).

42. Ibid., 37–40 no. 16. The inscriptions incised over several of the figures are probably modern (39).

43. Ibid., 37.

44. Ibid.: ". . . zeigt vier Frauenfiguren" (". . . shows four figures of women").

45. Liepmann, *CSE* BRD 2, 21–22 no. 3 (supra n. 4); no specific context. P. Jacobsthal and A. Langsdorf (*Die bronze Schnabelkannen* [Berlin, 1929], 69, 73) questioned the provenience of individual objects in the collection, indicating that Stutzel purchased these (including the mirrors) from various sources.

46. Rebuffat-Emmanuel, *Le Miroir étrusque*, 98–102 no. 13 (supra n. 12).

47. Numerous Etruscan mirrors represent Hermes (*Turms*) wearing such a hat (sometimes with the characteristic wings). For a few examples, see de Grummond, *Guide to Etruscan Mirrors*, 95 (supra n. 1); Rebuffat-Emmanuel, *CSE* France 1, no. 7 (supra n. 11); R. V. Nicholls, *CSE* Great Britain 2: Cambridge (Cambridge, 1993), no. 13; De Puma, *CSE* USA 2, no. 28 (supra n. 1); Vatican Museums, inv. 12665; Siena, Chigi Collection (*ES* 5:103.2). Often he is juxtaposed in a symmetrical composition with another figure, echoing like works showing the Dioskouroi; see De Puma, *CSE* USA 1, no. 17 (supra n. 32); DePuma, *CSE* USA 2, no. 34 (supra n. 1).

48. A Praenestine *cista* in Berlin (Staatliche Museen, inv. 3467) represents a changed version of the judgment of Paris. Paris (*Alixente[r]*) stands with his leg resting on a rock in a position resembling that of Hermes on the Cabinet des Médailles mirror (G. Foerst, *Die Gravierungen der praenestinische Cisten* [Rome, 1978], no. 7).

49. This gesture occurs on all four of the mirrors in this group, with and without drapery, regardless of logical consequences.

50. Siena, Chigi Collection (*ES* 5:103.2); *LIMC* 2:172 no. 20, s.v. "Aphrodite/ Turan."

51. Vatican Museums, inv. 12665; *ES* 1:192; *LIMC* 1:207, 211–12 no. 109, s.v. "Achle," third century B.C.

52. For example, from Chiusi (*ES* 4:368); Volterra, Guarnacci Museum, inv. 922 (G. Cateni, *Volterra: Museo Guarnacci* [Pisa, 1988], 89, 90, dis. 2); Paris, Cabinet des Médailles, inv. 1294 (Rebuffat-Emmanuel, *Le Miroir étrusque*, pl. 12 [supra n. 12]); Esslingen, Ger., in a private collection (Freytag Löringhoff, *CSE* BRD 3, no. 19 [supra n. 4]).

Greek Mythology in Etruria: An Iconographic Analysis of Three Etruscan Relief Mirrors

ALEXANDRA CARPINO

Among the over four thousand extant Etruscan mirrors are a very few whose principal decoration on the reverse is not engraved but cast in relief and sometimes embellished with metal inlays.[1] There are no antecedents for this rare type of mirror in the Near East, Egypt, or Greece, suggesting that it is an Etruscan invention. Of the sixteen known examples, fourteen reside in European collections and two in the United States. (These figures do not include two mirrors whose subjects are cast in sunk relief.) Three of the relief mirrors date between 500 and 475 B.C.; seven fall between the mid-fifth and early third centuries B.C.; and the remaining six are of uncertain antiquity.[2] These unique artifacts document the Etruscans' wealth, creativity, and metallurgic skill during the Archaic and Classical periods. Furthermore, their small number suggests that they were specific commissions designed to augment the social status of a selected group of aristocratic Etruscans. They are larger, heavier, and more elaborately decorated than their engraved counterparts; but like them, they also had a symbolic function: all, eventually, were interred in tombs where, as

FIGURE 1. Etruscan relief mirror, *Machaon's (Machan's) Healing of Philoktetes (Pheltuse)*, ca. 460–450 B.C., Bologna, Museo Civico Archeologico, inv. 273. *Photo by author; used by permission of Museo Civico Archeologico.*

| 65 |

gifts, they may have helped the souls of the deceased to be transported into the afterlife.[3]

The subjects on the reverses of seven of these relief mirrors originate in Greek mythology and literature, but none represent direct copies of this material. Instead, they depict unique or unusual themes, such as the delivery of Helen's egg (figure 2),[4] Talos' triumph over the Boreads (figure 3),[5] or Machaon's healing of Philoktetes (figures 1 and 4).[6] Scholars have often interpreted these variant representations in two ways: either they indicate the Etruscans' inability to fully comprehend their sources, or they represent copies of now-lost Greek or Magna Graecian paintings or sculptures. When the mirrors' subjects are analyzed in the context of Etruscan cultural and religious traditions, however, their differences are more easily understood.

The iconography of many Etruscan mirrors indicates that the Etruscans had a sophisticated knowledge of Greek mythology but that they often changed or added characters to the stories they assimilated

FIGURE 2. Etruscan relief mirror, *The Delivery of Helen's Egg,* ca. 350 B.C., Boston, Museum of Fine Arts, inv. 1971.138. William E. Nickerson Fund No. 2. *Photo courtesy of Museum of Fine Arts, Boston.*

FIGURE 3. Etruscan relief mirror, *Talos and the Boreads*, from Rome, ca. 420–400 B.C., Antikensammlung, Staatliche Museen zu Berlin, inv. 30480. *Photo by Saturia Linke.*

FIGURE 4. Line rendering of *Machaon's (Machan's) Healing of Philoktetes (Phletuse)*, figure 1. *Drawing from G. Sassatelli, CSE Italia 1—Bologna, Museo Civico, fasc. 1 (Rome: "L'ERMA" di Bretschneider, 1981), fig. 14a.*

from visiting Greek merchants, immigrants, and artists.[7] On the relief mirror now in Boston (figure 2), for example, the depiction of Hermes delivering Helen's egg to Leda and Tyndareos, although unusual, demonstrates a clear familiarity with the Greek myth. While most ancient authors agreed that Helen of Troy was fathered by Zeus and hatched from an egg in the care of Leda, they differed in their identification of her mother. The Spartans believed that Leda was Helen's mother, while the Athenians claimed that Helen was the daughter of Zeus and Nemesis, an Attic fertility deity with a shrine at Rhamnus.[8] Because of the popularity of the cult of Nemesis in Athens, images of Helen's egg were particularly in vogue in Greece during the fifth and fourth centuries B.C.[9] A red-figure *krater* by Polion from the late fourth century B.C.,[10] for example, depicts Leda looking at the egg with her arms raised in surprise, as if she had never seen it before. It sits on an altar, resting on warm ashes. Tyndareos stands behind Leda, and her two sons before her. To the right of the altar, a column topped by a miniature statue of Zeus suggests that the setting is a sanctuary dedicated to the god—an appropriate location, since Zeus was Helen's father. The bearded god holds a scepter and a phiale in his outstretched hand, as if offering a libation to his daughter's egg.

In the Greek colonies of southern Italy, vase painters departed from the tradition of the motherland by preferring to depict the actual moment of Helen's birth, with the egg cracking and the baby springing out of it. An Apulian *pelike* by the Painter of Athens 1680,[11] for example, shows Helen sitting in the partially broken shell on an altar, while a late fourth-century B.C. bell krater by the Caivano Painter has Helen completely hatched and spreading her arms out to greet her foster parents.[12] Several scholars have suggested that the iconography of these southern Italian images relates specifically to the popularity of the Orphic and Dionysiac cults in this region between the early Classical and Hellenistic periods, since followers of these cults believed that Kronos formed an egg in *aether* (sky) from which Phanes, the bisexual creator and first king of the gods, sprang forth.[13]

The Boston relief mirror indicates that the Etruscans were also interested in Helen's egg but that they chose to modify the myth when they began to represent it on their mirrors and vases in the fourth century B.C. Unlike the Greek and Magna Graecian images, the Etruscan versions focus primarily on a preliminary event: the egg's delivery by Hermes (figures 2 and 5) or one of the Dioskouroi (figures 6 and 7).[14] These characters could easily be interchanged in the minds of the Etruscans, since the Dioskouroi shared between them a single immortal existence and therefore moved easily between the worlds of the dead and the living, as did Hermes, the god responsible for trans-porting the souls of the dead to the afterlife.

L. Bonfante suggests that these Etruscan delivery scenes reflect the importance of the family in Etruscan society, since the arrival of the egg is an event that naturally brings about the assembly of all the family members.[15] This alone, however, does not entirely explain the Etruscan modification, since the Greek images also focus on the fam-ily, albeit gathered around an altar. Instead, what seems to connect all of the Etruscan scenes to each other is the overriding interest in the egg itself: usually it is quite large and dominates the center of the composition. Although no texts have survived which provide insights into the function and meaning of eggs in Etruria, many works of art

FIGURE 5. Etruscan engraved mirror, *Delivery of Helen's Egg,* from Avenches, Switzer-land, fourth century B.C., Lausanne, Musée Cantonal d'Archéologie et d'Historie, inv. 82. *Drawing by Shawn R. Skabelund after Gerhard.*

demonstrate that they played an important role in Etruscan religious life. Numerous Tarquinian tomb paintings, for example, illustrate the deceased either holding eggs or offering them to others to eat or contemplate, suggesting that they functioned as a provision which gave the deceased eternal energy and life in the underworld.[16] African ostrich eggs, as well as eggs made out of stone, terracotta, and alabaster, also appear in Etruscan tombs between the seventh and third centuries B.C., demonstrating that their presence was often symbolic.[17] In the Near East, eggs were considered symbols of fertility, life-giving power, and, ultimately, resurrection; and the Etruscans' paintings and artifacts suggest that they, too, viewed the egg as a chthonian motif.[18]

In view of these associations, it is possible to interpret the Etruscans' interest in the delivery of Helen's egg as indicative of their ideas about birth and rebirth, especially since all of the extant artifacts depicting the story were eventually interred with their owners. The ultimately funerary nature of these images is also accentuated by the presence of the fish in the exergue of the Boston relief mirror, a

FIGURE 6. Etruscan engraved mirror, *Delivery of Helen's Egg*, prob. from Orvieto, early third century B.C., Orvieto (from Mancini collection). *Drawing by Shawn R. Skabelund after Klügmann and Körte.*

motif also found on an engraved mirror of the late fourth century B.C. from Porano with the same subject (figure 7).[19] In many Etruscan tombs, fish signified the sea, or the water that one must traverse to reach the afterlife. Their appearance on these two mirrors suggests that they symbolize the journey which preceded Helen's arrival in her foster home.

Thus, these delivery scenes not only depict the origin of one of the Etruscans' favorite heroines, but they also exemplify for their owners the hope of a fertile and productive existence, both during their lifetimes and after their deaths. This modification of the Greek myth, therefore, not only considers the multiple functions of Etruscan mirrors and vases, but it also underscores their talent for transforming Greek stories into expressions of local belief.

A late fifth-century B.C. relief mirror now in Berlin[20] (see figure 3) also depicts a Greek story that has been cleverly modified by an Etruscan artist, perhaps at the insistence of the patron. Here, a centrally placed nude man fashioned in a figural style reminiscent of Myron or

FIGURE 7. Etruscan engraved mirror, *Delivery of Helen's Egg*, from Porano, late fourth century B.C., Perugia, Museo Archeologico, inv. 847. *Drawing by Shawn R. Skabelund after Klügmann and Körte.*

Polykleitos has his arms wrapped around the necks of two winged men. He seems to be ready to crush them to his chest. One of the winged men grasps the central figure's upper thigh, while the other has his arms wrapped around his opponent's waist. Both bend from the pressure of their entrapment. They have thick mustaches and beards, and the fillets holding their hair in place are articulated with two flaps that hang down their cheeks. In her discussion of a Hellenistic cinerary urn from Chiusi, now in New York, Bonfante notes the presence of similar fillets on severed heads and suggests that they functioned as a visual motif indicative of the deaths or impending deaths of those wearing them.[21] Considering the nature of the fight shown, it is more than likely that these fillets have a similar meaning on this mirror.

The fight takes place in a rocky environment. A large boulder appears in the foreground, helping to steady one of the winged men. A frontally positioned silen head with large eyes, a pug nose, a furrowed brow, and a bushy beard sits beneath the central figure's feet. Although L. Curtius suggests that it functioned to localize the fight at a spring,[22] the absence of spouting water makes this hypothesis unlikely. As an engraved Praenestine mirror now in Toledo (figure 8) illustrates, silen-headed springs generally emit water.[23] O. Brendel believes that the head represents an original Etruscan motif imbued with chthonian connotations;[24] and the nature of the fight makes this hypothesis seem more likely. Moreover, an engraved mirror from Palestrina (figure 9) similarly includes a silen head in a scene which G. Sassatelli has identified as an obscure account of Ariadne's imminent death.[25]

The tang of the Berlin relief mirror contains a cast siren. A careful analysis of this element, however, indicates that it was a later addition, dating perhaps to the Roman period. Nevertheless, given the overt theme of impending death on the mirror, the repairer's use of this particular motif may indicate that the original tang contained either an engraved or cast siren. A similar juxtaposition, moreover, appears on a mirror from Vulci, dating to the late fifth century B.C., on which two warriors battle above a siren in the exergue.[26]

Curtius identifies the figures on the Berlin relief mirror as the Cretan giant Talos and the twin sons of Boreas: Kalais and Zetes.[27] According to Apollonius Rhodius, Talos "was of the stock of bronze,

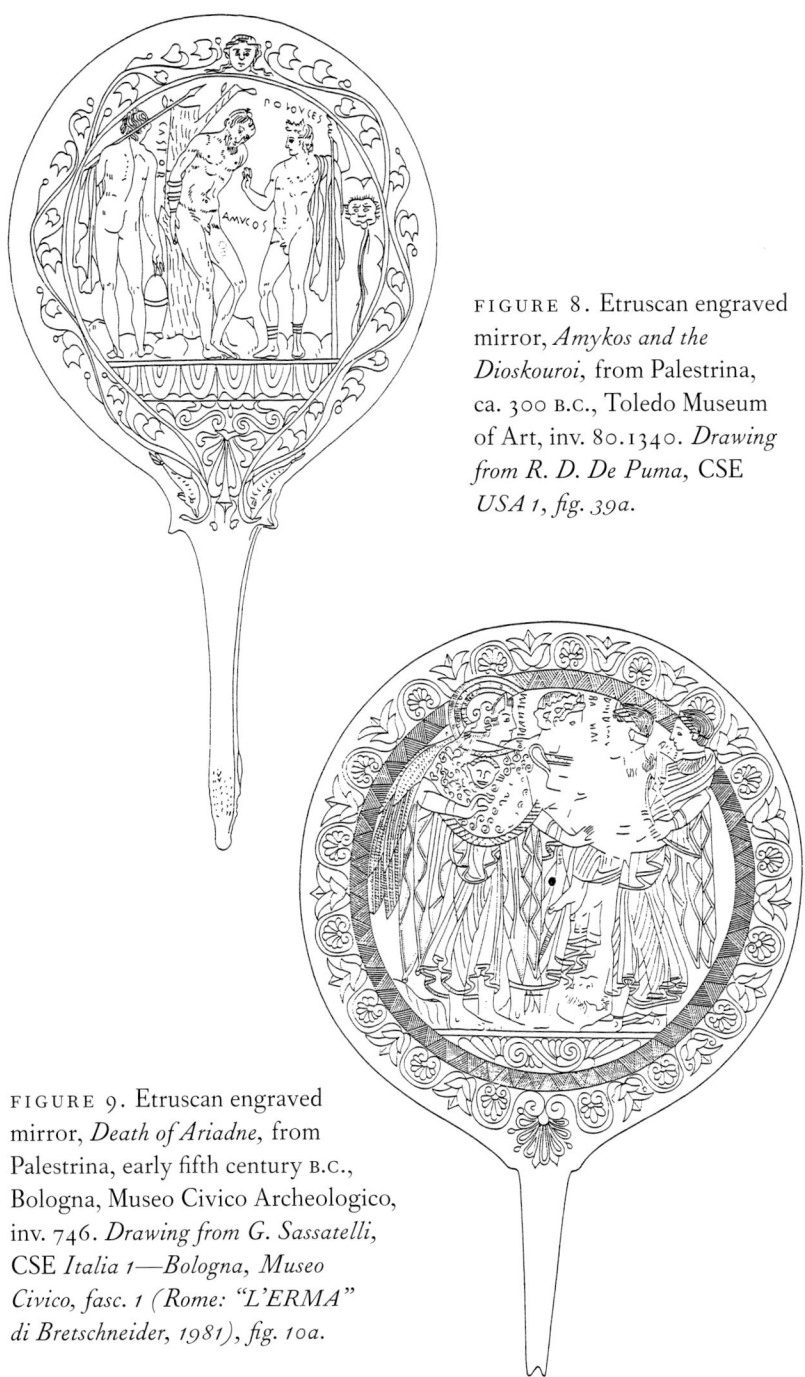

FIGURE 8. Etruscan engraved mirror, *Amykos and the Dioskouroi*, from Palestrina, ca. 300 B.C., Toledo Museum of Art, inv. 80.1340. *Drawing from R. D. De Puma*, CSE USA 1, *fig. 39a*.

FIGURE 9. Etruscan engraved mirror, *Death of Ariadne*, from Palestrina, early fifth century B.C., Bologna, Museo Civico Archeologico, inv. 746. *Drawing from G. Sassatelli*, CSE *Italia 1—Bologna, Museo Civico, fasc. 1 (Rome: "L'ERMA" di Bretschneider, 1981), fig. 10a*.

of the men sprung from ash-trees, the last left among the sons of the gods." He writes that "the son of Kronos gave him to Europa to be the warden of Crete and to stride round the island thrice a day with his feet of bronze."[28] By circumambulating the island in this way, Talos protected it from strangers. Whenever he caught trespassers, he smothered them to death by crushing them to his molten chest.[29] Despite his size and strength, the giant had one weak spot: one of the veins in his heel was secured with a bronze pin which, if removed, would cause him to bleed to death.[30] Brendel believes that the triangular projection near Talos' right heel on the Berlin relief mirror indicates the location of this vulnerable vein, since his feet are covered with boots;[31] but this may only be part of the giant's foreshortened foot.

In Greek art and literature, Talos appears in connection with the adventures of the Argonauts. Apollodorus writes that he died "from the deceits of Medea" after refusing to allow the *Argo* to land on Crete.[32] The Talos Painter's late fifth-century B.C. *volute* krater from Ruvo records this event.[33] On it, the Dioskouroi capture the giant for Medea by grabbing him from behind with the help of their horses. Talos leans back with his arms outstretched and his legs crossed in front of him. His white skin confirms his identity as the man of bronze. Medea stands to the figures' right, holding a basketful of potent herbs. She seems ready to fix the giant with her evil eye and mutter her fatal formula. In the background, several reclining figures watch the proceedings; these include Poseidon, Jason, and the sons of Boreas, shown as young men. A vase fragment from Spina[34] and a krater from Montesarchio[35] depict similar scenes; these, however, show Jason and Medea reaching for the opening in Talos' foot while Thanatos, the Greek god of death, sits beside him, indicating that his death is imminent.

Unlike these Greek images, the Etruscan relief mirror depicts a victorious Talos, a man who is about to overcome his two antagonists, who are burdened with large enveloping wings. Medea is absent, and the Dioskouroi seem to have been replaced by the Boreads, Kalais and Zetes, pictured as older men.[36] This substitution suggests that the mirror's iconography does not reflect a specific literary story, even though Talos is about to kill his antagonists by smothering them to his chest. The Boreads, after all, were supposed to have died long before the Argo ever reached Crete, being killed by Herakles on the island of Tenos after Hylas' disappearance at the spring.[37] Nevertheless, the Ruvo krater indicates that even the Greeks sometimes disregarded this fact, since it includes the Boreads as onlookers in the background. Although T. Dohrn identifies the men on the Berlin relief mirror as the Dioskouroi,[38] most scholars have accepted the hypothesis proposed by Curtius, especially since similar representations of the sons of Boreas appear on Greek and Etruscan artifacts from the fifth century B.C.[39] The latter hypothesis is also strengthened by the fact that the Dioskouroi never appear bearded in Etruscan art, although they sometimes have wings.[40]

Since ancient artists often intermixed and combined the adventures of the Dioskouroi and the Boreads, the specific identity of Talos' antagonists does not seem to be crucial to an understanding of the mirror's iconography, except for the realization that they are not the sons of Zeus. The Etruscans were well aware of the traditional Greek story and depicted it on several engraved mirrors which date to the fourth century B.C., including an example from Chiusi (figure 10).[41]

FIGURE 10. Etruscan engraved mirror, *Castor, Polydeukes, Talos, Aphrodite, and Athena*, from Chiusi, late fourth century B.C., British Museum, inv. 629. *Drawing by Shawn R. Skabelund after Gerhard.*

Here, the four figures are identified either by inscriptions or their attributes. Talos is inscribed *Chaluchasu,* a name that seems to represent an Etruscan interpretation of the Greek epithet for "man of bronze."[42] Unlike the scene on the Ruvo krater, the Etruscan Dioskouroi are horseless. They grab Talos around his chest, while he wraps his arms around their necks. Their gestures are very similar to the ones which appear on the Berlin relief mirror. A helmeted Athena stands quietly to the left, perhaps functioning as the protector of the twins, while the fifth figure, inscribed *Turan* (the Etruscan Aphrodite), bends over a box on the right. R. Bloch sees her as the protector of Talos, since he had been created by her husband, Hephaistos;[43] but it is also possible that the person who inscribed her name confused her with Medea, the woman traditionally associated with the giant's death.

A late fourth-century B.C. mirror now in Paris (figure 11) contains a scene which has also been identified as Talos' fight with the Dioskouroi. On this variant, the giant stands in a three-quarter

FIGURE 11. Etruscan engraved mirror, *Talos and the Boreads (?),* fourth century B.C., Paris, Bibliothèque Nationale, Cabinet des Médailles, inv. 1304. *Drawing from D. Rebuffat,* Le Miroir étrusque d'après la collection du Cabinet des médailles *(Rome, 1973), pl. 22.*

position, facing left. His right arm is raised in a gesture of surprise, and the twins each have an arm stretched behind his back. D. Rebuffat-Emmanuel suggests that the mirror depicts a moment before the Dioskouroi have seized the giant. They seem to be telling him either to allow the Argo to land or to suffer the consequences. The quiet concentration and figural gestures give the scene a sense of psychological drama, with the action of the two mirrors mentioned above replaced by a more contemplative image that focuses on a man's reaction to his fate and impending death.[44]

Yet another variant might appear on a second engraved mirror in Paris (figure 12) where the Dioskouroi struggle with a figure inscribed *Itas*. The surprised Itas stands with his arms raised, clutching a stone, his only means of protection. Because Apollodorus mentions that Talos often kept strangers off Crete by throwing stones at them,[45] it is possible that the inscription is a mistake and that this character actually represents the Cretan giant.[46]

FIGURE 12. Etruscan engraved mirror, *Polydeukes, Castor, and "Itas" (Talos?)*, late fifth century B.C., Paris, Bibliothèque Nationale, Cabinet des Médailles, inv. 1312. *Drawing from Gerhard, ES 1:58.*

These three mirrors all make reference to the traditional Greek story recorded by Apollodoros that emphasizes the impending death of Talos. The Berlin relief mirror differs from these examples in that it shows Talos as the protagonist, gaining the upper hand in his confrontation with the two winged men. This version of the Talos story also appears on a late fourth-century B.C. engraved mirror from Tuscania (figure 13), also in Berlin.[47] Interestingly, the bearded men on this mirror wear fillets similar to the type found on the relief mirror from the fifth century B.C. Because it lacks the silen head and contains some additional motifs (a large flower, a seven-pointed star, and a crescent moon),[48] the later mirror cannot represent a direct copy of the earlier one. Rather, both seem to make reference to a local myth that viewed Talos as a positive figure, a man whose strength and invincibility help to overpower unwanted trespassers or strangers.

To date, scholars have not commented on this unusual representation of Talos, except to say that the scene may copy a now-lost Greek original. This idea fails to account for the fact that both mirrors depict an inversion of the Greek story, one that may reflect specifically

FIGURE 13. Etruscan engraved mirror, *Talos and the Boreads,* from Tuscania, late fourth century B.C., Antikensammlung, Staatliche Museen zu Berlin, inv. 150. *Drawing from G. Zimmer,* Spiegel in Antikenmuseum: Bilderheft des Staatlichen Museen Preussischer Kulturbesitz, *heft 52 (Berlin, 1987), fig. 10.*

local—that is, Etruscan—concerns. An analysis of the historical circumstances in Etruria between 450 and 400 B.C., the time during which the mirror was manufactured, suggests a reason for the portrayal of a victorious Talos. During this period, the economic distress of the coastal cities of southern Etruria, caused by their military and naval defeats in the late sixth and early fifth centuries B.C., had lessened, only to be replaced by an even greater menace: the rising Roman Republic, which slowly began to make inroads into Etruria. Although Veii and her immediate neighbors allied themselves together to resist this aggression, they could not overcome the force of the Roman attacks; and early in the fourth century B.C. Veii succumbed after a long siege. Etruscan lands in Latium and Campania were also threatened at this time by invading Italic tribes, who advanced into these coastal plains and successfully overturned their rule.[49]

While their southern neighbors were experiencing economic decline, many of the inland communities of Etruria prospered, since their economies were supported by agriculture and the trade routes leading to the Adriatic coast. Nevertheless, they faced similar problems with foreign encroachments when the Etruscan settlements in the Po River valley came into conflict with Gallic invaders in the second half of the fifth century B.C. In the early fourth century B.C., a Gallic army crossed the Apennines and attacked Clusium; the inhabitants of this city-state prevailed, however, after receiving help from Rome. In return, the Gauls marched on Rome and burnt the city in 390 B.C. Westward incursions of eastern Italic, Oscan-Umbrian-speaking peoples also threatened many central and northern Etruscan city-states, whose soldiers bravely defended their settlements and blocked the invaders' path westward.[50]

This brief historical overview demonstrates that the mid– to late fifth century B.C. was characterized both by the loss of previously held Etruscan territories and by the widespread movement of outsiders into Etruria—the Romans, Gauls, and other native Italic tribes. If the iconography of these two mirrors in Berlin is viewed in light of these circumstances, it makes more sense. Unlike the Greek Talos, who was seen as a nuisance, this particular man of bronze is self-assured and invincible, a being created by the gods for the express purpose of protecting his land from intruders, trespassers, or strangers. Indeed, he may even represent the Etruscans' desire to remain free and independent from these unwanted encroachments of foreigners. The Etruscan inversion of the Greek story may also contain a warning that the result of such aggressive acts was certain death, an idea further emphasized on the mirrors by the inclusion of the silen head, the fillets, and/or the siren. It is not unusual for Etruscan mirrors to contain narratives that reflect their owners' personal experiences, as R. D. De Puma suggests in his study of Eos and Memnon on a group of mirrors from the early fifth century B.C.[51] Therefore, it is possible that these two mirrors belonged to wealthy aristocratic families who had successfully defended their city-states from foreign invasions and who likened their efforts to those of Talos on Crete.

The third relief mirror under consideration in this essay is now in Bologna and dates to the mid–fifth century B.C. (figures 1 and 4). It does not contain a unique subject but one rarely found on extant Greek artifacts: Machaon's healing of the Greek archer Philoktetes.[52] Cast inscriptions in Etruscan lettering identify these characters—who are better known by their Greek names—as *Machan* and *Pheltuse.* Machaon is shown in the very process of curing Philoktetes' wound: he leans over a folding stool topped with medical supplies as he applies a bandage to the swollen ankle. The slender, heroically nude archer, dramatically foreshortened in a nearly frontal pose, has a mantle draped over his shoulders and upper arms. His bearded head appears in profile, and he looks over his shoulder to watch Machaon's work, steadying himself with a long staff. In his left hand he holds a bow, and behind his right foot is a bearded snake with a large head, presumably a reference to the initial cause of his wound.[53]

Surrounding the composition is a border of waves topped by curvilinear dolphins. The archaeological record indicates that Etruscan artists often used this motif to represent water or the sea.[54] Although the borders of Etruscan mirrors do not necessarily relate to their subjects, the use of this particular motif here may not have been arbitrary. In one sense, it reminds viewers that Philoktetes suffered a ten-year exile on an isolated island. But it also has a more positive connotation, since the archer journeyed across the sea to be healed, an event which signaled his return to life. Because the Etruscans believed in the restorative power of water, locating many of their healing sanctuaries near springs and wells,[55] this border motif may be a sophisticated decorative device intricately connected to the mirror's subject.

Philoktetes' story had been part of the Greek epic tradition as early as Homer's *Iliad*.[56] There, the poet records that while traveling to Troy, Philoktetes was bitten by a water snake and abandoned on the island of Lemnos. The *Cypria* mentions that the hero had been bitten during a banquet and that "because a disgusting stench emanates from his wound, he is abandoned on Lemnos."[57] The *Little Iliad* summarizes the end of the story, ten years after the initial abandonment, and indicates that Philoktetes was rescued because Helenus, a Trojan seer, determined that his presence was necessary for the final destruction of Troy.[58] Although the *Little Iliad* does not explain in depth why Philoktetes was needed at Troy, a reason appears in the play about him written by Aeschylus in the early fifth century B.C. In it, Philoktetes has a coveted weapon: the bow and poisoned arrows of Herakles, gifts that he received as the latter lay dying on his funeral pyre.[59] This story not only gives the Greeks the advantage of Herakles' help at Troy, especially since Achilles and Ajax are dead by this time, but it also clarifies the apparent need for Philoktetes at the fall of Troy. Likewise, it provides the Greeks with a concrete reason for rescuing him. The presence of the bow on the Bologna relief mirror indicates that the Etruscan artist was well aware of this attribute's importance.

In his late fifth-century B.C. drama *Philoktetes*, Sophocles links the archer's healing with the promise of a divine cure and immortal glory—an offer the embittered man cannot refuse, although he agonizes greatly over his decision. Near the play's end, Neoptolemos persuades Philoktetes with the following words:

> Be certain you will never find relief
> from your hard illness . . .
> . . . until you come
> of your own will to Troy, where you will find
> the children of Asclepius among us,
> and they will soothe your illness; then, with me,
> and with your bow, you will demolish Troy.[60]

Like a good hero, Philoktetes accepts this "fair reward to be acclaimed / the noblest of the Greeks" and eventually finds his way to the waiting "healing hands."[61]

Surprisingly, Greek artists rarely portray Philoktetes as a man whose perseverance and patience give him the rewards mentioned in Sophocles' play. Instead, the two subjects they depict most frequently concern either his psychological state during his years of exile[62] or the difficulties the Greeks encountered when they returned to Lemnos. A Paestan bell krater now in Syracuse illustrates the second theme.[63] Philoktetes sits in a grotto, holding his bow in his left hand and leaning his right arm on his wounded leg. He uses a feather to help fan away the stench of his wound. Athena, a bearded warrior (possibly Odysseus), a youth (perhaps Diomedes or Neoptolemos), and a young woman stand behind the grotto. The obverse of an Early Imperial silver cup from Hoby, now in Copenhagen, also depicts Philoktetes before the Greek envoys.[64] In this scene, perhaps a copy of a now-lost fourth-century B.C. monumental painting,[65] the hero appears as the epitome of an abandoned man; his shaggy beard, overgrown locks, bent body, and lined face all reinforce his melancholy, and he ignores Odysseus, who sits before him. In the background, a youth reaches for his bow, an action which seems to underscore the Greeks' true motive for his rescue.

In his 1879 study of Philoketes in classical literature and art, L. A. Milani notes that the hero's healing was one of the least-portrayed subjects in the Greek visual repertoire.[66] Only the reverse of the Hoby silver cup seems to illustrate this event.[67] Here, the unkempt melancholic man on the cup's obverse has been transformed into a youthful athlete who sits on a flat, rocky ledge while the physician bandages his wound. A snake lies curled in the foreground, while hanging from a tree on the far right is Philoktetes' quiver.

The Bologna relief mirror, on the other hand, seems to be the oldest extant image of Philoktetes' healing in either Greece or Etruria. The mirror's cast inscriptions, along with the bow and the snake, indicate that someone—most likely the patron—desired this specific narrative to be understood and contemplated. Judging by the mirror's date, the patron may have been a woman whose husband, lovers, or children were engaged in the Etruscans' military difficulties of the early fifth century B.C. To such a person, Philoktetes' story would have offered both reassurance and hope, serving as a reminder that the gods and their emissaries on earth were capable of healing all wounds—even those deemed incurable. The Bologna relief mirror also depicts a man whose patience and endurance were rewarded not only with a divine cure but with immortal glory. This second reward, the hope of all Etruscans, clearly outweighs his years of agony and pain and is communicated visually by his heroically nude body and energetic pose: he stands, almost precariously, on one foot, ready to spring to action with the help of his bow.

A similar correlation, interestingly, appears on a Greek *kylix* by the Sosias Painter,[68] found interred in an Etruscan tomb at Vulci, the place where most scholars believe the relief mirror was manufactured. In the *tondo*, the wounded Patroklos clenches his teeth as Achilles bandages his arm. Achilles makes an appropriate physician, since he learned the art of medicine from his foster father and teacher, the centaur Cheiron.[69] On the exterior of the kylix, Herakles stands in a procession of the gods, an event signifying the end of his earthly life and the beginning of his new life among the Olympians. Because the Etruscans believed the dead were perpetually alive, living a second life in the underworld,[70] the imagery on the kylix accentuates this link between healing and the attainment of immortality. For just as the healing of Patroklos gives him additional opportunities to gain glory at Troy, Herakles' physical death on the pyre is exchanged for a better life among the gods. Because the Sosias Painter's kylix was an Etruscan import, its owner must have been aware of the importance of this juxtaposition. Therefore, it is not surprising that the Bologna relief mirror manifests a similar idea, especially since Philoktetes' healing and subsequent renewed life would have given the mirror's owner a sense of hope and continued health both during her lifetime and after her death, when the mirror became one of her tomb gifts.

The unusual iconography of the Bologna relief mirror may also indicate that its owner was connected to a healing cult. In a recent essay, Nancy Thomson de Grummond suggests a link between mirrors and healing cults in connection with Pausanias' discussion of an oracle at Patria in Greece, where mirrors were used in healing rituals.[71] Pausanias writes that this oracle was meant primarily for sick people. Those consulting the oracle would tie a mirror

> to a fine cord and let it down [a well], judging the distance so that it does not sink deep into the spring, but just far enough to touch the water with its rim. Then they pray to the goddess [Demeter] and burn incense, after which they look into the mirror, which shows them the patient dead or alive.[72]

Although the precise function of the Bologna relief mirror remains elusive, an examination of the archaeological record in Etruria reveals the importance of healing cults and sanctuaries as early as the sixth century B.C. The Cannicella sanctuary in Orvieto, for example, contained deposits dating to this period, suggesting that the deity had a healing power. Two water basins and a well found at the site also confirm the association between healing and the restorative powers of wells and springs.[73] The many anatomical votives from the Classical and Hellenistic periods also attest to the continuing popularity and importance of healing cults in Etruria and indicate the Etruscans' growing concern for their personal welfare.[74] Several gems and mirrors from this period make healing their focal point. For example, a late fifth-century B.C. carnelian scarab from Chiusi illustrates a scene which several scholars have identified as Philoktetes' healing,[75] while a mirror now in New York portrays Asklepios curing Prometheos.[76]

A. Pfiffig notes that within the pantheon of Etruscan healing deities there were many nameless local gods with affinities to better-known figures such as Apollo, Silvanus, or Asklepios.[77] On the Bologna relief mirror, however, the identity of the physician is never in doubt; he is the son of Asklepios, the great Greek healer known for his abilities to both cure people and bring back the dead. Although not much is known about Machaon's role in Etruscan religion or healing cults, the Bologna relief mirror reinforces the idea of a divine cure in its completely unique depiction of Philoktetes. Interestingly, several late Hellenistic cinerary urns from Volterra which illustrate Philoktetes' confrontations with the Greek envoys show Odysseus seizing the archer's wounded leg.[78] F.-H. Pairault has interpreted the gesture as Odysseus' attempt to persuade Philoktetes by the promise of a cure.[79] But in view of the clandestine activities of the men behind the hero, who are attempting to steal his bow, it may merely be a means of distracting his attention from the thieves. These urns depict Philoktetes in the Greek fashion as the epitome of the wronged exile, an image that is very different from the one shown on the relief mirror. Thus, although the characters found on the three relief mirrors discussed in this paper originate in Greek mythology and legend, all of them have been transformed into uniquely Etruscan figures who participate in narratives rarely or never found on Greek artifacts. This manipulation of myth not only indicates both the patrons' and the artists' sophisticated knowledge of their source material, but it also demonstrates a desire to reinterpret the stories according to local religious beliefs or contemporary historical circumstances. Brendel summarizes this understanding of Greek mythology in Etruria very well with his reminder that "myths have neither author nor copyright; they are common property, ready for everyone to reshape or vary their plots and decipher their meanings."[80] The modifications visible on these three relief mirrors, therefore, cannot be viewed as misinterpretations of the original source material. They are, instead, very personal scenes imbued with various layers of distinctly Etruscan meaning.

NOTES

1. Not all of the extant Etruscan mirrors have cast or engraved narratives on their reverses. Many are undecorated or have only simple floral patterns in the extension (the area between the disc and tang) on the obverse.

2. For a more in-depth discussion of these mirrors, see A. Carpino, "Etruscan Relief Mirrors: Origins, Functions, and Cultural Significance" (Ph.D. diss., University of Iowa, 1993).

3. See N. T. de Grummond, ed., *A Guide to Etruscan Mirrors* (Tallahassee, Fla., 1982), 183–84.

4. Boston, Museum of Fine Arts, inv. 1971.138; M. Comstock and C. Vermeule, *Greek, Etruscan, and Roman Bronzes in the Museum of Fine Arts, Boston* (Greenwich, Conn., 1971), vol. 4 no. 376a; R. D. De Puma, *CSE* USA 2: Boston and Cambridge (Ames, Iowa, 1993), no. 28.

5. Berlin, Antikenmuseum, inv. 30480; G. Zimmer, *Spiegel in Antikenmuseum: Bilderheft des Staatlichen Museen Preussischer Kulturbesitz*, heft 52 (Berlin, 1987), color pl. 3.

6. Bologna, Museo Civico Archeologico, inv. 273; *ES* 4:394 no. 2; G. Sassatelli, *CSE* Italia 1 (Rome, 1982), no. 14.

7. See I. Krauskopf, *Der Thebanische Sagenkreis und andere griechischen Sagen in der etruskischen Kunst* (Mainz am Rhein, 1974), 35–36; N. Spivey and S. Stoddart, *Etruscan Italy* (London, 1990), 98–106.

8. See Apollod. 3.126–27. For information on Nemesis, see *OCD*, 601, s.v. "Nemesis." Pausanias (1.33.7) also cites Nemesis as Helen's mother in his discussion of the base of the goddess's cult statue at Rhamnus; but he also records (3.16.1) that the egg was still in Sparta when he visited the place in the second century A.D. and, in this account, cites Leda as Helen's mother.

9. See F. Chapouthier, "Léda devant l'oeuf de Némésis," *BCH* 66–69 (1942–43): 1–21. Although the story of Helen's egg had been recorded in the literature of the sixth century B.C., there are no visual representations of the theme until the late fifth century B.C., a time which coincides with the beginning of the Peloponnesian War. The sanctuary of Nemesis had been destroyed by the Persians in the early fifth century B.C. and was restored just prior to the war. During this conflict there was a revival in her cult, and this may explain the new interest in Helen's egg.

10. Bonn, Akademisches Kunstmuseum, inv. 78; *ARV²* 1171, 4. See *LIMC* 3:583 no. 185, s.v. "Dioskouroi."

11. Kiel, Ger., Kunsthalle, inv. B 501; *LIMC* 4:503 no. 6, s.v. "Helen."

12. Naples, Museo Nazionale, inv. 147950; *LIMC* 4:504 no. 9, s.v. "Helen."

13. For further discussion, see *OCD*, 627, s.v. "Orphism"; A. Bottini, "Elena in Occidente: Una tomba dalla chora di Metaponto," *BA* 73 (1988): 1–18, pls. 1–20. In the latter work, Bottini discusses a recently discovered late fifth-century B.C. tomb in Metapontum which contained both a small terracotta egg and a limestone statuette of Helen within a cracked terracotta eggshell which had been placed inside a small *pyxis*.

14. For a listing of these artifacts, see *LIMC* 6:247 nos. 2–7, s.v. "Leda (in Etruria)"; G. Heres, *CSE* DDR 1 (East Berlin, 1986), 31–33 no. 13, 43–46 no. 32. The Dioskouroi were known in Etruscan as Tinas Cliniar, and numerous inscriptions and artifacts found in Etruria attest to their importance in Etruscan religion and culture.

15. L. Bonfante, "Daily Life and Afterlife," in de Grummond, *Guide to Etruscan Mirrors*, 80 (vol. supra n. 3).

16. For the representation of eggs on the walls of Etruscan tombs, see S. Steingräber, *Etruscan Painting: Catalogue Raisonné of Etruscan Wall Paintings*, English language ed., ed. D. Ridgway and F. R. Ridgway (New York, 1986).

17. The Isis Tomb from the Polledrara Cemetery in Vulci also contained an ostrich egg carved in low relief; others have been found in tombs at Cerveteri,

Tarquinia, Vetulonia, and Populonia. See A. J. Pfiffig, *Religio etrusca* (Graz, Austria, 1975), 193; M. Martelli, "La cultura artistica," in *Gli etruschi: Una nuova immagine*, ed. M. Cristofani (Florence, 1984), 172. F. Messerschmidt ("Disiecta membra: Masken und Schauspieler Terrakoten in Gräber von Vulci und Tarquinia," *MDAI(R)* 46 [1931]: 47–59) also discusses the presence of numerous egg-holding vessels from the Hellenistic period found in tombs at Vulci and other centers.

18. This idea is further emphasized by the decoration of a mirror once in Berlin (Staatliche Museen, Antikensammlung, inv. 16; Heres, *CSE* DDR 1, no. 1 [supra n. 14]) on which a siren, one of the messengers of the afterlife, holds two eggs. R. D. De Puma (*CSE* USA 1: Midwestern Collections [Ames, Iowa, 1987], no. 42) cites a mirror with similar iconography now in Cincinnati (Art Museum, inv. 1884.194) which may have come from a tomb in Palestrina.

19. Perugia, Museo Archeologico, inv. 847; *ES* 5: pl. 77; *LIMC* 6:247 no. 7, s.v. "Leda (in Etruria)."

20. See n. 5 above.

21. L. Bonfante, "Human Sacrifice on an Etruscan Funerary Urn," *AJA* 88 (1984): 531–39. According to the Hellenistic author Lucretius (1.84–100), similar fillets also adorned the head of Iphigenia prior to her sacrifice. Both Bonfante (537) and commentators on the ancient text such as C. Bailey, ed. and trans., *Titi Lucreti Cari De Rerum Natura Libri Sex* [Oxford, 1947], commentary, 2, 614) have suggested that he may have been inspired by well-known paintings or sculptures on view during his lifetime.

22. L. Curtius, "Neue hermeneutische Miscellen," *AA* 63–64 (1948–49): 63.

23. Toledo, Museum of Art, inv. 80.1340; *ES* 5:90; De Puma, *CSE* USA 1, no. 39 (supra n. 18).

24. O. Brendel, *Etruscan Art* (Harmondsworth, Engl., 1978), 373.

25. Bologna, Museo Civico Archeologico, inv. 746; Sassatelli, *CSE* Italia 1, no. 10 (supra n. 6). Silen heads also appear on mirrors from the fourth century B.C., including the famous Cacu mirror now in London (British Museum, inv. 633; *ES* 5:127), in which the head appears on a rocky ledge behind the main protagonists.

26. Bologna, Museo Civico Archeologico, inv. 1070; *ES* 4:395; Sassatelli, *CSE* Italia 1, no. 40 (supra n. 6).

27. Curtius, "Neue hermeneutische Miscellen," 63 (supra n. 22). Brendel (*Etruscan Art*, 370–73 [supra n. 24]), U. Fischer-Graf ("Spiegelwerkstätten in Vulci," *Archäologische Forschungen* 8 [1980]: 3), Bonfante ("Human Sacrifice," 538 [supra n. 21]), and Zimmer (*Spiegel in Antikenmuseum*, 21 [supra n. 5]) agree.

28. A.R. 4.1638–45 (R. C. Seaton, trans., *The Argonautica* [1912; reprint, London and Cambridge, Mass., 1955], 407.) Apollodorus of Athens writes that "this creature some say was one of the bronze generation and was actually a bronze man; others hold that he was given to Minos by Hephaestus and was a bull" (1.140–42; K. Aldrich, trans., *The Library of Greek Mythology* [Lawrence, Kans., 1975], 26).

29. *OCD*, 878, s.v. "Talos."

30. Apollonius Rhodius records, "Now in all the rest of his body and limbs was he fashioned of bronze and invulnerable; but beneath the sinew by his ankle was a blood-red vein; and this, with its issues of life and death, was covered by a thin skin" (4.1645–49; Seaton, *Argonautica*, 407 [supra n. 28]) Apollodorus writes, "He had one blood vessel that extended from his neck down to his ankles, the lower end of which was held in place by a bronze stud" (1.140–41; Aldrich, *Library of Greek Mythology*, 26 [supra n. 28]). A. B. Cook (*Zeus: A Study in Ancient Religion* [Cambridge, 1914], 1:723) writes that "it is tempting to explain certain traits in the myth of Talos along rationalistic lines. The single vein running from his neck to his ankles and closed by a bronze nail thrust through it vividly recalls the *cire perdue* method of hollow casting. . . . In this technical process, the hollow from head to toe, pierced with its bronze pins, was—one may suspect—the fact underlying the fiction of Talos' vein."

31. Brendel, *Etruscan Art*, 370 (supra n. 24).

32. Apollod. 1.141 (supra n. 28).

33. Ruvo, It., Sammlung Jatta, inv. 1501; *ARV²* 1338, 1; H. Sichtermann, *Griechische Vasen in UnterItalien: Aus der Sammlung Jatta in Ruvo*, Deutsches Archäologisches Institut, 3/4 (Tübingen, Ger., 1966), figs. 24–34; K. Schefold and F. Jung, *Die Sagen von den Argonauten, von Theben und Troia in der klassischen und hellenistischen Kunst* (Munich, 1989), figs. 17a–b; *LIMC* 7:835 no. 4, s.v. "Talos" [J. Papadopoulas].

34. Ferrara, Museo Nazionale, inv. 3092; *ARV²* 1340; Schefold and Jung, *Die Sagen von den Argonauten*, n. 65 (supra n. 33); *LIMC* 7:835 no. 5, s.v. "Talos."

35. Benevento, It., Museo del Sannio. See also Schefold and Jung, *Die Sagen von den Argonauten*, fig. 18 (supra n. 33); *LIMC* 7:835 no. 6, s.v. "Talos."

36. As K. Schefold (*Die Göttersage in der klassischen und hellenistischen Kunst* [Munich, 1981], 323) has observed, there seems to be little consensus in ancient art about the appearance of the Boreads. Sometimes they appear as nude athletes, with or without wings, while at other times they appear as older bearded men—again, with or without wings.

37. See H. J. Rose, *A Handbook of Greek Mythology: Including Its Extension to Rome* (New York, 1959), 200.

38. T. Dohrn, *Die etruskische Kunst im Zeitalter der griechischen Klassik: Die Interimsperiode* (Mainz am Rhein, 1982), 38.

39. See the krater from Spina by the Eucharides Painter, dated to the early fifth century B.C. (Ferrara, Museo Nazionale, inv. 2666; Schefold, *Die Göttersage*, figs. 470–71 [supra n. 36]) or the Briseis Painter's neck amphora from Nola (British Museum, inv. 1928.1-17.56; *ARV²* 409, 48). For a complete list, see *LIMC* 3:126–33, s.v. "Boreadei."

40. See *LIMC* 3:606, s.v. "Dioskouroi/Tinas Cliniar."

41. British Museum, inv. 629; *ES* 1:56; *LIMC* 3:606 no. 77, s.v. "Dioskouroi/ Tinas Cliniar"; *LIMC* 7:836 no. 8, s.v. "Talos."

42. D. Rebuffat-Emmanuel, *Le Miroir étrusque: D'après la collection du Cabinet des Médailles*, Collection de l'Ecole française de Rome, 20 (Rome, 1973), 511. J. D. Beazley (*Etruscan Vase Painting* [Oxford, 1947], 199), however, associates this name with Calchas, the seer who appears on a mirror from Vulci divining a liver (Vatican Museums, inv. 12240). Fischer-Graf ("Spiegelwerkstätten in Vulci," 43 [supra n. 27]) follows this attribution, but it does not make much sense to associate this name with the mythological Trojan seer/priest. Talos seems to be a more logical translation.

43. *LIMC* 2:27, s.v. "Turan."

44. Paris, Cabinet des Médailles, inv. 1304; Rebuffat-Emmanuel, *Le Miroir étrusque*, 510, pl. 22 (supra n. 42); *LIMC* 3:604 no. 78, s.v. "Dioskouroi/Tinas Cliniar."

45. Apollod. 1.141 (supra n. 28).

46. Paris, Cabinet des Médailles, inv. 1312; *ES* 1:58; Rebuffat-Emmanuel, *Le Miroir étrusque*, pl. 30 (supra n. 42); *LIMC* 3:605 no. 83, s.v. "Dioskouroi/Tinas Cliniar."

47. Berlin, Antikenmuseum, inv. 150; *ES* 3:255; Zimmer, *Spiegel in Antikenmuseum*, fig. 10, pl. 12 (supra n. 5); *LIMC* 7:836 no. 11, s.v. "Talos."

48. Although some scholars have associated the star and moon with the Dioskouroi, they can be connected with Talos since he was an astral deity associated with both Zeus and the sun. See Cook, *Zeus: A Study*, 1:720 (supra n. 30); Rebuffat-Emmanuel, *Le Miroir étrusque*, 511 (supra n. 42).

49. See S. Haynes, *Etruscan Bronzes* (London, 1985), 29–31; M. Pallottino, *A History of Earliest Italy*, trans. M. Ryle and K. Soper, Jerome Lectures, 17th ser. (Ann Arbor, Mich., 1991), 106–12. It is important to remember that some Etruscan cities—Caere, for example—seemed to support Rome during this period; see, in this volume, the essay by John F. Hall, 153 and n. 21.

50. See Haynes, *Etruscan Bronzes*, 32–35 (supra n. 49).

51. R. D. De Puma, "Greek Gods and Heroes on Etruscan Mirrors," in de Grummond, *Guide to Etruscan Mirrors*, 100 (vol. supra n. 3). He notes that the popularity of scenes in which a grieving Eos cradles the body of her dead son Memnon might reflect the anguish many mothers would have felt if they had lost children during the Etruscans' attempt to defend their supremacy in the Tyrrhenian Sea in the early fifth century B.C.

52. See n. 6 above.

53. G. Pfister-Roesgen (*Die etruskischen Spiegel des 5. Jhs. v. Chr.* [Frankfurt am Main, 1975], 67), however, suggests that the snake alludes to Machaon's parentage, since he was a son of Asklepios.

54. Similar framing bands appear on a variety of mirrors from the early fifth century B.C., including examples in Boston (Museum of Fine Arts, inv. 95.72; De Puma, *CSE* USA 2, no. 4 [supra n. 4]), Rome (Museo di Villa Giulia, inv. 1091; G. A. Mansuelli, "Materiali per un supplemento al 'Corpus' degli specchi etruschi

figurati," *SE* 17 [1943]: 492 fig. 2, pl. 31), and Copenhagen (Nationalmuseum, inv. 3403; *ES* 4:468 no. 1; H. Salskov Roberts, *CSE* Denmark 1 [Odense, 1982], no. 22).

55. Pfiffig, *Religio etrusca*, 269 (supra n. 17).

56. Hom., *Il.* 2.716–33.

57. The *Cypria* is summarized by Proclus in the Biblioteca of Photius (ninth century A.D.). For a translation of this section, see O. Mandel, *Philoctetes and the Fall of Troy: Plays, Documents, Iconography, Interpretations Including Versions by Sophocles, André Gide, Oscar Mandel, and Heiner Müller* (Lincoln, Neb., 1981), 9.

58. The *Little Iliad*, from *Homeri Carmina et Cycli Epici Reliquiae*. This section is translated by Mandel in his *Philoctetes and the Fall of Troy*, 9–10 (supra n. 57).

59. See J. Boardman, "Herakles in Extremis," *Studien zur Mythologie und Vasenmalerei: Festschrift für Konrad Schauenburg* . . . (Mainz am Rhein, 1986), 128. Boardman notes that only a few Attic vases, all of which date after 460 B.C., depict this event; Philoktetes is shown either receiving the weapons or departing with them.

60. S., *Ph.* 1329–35. The translation used here is that of Mandel (*Philoctetes and the Fall of Troy*, 90 [supra n. 57]).

61. Ibid., 1344–47 (91).

62. An example of this type appears on a *lekythos* of the mid–fifth century B.C. now in New York (Metropolitan Museum of Art, inv. 56.171.58); see L. Séchan, *Études sur la tragédie grecque dans ses rapports avec la céramique* (Paris, 1926), fig. 143. Several Etruscan gems also show a solitary Philoktetes who stands or sits and who supports himself with a staff. These gems probably reflect his abandonment on Lemnos. See A. Furtwängler, *Die antiken Gemmen: Geschichte der Steinschneidekunst im klassischen Altertum* (Leipzig and Berlin, 1900), 1: pl. XVII no. 50, pl. XVIII no. 64; P. Zazoff, *Etruskische Skarabäen* (Mainz am Rhein, 1986), nos. 1195, 1198.

63. Syracuse, Museo Nazionale, inv. 36319; *CVA* Italia Syracuse 1, fasc. 4E, pl. 8, 1–2.

64. Copenhagen, Nationalmuseum, inv. 9120; *LIMC* 1:154 no. 687, s.v. "Achilleus," 7:383 nos. 69, 74, s.v. "Philoktetes"; Schefold and Jung, *Die Sagen von den Argonauten*, fig. 242 (supra n. 33).

65. See Schefold and Jung, *Die Sagen von den Argonauten*, 270–71 (supra n. 33).

66. See L. A. Milani, *Il mito di Filottete nella letteratura classica e nell'arte figurata* (Florence, 1879).

67. Schefold and Jung, *Die Sagen von den Argonauten*, 271 fig. 243 (supra n. 33). M. Pipili (*LIMC* 7:383 no. 74, s.v. "Philoktetes") argues that this scene represents Philoktetes' wounding rather than his healing, since he is pictured at different ages on the two sides of the cup.

68. Berlin, Antikenmuseum, inv. 2278. See *LIMC* 1:115, s.v. "Achilleus." The kylix dates to the late sixth century B.C.

69. Hom., *Il.* 2.831–32.

70. See E. Vermeule, *Aspects of Death in Early Greek Art and Poetry*, Sather Classical Lectures, 46 (Berkeley, Calif., 1979), 118.

71. N. T. de Grummond, "Mythology, Iconography, Religion" in *Antichità dall'Umbria a New York*, ed. F. Roncalli and L. Bonfante (Perugia, It., 1991), 100.

72. Paus. 7.21.12. The translation is that of W. H. S. Jones (*Description of Greece*, Loeb Classical Library, 168 [London and Cambridge, Mass., 1939], 297).

73. Pfiffig, *Religio etrusca*, 68 (supra n. 17).

74. Haynes, *Etruscan Bronzes*, 33–34 (supra n. 49).

75. British Museum, inv. 65.7-12.94/730; Pfister-Roesgen, *Die etruskischen Spiegel*, 163 (supra n. 53); Zazoff, *Etruskische Skarabäen*, 184 no. 1043 (supra n. 62); *LIMC* 7:383 no. 72, s.v. "Philoktetes." Although inscriptions identify these figures as "Epetus" and "Acheos," G. M. A. Richter (*Engraved Gems of the Greeks, Etruscans, and Romans* [London, 1968–71], 1:204 no. 829) suggests that these may be either invented names for the characters or references to the gem's owner. Previous scholarship held that the scene depicts the healing of Telephos, perhaps due to the absence of the bow. Milani (*Il mito di Filottete*, 104–5 [supra n. 66]), however, believes that the scene on the scarab depicts an alternate version of the myth, one where Philoktetes kills Paris before he is healed. This hypothesis seems unlikely.

76. New York, Metropolitan Museum of Art, inv. 03.04.3. See R. D. De Puma, "Mirrors," in *Antichità dall'Umbria*, 281–82 fig. 6.8 (vol. supra n. 71).

77. Pfiffig, *Religio etrusca*, 269–71 (supra n. 17).

78. F.-H. Pairault, *Recherches sur quelques séries d'urnes de Volterra à représentations mythologiques*, Collection de l'Ecole française de Rome, 12 (Rome, 1972), 133–41, 199–208.

79. Ibid., 134.

80. Brendel, *Etruscan Art*, 365 (supra n. 24).

A Storage Vase for Life:
The Caeretane Dolio and Its Decorative Elements

LISA PIERACCINI

The pottery produced by the Etruscans has contributed much to our understanding of their fascinating and unique culture.[1] Among the most prevalent of pottery finds around the ancient southern Etruscan city of Caere (modern Cerveteri) is the *dolio*, a large vase similar in shape and probable function to the Greek storage vase known as the *pithos* (figure 1).[2] Most of these vases have been found in the cemeteries of ancient Caere—namely the Banditaccia, Monte Abatone, and Bufolareccia—and in the rich Regolini-Galassi tumulus in the Sorbo area of Caere, where they presumably served the funerary purpose of holding items that the deceased could use in afterlife.[3] In addition, it appears that dolii served in Etruscan households and sanctuaries as practical storage vessels for grain, oil, and wine, being similar in function to other storage vessels common in the ancient Mediterranean. The majority of these Caeretane vases eventually became part of several large private collections—the Castellani, Campana, and Campanari—all of which were later purchased by museums, including the British Museum, the Louvre, the Berlin Museum, the Hermitage, and the Villa Giulia Museum.[4] Although Caeretane dolii are well represented in museums and museum storage rooms throughout central Italy, they

FIGURE 1. Metope-stamped dolio, from Tomb 4 on the periphery of the Regolini-Galassi tomb, Cerveteri, late sixth to early fifth century B.C., Vatican, Museo Gregoriano Etrusco, inv. 36589. *Photo by A. De Luca; courtesy of Monumenti Musei e Gallerie Pontificie.*

have not received the attention they deserve. But whatever the degree of historical importance that has been ascribed to them as functional storage vessels with a long tradition in the ancient Mediterranean, even cursory examination of these handsome objects indicates that the artisans of ancient Caere took great pride in both their craftsmanship and artistic decoration—matters that will be the primary focus of this essay.

Caeretane dolii were made between the seventh and fifth centuries B.C.—roughly the first centuries of the Etruscan period—as can be dated by their appearance in Etruscan tombs. The abundance of tombs at Caere dating to this period makes it a relatively easy task to date these vessels by comparing them with other items found in the same tombs—that is, comparing dolii with other types of well-dated pottery such as Etruscan, Etrusco-Corinthian, and Attic. Of course, the ideal situation would be to establish for these vessels a dating chronology of their own, one that does not rely on external evidence. Since, as noted above, most of the extant dolii have been discovered in Etruscan tombs at Caere, it is widely accepted that these vessels were manufactured there.[5] Although workshops dating from that time period have not yet been excavated at Caere, M. A. Del Chiaro convincingly argues that, because there were several workshops at this Etruscan center producing pottery at a much later date, the tradition of ceramic workshops most likely existed earlier.[6] Although most dolii are found in the vicinity of Caere, they have also been unearthed at Pyrgi (the port city of Caere), as well as Blera, Tuscania, and Tarquinia,[7] and were perhaps used in functional areas of sanctuaries, suggesting that dolii had a ceremonial significance beyond mere practical use. Recent excavations of the ancient Etruscan city of Caere have yielded finds of dolii in the city's municipal areas (Archaic habitation and late Archaic temple sites), almost none of which, interestingly enough, are stamped or decorated.[8]

In the past, archaeological excavations at Caere have concentrated on tombs rather than habitation sites; thus, dolii in Caeretane habitation and urban areas have only recently been discovered.[9] Additionally, because of looting through the centuries and haphazard excavations during the nineteenth and early twentieth centuries, it is also only recently that dolii have been scientifically recovered. For example, most of the large number of dolii found in the necropoli of Caere were, unfortunately, excavated after the tombs had been disturbed and sacked by looters and when no particular attention to appropriate archaeological method was demanded. Data on how dolii were originally arranged in the tombs might have led to reliable conclusions about their presence there and their contents. Still, the sheer quantity of extant Caeretane dolii, even without specific tomb reference, suggests that these vases were widely used during the period when Caere's population was at its height and it ranked as the most powerful southern Etruscan city. Consequently, the Caeretane workshops must have enjoyed a good local market. The abundance of dolii found in tombs may mean that they were valued enough as funerary objects that the wealthier classes may have commissioned craftsmen to make dolii specially to order—a tradition similar to that of the custom-made tombs so common at Caere.

Caeretane dolii are among pottery often described as Etruscan "Red Ware," [10] or in Italian as *impasto ceretano stampigliato* (meaning stamped Caeretane impasto), [11] with stamping referring to the method of decoration and impasto to an unrefined clay with gritty particles that contributed to its adhesive quality. This coarse, reddish clay proved most suitable for these large vessels because it enabled them to withstand their own considerable weight, both before firing and thereafter. For the most part they are consistent in form, standing 70 to 90 centimeters high with a width at the widest part of the vessel measuring usually half that of the height. [12] The body of the vase is eggshaped, with the wider portion at the top and a somewhat narrower flat base, with the overall shape being quasi-oval, gracefully curved and tapered. There are no handles on the stamped decorated dolii—a characteristic that sets them apart from other storage vases in the ancient Mediterranean—and it is difficult to discern whether they had clay lids due to the lack of solid archaeological data. [13] The mouths, wide and flared, are connected to a relatively narrow and short neck. The thickness of the clay generally ranges from half an inch to an inch and a quarter and, as a result of the denseness of the impasto, these vessels are very solid and heavy.

Dolii have often been associated with another item of Caeretane "Red Ware" known as the *braciere* (brazier). Bracieri are large, dish-like vessels constructed of the same type of clay as dolii and decorated in the same manner, commonly with the exact same stamp patterns used on dolii.[14] This alone affirms that these vessels were indeed produced in the same workshop. To some scholars this similarity, along with their contemporary time frame and their frequent appearance in the same tombs, implies that the dolio and braciere functioned together, the dolio being placed within the braciere, which acted as a kind of base plate.[15] Many museums—including the Louvre—have displayed dolii and bracieri in this fashion (figure 2). But although the two have been occasionally found in the same tombs, there is no conclusive evidence that they were used together in this manner or even designed as a unit. On the contrary, there is considerable evidence to suggest that they were used as separate entities (figure 3).[16] For this reason bracieri, in spite of their similarities to dolii, are not discussed further in this essay.[17]

FIGURE 2. Dolii and bracieri, Louvre, Galerie céramique, salle C. *Photo from E. Pottier,* Vases antiques du Louvre, salles A–E *(Paris, 1897), pl. 2; reproduced courtesy of Louvre.*

FIGURE 3. Braciere in situ, from Tomba III Maroi, Banditaccia Cemetery, Cerveteri, second half of sixth century B.C., Rome, Museo di Villa Giulia. *Photo courtesy of Museo di Villa Giulia.*

Dolii were created on potting wheels,[18] most likely in two or three parts, the mouth of the vase being placed down on the wheel and the shoulders being made to flare out by controlling the clay and wheel. The bottom of the vase would have been created on the wheel with the base being placed flat on the wheel and the sides being shaped to flare out gradually. The center of the vase, the most crucial part, was fashioned by joining successive clay coils[19] (a process known in Italian as *a colombino*) to the slightly hardened bottom part of the vase (figure 4) and securing them by hand, working the clay to flare it out slightly and tooling it to a smooth surface, which was then vertically fluted or ribbed for strength (figure 5). The top part of the vase, also slightly hardened, was then placed onto the coiled midsection (figure 6) and secured with a clay band (figure 7). This band, further described below, was then often decorated with stamping (figure 8), in which case its placement at the widest part of the vessel may have been designed to do triple duty: to hide the seam, reinforce it, and decorate the finished product.[20] Before firing, the surface of the completed vase was burnished to that rich red-brown finish that distinguished much of early Italic pottery.[21]

Though handsome and imposing in general shape, color, and finish, dolii were additionally enhanced with elegant decoration. The motifs used indirectly reflect the Near Eastern artistic influences which were arriving in Italy on trading ships carrying goods from Greece and elsewhere in the east during the early seventh and early sixth

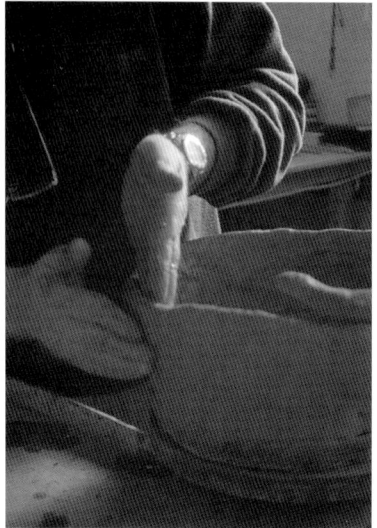

FIGURE 4 *(above, left)*. Shaping the midsection of the dolio using the *a colombino* process. *Photo by author.* FIGURE 5 *(above, right)*. Assembling the three parts of a dolio; the vertical fluting of the exterior was intended both for decoration and for added strength of the tripartite vessel. *Photo by author.*

FIGURE 6. Walter Brandolini, *artigiano ceramista*, creates modern dolii using the ancient techniques, as far as they are known. *Photo by author.*

FIGURE 7. Applying the decorative clay band. *Photo by author.*

FIGURE 8. Impressing the clay band with a cylinder stamp. *Photo by author.*

centuries B.C.—constituting the movement in Etruscan art known as the Orientalizing phenomenon. On many of the dolii tooled clay was laid over the shoulder above the stamped area in a graceful design resembling looped drapery tassels (figures 1 and 9), a zigzag formation (figure 10), or interlocked cables. These draped ornamental motifs are perhaps a result of Greek influences, as seen on Etrusco-Corinthian pottery bearing cablelike patterns. In addition, triangular forms at the foot and shoulder of some vessels recall characteristics of Minoan pithoi—an interesting parallel in light of other, similar circumstantial evidence.[22] The clay bands mentioned above, added at the widest part of the vase and decorated by impressing them with stamping tools

FIGURE 9. Detail of metope-stamped dolio, Rome, Museo di Villa Giulia, Castellani Collection. *Photo by author; used by permission of Museo di Villa Giulia.*

FIGURE 10. Detail of cylinder-stamped dolio, Rome, Museo di Villa Giulia, Castellani Collection. *Photo by author; used by permission of Museo di Villa Giulia.*

bearing artistic elements in relief, are perhaps the most striking and important aesthetic enhancement of most dolii.[23] The stamps were employed while the clay of the band was still damp, yet of a leathery consistency firm enough to maintain its shape under the pressure of the stamp.

As F. Serra Ridgway has pointed out, the use of seals for stamping purposes was common in the Near East and in Greece; but the direct inspiration for the application of a relief stamp to a large container for ceremonial, funerary, or votive purposes came more from Corinth, the source of many ideas, styles, and objects that reached Italy in the seventh century B.C.[24] On dolii, two general types of stamps were used— *metope* (figure 9) and cylinder (figure 10).[25] The impressions produced by both varieties of stamp vary widely according to the design complexity and depth of relief of the stamps. Some produced a single-level relief similar to a flat cookie cutter, and others were cut to varying depths to allow the intricate detailing of such minute items as hair and teeth. Unfortunately, archaeological excavations at Caere have not uncovered any stamping tools to date; this may imply that the material from which the tools were made was a perishable one, such as wood, bone, or wax, but it seems plausible that the stamps were made out of a more durable medium such as terracotta, bronze, or lead.[26]

The earlier type of stamp, the metope, dates to roughly the last quarter of the seventh century B.C.[27] It was pressed or punched into the partially damp clay in impressions repeated side by side along the band and entirely around the vase (figure 11). Although there are examples of different metope stamps used on a single vase, on many vases a single metope stamp, with a single primary design element,

FIGURE 11. Detail of metope-stamped dolio, Rome, Museo di Villa Giulia, Castellani Collection. *Photo by author; used by permission of Museo di Villa Giulia.*

was repeated around the entire circumference, sometimes precisely and sometimes rather unevenly—as if the craftsman was either in a hurry or not concerned about precision (figure 12). For the most part, the relief friezes face to the right. However, on occasion the impression does not follow the apparent given course, possibly because the impression could not be made to fit the pattern, or, again, because of imprecision on the part of the craftsman. Some metope reliefs include a frame around the primary element or icon of the stamp. The framing around the stamps shown in figures 11 and 12 is quite detailed, involving a border within the frame. Likewise, the impression pictured in figure 9 exemplifies the high-quality relief that the stamp matrix produced. Although no frame is inscribed on the metope relief, the artisan has punched the stamp deeply into the clay, using the edges of the stamp itself to create a cleanly defined frame.

The primary relief elements or icons of most metope stamps are animals, hybrid animals (mythological creatures typical of Orientalizing art), or man, all in general being subjects characteristic of Archaic art. There are several ways in which the human figure was rendered on the metope stamp; the most common depicts a man on a horse (figure 13) or running in a posture calling to mind a swastika, better known in Greek art as the Archaic running man or the "knielauf position"[28] (figure 14). Indeed, Etruscan pottery design was directly influenced by Greek pottery; as J. Gy. Szilágyi points out, the emergence of Etrusco-Corinthian ware in the seventh and sixth centuries B.C. attests to the wide appeal of Corinthian pottery styles among Etruscans.[29] The imported Greek wares relied heavily on motifs typical of the Orientalizing period, such as hybrid animals, rows of animals, or animals in a procession, which are the primary subject matter impressed on so many of the extant dolii. As pointed out in other essays in this volume, the Etruscans were quick to adopt artistic motifs from designs seen on Greek goods; they then adapted these designs by altering elements to reflect their own cultural and artistic preferences, creating something uniquely Etruscan.[30]

One of the favorite themes of the metope stamp was the "horse, bird, and man" (figure 15), which coincides with themes from early Greek art brought to light by J. L. Benson in his book of the same

FIGURE 12. Detail of metope-stamped dolio, Rome, Museo di Villa Giulia, Castellani Collection. *Photo by author; used by permission of Museo di Villa Giulia.*

FIGURE 13. Detail of metope-stamped dolio, Cerveteri–Scavi Brizi, Cava della Pozzolana. *Photo by author; used by permission of Museo di Villa Giulia.*

FIGURE 14. Detail of metope-stamped dolio, Cerveteri–Scavi Brizi. *Photo by author; used by permission of Museo di Villa Giulia.*

FIGURE 15. Horse, bird, and man
metope stamp. *Drawing by Chad Hofheins.*

name.[31] Horses are an ancient symbol of power and wealth, and man's
domination of the horse in a riding position emphasizes this meaning.
In this context, the bird is most likely a symbol of flight or motion signifying the movement of the horse and rider—as in Greek vase painting representations—rather than an icon of purely Etruscan design.

The centaur is another popular image for the metope stamp
(figure 9).[32] This half-man/half-horse figure is more often than not
depicted with human front legs, giving it a more anthropomorphic
appearance similar to that echoed in Protocorinthian vases and
Corinthian and Rhodian relief vases.[33] The length of the tail also
recalls early Greek geometric art. The centaur is portrayed with his
traditional attributes—the rock in one hand and the branch in the
other—hence the frequent reference to centaur-dendrophoros.[34]
Other common subject matter for the metope impressions includes the
griffin, sphinx, panther, and bearded figure, whose treatment of hair
recalls depictions of the "daedalic" figures represented in early Greek
art (figure 11). A very rare metope stamp on a dolio from the sixth
century B.C., belonging to the Castellani collection in the Museo
di Villa Giulia, shows the face of a hybrid creature (figure 16).
P. Mingazzini identifies it as the Greek river god Achelous.[35] The
god's face is shown with an open mouth and glaring eyes. Each metope
is separated by delicately fashioned floral circles composed of eight
petals—a commonly used icon on Protocorinthian vases.[36] In addition, the careful detail of this floral border illustrates the fine craftsmanship of the Caeretane workshops. The subject matter of this stamp
is unique, if not one of a kind, and it clearly exemplifies the adoption
of Greek art motifs based on Greek mythology.

Although there are numerous examples of male figures in metope- and cylinder-stamped designs on extant dolii, I have not encountered depictions of females. This is of particular interest since, if women were in fact never included in dolio decoration, such would have been a significant departure from the norm of the other forms of Etruscan artistic representation—as amply demonstrated in other essays in this volume.[37] Moreover, since it is known that at this time in Etruria great quantities of Greek vases depicting women were imported into Italy, it is interesting that the Caeretane craftsmen of red ware chose not to depict females. Perhaps the craftsmen were adhering to a closer artistic theme or genre still heavily influenced by Protocorinthian and Corinthian vases, whose subject matter was confined primarily to animals and men.

The other type of stamp, dating from around the end of the seventh to the beginning of the sixth century B.C., was a cylinder into which an extended relief design was inscribed.[38] The design was impressed by rolling the cylinder along the clay, thereby rendering an uninterrupted frieze (figure 10). Cylinder stamps were generally more elaborate and complex than metope stamps, and, owing both to the complexity of the design and to the rolling technique, the relief friezes were normally impressed less deeply than was the case with most metope applications. They were generally also vertically smaller in size.

While metope stamps possessed their own frame within the stamp, or the edges of the stamp itself created a kind of frame, cylinder stamps more often than not included intricate borders within the

FIGURE 16. Detail of metope-stamped dolio, Rome, Museo di Villa Giulia, Castellani Collection. *Photo by author; used by permission of Museo di Villa Giulia.*

stamp, although it appears that some cylinder stamp friezes seem to have been framed with a separate stamp (figure 10). The astragal or metope border, when not included within the cylinder stamp itself, was probably executed with a tool resembling a contemporary single ravioli cutter. Irregularities such as carelessly applied borders reveal the use of this technique (figure 17). Still, in many cases this "framing stamp" was as intricately and elegantly rendered as the cylinder stamp itself. Some dolii demonstrate a rich combination: a delicate and complex frieze bordered above and below by equally delicate and complex framing separately applied, above which the craftsman has added elegant tooling in looping design. The result is a vase of great beauty.

In general, while metope stamps tend to depict subject matter without a narrative theme (figure 1), cylinder stamps involve scenes of motion and action, such as a chariot race or a hunt (figure 10). However, the early cylinder stamps (figure 18), which may mark the

FIGURE 17. Poorly made dolio, Rome, Museo di Villa Giulia, Castellani Collection, inv. 50602. *Photo courtesy of Museo di Villa Giulia.*

transition from the metope stamp to the refined cylinder stamp, resemble metope stamping in that they portray large scenes of animals in procession and are, for the most part, without a narrative theme.[39] On the whole, the iconography of both types of stamps deals predominantly with animals and frequently pictures them being hunted by other animals or men.

One cylinder stamp, dating from the second quarter of the sixth century B.C., represents a significant departure from the more usual scenes of the hunt or battle in that it depicts an involved banquet scene (figure 19). Viewing from left to right, a man reclining on a couch with two pillows appears to be holding a cup; under his couch are two ducks—perhaps picking at crumbs from the banquet. A plant is next and then a column crater vase with yet another vase on top of it. A man, possibly nude, runs to the left with an ax in his hand. To the right of him is another reclining man with what appears to be a

FIGURE 18. Etruscan dolium (pithos), terracotta, ca. 600 B.C., height 69 cm, diameter of mouth 32 cm, cylinder-stamped. Collection of the J. Paul Getty Museum, Malibu, California, inv. 71.AE.287. *Photo courtesy of J. Paul Getty Museum.*

FIGURE 19.
Cylinder-stamped
dolio showing
banquet scene.
Photo by author;
used by permission
of Museo di Villa
Giulia.

footstool under his couch. Two men are pictured next; the one facing the left appears to be dancing, while the other faces right and plays the *tibiae*.[40] The entire scene is framed in an astragal border. This subject matter, although not rare for Etruscan artists, is relatively rare for these large vases. The entire frieze, which is 3.5 centimeters high and 18.7 centimeters in length, illustrates well the great detail and elaborate themes that could be achieved in a relief stamp of this kind.

Although the more detailed cylinder stamps appeared after the more simple metope stamping, plainer overall vase decoration—which of course existed before the highly decorated style—seems to have become more prevalent in the later part of the Etruscan period (figure 20). Nevertheless, it would be erroneous to assume that the highly decorated style gave way entirely to the plainer style. There are, in fact, examples of dolii with stamped relief decoration dating from well into the late sixth and early fifth centuries B.C.—that is, near the end of the period that dolii were known to have been constructed. The plainer style, while it reveals less than the more highly decorated style about the sources of influence upon its producers, still displays a generally high quality of craftsmanship, particularly in the shaping of the vase, which yields an appearance of lightness very pleasing to the eye. It was during this period (sixth century B.C.) that these vases were being produced in mass; during the earlier period they were much cruder in form and decor, as the contrast between figures 20 and 17 clearly demonstrates.

The interest of Etruscan dolii is clear: their graceful shape, warm color, and elegant decoration well demonstrate the level of skill and artistry of the Caeretane craftsmen as well as representing the result of Near Eastern and Greek influences during the Orientalizing period in the pottery workshops at Caere. But as important as these objects may be as functional vases, their qualities places them among the most striking and successful pottery forms produced by the Caeretane artisans. Like the graceful and comfortable beauty of the Caeretane tombs, where most of these vases have been found, their aesthetic appeal remains universal and timeless.

FIGURE 20. Plain dolio. *Photo courtesy of* Etruscan, Greek, and Roman Artifacts in the Frank V. de Bellis Collection of the California State University: A Catalog, *by Andreina L. Becker-Colonna, rev. and ed. by Rosefannie Grabstein (San Francisco, Calif.: San Francisco State University, 1976).*

NOTES

The impetus for this paper was born out of the recommendation of Dr. Mario Del Chiaro during his graduate seminar in Etruscan art in the fall of 1992 at the University of California–Santa Barbara. I gratefully acknowledge my debt to Dr. Del Chiaro for his guidance and insightfulness during my graduate studies; it has been a great honor to work with him. Parts of this text were revised and updated during my 1994–95 Fulbright year in Rome. These pertinent revisions would not have been possible without the constant support of the Soprintendente archeologico per l'Etruria meridionale–Direttore del Museo Nazionale di Villa Giulia, Dr. Giovanni Shichilone, who inspired me to choose the field of archaeology as a career many years ago; and Dr. Giuliana Nardi, whose expertise on bracieri and dolii from Caere as well as her pertinent suggestions concerning this text proved to be indispensable. I wish to express my gratitude to Dr. Maria Antonietta Rizzo for kindly allowing me to take part in the excavation at Caere last fall, to Dr. Apostolos Athanassakis for his early revisions of this paper, to Dr. Francesca R. Serra Ridgway for her comments and advice, and to Ercole Zapicchi for his continual assistance at Caere. I accept full responsibility for any errors.

1. M. Martelli, *La ceramiche degli Etruschi: La pittura vascolare* (Novara, It., 1987).

2. For purposes of clarity, the ancient name of Caere will be used throughout this essay, whether the context of the use is primarily historical or modern. Also, there are four variants of the adjectival form of the city's name; of these, "Caeretane" has been chosen for use throughout the volume for the sake of editorial consistency. There is an Etruscan inscription on a dolio from Caere with reference to the vase itself as *larnas*, which seems to come from the Greek word λαρναξ. This word can mean coffer, box, chest, cinerary urn, ark, or drinking trough and is similar to the word πιθοσ. See G. Colonna's report on Caere in M. Cristofani, ed., "Rivista di epigrafia etrusca," *SE* 46 (1978): 350 ff., n. 103. I am not aware of any scientific research on the actual contents of dolii, but it has been generally accepted that they were containers for grain, wine, and oil. Further research and scientific analysis on these vases as they are found in situ will likely shed light on their contents. However, there is a possible reference inscribed on a dolio referring to the contents inside; see G. Colonna's report on Caere in M. Cristofani, ed., "Rivista di epigrafia etrusca," *SE* 52 (1984): 317 ff., n. 71.

3. S. P. Boriskovskaya, "Etruscan Relief Pithoi from Caere," *Wissenschaftliche Zeitschrift der Universität Rostock* 19 (1970): 567 ff.; L. Pareti, *La tomba Regolini-Galassi del Museo Gregoriano Etrusco e la civiltà dell' Italia centrale nel sec. VII A. C.*, Monumenti vaticani di archeologia e d'arte, 8 (Rome, 1947).

4. Boriskovskaya, "Etruscan Relief Pithoi," 567 (supra n. 3).

5. Ibid., 567 ff.; M. Del Chiaro, "Etruscan Vases at San Simeon," *California Studies in Classical Antiquity* 4 (1971): 115 ff.; F. R. Serra Ridgway, "Impasto ceretano stampigliato: Gli esemplari del British Museum: Origini e affinità," in *Italian Iron Age Artefacts in the British Museum: Papers of the Sixth British Museum Classical Colloquium*, ed. J. Swaddling (Oxford, 1986), 283 ff.

6. For evidence of Etruscan workshops at Caere during the fourth century B.C., see M. Del Chiaro, *Etruscan Red-Figured Vase-Painting at Caere* (Berkeley, Calif., 1974).

7. Serra Ridgway, "Impasto ceretano stampigliato," 287 (supra n. 5).

8. This may imply that when dolii were used as household or ceremonial vases, functionality was more important than decoration. In short, perhaps the highly decorated vases were used only in the tombs. For recent archaelogical finds of dolii at Caere, see G. Nardi, "Dolii," in *Caere 3.2: Lo scarico arcaico della vigna parrocchiale*, ed. M. Cristofani (Rome, 1993), 351 ff. (vol. hereinafter cited as *Caere 3.2*).

9. For the most recent excavation reports on the ancient city of Caere, see M. Cristofani, "L'area urbana," in *Caere 1: Il parco archeologico*, ed. M. Cristofani (Rome, 1988), 85 ff.; M. Cristofani, ed., *Caere 3.1–2: Lo scarico arcaico della vigna parrocchiale* (Rome, 1992–93), with primary bibliography (vol. 2 supra n. 8).

10. Boriskovskaya, "Etruscan Relief Pithoi," 567 (supra n. 3).

11. Serra Ridgway, "Impasto ceretano stampigliato," 283 (supra n. 5).

12. Ibid.

13. Many of the plainer dolii described later in this paper do have small handles and may even be older than the highly decorated ones. There are a few examples of dolii displayed with clay lids, but their placement may be spurious. See Pareti, *La tomba Regolini-Galassi*, 438, n. 641, tav. 69 (supra n. 3).

14. However, it is of interest to note that bracieri are almost always decorated only with cylinder stamping and not metope stamping.

15. R. D. De Puma, *Etruscan and Villanovan Pottery: A Catalogue of Italian Ceramics from Midwestern Collections* (Iowa City, Iowa, 1971), 11 ff.; R. D. De Puma, *Etruscan Tomb Groups: Ancient Pottery and Bronzes in Chicago's Field Museum of Natural History* (Mainz am Rhein, 1986), 84.

16. I have seen a number of unpublished bracieri in the storage rooms at Caere excavated within the past few decades with coals and burned contents still inside. Moreover, there are photographs at the Museo di Villa Giulia in Rome of excavated bracieri with remains of coals in them. This supports the theory that the braciere acted as a type of portable hearth in the tomb. There is on display at the Museo di Villa Giulia an example of a braciere found in situ with coal and eggs still remaining within it. See G. Proietti et al., *Cerveteri* (Rome, 1986), 125. I am currently researching bracieri at Caere; publication of my finds and conclusions is forthcoming.

17. For further information on bracieri, see P. Mingazzini, *Vasi della collezione Castellani: Catalogo* (Rome, 1930); Serra Ridgway, "Impasto ceretano stampigliato," 238–88 (supra n. 5); G. Nardi, "Bracieri," in *Caere 3.2*, 399 ff. (vol. supra n. 8).

18. Serra Ridgway, "Impasto ceretano stampigliato," 285 (supra n. 5).

19. For a thorough description of ancient vase-making techniques, see N. Cuomo di Caprio, *La ceramica in archeologia: Antiche tecniche di lavorazione e moderni metodi d'indagine* (Rome, 1985).

20. In examining many dolii and fragments of dolii in the storage rooms at the Banditaccia and at the Museo di Villa Giulia I have noted that these vases tend to break and crack in the widest area of the vase and that often a faint seam can be seen in the clay. In addition, I have seen fingerprints left in the inside of the vases, from the artisan's attempts to join and smooth the clay (in a dolio from Monte dell'Oro and on a fragment from Monte Abatone tomb 136; both pieces are located in the storage rooms in the Museum of Caere). Studying scientifically the evidence shown by seam traces will further increase our knowledge of the techniques used by the Caeretane craftsmen.

21. Del Chiaro, "Etruscan Vases," 116 (supra n. 5).

22. See F. Courby, *Les Vases grecs à reliefs* (Paris, 1922), pls. I–III; A. Evans, *The Palace of Minos . . . at Knossos*, 4.2 (London, 1935), 636 ff., figs. 625a–b. Decorated stamped pithoi are found outside Etruria in various areas of the Hellenic world, namely Rhodes, Boeotia, and Crete; see Serra Ridgway, "Impasto ceretano stampigliato," 285 (supra n. 5). For possible east Greek influences, see D. Feytmans, "Les Pithoi à reliefs de l'île de Rhodes," *BCH* 74 (1950): 135–80, pls. XX–XXIX.

23. Quite possibly the artisans intended to imitate metal, although appropriate models have not been found to offer conclusive evidence for this idea. See Serra Ridgway, "Impasto ceretano stampigliato," 285 (supra n. 5).

24. Ibid., 286.

25. Stamping in clay was not new to the Mediterranean at this time; in fact, it had a long tradition in the ancient Near East. See D. Collon, *First Impressions: Cylinder Seals in the Ancient Near East* (London, 1987). The Greeks, especially the Corinthians, adopted this type of decoration perhaps directly from Crete, which inherited relief ware techniques from the Minoans; see S. S. Weinberg, "Corinthian Relief Ware: Pre-Hellenistic Period," *Hesperia* 23 (1954): 111–37; L. H. Anderson, "Relief Pithoi from the Archaic Period of Greek Art," Ph.D. diss. (University of Michigan, 1977). For further Greek relief ware, see Courby, *Les Vases grecs à reliefs* (supra n. 22); E. Pottier, "Les Vases archaïques à reliefs," *BCH* 12 (1888): 491–510.

26. A clay cylinder stamp matrix depicting a floral motif has been discovered north of Caere at Roselle; see C. B. Curri, "Un cilindretto etrusco di Roselle," in *Studi di antichità in onore di Guglielmo Maetzke* (Rome, 1984) 2:243–49. Another has been discovered in Sicily; see N. Allegro, "Louteria a rilievo da Himera," *Secondo quaterno imerese (Studi e materiali dell'Istituto di archeologia dell'Università di Palermo)* 3 (1982): 122, n. 40.

27. Boriskovskaya, "Etruscan Relief Pithoi," 567 (supra n. 3); Serra Ridgway, "Impasto ceretano stampigliato," 286 (supra n. 5).

28. Weinberg, "Corinthian Relief Ware," 113, pl. 25c (supra n. 25).

29. J. Gy. Szilágyi, *Etrusko-korinthosi Vázafestészet* (Budapest, 1975); J. Gy. Szilágyi, *Ceramica etrusco-corinzia figurata*, trans. E. S. Graziani, Monumenti etruschi, 7 (Florence, 1992).

30. See, in this volume, the essays by Helen Nagy, 45 ff., and Alexandra Carpino, 65 ff.

31. J. L. Benson, *Horse, Bird, and Man: The Origins of Greek Paintings* (Amherst, Mass., 1970).

32. For a thorough study of the centaur in ancient art, see P. V. C. Baur, *Centaurs in Ancient Art: The Archaic Period* (Berlin, 1912).

33. Boriskovskaya, "Etruscan Relief Pithoi," 569 (supra n. 3); Weinberg, "Corinthian Relief Ware," pl. 25c (supra n. 25); Baur, *Centaurs in Ancient Art*, 84–86 (supra n. 32).

34. Boriskovskaya, "Etruscan Relief Pithoi," 568 (supra n. 3).

35. Mingazzini, *Vasi della collezione Castellani*, 78 ff., n. 252, tav. IX, 1 (supra n. 17). Achelous was a popular icon in Etruscan art, as can be seen by his appearance on gold work, bronze, and clay. He was a hybrid Greek mythological figure with a human face and the horns and torso of a bull. He acquired his name from the longest river in Greece, the Achelous, which has its source in central Epirus and empties into the Corinthian Gulf.

36. Floral rosettes are commonly found on Cretan pithoi; see D. Levi, "Early Hellenic Pottery of Crete," *Hesperia* 14 (1945): 1–32, pl. XXX; Weinberg, "Corinthian Relief Ware," 114–15 (supra n. 25); Serra Ridgway, "Impasto ceretano stampigliato," 286 (supra n. 5).

37. For descriptions and representations of women in Etruscan art, see, in this volume, the essays by Helen Nagy, 47 ff.; Alexandra Carpino, 65 ff.; Robert L. Maxwell, 273 ff.; Harrison Powley, 289 ff.; Steven Bule, 318 ff.; and Nancy Thomson de Grummond, 358 f. To date, I have not encountered any clearly defined depictions of women on bracieri or dolii.

38. Boriskovskaya, "Etruscan Relief Pithoi," 567 (supra n. 3).

39. In a few cases dolii share both types of stamps, suggesting that there was not a significant time span between the two types.

40. For more on tibiae, see, in this volume, the essay by Harrison Powley, 293 ff. and fig. 7 on p. 297.

Etruscan Domestic Architecture: An Ethnoarchaeological Model

DOROTHY DVORSKY ROHNER

Perhaps the most compelling of many reasons archaeologists offer for excavating and examining the remains of long-vanished civilizations is to find out how the people within them conducted their lives from day to day. This is not surmised by examining artifacts alone; situation, provenience, and context are all very important in formulating interpretations of what is found. And recognition of the importance of studying the homes themselves—the domestic structures that housed these people and their possessions—is steadily growing. In the case of ancient Etruria, scholars in general agree that the arrangement of domestic living space is reflected in the arrangement of this culture's tomb structures and temple forms;[1] and the organization evident in the tomb complexes, in turn, reflects the pattern of Etruscan urban development. To fully appreciate and understand this dynamic, it is important to reexamine the Etruscan home itself as well as the rationale behind scholars' interpretations of this culture's domestic architecture. In addition, it is helpful to compare the domestic forms of Etruria to those of the contemporary Greek culture and the Roman culture which derived from the Etruscan, thereby highlighting the distinctive identifying marks of these Etruscan forms. Close examination reveals domestic structures to be a symbolic paradigm that sheds light on the arrangement of Etruscan affairs in general.

FIGURE 1. Dorothy D. Rohner, representation of Etruscan home life, mixed water media on paper, 1995. *Photo by John Rohner.*

An ethnoarchaeological tool known as the predictive model provides the method for this examination. A predictive model structures and organizes the physical expressions of a specific culture, producing a formula which may be used to interpret the abstract ideas of that culture. The model demands that the data be consistent; otherwise its predictive purpose is thwarted. Each model has a specific focus, such as the cause of sedentism, the course of rural-to-urban migration, or—as in this instance—the use of domestic space. In other words, the predictive model presented here discusses the importance of the "domestic idea" within Etruscan society. Examination of architecture and material remains, the observable cultural forms with which the model deals, stimulates questions, such as what importance the domestic idea held within the Etruscan culture at large, whether status was reflected in this domestic idea, whether this status carried over into the general society, whether a change of domestic form coincided with a historical or economic event that may have influenced the change, and how important the domestic idea was in Etruria as compared to other contemporary cultures.

The controversy surrounding the issue of whether or not architectural units in the prehistoric archaeological record can reliably designate specific social interrelationships—between individual and family, male and female, household members of differing social status and age—need not be discussed here, as R. E. Tringham has already dealt with this topic extensively.[2] Rather, this research proceeds from that of Tringham, S. Kent, and others who seek to provide a reading of a culture which does not compete with other interpretations but instead contributes to a vibrant scholarly dialogue.[3] Tringham's work addresses the tension between the observer as recorder of a prehistoric society and as mediator translating for the prehistoric participant's viewpoint.[4] In her discussion of the two Neolithic sites of Divostin and Opovo in Yugoslavia she sets out to provide "a case study of humanized prehistory,"[5] her hypothesis being that inquiry into the point of view of the participant in an architectural setting is valid. Tringham uses two- and three-dimensional illustrations to visualize and imagine the buildings of the past and their inhabitants.[6] In this way she develops an interpretation of the space as it relates to individuals and their actions in a society.[7] Figure 1 of this essay is a similar attempt. This analysis is readily done in the study of contemporary cultures, but obvious difficulties exist in the interpretation of domestic space in prehistoric cultures or those ancient cultures which have not left explicit or comprehensive records of their domestic life. For the purpose of this study, then, the Etruscan house model develops primarily from archaeological remains—that is, the architecture, findings, and artifacts and their expression within several sites. In addition, ancient texts provide supporting evidence when available.[8] The model, as it has been developed, establishes a formulaic pattern against which the various sites may be first analyzed and compared and then interpreted. The preliminary research does find constancy of space use and consistency of space form from structure to structure and site to site through a chronological span and shows interaction between interior domestic space and greater community space. In addition, comparison of the domestic architectural plan to both burial and religious structures shows that these forms are also consistent with the developed domestic pattern.

Before further discussion of the model or its application, it should be stated for the sake of clarity that, as used in this essay, the term *domestic architecture* refers to the actual material and physical remains of a structure which has been identified as being a *domus* (residence) through the study of the artifacts and findings located within and in conjunction with it. *Living space* as used here is that area which is bounded by this domestic architecture and contains the activities relating to the daily life of the individuals who inhabit it. In addition to defining living space, the walls and other physical boundaries of domestic architecture signal to the greater community the opportunity (or lack thereof) to participate in the inhabitants' relationships.[9] Such factors as the arrangement of the rooms, the activities within those rooms, what activities are brought into that space from the greater community, ease of egress and ingress, and the accessibility of the center of the house to an individual outside the household unit act as a physical embodiment of that culture's perception of domesticity and the interactions within it. That is to say, living space and domestic architecture as viewed through the predictive model provide a key to determining the relationships of individuals to one another with regard to gender, age, and class, as well as designating their relationships to the greater community. If similarities to domestic architecture are present in cultural architectural expressions outside the domestic arena, it can be hypothesized that the domestic idea continues into cultural spheres in which domestic activities are not necessarily the primary function.

Just as the relationships of house structures to the whole of the community are shown in the archaeological site plan, so the structural remains of each house record the arrangement of the rooms in relation to one another—acting as the physical blueprint, so to speak—and the material remains, such as pottery and loom weights, help to determine the functions of the rooms.[10] In order to aid in interpreting these remains, illustrations for the Etruscan domestic predictive model developed in this essay are labeled with an alphanumeric system, the numeric portion of which is based on the connection of one living space to another. Starting at 6 for the communal area, the system moves toward smaller numbers to indicate more private space. Arrows indicate the main access to each house and offer an idea of visual direction and range—the line of sight of an individual standing at the front doorway and looking into the dwelling. It is primarily this line of sight that determines the numerical ranking assigned to each area. Thus, the larger the numbers observed in a house plan, the more open that plan is to the community at large.[11] Lowercase letters in the various areas of a house indicate consistency of space arrangement and usage as compared with other houses from the same site. All rooms labeled "a," then, had counterpart rooms that were located similarly in other houses at the same site and contained similar types of artifacts. Uppercase letters indicate constancy of space arrangement and usage in houses from different periods of time and different sites. Examination of the drawings shows that only one area demonstrates this kind of constancy in placement and usage from one site to another and from early constructions to later ones: the central courtyard, or communal area, about which more will be said later. Private, noncommunal outside space—that is, space which opens into an outdoor but enclosed area not easily accessed by the community, unlike the court-yard space—is labeled as such on each diagram.

The alphanumeric code used in the diagrams is supplemented by chart 2 (see p. 132), which summarizes the ease of access and con-stancy of use for each site discussed. The overall ease with which an outsider can recognize the plan layout upon entry is also designated, with plus/plus ($+/+$) meaning easily read, plus/minus ($+/-$) meaning partially easy to read, and minus/minus ($-/-$) meaning not easily read. In addition, it states whether or not areas are recognizable, through artifact finds, as gender-, age-, or class-specific; and whether areas can be identified, again through artifact finds, as mono- or multi-functional in activity.

The analysis presented in this essay begins with the early Archaic site of Acquarossa, with supporting evidence from the contemporary sites of Veii, Vetulonia, and San Giovenale.[12] The later Archaic transi-tional houses from Acquarossa and the urbanized structures of Marzabotto are analyzed using the same model and are compared to the early Archaic type.

The arrangement of the Archaic houses of Acquarossa show a general similarity in their spatial relationships within each unit and to one another. The house units of the Acquarossa zone B area—the early Archaic structures (figure 2)—have a central communal area (c6), around which quasi-rectangular buildings are arranged with a long side facing toward the open area. Entry to each of the houses is by a door in this long side of the structure, with the line of sight lead-ing directly into the interior and, in most cases, all the way to the back wall. Houses I and II have an open porch or enclosed vestibule. There is easy access from the communal plaza (c6) to any of the houses. The ease of access to the center of the home is noted by the numeric code 5 or 4 or, in two cases, 3 in each of the living areas.

A tripartite arrangement of rooms sits at the rear of houses II and III. The actual enclosed living space in house III is sixty square meters; the average living space may be somewhat larger. Accommo-dations for storage, sleeping, cooking, and toilet facilities would, of course, be necessary for the inhabitants. The material remains found in each of the tripartite rooms of houses II and III suggest all these various functions by the presence of sleeping benches, deposits from storage, and artifacts specific to activities such as meal preparation and craft work. Moreover, many Etruscan mirrors are decorated with depictions of family conferences, symposia, maternal scenes, musical entertainments, lovers' rendezvous, and women putting on their jewelry, all of which represent living activities carried on in the domestic area.[13] At the back of both houses II and III a door from one of the three rooms opens into what F. Prayon terms a back courtyard or garden behind the house.[14] Frequently it is this room that reveals a higher concentration of deposits related to water storage and cooking pottery.[15]

Typically, houses of Acquarossa from the seventh to the end of the sixth century B.C. occur in clusters such as that pictured here. The easy access home dwellers enjoyed to and from the communal space infers that the inhabitants of the single dwellings expanded their living

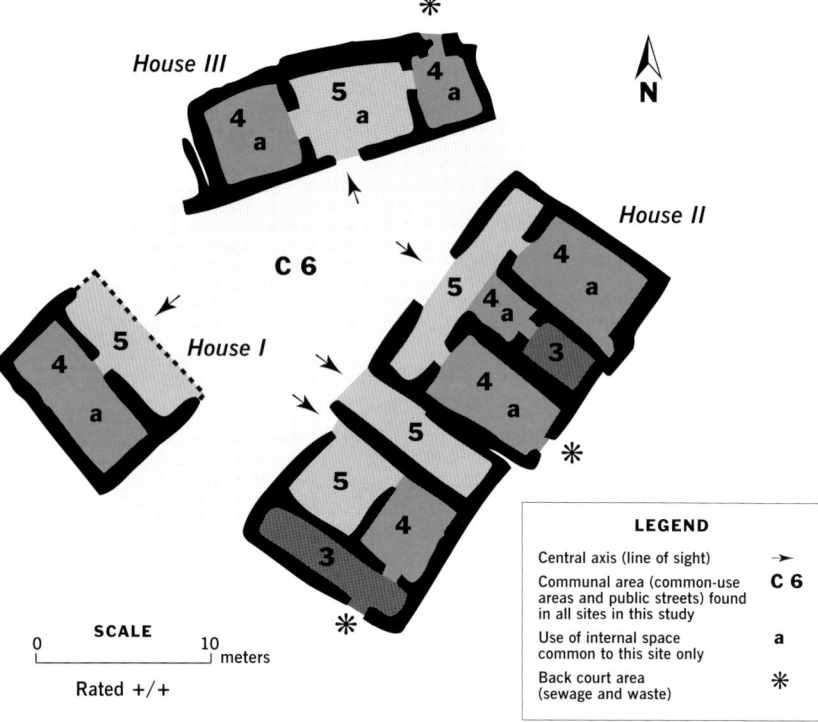

FIGURE 2. Early Archaic houses, zone B, Acquarossa, ca. 600 B.C., plan. *Drawing by author after Prayon.*

space into the open communal area. Indeed, many domestic activities could be carried out in the area immediately adjacent to the entryway of the house. Servants or slaves may have slept there, *dolii* may have been stored there (and have, in fact, been found there in situ), family barbecues might easily have been held as children played and ran between homes.[16] Cooking outdoors on portable stands is most probable, as these stands are frequently found as artifacts and therefore can be considered an integral part of the Etruscan domestic scene.[17] This semiprivate/communal area and its associated activities were important in the later development of the Etruscan house, when this space was moved right into the house itself as a part of the floor plan. The back court's most practical function at this early stage was the disposal of kitchen garbage (evidenced by bones of fish and other food animals) and, very likely, human waste. For the sake of sanitation and the close proximity of neighbors, the wastes of the household could not be dumped out the front door into the communal area; hence this back court area off what was probably primarily a kitchen/bath area was reserved for sewage.

So, in general, the house plan most common at the site is oriented with its main entrance fronting a communal space. The rooms—three, generally—are arranged along the back of the dwelling, and the line of sight from the entrance leads directly into this interior arrangement. A small back court opens from a corner room that often contains artifacts common to a kitchen/bathroom. The easy accessibility of every area within the home to any and all seems to indicate that activities were not gender-, age-, or class-specific in designated areas; the simple and unobstructed traffic pattern of the plan would not have allowed for this. The Archaic houses of Acquarossa are thus characterized by openness of private space to the communal space and nonspecific functional areas within the structures.[18]

The house areas of Veii (figure 3) and Vetulonia (figure 4) do not have the same cluster arrangement as Acquarossa. This is in part a reaction to the topography of the region.[19] In the case of Vetulonia it may also be an arrangement based on commercial needs, as the westernmost buildings on the stretch of winding road pictured (represented by house 1) have been identified as *tabernae*.[20] The domestic architecture

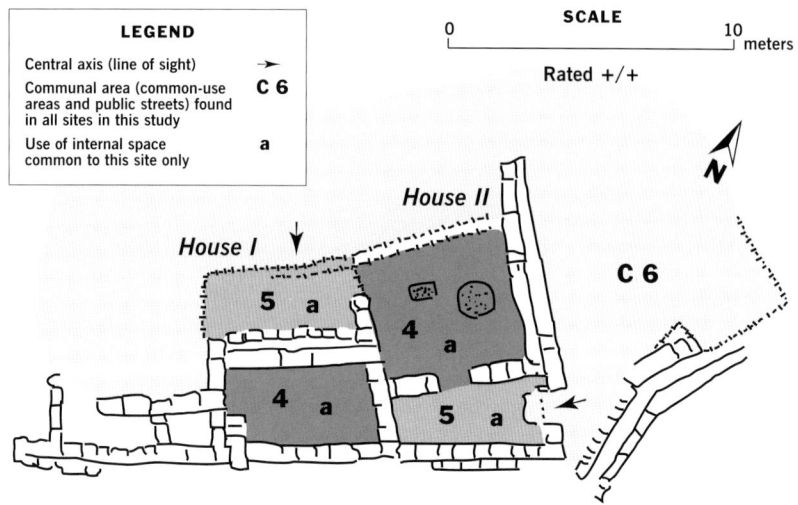

FIGURE 3. Early Archaic houses, Veii, ca. 600 B.C., plan. *Drawing by author after Boëthius.*

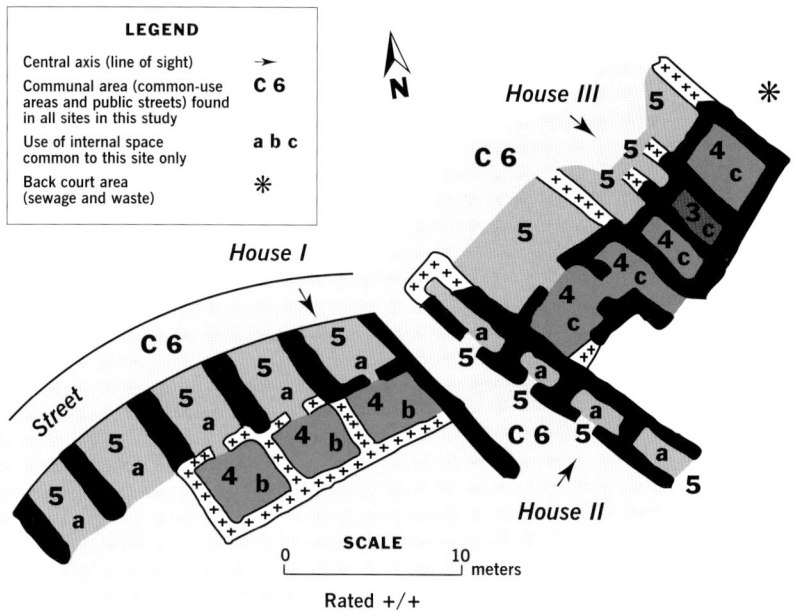

FIGURE 4. Early Archaic houses, Vetulonia, ca. 600 B.C., plan. *Drawing by author after Boëthius.*

in both plans, however, reiterates the characteristics of ready access to the home from a communal space, easy readability of the plan to an outsider, and constancy of rooms. These plans, as in the Acquarossa arrangement, do not accommodate gender-, age-, or class-specific areas, nor are there monofunctional use areas for the family; the only areas demonstrating monofunctional use are those comprising the commercial area.

Vetulonia contains typically identifiable Etruscan house plans in houses I, II, and III (figure 4). The so-called *megaron* house of Veii (house II in figure 3) is found as house I at Vetulonia. The megaron form, as discussed by A. Boëthius,[21] appears to be an arrangement for Etruscans of a lower economic level. The longitudinal-axis arrangement of Acquarossa (house II in figure 2) is found at house II and its neighbors at Vetulonia, according to the excavator; and the later Marzabotto form is seen in Vetulonia as house III.[22] Vetulonia may be considered an early attempt at urban planning by working with established Etruscan house forms with an additional commercial purpose in a steeply graded and oddly shaped geographic site.

San Giovenale (figure 5) provides material evidence of the Etruscan penchant for nonspecific task areas. As shown in chart 1, the distribution of the ceramic material in all three rooms is indiscriminate:

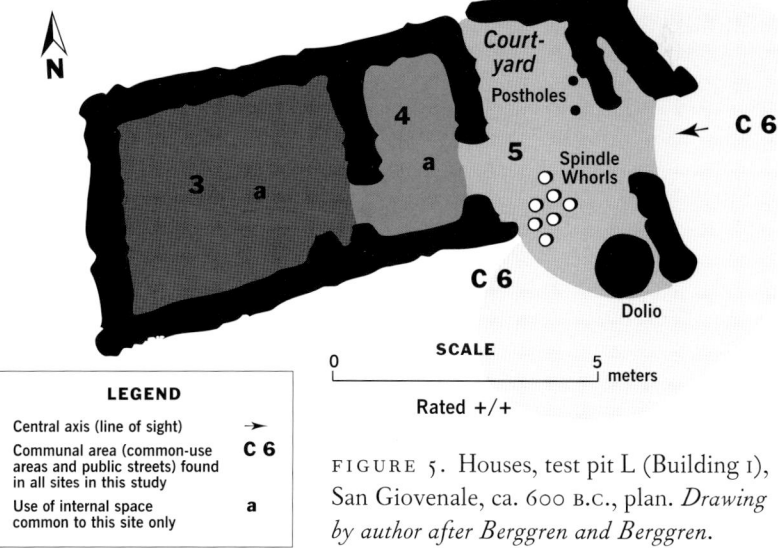

LEGEND

Central axis (line of sight)

Communal area (common-use areas and public streets) found in all sites in this study   **C 6**

Use of internal space common to this site only   **a**

FIGURE 5. Houses, test pit L (Building I), San Giovenale, ca. 600 B.C., plan. *Drawing by author after Berggren and Berggren.*

for instance, fine glazed wares are present in each of these areas along-side rougher kitchen vessels, and in the same stratum.

STRATUM	BACK ROOM	CENTER ROOM	COURTYARD
4	Primitive Impasto	Primitive, Advanced Impasto	Primitive, Transitional, Buccheroid, Brown Impasto; Kitchen; Red Slip
3	Primitive, Transitional, Advanced, Buccheroid Red Impasto; Internal Red Painted; Kitchen	Painted, Transitional, Advanced, Buccheroid, Brown Impasto; Red Slip	Sub-Apennine; Primitive, Transitional, Advanced, Buccheroid Impasto
2	Primitive, Transitional, Advanced, Buccheroid Impasto; Red Slip; Etrusco-Corinthian; Black Glaze	Primitive, Transitional, Advanced, Buccheroid, Red Impasto; Red Slip; Fine Creamware; Plain White Ware	Primitive, Transitional, Advanced, Buccheroid, Red Impasto; Red Slip; Etrusco-Corinthian; Plain White Ware

CHART 1. Distribution of Ceramics in Building 1, San Giovenale[23]

The excavators found spindle whorls and bobbins, noted by the tiny circles in the courtyard.[24] Based on these deposits, they consider this area to be a refuse dump. However, in this same area postholes were found, as indicated by the two black circles. The spindle whorls appear to be close enough to the postholes to suggest a loom and textile manufacturing area. This is most plausible, as the courtyard fits the requirements for light and sufficient space to set up a permanent loom and it is possible that only half or partial walls existed to the east and south.[25] The architectural arrangement of the San Giovenale plan, therefore, reaffirms the apparent Etruscan preference for several con-sistent characteristics: a domestic environment characterized by open-ness to communal areas; nonspecific areas for tasks, such as cooking, that would seemingly call for a monofunctional area, the only excep-tion possibly being the loom area; ease of entry to the center of the home; and no gender-, age-, or class-specific areas. The nature and location of material remains support these conclusions as well.

Use of the three-*cellae* longitudinal organization at these early sites did not stem from construction needs or lack of technology required to build a square form; the monumental, possibly sacral, square structure at Poggio Civitate dating to 575 B.C. is evidence of this.[26] Instead, the Etruscan house model seems specifically to prefer the architectural forms of the longitudinal back tripartite room arrangement as seen at early Acquarossa and the so-called megaron form of early Veii and Vetulonia.[27] The megaron form fits within the parameters of the model in every category except in room arrangement. Although both forms existed simultaneously, the tripartite arrangement was used more frequently overall, even at the early stage of house development; and in the later stages the megaron form disappeared entirely. It seems to have been a logical step for the household with a megaron-style home to add rooms onto the sides when it became economically feasible in order to give it the more customary longitudinal three-cellae form.[28] For the inhabitants, this familiar arrangement, with its ease of access to the household center, seems to have been the optimum in domestic architecture.

The later sixth-century B.C. complex at Acquarossa (figure 6) shows an arrangement of rooms around a large courtyard. The architectural structure maintains the scheme of domestic space which

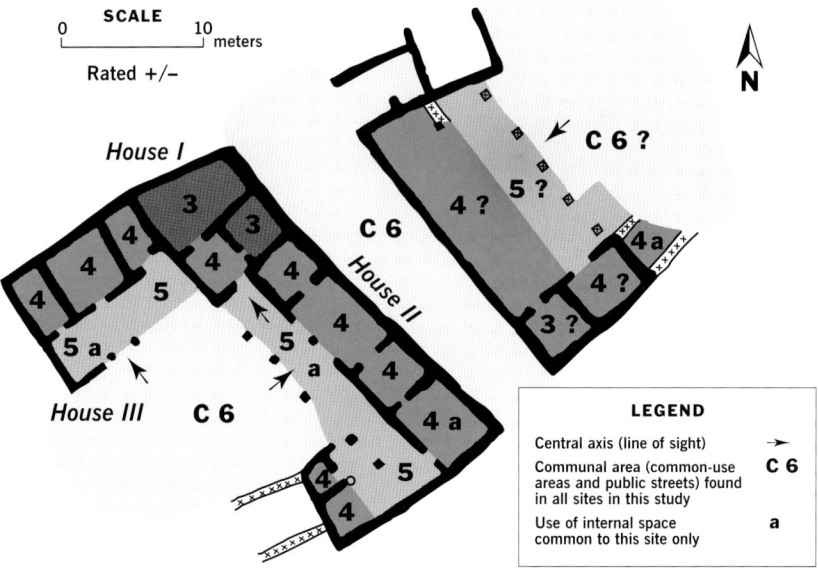

FIGURE 6. Houses, zone G, Acquarossa, ca. 550 B.C., plan. *Drawing by author after Sgubini Moretti.*

occurred earlier at Acquarossa. The domestic form pictured here comprises houses I, II, and III. The expansion and joining together of these former smaller one-unit house structures is the next developmental step of the Etruscan residence. These joined units necessitated the placing of additional rooms on the sides of the square in order to surround the communal plaza, but this did not in any way change the orientation of the main three cellae on a longitudinal axis with one long side fronting the communal area. Moreover, the added corner rooms are nearly as accessible to the courtyard as any of the other rooms lining it. Another house complex to the east of this better-preserved structure may be built virtually in its mirror image, with joined domestic units organized around another communal area, although due to damage and the presence of only partial walls this is difficult to determine. This expansion of the Etruscan home most probably reflects the increasingly prosperous economic life of this period, as well as indicating the presence of the newly developing Etruscan aristocracy.

There is disagreement as to the function of this complex, although the domestic house forms are present. Scholars have attempted to define its character by the iconography with which it is associated. Terracotta decorative plaques depict a procession and figures which F. Coarelli identifies as scenes from the labors of Herakles (figure 7).[29] A second group of plaques, which he states are of a later date (ca. 530–500 B.C.) and crafted by a different artist's hand, depict a *symposium* and *komos*. G. Säflünd reads Coarelli's Herakles interpretation rather

FIGURE 7. Plaque, terracotta, from Acquarossa, ca. 600 B.C. *Drawing by author.*

as the iconography of a wedding ceremony comparable in depiction to a Corinthian *aryballos* portraying Herakles with his bride, Hebe, in their wedding procession, as indicated by the epigraphy and the presence of the Charitides, Aphrodite holding a pomegranate, and Athena with a wreath (figure 8).[30] Säflünd believes that the iconographic depiction of a wedding theme in this complex connotes a restricted use of it for festal, public, and ceremonial activities.[31]

In contrast to Säflünd's identification, A. M. Sgubini Moretti believes that the building functioned as a residence as well as a civil structure of a local dynasty.[32] A closer look at Coarelli's reading of the terracotta plaques in comparison to the aryballos scene supports this contention. Coarelli sees the male figure standing in the chariot as Herakles and the female at his side as Athena, his protectoress. The single male figure with a staff of authority standing before the winged horses is possibly Eurytheus.[33] This scene conforms to other depictions of Heraklean labors in that the necessary characters are all present. Further, another plaque which directly precedes this section portrays another labor of Herakles: the vanquishing of the Nemean lion. One could surmise that the entire frieze of plaques was concerned with the labors of this hero.

Moreover, on the plaque with the chariot procession the necessary nuptial iconographic devices, such as those seen on the aryballos—the Charitides or Aphrodite with the pomegranate—are not present. The female and male figures in the chariot are the sole indicators of a

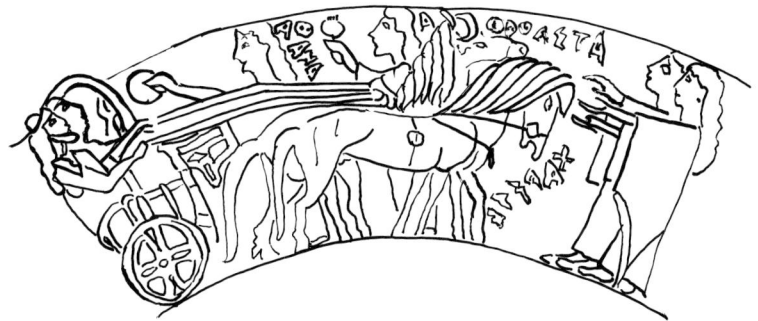

FIGURE 8. Corinthian aryballos, from Vulci, sixth century B.C. *Drawing by author after Pandolfini.*

conjugal union, and these do not present enough iconographic evidence to name it a marriage procession. The basis, then, for declaring the building a sacral building cannot be supported by the iconography of the decorative plaques, as the question of theme is not clearly understood as yet.

It is suggested that constructions like this complex of domestic units carried the Etruscan domestic idea into a transitional phase of expansion in response to economic and demographic pressures. The courtyard continued to act as extended living space for the inhabitants. The domestic architectural plan preserved the three cellae/megaron forms by the joining of the structures along an L shape. The numeric progression from public space to private is 6 to 5. The complex is rated plus/minus, because to a great extent the rooms are identifiable to an outsider and there is still easy access to the main tripartite division, which remains constant in location and arrangement. Judging from the artifacts, the plan continues to be nonspecific in areas for gender, age, and class, although with the expanded house plans certain areas are now monofunctional: the corner rooms seem to have been used exclusively for storage.

The communal area is easily accessed from other building complexes in the area, each with its own communal space, in an arrangement similar to the hacienda complexes and Native American pueblos of the American Southwest and Mexico. The Acquarossa complex appears to have housed an extended family who shared the communal area as an extension of living space and in cooperation with other extended families of the greater community for mutual activities. This more expansive plan at Acquarossa does not change the function of the domestic or communal space nor their orientation to one another; the general layout is in full agreement with the earlier Acquarossa Archaic structures, as well as those of the previous sites mentioned.

The sacrificial pit found in this area does not by its presence argue against interpretation of the architecture as domestic space.[34] Rather, it reinforces the fact that the Etruscans expressed their religious rites and ancestral devotion in an intimate fashion. This use of the courtyard by the greater community as an area for religious functions or ceremonies was not a new expression, but rather a natural development progressing from the previous period.

The floor plans common in Archaic Acquarossa appear again in modified versions at the more urbanized site of Marzabotto. The plans are the same in that they still give direct access to the center of the house via the central axis, the traditional three cellae still face the central court area, and room identity and constancy remain intact for the traditional rooms. However, the additional side rooms do not fit into the constancy pattern, nor are they easily identifiable to a stranger. Material remains indicate that storage and possibly servant/slave quarters were in these rooms, most of which were situated at the front of the house.[35]

Additionally, floor plans had to be altered to accommodate Marzabotto's strictly laid out urban block format (see figures 9 and 10).[36] One of these alterations, according to Prayon, was the relocation of the back court from its traditional place off the kitchen/bathroom to a position in front of the tripartite cellae layout to form a central court. He argues that this was done to provide needed light in the center of the house.[37] This, however, may be an incorrect assumption; if it were so, the traditional back court space would have to have migrated across a side room, reoriented itself along the central axis, and become the focal point of activity. Further, its primary function would have changed from a sewage and garbage disposal area to the center of the home's living area. This would have been a rather striking—and therefore unlikely—transformation, philosophically and conceptually alien to the Etruscan domestic architectural mindset as demonstrated in the continuity of floor plans across both time and area. It is more probable that the central court of the houses in Marzabotto was a transformation of Archaic Acquarossa's central communal area.[38]

Virtually since its discovery, Marzabotto has been a prime site for the study of Etruscan urban development. In particular, Coarelli's analysis of its domestic drainage system reveals the sophistication that urban planning had achieved by circa 500 B.C.[39] The system, shown in figure 10, consists of north-to-south drainage ditches flowing into west-to-east drainage ditches, all following the main and secondary roads of the strictly rectangular townsite grid. These ditches make up an integrated system designed to take advantage of Marzabotto's

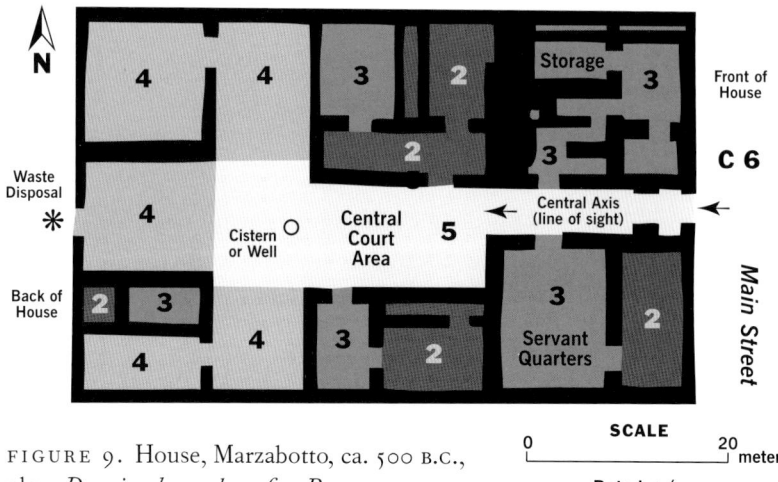

FIGURE 9. House, Marzabotto, ca. 500 B.C., plan. *Drawing by author after Prayon.*

SCALE
0 ———————— 20 meters

Rated +/–

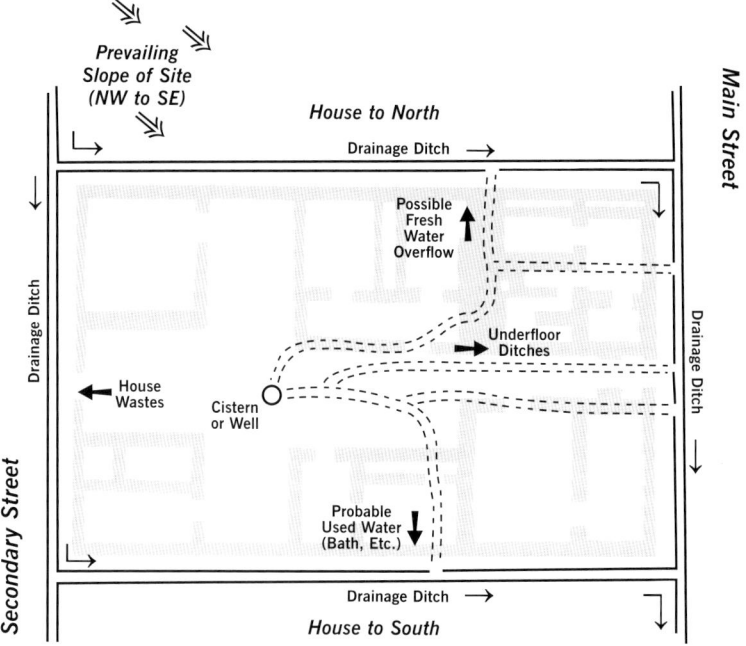

FIGURE 10. Drainage system around Marzabotto house, ca. 500 B.C., plan. *Drawing by author after Prayon.*

topography, which slopes downward from the acropolis area northwest of the townsite to the lower portion of the site at the southeast. To complete the system, additional ditches were channeled from west to east between each of the houses.[40] Rainwater, culinary waste water, and any other water sources flowing through the system flushed the entire site's combined waste away to the southeast.[41]

Rain provided the primary water supply for both the site's drainage and culinary needs, and most of this water was channeled or collected from the roofs of the site's individual houses. Constructed in the *displuvium* style, these roofs routed rainwater in two primary directions (figure 11). Most of it was directed outward, where it poured from the eaves into the ditches surrounding each house; but some was directed inward toward the open-air central court of each house, where it was caught and stored in a well or cistern.[42] Channels underneath the house floor carried away any overflow from the well or cistern (along with used culinary water, such as bath- or washwater) and emptied it into the city's drainage system. According to Coarelli, sewage was also dumped into these channels and so made its way into the grid of drainage ditches.[43] But this assessment, like

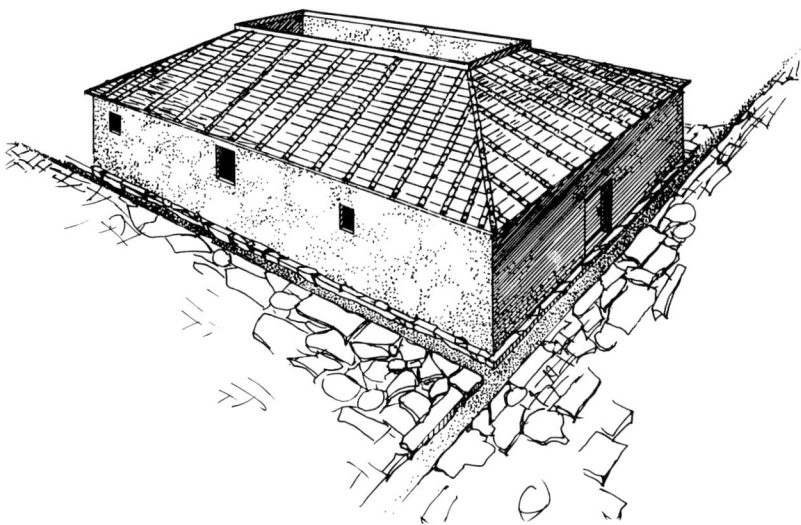

FIGURE 11. Artist's conception of typical Etruscan house in Marzabotto, ca. 500 B.C. *Drawing by Carleton Christy.*

Prayon's, raises problems. Channeling sewage under the house floor would probably have presented the unpleasant consequence of periodic clogging and possibly flooding; odors, too, might have caused annoyance if there was not sufficient water flowing through the channels to carry the sewage away quickly and completely. It is more likely that household sewage, as had been the case at earlier sites, was disposed of directly out the back door into the drainage ditch running along the back of the house.

This survey of Etruscan house plans shows these several characteristics to be significant enough to recur throughout their developmental history: the predominance of the longitudinal three-cellae pattern; easy accessibility of both family and outsider to the interior; multifunctional use for rooms except for sleeping benches and quasi-kitchen/bath areas; sewage and waste disposal off a tripartite room; ease of "reading" the house plan; lack of gender-, class-, or age-specific areas; and constancy of room and court arrangement. Chart 2 shows the incidence of these traditional characteristics in houses of the Archaic period.

SITE	EASE OF ACCESS	IDENTIFI- ABILITY	CON- STANCY	NON-GENDER-, AGE-, CLASS- SPECIFICITY	MONO- FUNCTIONALITY
Acquarossa	6	+ / +	yes	yes	no
Acquarossa (later)	5	+ / –	yes	yes	partial
Veii	6 to 5	+ / +	yes	yes	no
Vetulonia	6 to 5	+ / +	yes	yes	no
San Giovenale	6 to 5	+ / +	yes	yes	no
Marzabotto	5 to 4	+ / –	yes / no	yes	yes

CHART 2. Characteristics of Etruscan Homes

Detailed discussion of the domestic form as observed in sacral and burial architecture is a broad enough topic to fill a study of its own and can only be briefly alluded to in this essay. It can be demonstrated, however, that the three-cellae pattern coupled with the frontal communal access of the house is clearly reiterated in temple and tomb structures from Veii (figure 12) and Caere (figure 13). This sense of three thus continues as some seemingly inherent requirement or concept within the Etruscans, not only for the domestic form but for other architectural expressions.

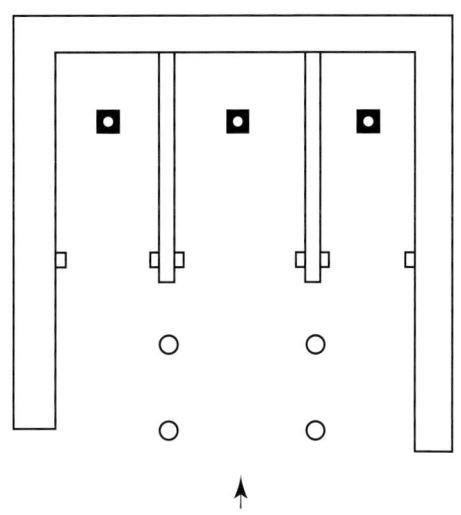

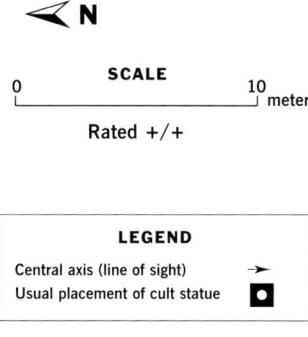

SCALE

0 _____ 10
meters

Rated +/+

LEGEND

Central axis (line of sight) →
Usual placement of cult statue ▣

FIGURE 12. Portonaccio Temple, Veii, ca. 500 B.C., plan. *Drawing by author after Boëthius.*

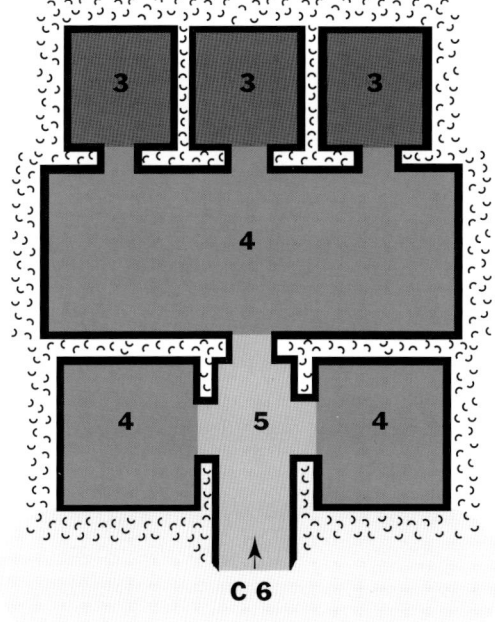

FIGURE 13. Tomb of the Greek Vase, Caere, sixth century B.C., plan. *Drawing by author after Boëthius.*

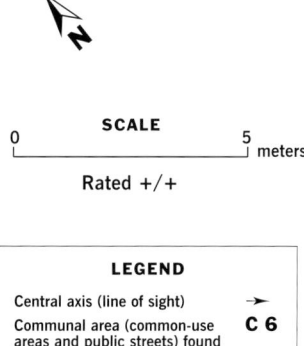

SCALE

0 _____ 5
meters

Rated +/+

LEGEND

Central axis (line of sight) →
Communal area (common-use areas and public streets) found in all sites in this study **C 6**

These characteristics of the Etruscan domestic form become even more distinctive when compared to the domestic arrangements of the contemporary Greek culture. Chart 3 shows the characteristics of Archaic houses of Thorikos (figure 14), Archaic and Classical homes in the Agora in Athens (figure 15), and Classical houses of Olynthus as compared to those of the Etruscan Archaic dwellings surveyed in chart 2.

SITE	EASE OF ACCESS	IDENTIFI-ABILITY	CON-STANCY	NON-GENDER-, AGE-, CLASS-SPECIFICITY	MONO-FUNCTIONALITY
Archaic Agora	6 to 0	− / −	no	no	yes
Archaic Thorikos	6 to −2	− / −	no	no	yes
Classic Agora	6 to 1	− / −	no	no	yes
Olynthus	6 to 1	− / −	no	no	yes

CHART 3. Characteristics of Greek Houses

As can be seen, all of these exhibit characteristics of compartmentalization, unreadability of the plan to an outsider, and lack of accessibility to an outsider; the alphanumeric accessibility code moves from 6 to 1 at best and 6 to −2 in the most extreme case. Both artifact finds and the literary record indicate monofunctional areas and boundaries of space for specific gender and age groups: certain front rooms were reserved for the elder males of a household, while women's and children's quarters were at the back of the house. Rooms are not oriented to a central axis; main entrances are uncertain and move into the structures at angles.[44] The isolated locations of the Greek rooms in relation to one another and the community area, in addition to showing how different a Greek house was from an Etruscan one, emphasize how remarkably similar Etruscan homes were to each other.

Moreover, Greek temples and funerary structures show no similarities to the typical Greek domestic plan.[45] Temples, interestingly, tend to be far simpler architecturally than Greek homes: they are rectangular in form, are accessible from all sides, and follow a simple *pronaos*-cella plan, with the image of the deity situated at the far end of the cella; if there is a back room (*opisthodomos*), it is usually sealed off from the cella and must be accessed through a separate entrance at the back of the temple (figure 16). Almost invariably, a temple was

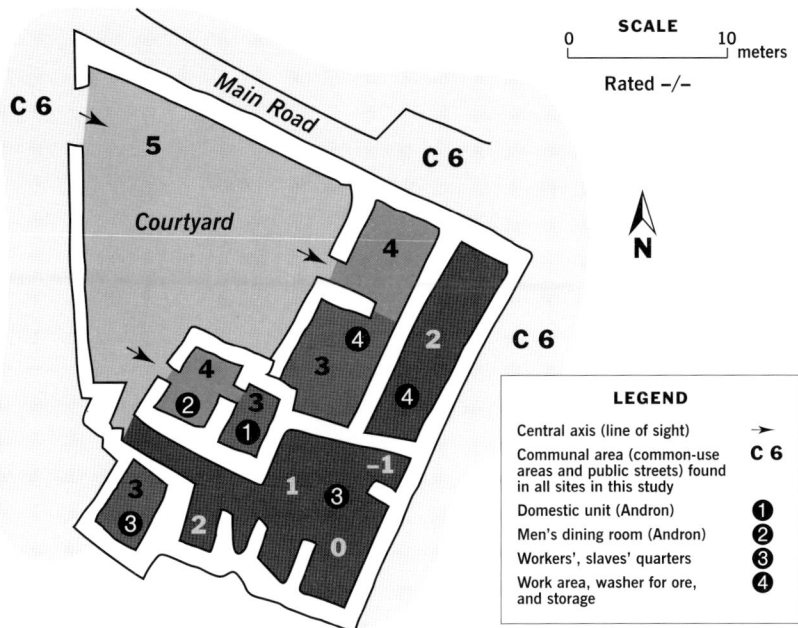

FIGURE 14. Archaic house, Thorikos, mid–sixth century B.C., plan. *Drawing by author after Donnay.*

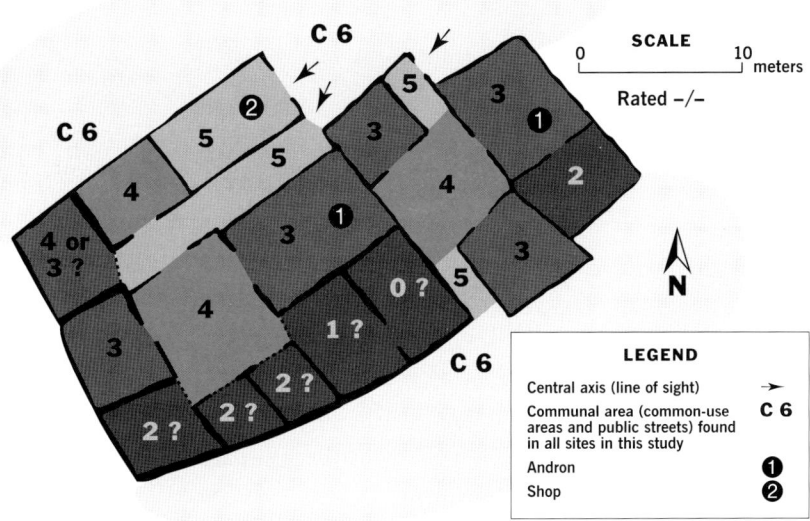

FIGURE 15. Archaic house near Agora, Athens, 500 B.C., plan. *Drawing by author after Kriesis.*

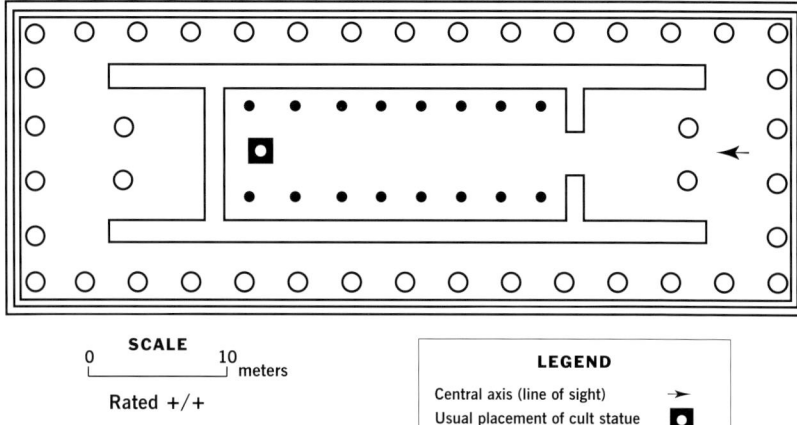

FIGURE 16. Greek temple, plan. Layout is representative and does not picture any particular site. *Drawing by author after Richter.*

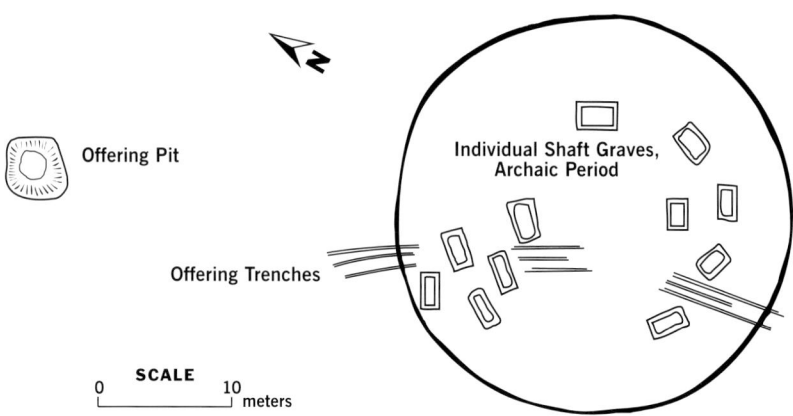

FIGURE 17. Grave mound in Kerameikos area, Athens, ca. 600 B.C., plan. *Drawing by author after Karo and Scheibler.*

dedicated to and occupied by a single deity, mirroring the separateness of men and women in Greek society.[46] From the Proto-Archaic period on, deceased Greeks were interred within family *tumuli*, but in separate gravesites (figure 17);[47] in Archaic times, separate statues or stelae were added as grave markers. These tumuli were simple mounds of earth which bore no resemblance to the Greek house; neither did the graves within them.[48] Certainly, it is natural to infer from these architectural differences a corresponding difference in world view.

The development of the Roman house and its similarities to the Etruscan are also ample subjects for another study and cannot be dealt with in depth here. For the purposes of this essay, it is sufficient to say that the Roman house form very closely follows the Etruscan paradigm (figure 18). To cite just a few of the similarities, an entrance to the Roman home comparable to that of the later Marzabotto Etruscan style is seen by the direct entry into the interior of the house through the hall, or *fauces*. This hall leads into the atrium with its *impluvium*, which is the Roman version of the Etruscan courtyard with its well or cistern. The tripartite set of rooms at the back of the atrium reproduces the Etruscan arrangement as well. And because the Roman house form developed after urban organization was well established, it

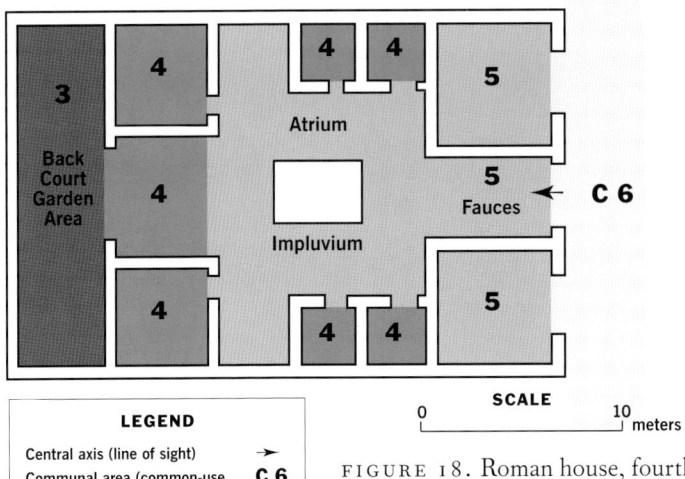

LEGEND

Central axis (line of sight) →
Communal area (common-use **C 6**
areas and public streets) found
in all sites in this study

Rated +/–

FIGURE 18. Roman house, fourth to third century B.C., plan. Layout is representative of time period and does not picture any particular site. *Drawing by author after Brown.*

is not surprising that homes were also arranged in blocks, or *insulae;* Roman urbanization did, after all, originate with the Etruscans.[49]

As to funerary architecture, the burial practices of Romans resemble the Etruscan tradition of family interments, with individual family members in their sarcophagi resting together in a family monument, such as that of the Scipii.[50] The mausoleum of Augustus represents a continuation of this custom (figure 2 on p. 219).[51] And in the area of religion, the architecture shows that the triad of major divinities, like the Etruscans who worshipped them, were not isolated from one another but shared their temple home. In fact, they comprised a family: a father, Tina; a mother, Uni; and a child, Minerva, as represented in the recently rediscovered Capitoline statue.[52] The Capitoline Temple of Jupiter, with its arrangement of three cellae for the deities Jupiter, Juno, and Minerva,[53] is representative of the Etruscan temple style from which the Romans derived their own (figure 19). Other examples include the Archaic temple to Fortuna and Mater Matuta from circa 264 B.C., the Temples of the Arx at Cosa from the third to second centuries B.C., and temples A and C in the Largo Argentina area of Rome from the Republican period.[54] All this is in striking contrast to the

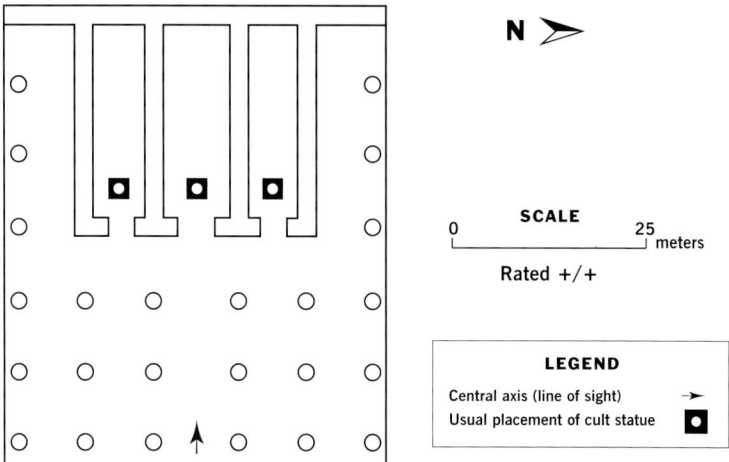

FIGURE 19. Capitoline Temple, Rome, 509 B.C., plan. *Drawing by author after Sear.*

Greeks, who had no symbol of home or family in either their sacral or their burial practices: they worshipped separate gods separately while they lived; and when they died they slept eternally separated, just as they had lived out their mortal days.

In general, then, the preliminary conclusion of this study is that the predictive model proposed herein appears to have further use in comparative studies of domestic architecture.[55] On a more specific level, observations illustrate that Etruscan house forms followed a line of development which apparently satisfied Etruscan living requirements eminently well and did not readily admit outside influences, even from the Greek culture that may have influenced other areas of Etruscan life. In fact, the one common domestic arrangement that may have originated in Greece—the megaron form—seems to have been used only until its Etruscan occupants could afford to expand it into the preferred tripartite form. Other inferences may be suggested: namely, that the Etruscan domestic plan encourages the intermingling of individuals regardless of gender, age, or class; that the center of the home opens to the greater community due to some viewed communality of those outside the immediate family unit; and that the three-cellae pattern replicated in burial and temple structures proclaims the domestic arena as inseparable from the sacral and the immaterial world. That these ideas carry over into the abstract concepts of the culture is evident in the social position of women and children in the family and community, the importance of the relationship between mother and child, and the obvious devotion to family and clan, in addition to their willingness to take into the center of their culture the Greek pantheon, the Greek alphabet, and certain expressions of Greek art.[56]

Domestic architecture reveals the underlying psyche of a culture. Individuals within a culture both act and are acted upon by unconsciously held cultural clues which are physically expressed in the domestic architecture and living space that comprise the community. This examination of how the Etruscan people organized and used domestic space, what variables potentially influenced their use of it, and its interrelationship with material artifacts and other aspects of culture outside the domestic sphere reveals a fundamental and unique manifestation of Etruscan cultural identity.

NOTES

1. L. Bonfante, "Daily Life and Afterlife," in *Etruscan Life and Afterlife: A Handbook of Etruscan Studies*, ed. L. Bonfante (Detroit, 1986), 232–34; A. Boëthius et al., *Etruscan Culture, Land, and People* . . . , trans. N. G. Sahlin (New York and Malmö, Swed., 1962), 71; F. Prayon, "Architecture," in *Etruscan Life and Afterlife*, 174 (vol. supra this n.).

2. R. E. Tringham, "Households with Faces: The Challenge of Gender in Prehistoric Architectural Remains," in *Engendering Archaeology: Women and Prehistory*, ed. J. Gero and M. W. Conkey (Oxford, 1991); R. E. Tringham, "Architectural Investigation into Household Organization in Neolithic Yugoslavia" (paper presented at the Eighty-third Annual Meeting of the American Anthropological Association, Denver, 1984); R. E. Tringham, "Experimentation, Ethnoarchaeology, and the Leapfrogs in Archaeological Methodology," in *Explorations in Ethnoarchaeology*, ed. R. A. Gould, School of American Research Advanced Seminar Series (Albuquerque, 1978) (vol. hereinafter cited as *Explorations*).

3. R. E. Tringham, "Men and Women in Prehistoric Architecture," *Traditional Dwellings and Settlements Review* 3.1 (1991): 17; S. Kent, *Analyzing Activity Areas: An Ethnoarchaeological Study of the Use of Space* (Albuquerque, 1984); S. Kent, ed., *Method and Theory for Activity Area Research: An Ethnoarchaeological Approach* (New York, 1987); S. Kent, ed., *Domestic Architecture and the Use of Space: An Interdisciplinary Cross-cultural Study*, New Directions in Archaeology (Cambridge, 1990).

4. Tringham, "Men and Women," 2–28 (supra n. 3).

5. Ibid., 14. Both sites date from Late Neolithic/Early Neolithic Vinca culture (ca. 4400–4000 B.C.).

6. Ibid., 11.

7. Tringham discusses the variance of the domestic scene between the two sites of Divostin and Opovo through the eyes of a woman moving from a family unit at one site into a family unit at the other (ibid., 18–19).

The concept that the form and arrangement of domestic architecture and the associated living space reinforce a specific world view for those who inhabit it is not new within the discipline of contemporary ethnoarchaeology. For instance, M. Jasnosky of George Washington University points out that Eskimos coming from the traditional igloo home have difficulty in drawing or conceptualizing the right angle; she feels that the homes in which people grow up affect not just their preferences but their modes of thought ("Professor Finds Home Affects Moods, Culture," *Denver Post*, 24 January 1994; see also M. Jasnosky, "The Physical Environment Affects Quality of Life Based upon Environmental Sensitivity," *Journal of Applied Developmental Psychology* 13.2 [1992]: 139–42). In her comparative study of Euroamerican, Hispanic, and Navajo households, Kent found that the arrangement of the domestic activity areas and the functions carried on within those areas form patterns which continue by extension in the general culture of each group. She also determined that the domestic space of Navajos and the activities carried on within it by the family unit were nonspecific with regard to sex-oriented tasks, single-task space designation, and definition of generational space (Kent, *Method and Theory*, 535 [supra n. 3]). I can confirm this from my personal observation of a traditional Navajo family unit in which the working of silver was done by males or females; tasks such as spinning, weaving, or cooking were not relegated to one designated area; and intergenerational activities were the norm (D. D. Rohner, personal observation of Sara and Leo Natani and children at home, Shiprock, Arizona, fall 1990).

Kent's studies are reinforced by findings of a number of other anthropologists and ethnoarchaeologists: L. R. Binford, "Willow Smoke and Dogs' Tails: Hunter-Gatherer Settlement Systems and Archaeological Site Formation," *American Antiquity* 45.1 (1980): 4–20; M. B. Schiffer, "Methodological Uses in Ethnoarchaeology," in *Explorations*, 229–47 (vol. supra n. 2); R. A. Gould, "From Tasmania to Tucson: New Directions in Ethnoarchaeology," in *Explorations*, 1–10 (vol. supra n. 2); R. Ascher, "Time's Arrow and the Archaeology of a Contemporary Community," in *Settlement Archaeology*, ed. K. C. Chang (Palo Alto, Calif., 1968), 43–52; M. B. Stanislawski, "Ethnoarchaeology and Settlement Archaeology," *Ethnohistory* 20.4 (1973): 375–92; J. O'Connell, "Site Structure and Dynamics among Modern Alyawara Hunters" (paper presented at the Forty-fourth Annual Meeting of the Society for American Archaeology, Vancouver, Wash., 1979); J. E. Yellen, *Archaeological Approaches to the Present: Models for Reconstructing the Past* (New York, 1977). Their research shows that the pattern of domestic space use is reiterated in the general culture and finds expression in male/female relationships; task differentiation; and age, gender, and class status. These results lead Kent to state that "culture, behavior, and cultural material are not discrete entities independent of one another. Behavior (social actions interpreted within a system of meaning) is not separate from culture (a system of meaning and symbols) or from cultural material (the tangible products of behavior) any more than culture and cultural material are separate from . . . one another" (Kent, *Analyzing Activity Areas*, 12 [supra n. 3]; punctuation altered for clarity).

8. Only Vitruvius offers specific insight into Etruscan domestic architecture in his *De Architectura*, especially at 6.3, which concerns the plan of a house, and 6.4, which discusses various suites of rooms. Others of the ancients whose writings shed light indirectly on the topic are Livy in his *History of Rome*, the first book of which discusses contacts between Romans and Etruscans; Diodorus Siculus, who in his *Library of History* (esp. 10.20–22, 11.88, 14.113–17, 15.14, 19.106, 20.11, 61, 64, 21.3) discusses pillage and warfare with the Tyrrhenians; Pliny the Elder in his *Natural History* (esp. 2.138–42); and Polybius (2.18–22, 6.53).

9. Tringham states that "the wider view of the house in the context of its landscape [reminds observers] that the social arena of domestic space is not restricted to the dwelling itself, but includes the areas immediately outside, including the garbage pits, and the fields, woods, and marshes beyond" ("Men and Women," 20 [supra n. 3]).

10. As mentioned, the functions of various areas are inferred according to the array of artifacts they are found to contain. Monofunctional areas contain specific kinds of artifacts relative to a single specific task, while multifunctional areas contain artifacts relative to a variety of specific tasks. For instance, a preponderance of cooking

ware associated with a charcoal hearth, scrapers, and food remains indicates a cooking area; but if the cooking ware and food scraps are found together with dining utensils, textile scraps, sewing implements, and toys, it is likely that more than one activity regularly occurred in this area. In this fashion, areas are interpreted as mono- or multifunctional. Likewise, an area would not be considered gender-, class-, or age-specific if found to contain artifacts of both genders, all age groups, and all classes (this last would more likely be known through literary sources than artifact finds).

In regard to the structural remains of a house as a "physical blueprint," it should be noted that there are limitations to what archaeologists can understand with certainty from such a limited record. For instance, the placement of doorways is not always obvious merely from the foundation stones, since only the thresholds remain and these were often made of the same materials and in the same manner as the walls. Likewise, walls, windows, and roofs may be missing entirely. This situation can and does lead to varying interpretations of the same building. Unless otherwise noted, the diagrams accompanying this essay are based on what I consider to be the most accurate interpretations made so far of specific structural remains. The locations of the doorways have often been surmised from the overall layout of the foundations and from artifact evidence because no solid architectural evidence remains.

11. P. Bourdieu, "The Berber House," in *Rules and Meanings: The Anthropology of Everyday Knowledge*, ed. M. Douglas (Harmondsworth, Engl., 1973).

12. The portion of my research which focuses on the Etruscan home is indebted to and progresses from previous work by E. Berggren, K. Berggren, A. Boëthius, L. Bonfante, J. Clarke, F. Coarelli, W. Dinsmoor, N. T. de Grummond, F. Prayon, E. Richardson, and others whose scholarly efforts have greatly assisted me.

13. N. T. de Grummond, ed., *A Guide to Etruscan Mirrors* (Tallahassee, Fla., 1982), 79–86.

14. Prayon, "Architecture," 190–91 (supra n. 1).

15. E. Berggren and K. Berggren, *Excavations in Area B, 1957–60*, vol. 2 fasc. 2 of *San Giovenale: Results of Excavations . . .* , Skrifter Utgivna av Svenska Institutet Rom, 4°, 26 (Stockholm, 1981), 22; hereinafter cited as *San Giovenale*.

16. Ibid., 19 fig. 10, 21 fig. 14; F. Buranelli, *The Etruscans: Legacy of a Lost Civilization: From the Vatican Museums*, trans. N. T. de Grummond (Memphis, Tenn., 1992), 39.

17. C. Scheffer, *Cooking and Cooking Stands in Italy 1400–400 B.C.*, vol. 2 pt. 1 of *Acquarossa: Results of Excavations . . .* , Skrifter Utgivna av Svenska Institutet Rom, 4°, 38 (Stockholm, 1981), 109.

18. The Etruscan arrangement parallels the distribution of materials and people in the traditional Hispanic home and Navajo hogan. Family members live together as an intimate, close-knit group and not simply as individuals who happen to be a family (Kent, *Analyzing Activity Areas*, 195, 197–98 [supra n. 3]).

19. A. Boëthius, *Etruscan and Early Roman Architecture*, 2d ed. rev., The Pelican History of Art (Harmondsworth, Engl., 1978), 75.

20. Ibid., 76.

21. Boëthius also states that the megaron shape is seen in chamber tombs and ash urns modeled in the shape of houses (ibid., 75).

22. Ibid., 74–76.

23. Berggren and Berggren, *San Giovenale*, 15–17 (supra n. 15). Stratum 4 is the earliest of the three, with stratum 2 containing some medieval deposits.

24. Ibid., 17.

25. Ibid., 15.

26. F. Coarelli, ed., *Etruscan Cities*, trans. C. Atthill et al. (London, 1975), 264.

27. Prayon, "Architecture," 180 (supra n. 1).

28. Boëthius infers this in his description of the site: "In the confusion of low foundations inside the regular rectangular blocks of Marzabotto, small rectangular houses can be distinguished. They often have party walls *(parietes communes)* and inner courtyards with wells. Rectangular houses are common, usually some 10–13 feet wide, with porches on the front toward the street and two rooms *en suite*. These houses resemble the Greek megara. *Often they had rooms added to their right and left flanks. Usually they had a door directly on to the street*" (Boëthius, *Etruscan and Early Roman Architecture*, 75; italics in last two sentences are mine [supra n. 19]). Since the megaron style is defined by the "en suite" arrangement of the rooms, once new rooms are added on the flanks these houses can no longer be considered true megara. He does not connect this alteration with the economic means of the inhabitants, which is my interpretation.

29. Coarelli, *Etruscan Cities*, 85 (supra n. 26).

30. G. Säflünd, *Etruscan Imagery: Symbol and Meaning*, Studies in Mediterranean Archaeology and Literature, 118 (Jonsered, Swed., 1993), 62–67.

31. Ibid., 60–62.

32. A. M. Sgubini Moretti, *Dizionario della civiltà etrusca* (Florence, 1985), 5.

33. Coarelli, *Etruscan Cities*, 307–8 (supra n. 26).

34. Säflünd, *Etruscan Imagery*, 62 (supra n. 30).

35. Although servants or slaves seem to have been quartered in this area, it was not, in a strict sense, a class-specific area. Its situation in the front of the house— between the communal area (in this case, the main street in front of the house) and the three cellae at the back—ensured that all classes would pass through it regularly, whether or not they engaged in any other activities there.

36. The controversy over the question of the origin of orthogonal urban planning is too complex to be discussed here, but it is given thorough treatment in J. Rich and A. Wallace-Hadrill, eds., *City and Country in the Ancient World*, Leicester-Nottingham Studies in Ancient Society, 2 (London and New York, 1991); J. E. Owens, *The City in the Greek and Roman World* (London, 1991); R. E. Wycherly, "Hippodamus and Rhodos," *Historia* 13 (1964): 135–39; A. Burns, "Hippodamus and the Planned City," *Historia* 25 (1976): 414–28; A. Kriesis, *Greek and Roman Town Building* (Athens, 1965); P. Grimal, *Roman Cities*, trans. and ed. G. M. Woloch, Wisconsin Studies in Classics (Madison, 1983), 10–27.

37. Prayon, "Architecture," 191 (supra n. 1).

38. Buranelli, *Etruscans: Legacy*, 39 (supra n. 16).

39. Coarelli, *Etruscan Cities*, 306–9 (supra n. 26).

40. Ibid., 308; P. Saronio, "Nuovi scavi nella città etrusca di Misano a Marzabotto: La campagna di scavi dell'estate 1964," *SE* 33 (1965): 385–416 and esp. fig. 1.

41. In working on the main north-south road fronting the houses of block one in Region IV of Marzabotto, excavators for the 1965 season found a stratum of river gravel beneath the street bed containing many animal bones, ashes, and fragments of ceramics in mixed association. This gravel bed would have provided a further filtration system in addition to the drainage ditches, which were also lined with this type of gravel. It is fairly certain, judging from the location of the find, that these deposits come from the same time period as the houses and not from what may be an earlier layer of settlement nearer the acropolis. It is not surprising that a find of this sort should occur underneath the street immediately adjacent to the houses, since it would be natural for some of the drainage ditches to overflow into the street at times of heavy rain. The rarity of this find also indicates, however, that the main dumping of household waste would most likely have been from the backs of the houses; otherwise, finds such as this at the fronts of houses would be more frequent and more extensive (Saronio, "Nuovi scavi," 391 [supra n. 40]).

42. Scholarly opinion varies on whether the water facilities found in the courtyards were actually wells with ground water as the source or cisterns storing only rainwater. In my opinion, they are more likely to be cisterns, because wells would cut through the gravel drainage layer below the house and might therefore risk contamination from waste water in that layer.

43. Coarelli, *Etruscan Cities*, 308 (supra n. 26). Some of the outward-flowing water may have been collected at the eaves and directed through pipes down the walls and inward to the well or cistern (Vitr. 6.3.2; see also Boëthius, *Etruscan and Early Roman Architecture*, 90–91 [supra n. 19]).

44. J. M. Camp, *The Athenian Agora: Excavations in the Heart of Classical Athens* (London, 1986), 44; G. Donnay, *Thorikos 1964: Rapport préliminaire sur la deuxième campagne de fouilles* (Brussels, 1967), 63–72, plan I; W. B. Dinsmoor, *The Architecture of Ancient Greece: An Account of Its Historic Development* (New York, 1975), 332–34. Dinsmoor states that Olynthus was built with the front of the house facing to the south. If the house was built on the south side of the street, this forces the entrances to the north or back of the house. This interpretation results in two plans: one with the entrance at the south, with or without a shallow vestibule and wooden screen which isolates the front part of the house from the back; or the other with the entrance at the north, which gives indirect access to a paved court through some room or passage.

45. On cemeteries, see I. Scheibler, *The Archaic Cemetery*, trans. S. C. D. Slenczka, German Archaeological Institute, Athens, Kerameikos, 3 (Athens, 1973), p. 4 fig. 3, p. 10; On temples, see Dinsmoor, *Architecture of Ancient Greece*, 36–112 (supra n. 44).

46. One of the extremely rare exceptions to this pattern is the Temple of Hephaistos and Athena in the Athenian agora, dating from ca. 420 B.C.

47. Large tumuli were abandoned as space became limited ca. 400 B.C. Family plots were smaller and hence the deceased were physically closer, but they were still separated in that they were buried as individuals apart from other members of the family.

48. In contrast are the famous tumuli of Cerveteri: these contain tomb chambers constructed in the form of the Etruscan house, in which family members were interred together. See fig. 13.

49. E. de Albentiis, *La casa dei romani* (Milan, 1990), esp. 261; Buranelli, *Etruscans: Legacy*, 38–39 [supra n. 16]. More excellent background on the Roman home is available in F. Sear, *Roman Architecture* (Ithaca, N.Y., 1982), 11; Vitr. 4.7; R. E. M. Wheeler, *Roman Art and Architecture* (London, 1987); J. B. Ward-Perkins, *Roman Imperial Architecture*, Pelican History of Art (Harmondsworth, Engl., 1985); F. Coarelli, *Guida archeologica di Roma*, ed. A. Mondadori (Milan, 1984); A. C. Carpiceci, *Pompeii Nowadays and 2000 Years Ago*, Edition Il Turismo (Florence, 1977); J. J. Dobbins, "Problems of Chronology, Decoration, and Urban Design in the Forum at Pompeii," *AJA* 98 (1994): 629–94; F. E. Brown, *Roman Architecture* (New York, 1982); R. Brilliant, "Roman Architecture," in *Roman Art from the Republic to Constantine* (London, 1974); R. Bianchi Bandinelli, "Problems of Pictorial and Architectural Space," in *Rome, the Center of Power: 500 B.C. to A.D. 200*, trans. P. Green (New York, 1970). See, in this volume, the essay by John F. Hall, 151 ff.

50. Bianchi Bandinelli, "Pictorial and Architectural Space," 26 [supra n. 49].

51. See, in this volume, the essay by Mark J. Johnson, 217 ff.

52. "Recovered," *Boulder Daily Camera*, 24 February 1994. The brief announcement includes a photograph of the twenty-four-inch-tall statue, which was stolen shortly after its excavation "from an archaeological site northeast of Rome" and recovered some eighteen months later. It has been dated to the third or second century B.C.

53. Sear, *Roman Architecture*, 11 (supra n. 49).

54. Coarelli, *Guida archeologica di Roma*, 249, 282–83; Brown, *Roman Architecture*, 52, fig. 5 (both supra n. 44).

55. In contrast, Tringham states, and many anthropologists and architects believe, that "any action that did not modify the archaeological record, or which cannot be identified as having modified it, cannot be reconstructed and is therefore not testable. Thus, [many scholars believe that such] aspects of the use and significance of space . . . [as] social relations, especially those based on gender and age, and the social action of individuals within space" cannot demonstrate verifiable conclusions (Tringham, "Men and Women," 11 [supra n. 3]). However, I find the evidence to the contrary, as discussed in this essay, to be very compelling.

56. See, in this volume, the essays by Helen Nagy, 49 ff.; Alexandra Carpino, 66 ff.; Steven Bule, 325 ff.; Nancy Thomson de Grummond, 355 ff.

ROMAN ITALY

MVNIF·PIL·IX·P·M·
AN·XVIII

From Tarquins to Caesars:
Etruscan Governance at Rome

JOHN F. HALL

Lars Porsena of Clusium
    By the Nine Gods he swore
That the great house of Tarquin
    Should suffer wrong no more.
By the Nine Gods he swore it,
    And named a trysting day,
And bade his messengers ride forth
East and west and south and north,
    To summon his array.

East and west and south and north
    The messengers ride fast
And tower and town and cottage
    Have heard the trumpet's blast.
Shame on the false Etruscan
    Who lingers in his home
When Porsena of Clusium
    Is on the march for Rome.

So read the opening lines of the poem popularly known as "Horatius at the Bridge." When British historian Thomas Babington Macaulay tried his hand at poetry more than a hundred and fifty years ago, the long poem "Horatius" comprised the central portion of his *Lays of Ancient*

FIGURE 1. Statue of Augustus, marble, Villa of Livia, Primaporta, 19–17 B.C., Vatican, Bracchio Nuovo, inv. 2290. *Photo by M. Sarri; courtesy of Monumenti Musei e Gallerie Pontificie.*

Rome. Though Macaulay's historical interests centered primarily upon England during the era of the Restoration, he was well acquainted with the history and historians of ancient Rome. Livy's pleasant tales of Rome under the seven kings comprised the source material for "Horatius" and Macaulay's other poems.[1] It is therefore not surprising that, as in Livy's account, Macaulay depicts Porsenna's efforts to retake Rome for Tarquin, a fellow Etruscan, as foiled by the courageous defense of the Sublician Bridge by the one-eyed Horatius and his two companions, Sp. Larcius and T. Herminius.[2] The irony, of course, is that Horatius, had he been a real person, might conceivably have been Etruscan as well. Moreover, Larcius and Herminius, who were most assuredly actual historical figures, were indisputably Etruscan.[3]

The methodologies of contemporary scholarship—source criticism, archaeological investigation, and analysis of political and religious institutions and practices—have facilitated acknowledgment among scholars of a monarchical Rome not only ruled by Etruscan kings but permeated by Etruscan culture. In light of these findings, further revision of traditional views is needed regarding the presence of Etruscans in the Roman state and their participation in its governance. This essay addresses the role of Etruscan citizens of Rome in the governance of the state, not only in the monarchical period but in the early Republic as well. Furthermore, considerable evidence exists to corroborate a periodic continued involvement of Etruscans at the highest level of Roman government in later eras, including the late Republic and early Empire.

The traditional accounts of early Roman history, preserved and propagated by a long line of annalists, are conveyed to the modern student of archaic Rome primarily through Livy, but also through sources such as Dionysius or Roman antiquarians including Varro, Pliny, and Florus. Efforts to differentiate fact from fiction in these traditional accounts are undertaken using the methodology of source criticism.[4] Most pertinent to the present consideration is work relating to Fabius Pictor, a main source on archaic Rome for both Livy and Dionysius. Several historical treatments of the period demonstrate the many problems arising from Pictor's tendency to alter the record on grounds of national and family reputation. Fragmentary remains of the works of other early annalists suggest that, like Pictor, their intent was to diminish the role of Etruscans in the development of Rome and its institutions.[5] Whether national pride and warfare with Etruscan cities in the late fourth and early third centuries B.C. contributed to such a motive, or whether the primary source material of the early annalists—the *annales maximi* and the Linen Books—or the less reliable family chronicles ignored the Etruscan presence, are matters for further consideration.[6] Whatever the reason, the fact is that, beyond acknowledging the rule of the Etruscan Tarquins in the sixth century B.C., Rome's annalistic tradition recognizes Etruscan influence only in the trappings of government and in the building projects undertaken by the city's Etruscan kings.[7] In striking contrast to this tradition, archaeological evidence provides strong corroboration of an extensive Etruscan presence at Rome.[8]

While abundant remains of Etruscan pottery and other artifacts could be the material record of a vigorous Etruscan trade rather than widespread inhabitation by Etruscans, other kinds of evidence would be expected only in the event of a well-established Etruscan populace: remains of Etruscan inscriptions, foundation ruins and architectural decorations of Etruscan-style temples, and Etruscan votives dedicated in those temples, for example. The great public works projects of the Tarquins witness the presence of skilled Etruscan workmen who possessed the technical expertise needed to construct the *cloaca maxima,* pave the forum, and erect the Capitoline monuments. Place-names such as the *vicus Tuscus* define neighborhoods that housed the engineers and builders who transformed the several mud-hut villages of earliest Rome into an urban center.[9]

Indeed, urban living was characteristic of Etruscan society in the sixth century B.C.[10] "Whereas the way of life of the Italic tribes did not necessitate or imply urbanization, the Etruscans promoted and implanted it everywhere," A. Alföldi asserts.[11] The newly urbanized Rome was a product of advanced Etruscan civilization. In the view of R. M. Ogilvie,

> the Etruscans came to Rome and settled in force as craftsmen, merchants, and rulers. They were city dwellers and their arrival at Rome and their fusion with the native population radically changed

the whole settlement. From an agglomeration of huts it became an architectured city with streets, public buildings, markets, shops, temples, etc.[12]

Archaeological remains provide strong evidence of the Etruscan presence in early Rome.[13] Several recent works are useful for interpretation and quite adequate in their presentation of Etruscan source materials,[14] including a monograph by J. C. Meyer, *Pre-Republican Rome*, which provides a competent interpretative survey of the whole tradition of archaeological work on early Rome from the nineteenth century to the present. Strikingly apparent from Meyer's analysis is the view that, though differences on dating and interpretation exist, all are agreed that the archaeological evidence attests to an Etruscan Rome.[15]

To extrapolate from the material remains of archaic Rome even the most conjectural knowledge about history, society, or the institutions of the city demands caution. A. Momigliano's assessment of the problems implicit in historical reconstruction from scarce substantive information is instructive in this regard:

> It is curious to speculate how much of the history of Early Rome we should know today if we had only the archaeological evidence to rely upon. Somehow we could guess the existence of separate villages. The transformation of the forum would probably suggest a political unification of the villages, and the sudden outburst of foreign art in the sixth century could be interpreted as foreign influence from Etruria. If we were to include archaic inscriptions . . . we should have the possibility of establishing the near (Etrusco-Latin) bilingualism of the society of the sixth century. . . . Not much else could be established with certainty. The political and social structure of Early Rome would remain to a great extent unknown; the religion, the moral ideas, the very names of the legendary kings would, of course, be unknown.[16]

Fortunately, though, some texts do survive. In them, the Roman annalists and antiquarians, although they downplayed Etruscan domination at Rome, were effusive in attributing to Etruscans such aspects of Roman government as form and trappings, as well as the wearing of the toga, many societal practices, and certain ceremonies and rites. In fact, the very word ceremony in Latin, *caeremonia*, reveals an etymology pointing to a Caeretane origin of societal and religious rites.[17] Religion was, of course, the area in which Rome was most heavily influenced by the Etruscans, from the anthropomorphization of divinities and the construction of temples to house them to the development of a ritual calendar and priestly colleges across the whole state.[18]

As with Etruria proper, the Etruscan presence at Rome is generally addressed in synchronic rather than diachronic terms due to the nature of the evidentiary sources. Diachronic history examines institutional, political, military, and cultural developments in the context of time reference, not uncommonly through a chronological survey of events. By contrast, synchronic history is not developmental; it tends to portray itself in descriptive analyses of society in general and treats social, cultural, and intellectual history without specific time reference. The Etruscan presence at Rome is usually dealt with synchronically as a result of inadequacies in traditional historical accounts and the limited diachronic reference available through archaeology. The best time reference that can be established through examination of such material is perhaps M. Pallottino's observation that the archaeological evidence is absolutely in line with the canonical dating of Etruscan dynasties at Rome and the legendary traditions linked to them.[19]

Analysis of Etruscan participation in Roman government seldom proceeds beyond the comparison of practices attributed to Etruscans at Rome with those same practices in the Etruscan states. The situation is further complicated by the tendency of Roman writers of the late Republic to consider the political institutions of Rome in the monarchy or early Republic as essentially the same as those of the late Republic, particularly if the later institutions retained the names of the earlier institutions.[20] An additional problem is that Roman writers customarily referred to the Etruscans at Rome as simply Etruscans. Does this practice indicate a homogeneity among Rome's Etruscans or rather a carelessness or lack of knowledge among Rome's annalists and antiquarians? Where a place of origin is specifically identified in the case of Tarquin, false etymology and fanciful fabrication provide an inaccurate tale. More reliable evidence associates the first Tarquin with Caere, suggesting that Caere functioned as mother city to at least some of Rome's Etruscan inhabitants.[21]

Accordingly, other methodologies must be used, such as the careful perusal of information in the written sources about Roman religion. The conservative nature of religious institutions and practices ensures that many aspects of cult and ritual being observed at Rome in the time of the authors of the written sources originated in an earlier era. Religious customs perpetuated in this manner tend to survive intact, although they are frequently not well understood by their later practitioners. Information thus provided has been skillfully employed by R. E. A. Palmer as a key to understanding the religio-political institutions of the archaic community of the Romans.[22] He has identified the curiate constitution as the principal basis of community organization during the monarchy and also as an essential component of early Republican government. It is upon Palmer's framework that the methodologies of prosopography and onomastics can be applied to demonstrate the extent of Etruscan involvement in Rome's monarchical and early Republican government, thus facilitating a diachronic treatment of Etruscans at Rome.

Tradition assigns the creation of the curias and the tribes to Rome's first king. The three tribes functioned as separate elements of the Roman army, each being commanded by a regimental colonel known as the tribal officer or *tribunus*. Muster from the curias supplied the tribes with their complement of troops. The tribes were not ethnic groupings, nor do they imply equal numbers of Latins, Sabines, and Etruscans in Rome's army or among Rome's populace.[23]

The curias were ultimately thirty in number. Membership in a curia constituted possession of the *ius Quiritium*, or full citizenship. Curias received their names on toponymous or gentilicial grounds—or possibly both. Their composition was geographic, but in earliest Rome this did not exclude organization by *gens*, since the *gentes* occupied land on a fairly contiguous basis. As new gentes entered the state, they were assigned to curias or new curias were created. Palmer demonstrates that the "curias of a united community represented disparate elements in the primitive state which had no common generic name unless it be Rome."[24]

"The curias met severally for religious and political purposes," according to Palmer.[25] Each was presided over by an elected *curion*, an office descended in function from the village or clan chieftain. Each curia had its own religious organization consisting of priests or priestly colleges charged with conduct of the curia's cult and ritual. Curias also owned common land and places of meeting for purposes connected to curial cultic practice.[26] They met together in comitia to approve legislation, including the *lex curiata de imperio*, by which selection of the king was approved by the citizen body composed of curia members, who were known as *Quirites*. This assembly could be summoned only by the king, his viceregent, or in interregnal periods by those with auspicial authority: the *curio maximus*, *interrex*, or, after the end of the monarchy, the chief pontiff. Each curion would have represented his curia in the regal senate. Only the curio-senators, or *patres*, could fill the office of interrex upon the death of the monarch when the *auspices ad patres redeunt*.[27]

There is no reason to suppose that Rome's curial government was not coterminous with the origin of the state. Certainly the system was well entrenched at the time of the Etruscan advent. Dionysius reports that Tarquin and his Etruscan followers joined tribe and curia, so coming to possess the *ius Quiritium* and, with it, full incorporation into the body politic. If the tradition is accurate in characterizing Tarquin's accession to the Roman kingship as a peaceful process, his election would very likely have followed the established procedure of the curias. Even if Etruscan control had been instituted as a result of military intervention—most likely by Rome's neighbor Caere, home city of the gens Tarchna—it is not improbable that Rome's constitutional machinery would have been employed to legitimize Tarquin's rule.[28]

For the most part, the relationship of Rome's Etruscan kings with the curias was not a happy one. Efforts by Etruscans to centralize the machinery of state (whether political, religious, or military) by necessity conflicted with the decentralized curial organization, dominated not by new Etruscan citizens but by Rome's leading old families, which were primarily Latin and occasionally Sabine. As early as the reign of the first Tarquin, one Attus Navius used augural authority to block the king's proposal to increase the number of cavalry units.[29] As Palmer has observed, though Livy identifies Navius as a member of the college of augurs, Dionysius claims that he was not an augur of the state, implying that "this augur had curial authority and used it to prevent the creation of new tribes or centuries."[30] It was likely Tarquin or one of his successors who created a state college of augurs, whose principal seat, or *auguraculum*, is known to have been located at the civic center of the Etruscan kings, the Capitoline. Palmer proposes that a "partial intention of the Servian reform was the supersession of the centuries over the curias." Servius' incorporation of curial augural seats in a "sacral itinerary" of state augurs "intended to undermine curial augurs by introducing the Roman augurs in their place."[31]

The Etruscan origin of Servius Tullius, also known as Mastarna, seems clear.[32] Nevertheless, however the events which connected him to Rome and brought him to power are interpreted, Servius Tullius pursued an active policy of governmental reform.[33] This may have been occasioned by Etruscan affinities for centralized government or by political exigencies deriving from Servius' uncertain position as a conqueror from Vulci, who at the head of either a Vulcentane army or a force of Etruscan mercenaries and adventurers had become master of Rome through military intervention.[34] Not only Rome's Latin inhabitants, but also Etruscans from Caere who migrated to Rome under Tarquin, may have been subjugated by Servius. Their respective attitudes toward the new ruler remain a mystery. How readily Etruscans from Caere and Vulci—or later arrivals from Veii or Clusium—may have cooperated in city politics as a result of Etruscan ethnicity is similarly unknown. Nevertheless, a volatile situation is manifested by the tradition, preserved by Livy, that Servius chose to rule, at least for a time, without the authorizing grant of *imperium* from the curias. This may have been either the result or the cause of the bad relations between Servius and Rome's curio-senators.[35]

The centuriate reform Servius initiated further betrays his disdain or distrust of the curial system or of those whose political influence was best exercised in it. In the recent monograph *King Servius Tullius*, R. Thomsen defends the military necessity of the Servian reform:

> In the second half of the sixth century Rome formed part of the Etruscan koiné, had Etruscan rulers, and participated in the wars of Etruscan states. In order to survive in these wars it was not advisable to have an antiquated military system, and so, since the armies

of the Etruscan states in this period were based on the superior hoplite system, it would be an obvious matter for Rome, especially in the reign of her Etruscan kings to bring her forces up to date by adopting the hoplite phalanx too. This, indeed, is what is stated explicitly by the unanimous ancient traditions that the centuriate system, and accordingly also the hoplite phalanx, was introduced by Servius Tullius, the Etruscan condotierre "Mastarna."[36]

In conjunction with his creation of the centuries, Servius Tullius organized new tribes—four urban and perhaps others in the country-side.[37] Though the name *tribe* was retained, the military function of the original three tribes had been assumed by the centuries, which formed collectively the *populus*, or army, of the Roman citizen body, the *Quirites*. The Servian tribes instead served as bodies for mustering the troops of the centuries, thus assuming a function previously belonging to the curias.[38] It is possible that the new assembly of the centuries, designed to comprise and organize the *populus*, gradually supplanted the curias in others of their functions. At some point during the reign of Etruscan kings at Rome, the creation of new curias seems to have been suspended.[39] In fact, Servius Tullius and his followers may have never been incorporated into the curial body politic, particularly since this action could not be accomplished by the kings but required authorization of the curias themselves met in assembly and, of course, the patres through exercise of their special *auctoritas* to approve or disapprove *acta* brought before the curias.[40] If, as seems likely, Servius Tullius engendered opposition from the curias or their leaders, he and his followers may have resolved the constitutionality of their participation in government by the creation of new governmental machinery, which thenceforth functioned along with the older bodies of Rome's government. New inhabitants—whether Etruscans of Vulci, Veii, or later of Clusium, as well as all other immigrants or whole peoples who may have been annexed to the Roman state—while not incorporated into the curias, would have been Roman by virtue of their inclusion in tribes and centuries. Accordingly, the last half of the sixth century B.C. witnessed the simultaneous functioning of two constitutional systems: one heavily comprised of Latins with some Etruscan participation, the other including not only Rome's old

Latin population but far larger numbers of Etruscans, as well as other new inhabitants.[41]

As noted in the introduction of this essay, one of the most problem-laden parts of the annalistic tradition pertains to the ousting of Tarquinius Superbus and the founding of the Republic. The last Tarquin is noted for both his vigorous foreign policy and his construction of the great temple to crown the Etruscan complex upon the Capitoline—and, of course, for a comportment which engendered opposition and dethronement.[42] Historical and archaeological sources link Tarquinius Superbus to Veii. Probably, Veientane craftsmen imported to assist with building projects remained in Tarquinian Rome. Alföldi suggests that the last Tarquin's associations with Veii mark an era of Veientane suzerainty in northern Latium which ended only when he was ousted at the hands of Lars Porsenna of Clusium and his supporters within and without the city of Rome. Porsenna's activities should be judged less in terms of Roman concerns and more on Etruscan political grounds.[43] The most convincing segment of Alföldi's monograph is his reconstruction of Porsenna's actual role in establishing Republican government at Rome. Alföldi goes beyond the annalistic tradition to adduce further sources, both Roman and Greek, in demonstrating that Tarquin was Porsenna's foe and that Porsenna's seizure of Rome displaced him. The Larcius and Herminius whom Livy includes among the staunchest defenders of Rome were not Tarquin's men but Porsenna's. It was to their care that the city and its new government were entrusted.[44]

The advent of the Republic makes available an important and generally reliable source. The *fasti consulares* provide in their listing of Roman magistrates the names of the Republic's leaders. The problems of fictive consuls in the initial years of the Republic and occasional tampering with the record elsewhere do not discredit the overall dependability of the *fasti*. Even the annalistic record for this period is more expansive, as it reports the activities of leading politicians.[45]

At the head of the legitimate *fasti* stand, as first consular praetors, none other than T. Herminius and Sp. Larcius, presiding magistrates of 506 B.C. Their role as lieutenants of Porsenna is evident despite efforts of Roman annalists to cast them as commanding Roman forces against him. Moreover, their gentilicia are not only clearly Etruscan but, significantly, occur repeatedly at Clusium, as attested by epigraphic evidence. Though Porsenna himself may have administered Rome during the period of war with Tarquin and his Latin allies, afterwards a Rome plainly associated with Clusium was administered by the city's new and old aristocracy—including numerous Etruscans, many of whom, like Larcius and Herminius, were no doubt of Clusine origin.[46]

Ogilvie makes clear that Rome, "as the names of her leading families and the tokens of her political institutions indicate, did not turn her back on her Etruscan past. . . . After Porsenna's assault Rome seems to have been governed by a succession of plebeian consuls most of whose roots were in Etruria."[47] The government of the early Republic, led by Rome's aristocrats—Etruscan as well as Latin—maintained certain monarchical institutions. Consular praetors were elected by the centuries, whose assembly appears to have become the new Republic's chief body of state—though the curias continued to function, as evidenced by an end to the Etruscan kings' moratorium on curia creation with the formation of three new curias in 495 B.C.: two for new territories brought into the state and one to accommodate the recently immigrated followers of Appius Claudius, consul of 495 B.C. There is no specific indication whether Etruscans who had taken residence at Rome under the last kings or with the coming of Lars Porsenna had been incorporated into the curial body. Such action is not impossible, though its motivation is hard to comprehend since the state functioned largely under a centuriate constitution. If incorporation were to have ultimately occurred, it is possible that this transpired in 495 B.C. at the time when the creation of new curias implies not only some kind of continued functioning of the curial system but an awareness of the need to include the citizen body in the curias.[48]

The identification of Roman leaders of Etruscan descent reveals the degree of Etruscan involvement in the governance of post-monarchical Rome. Etruscan descent can be determined in part through onomastics. Where onomastic evidence is corroborated by epigraphic or historical proof, the likelihood of Etruscan origin increases. Since the remainder of this essay is devoted to identifying Etruscans and assessing their

role in governing Rome, it is not inappropriate to consider the onomastic sources used to ascertain Etruscan origin or descent.

By itself, the study of onomastics constitutes the least certain of
the evidential methods for determining Etruscan presence. Nevertheless, the sheer preponderance of such evidence, especially when corroborated by epigraphic and historical means, is convincing. Despite
some controversy which has surrounded his study of Latin proper
names since its publication[49] and the validity of onomastics in general,
W. Schulze's work remains heavily used and has not been superseded
by more recent effort. His citation of epigraphic evidence is extremely
valuable and his onomastic observations insightful. J. Kaimio reflects
accurately that "Schulze's great theory about the Etruscan origin of
Latin nomenclature has on many points not yet been invalidated."[50]
Furthermore, in tandem with other recent contributions, Schulze's
work can be used with confidence that much of its onomastic analysis
remains sound.[51] R. Syme rightly argues for the authenticity of the
principle, utilized in the studies of Schulze and F. Münzer, that "the
advance of alien stocks such as Etruscans in the governing hierarchy
of Rome can be discovered from nomenclature."[52]

In the early Republic, from its founding until the year 367 B.C.,
seventeen gentes of Etruscan origin can be identified as attaining
an imperial magistracy as either consular praetor, consular tribune,
interrex, or dictator.[53] Specific evidence, whether onomastic, epigraphic, historical, or literary, for the Etruscan derivation of these
families is detailed in the notes of this essay. Evidence concerning
magisterial office is summarized in T. R. S. Broughton's *Magistrates of
the Roman Republic.*[54]

Not unexpectedly, Etruscan influence was strongest during the
earliest years of the Republic. Before 493 B.C., twenty-six consuls
(consular praetors)[55] are recorded in the *fasti*; seventeen were Etruscan.
Four dictators are listed for the period; three were Etruscan. The Larcii
held three consulships (consular praetorships) and two dictatorships.[56]
Postumii were consular praetors three times and dictator once.[57] The
gens Verginia supplied three consuls (consular praetors)[58] and the
Veturii two.[59] Five other Etruscan clans rose to imperial rank with
a single consul from each: Aebutius,[60] Cominius,[61] Herminius,[62]

Lucretius,[63] and Menenius.[64] Ogilvie claims that so strong an Etruscan presence in the leadership of Rome explains the events of the period by implying "a policy of subservience to Etruria and expansion at the expense of Latium."[65] The successful functioning of the newly organized *res publica* and the triumphal assertion of Roman arms in conflict with neighboring Latins are owed in large part to Republican Rome's Etruscan leaders. Little doubt can exist as to the central role of these Etruscan gentes in the governing oligarchy.

From 493 B.C. to the institution of the consular tribunate in 444 B.C., more than half of all magistrates but only a third of all consuls (consular praetors) derived from Etruscan families. Sp. Larcius Flavus was consul for the third time in 490 B.C., and Postumus Cominius reiterated the consulship in 493 B.C.[66] The consul of 448 B.C. was possibly a grandson of T. Herminius.[67] The Verginii contributed seven consuls, the most of any gens in the period.[68] The Menenii,[69] Postumii,[70] and Veturii[71] were each represented by two consuls. An Aebutius and a Lucretius also maintained imperial honors for their respective gentes.[72] Etruscan gentes which attained to imperial rank in this period were the Manlii, with two consuls,[73] and—with a single consular or other representative with imperium from their gentes—the Aquilii,[74] Aternii,[75] Romilii,[76] Sicinii,[77] Tarquitii,[78] and Volumnii.[79] In sum, fifteen Etruscan gentes had become imperial families by 444 B.C.

Several Etruscans were among the *decemviri* charged with reconstituting Roman government in 451 and 450 B.C.[80] Other offices were also occupied by Etruscans at Rome. The office of plebeian tribune is traditionally held to have originated at the time of the first seccession of plebs in 493 B.C. Three of the first six tribunes were Etruscan, establishing what would be a long association of certain Etruscan gentes with the tribal assembly.[81] Between 493 and 444 B.C., the Verginii, Sicinii, and Licinii had already held a number of tribunates;[82] and representatives of the Canuleii,[83] Laetorii,[84] and Maecilii[85] had also served as plebeian tribune. Of course, the records for this office, or any other except consul, are extremely irregular for this period and only a small number of plebeian tribunes are known. Still, with so many Etruscans occupying the chief offices of state, it is reasonable to expect that lesser offices would be similarly held by those of Etruscan origin or descent.

The evidence, then, establishes the fact of enduring Etruscan presence at Rome and inclusion among the state's most important leaders. Unquestionably, the Etruscans did not leave Rome with Tarquin. Instead, since his exile was the work of an Etruscan ruler of Clusium, no doubt with the support of many leading Roman families—including those of Etruscan derivation—the Etruscans would certainly have remained in their homes at Rome and contributed to the development of their city, many of them being included among the ruling families of state.[86]

The years from 444 to 367 B.C., however, witnessed the decline of many Etruscan families in their possession of high state offices. Only the Manlii and Postumii increase in the number of imperial magistracies held. Before 444, the gens Manlia held two such magistracies. Afterward, eighteen imperial magistracies were possessed by ten Manlii.[87] Few gentes surpassed this number. As for other Etruscan families, the Postumii attained eleven imperial magistracies,[88] the Lucretii eight,[89] the Menenii five,[90] the Veturii five,[91] and the Verginii four.[92] A new imperial gens, the Licinii, not only held two magistracies with imperium during this period, but occupied the plebeian tribunate more extensively than any family, particularly due to the decade-long tenure of the famous tribune C. Licinius Stolo in that office from 376 to 367 B.C.[93] By contrast, other Etruscan families disappeared from the *fasti*. The Larcii, Herminii, and Aebutii held no imperial offices, nor did the Aternii, Romilii, Tarquitii, or Volumnii reiterate the single magistracies which made their gentes imperial. Fifty-three of 386 imperial magistracies between 444 and 367 B.C. were occupied by Etruscan families—only 14 percent of the total.

In chronicling the internal affairs of the early Republic, the Roman annalists devote virtually all their attention to the so-called struggle of orders. My own ongoing study of the role Etruscan families may have exercised in these events, although as yet incomplete, yields some observations of value here. I accept that the patriciate *per se* did not exist under the monarchy. Instead, it took form during the early Republic as certain aristocratic families, which had attained imperial office, sought to exclude from the prerogatives of those offices other aristocratic or near-aristocratic families, in particular those whose members had held an office granted by the plebeian assembly.[94] Palmer has demonstrated that at the resolution of this struggle by the Licinian-Sextian rogations of 367 B.C., the official criterion employed to distinguish the patrician and plebeian gentes entailed this very principle.[95]

How may this competition among leading families, which came ultimately to involve virtually the entire citizen body, have affected the role of Etruscan families in the governance of Rome? It is perhaps significant that the Etruscans seemed to exercise reasonable influence until the chaotic period of 449 to 444 B.C. Only the first decemviral commission contained Etruscans, who may have designedly been excluded from the second for not agreeing to the patrician-plebeian distinctions which appeared to be the object of governmental reform. The curtailment of Etruscan offices after 444 B.C. may be related to the change of government effected in that year.

Palmer has shown that a restoration of the old curiate constitution occurred in 444 B.C. While the centuries seem to have functioned occasionally to elect consular praetors between 444 and 367 B.C., in most years consular tribunes were elected by the curias.[96] Frequent interregna made possible by this system enabled several powerful families with much influence in the curias to control the composition of colleges of consular tribunes. These families were invariably from the old Latin aristocracy. Indeed, many of the important Etruscan families may have had no place in the curias, much less influence with them.

There is reason to connect certain Etruscan ruling gentes with the plebeian organization and effort. Not only were Licinii among the first tribunes, but it was a Licinius who repeated his tribunate for a decade, brought to a standstill Roman government, precipitated constitutional if not civil anarchy, and successfully terminated curial government, replacing it with the foundations of the classical Roman constitution as legislated in the Licinian-Sextian rogations.[97] The events surrounding this bloodless revolution are muddled in the historical accounts;[98] but it is clear that, after much opposition by leading Latin curial families, an Etruscan *dictator seditiones sedandae et rei gerendae causa,* one P. Manlius

Capitolinus, with the Etruscan Licinius Calvus as his *magister equitum*, enabled the tribune Licinius Stolo to enact his legislation.[99] It should also be remembered that it was an Etruscan—the former consular praetor and dictator Menenius Agrippa—who brought to an end the plebeian secession of 493 B.C.[100]

While the mass of the Roman plebs may have been small farmers with ties to aristocratic Latin *patroni*, perhaps the plebs most concerned with organization and change were the wealthier shopkeepers, craftsmen, artisans, and businessmen—the urbanites rather than the rural *pagani*. Many of this rising urban class were in all likelihood Etruscan. No doubt they contributed much to the plebeian movement and would have politically supported leading Etruscan gentes.[101] It is by no means improbable that an important ethnic element influenced, at least in part, the events described as the struggle of orders. The reforms of Licinius were largely ineffectual in restoring Etruscan participation in Roman government, and they were no more efficacious in increasing the number of plebeian aristocrats in the state's ruling bodies. After 367 B.C., few Etruscan families were part of the new senatorial aristocracy.

From 311 to 284 B.C., Etruria was brought increasingly into the Roman sphere of control. By 283 B.C., despite the official federate or ally status of several Etruscan cities, Etruscan independence was ended and the Etruscans were encompassed in the empire of the Roman people.

Between 284 and 91 B.C., during the late Republican era, a number of families from the towns of Etruria became active in government at Rome. Several acquired senatorial status and consular rank. But by this time the surviving Etruscan gentes at Rome were long since thoroughly assimilated. Their Etruscan origin would have been only a matter of heritage, if even remembered. By contrast, the new wave of Etruscan participants in Roman government, the *domi nobiles* of Etruria's cities, were very much aware of their Etruscan background, despite Romanization and cultural assimilation.[102] Since the participation of this Etruscan municipal aristocracy in politics at Rome has been the topic of a number of my previous publications, it is perhaps necessary in this essay simply to summarize the extensive influence of this group upon Roman governance.[103]

The general enfranchisement of Etruria did not, of course, occur until the Social War, with the region's incorporation into the Roman body politic under the terms of the Lex Iulia of 90 B.C.[104] Before 91 B.C., though, there were Etruscans who not only possessed citizen rights but had attained senatorial rank and, in the case of the powerful Perpernae, had already acquired consular insignia.[105]

While insufficient documentation exists to hazard an estimate of how many Etruscan families had acquired Roman citizenship by the beginning of the second century, a few families who were active in either the political system or the Roman army are identifiable. In addition, information concerning their places of residence allows the formulation of tenuous views as to how their enfranchisement came about. For example, the Aelii Tuberones[106] and Licinii Sacerdotes[107] from Veientane territory may be presumed to have received citizenship as a part of the Roman disposition of the area; and the Caeretane Aburii,[108] Campatii,[109] or Egnatii[110] held their citizenship probably as a result of the special position of Caere vis-à-vis Rome. On the other hand, there is reason to associate the citizenship of the Cornelii Sisennae,[111] Numisii,[112] and Fulcinii, as well as the Perusine families of the Nigidii,[113] Vibii Pansae,[114] and Volcacii Tulli,[115] with services rendered during the Second Punic War. The particular situations of three families suggest that special citizenship grants were brought through the influence of C. Marius. The Norbani are clearly to be linked to Marius as a result of attacks on the citizen status of Marius' political ally, C. Norbanus.[116] Similarly, the known Marians C. Carrinas[117] and the prosecutor Curtius[118] provide cause for connecting Marius with the enfranchisement of their gentes. The role of Etruscans in the events before and after the Social War has formed the subject of several studies which demonstrate the immersion of Etruscan municipal aristocrats in Roman politics thenceforth.[119] Their general alignment with the Marian and Cinnan cause in the wars against Sulla resulted in Sullan reprisals against Etruria and its aristocracy.[120]

The recurrent rebellions and seditions which burgeoned in Etruria during the last decades of the Republic bespeak extreme discontent and frustration among a considerable portion of the region's population. Such feelings derived in large measure from the lack of redress conceded to Etruria following Sulla's political settlement of this area in which he encountered such enduring and obdurate resistance. It is doubtful whether Caesar would have commanded what Etruscan support accrued to him had it not been for the still-lingering effects of Sulla's harsh retribution against Etruria and many of its leading citizens.[121]

Views on the extent and strength of Caesar's Etruscan support range from the opinion that Caesar possessed but a single follower from the Etruscan municipal aristocracy[122] to more moderate estimations that he could command reasonably significant Etruscan support—perhaps even the large and zealous following which is considered by some to have been Caesar's inherited Marian clientele.[123] Certainly it would seem that, in Caesar, many Etruscans discerned the champion with the best opportunity to effect change and compensate for past injustices to individuals and the region. The loyalty of many anti-Sullans can be expected to have been offered Caesar, all the more on account of his pledge to restore the rights of the proscribed and their children. The extension in 49 B.C. of full civic rights to many such individuals would have guaranteed their support in the following years.[124] Still, the support that Caesar received from Etruria did not derive entirely from the concerns of anti-Sullans; personal ties and connections to the region may also have provided him with the allegiance of additional Etruscans.[125]

In view of his conciliatory pledge, it is not surprising that anti-Sullans figured prominently among Caesar's Etruscan followers and, after the restoration of their citizenship, were in compensatory fashion rapidly advanced by him through offices and honors. Carrinas and Norbanus Flaccus, both sons of Cinnan commanders, had to be re-introduced by Caesar to political life at Rome, the former receiving a praetorship and the latter being elevated to praetorian rank in 43 B.C.[126] Similarly, Sex. Appuleius of Luna, later married to Caesar's niece, was quickly awarded political and priestly offices in keeping with the pattern of compensatory advancement allowed to sons of the proscribed.[127] The son of the proscribed Marian prosecutor Curtius, C. Curtius, was adlected to the senate under Caesar.[128] Another member of the gens Curtia, C. Rabirius Postumus, natural son of the wealthy equestrian C. Curtius and already a praetor by 49 B.C., held an influential position on Caesar's personal staff, both commanding troops and acting as one of Caesar's financiers.[129] With him on Caesar's staff were the Etruscan C. Vibius Pansa,[130] who espoused Caesar's cause and rose to praetorian and consular rank through his patronage; and C. Matius, a financial agent of Caesar's who also appears to have been of Etruscan origin.[131]

Representatives of other Etruscan gentes under Caesar seem to have entered public life, been adlected to the senate, or risen with his patronage. Some, such as L. Caesennius Lento,[132] the Hostilii Sasernae,[133] a Venuleius,[134] and D. Carfulenus,[135] served as Caesar's officers in Gaul or during the civil war. Other Etruscans are documented as simply supporting Caesar or receiving favor and advancement from him. They include C. Cestius, praetor of 44 B.C.; his brother L. Cestius, the praetor of 43 B.C.;[136] L. Critonius;[137] and perhaps the *haruspex* Spurinna.[138]

Within a short time of Caesar's death and the announcement of Octavian as his primary beneficiary and adopted son, a sparse assortment of supporters gathered around the young man. The participation of Etruscans in the party of Octavian Caesar, and their subsequent tenure of privileged positions in the Augustan regime, is a study too lengthy to consider here in detail, but an overview of names, ranks, and relationships provides some very compelling evidence of their presence and influence.[139] The wealthy equestrian Maecenas, of course, immediately springs to mind as a very prominent Etruscan supporter of Octavian. His ancestry from the kings of Arretium is well known, as are both his generous support of his friend Octavian at Arretium in the autumn of 44 B.C. and his activities influencing public opinion in ways favorable to Octavian's party.[140] Similarly, the poet Vergil played an important role among Octavian's supporters. He was, of course, of Etruscan descent and possessed the status of a municipal aristocrat.[141] Along with Maecenas, his brother-in-law C. Proculeius, Octavian's confidant and friend, must be counted Etruscan.[142] In Octavian's own family, his half-sister, Octavia (maior), was the daughter of the Etruscan Ancharia and wife of Sex. Appuleius, an

Etruscan of Luna, to whom she bore two sons, both of whom were elevated to consular rank under their uncle.[143]

Octavian's early political enterprises, including his personal sponsorship of the *Ludi Victoriae Caesaris*, were funded by Balbus and three Etruscans: C. Matius, C. Rabirius Postumus, and C. Hostilius Saserna.[144] Also prominent among Octavian's cadre of Etruscans in 44 and 43 B.C. were his mysterious agent Caecina of Volaterra[145] and the former Caesarian general C. Carrinas, a praetorian senator whom Octavian nominated in 43 B.C. to take his own place as consul.[146] Another Caesarian general of Etruscan origin, the ordinary consul of the same year, C. Vibius Pansa, seems also to have been counted as a friend of Octavian.[147] L. Cestius,[148] a praetor in 43 B.C., was of Etruscan descent and supported Octavian by a special coinage issue minted under his direction and that of his praetorian colleague, the Etruscan C. Norbanus, who is found in command of Octavian's camp at Philippi in the following year.[149] Moreover, it seems that many of the common soldiers filling the ranks of Octavian's forces and commanded by Etruscans like Carrinas and Norbanus were themselves Etruscan.[150] Among tribunes loyal to Octavian and instrumental in the conduct of his policy before the popular assembly was the Etruscan D. Carfulenus.[151] Perhaps the most valued of Octavian's Etruscan adherents, both early in his career and later when he became the emperor Augustus, was an individual who probably came from Pisa and may therefore be counted of Etruscan descent—M. Vipsanius Agrippa. His services to Octavian are too numerous to permit cursory elaboration.[152]

Other Etruscans are known to have belonged to the growing faction of Octavian at later times, and evidence may simply be lacking to demonstrate their association with the party as early as their fellows enumerated above. Those already mentioned do, nonetheless, constitute a large portion of the total support from the senatorial class enjoyed by Octavian in 44 and 43 B.C. As such, their role in the nascent party of Octavian must have been overwhelming, and it would not have been insignificant later in the Augustan councils of state.[153]

Nineteen men of Etruscan origin are identifiable, then, as proponents of Octavian during the period of his rise to power. Approximately a half dozen of these could be counted among his closest and most influential advisors, with Agrippa and Maecenas ultimately rising to occupy positions of great authority with Augustus. These Etruscan adherents together comprised a very large portion of the entire group of supporters known to have followed Octavian in this period, and it is rightly expected that their influence was proportionate to their number. As well, it surely follows, from either the Etruscans who later occupied posts under Augustus or the fathers and uncles of this next generation, that there were other Etruscan members of the *factio Octaviana*.

Etruscan proponents of Octavian in the period of his ascendancy remained prominent and influential participants in the Augustan regime. They and their families can be seen to have richly reaped the rewards of victory. Consular or praetorian office in Augustus' principate was most frequently attained, insofar as Etruscans were concerned, by those who were either kinsmen of Augustus or relatives of already important Etruscans. Augustus' own nephew, Sex. Appuleius, was consul of 29 B.C.,[154] and M. Appuleius was consul of 20 B.C.[155] C. Norbanus Flaccus, the son of Octavian's general Norbanus and son-in-law of the powerful Balbus, was consul of 24 B.C.[156] The valuable services of "quidam Caecina Volaterranus" were no doubt recompensed in the appointments of his son, A. Caecina Severus, as a suffect consul of 1 B.C.[157] and his grandson, A. Caecina Largus, as consul of A.D. 13.[158] Other third-generation adherents of Augustus were permitted by his long reign to reach similarly high magisterial office. Another son of Caecina Severus, Sex. Caecina, was a praetor in A.D. 12.[159] Yet another C. Norbanus Flaccus, grandson of the consul of 38 B.C., was praetor for A.D. 11. His brother, L. Norbanus Balbus, in order to qualify for his A.D. 19 consulate, must have also reached praetorian rank under Augustus.[160] Augustus' grandnephew, another Sex. Appuleius, was consul in the final year of his reign.[161] A son-in-law of Agrippa, the Etruscan Q. Haterius, certainly received his suffect consulate of 5 B.C. as a result of his relationship to Agrippa.[162] Similarly, two consuls from the Etruscan Aelii Tuberones—Q. Aelius Tubero, consul in 11 B.C., and Sex. Aelius Catus, a consul in A.D. 4[163]—seem to have been related to Maecenas' nephew and Augustus' praetorian prefect L. Seius Strabo,[164] and may have reached consular rank through the assistance of Maecenas. Additionally, Augustus' wife, Livia, possessed ties through a Claudian kinswoman of her father to the Volusii Saturnini of Ferentium. This connection to Augustus' own family no doubt accounts for the consulship of L. Volusius Saturninus in 12 B.C. and that of his son of the same name in A.D. 3.[165] Similarly, the Salvii Othones of Ferentium owed to Livia their introduction to Roman society, and through her influence the praetorship was offered to M. Salvius Otho.[166] P. Petronius, Etruscan son-in-law of Livia's close personal confidant, the Etruscan Urgulania, also held his praetorship under Augustus, followed by a consulate in A.D. 19.[167] Finally, it must not be forgotten that the children of Agrippa and Julia received an Etruscan heritage through their father. Therefore, in a certain sense, the many offices and honors of Gaius and Lucius Caesar qualify for inclusion among magistracies received under Augustus by men of Etruscan origin and ancestry.[168]

Space does not permit examination in this essay of the offices attained by the descendants of these men and by other Etruscans under Augustus' Julio-Claudian successors.[169] It is sufficient to say that the advancement of Etruscan municipal aristocrats to positions of political prominence was not restricted to the reign of Augustus, but continued uninterrupted under the patronage of his heirs. The Etruscan municipal aristocracy, then, is seen to have fared certainly as profitably as— if not more successfully than—the local nobility of any of Italy's regions in the political and social revolutions which characterized the last century B.C.

The Etruscans, then, did not cease to be involved in the governance of Rome at the time of Tarquin's ouster. On the contrary, Etruscan noble families continued to occupy the chief offices of state for more than a century. Although the next century witnessed a decline in their involvement, after Etruria became a part of the Roman state in 284 B.C. certain municipal aristocrats entered politics at Rome and played an important role in the events of the last century B.C. With Octavian Caesar, a small cadre of loyal Etruscan supporters rose to prominence, constituting a new ruling aristocracy of the empire under Augustus and his heirs. In a certain sense, Rome once again had Etruscan rulers.

NOTES

1. T. B. Macaulay, "Horatius," in *The Complete Poems of Thomas Babington Macaulay* (New York, n.d.), 5–6; see also vii–xxxvi.

2. The legendary incident at the Pons Sublicius is recounted in Liv. 2.10 and D.H. 5.23–35. In *A Commentary on Livy, Books 1–5* (Oxford, 1965), 258–59, R. M. Ogilvie explains it as an act of *devotio* to bless the bridge, from which a "simple ritual was enveloped with historical circumstances and from being a religious act became an historical fact."

3. The *gentilicium* Larcius is well established as derived from the Etruscan *larce* on the basis of onomastic arguments and abundant epigraphic evidence for both the Etruscan and Latin forms, as cited by W. Schulze in *LE*, 83, 109. See also *RE* XII, col. 796 [F. Münzer]. Herminius is similarly established as of Etruscan derivation by both onomastics and epigraphic attestation of the name and its variant forms in Etruria, with a significant number of examples found at Clusium. See *LE*, 173, for arguments and a listing of the epigraphic evidence. See also *RE* VIII, cols. 833–34. The case of Horatius is by no means sure. On the basis of onomastic theory Schulze allows the possibility of potential Etruscan antecedents for the Latin *nomen*. The role of the Larcii and Herminii as associates, rather than opponents, of Porsenna is proposed by A. Alföldi, *Early Rome and the Latins* (Ann Arbor, Mich., [1965]), 76.

4. Excellent summary discussions of the sources of the archaic period of Roman history and analyses of the problems of their usage include T. J. Cornell, "The Value of the Literary Tradition Concerning Archaic Rome," in *Social Struggles in Archaic Rome*, ed. K. A. Raaflaub (Berkeley, Calif., 1986), 52–76; Ogilvie, *Commentary*, 9–17 (supra n. 2); R. M. Ogilvie, *Early Rome and the Etruscans* (Glasgow, 1976), 15–29; E. Badian, "The Early Historians," in *Latin Historians*, ed. T. A. Dorey (London, 1966), 1–38; P. Fraccaro, "La storia romana arcaica," *RIL* 85 (1952): 85–118; and C. Ampolo, "La storiografia su Roma arcaica e i documenti," in *Tria corda: Scritti in onore di A. Momigliano*, ed. E. Gabba (Como, It., 1983), 9–26.

5. Most condemning of the accounts of Pictor and other Roman annalists is Alföldi's *Early Rome and the Latins*, 101–75 (supra n. 3). See also E. Rawson, "The First Latin Annalists," *Latomus* 35 (1976): 689–717. A different treatment of Pictor with exhaustive bibliography is D. Timpe, "Fabius Pictor und die Anfänge der römischen Historiographie," *ANRW* 1.2 (1972): 928–69.

6. For the *annales maximi*, see B. W. Frier, *Libri Annales Pontificium Maximorum: The Origins of the Annalistic Tradition*, Papers and Monographs of the American Academy at Rome, 27 (Rome, 1975). On the Linen Books, see R. M. Ogilvie, "Livy, Licinius Macer, and the *Libri Lintei*," *JRS* 48 (1958): 40–46.

7. Ogilvie, *Early Rome and the Etruscans*, 33–43 (supra n. 2); Alföldi, *Early Rome and the Latins*, 194–202, 318–35 (supra n. 3). See also C. Ampolo, "La grande Roma dei Tarquinii rivisitata," in *Alle origini di Roma*, ed. E. Campanile (Pisa, 1988), 77–87; H. H. Scullard, *The Etruscan Cities and Rome* (Ithaca, N.Y., 1967), 243–66.

8. Interpretations of the archaeological evidence to show minimal Etruscan influence on Roman society by scholars of several decades past (E. Gjerstad, *Early Rome*, 6 vols. [Lund, Swed., 1953–73]; I. S. Ryberg, *An Archaeological Record of Rome from the Seventh to the Second Century B.C.* [London and Philadelphia, 1940]) have given way to more recent views of an Etruscan permeation of Roman culture. Perhaps the best recent summary and analysis of the archaeological evidence is J. C. Meyer, *Pre-Republican Rome: An Analysis of the Cultural and Chronological Relations 1000–500 B.C.* (Odense, Den., 1983), esp. 139–69. See also L. Quilici, *Roma primitiva e le origini della civiltà laziale* (Rome, 1979); D. Ridgway, "Early Rome and Latium: An Archaeological Introduction," in *Italy before the Romans: The Iron Age, Orientalizing, and Etruscan Periods*, ed. D. Ridgway and F. Ridgway (London, 1979), 187–96; M. Pallottino, "The Origins of Rome: A Survey of Recent Discoveries and Discussion," in *Italy before the Romans*, 197–238 (vol. supra this n.); H. Müller-Karpe, *Vom Anfang Roms* (Heidelberg, 1959); H. Müller-Karpe, *Zur Stadtwerdung Roms* (Heidelberg, 1962).

9. Meyer, *Pre-Republican Rome*, 139–69 (supra n. 8), summarizes the evidence. See also Pallottino, "The Origins of Rome," 197–238 (supra n. 8); M. Pallottino, "Fatti e legende (moderne) sulla più antica storia di Roma," *SE* 31 (1963): 3–37; G. Colonna, "S. Omobono: La ceramica etrusca dipinta," *BCAR* 77 (1962): 125–43; A. Alföldi, *Römische Frühgeschichte: Kritik und Forschung seit 1964* (Heidelberg, 1976), 190–95; G. Colonna, "Preistoria e protostoria di Roma e del Lazio," in *Popoli e civiltà dell'Italia antica* (Rome, 1974), 2:275–93; C. de Simone, "Gli Etruschi a Roma: Evidenza linguistica e problemi metodologici," in *Gli Etruschi e Roma: Atti dell'incontro di studio in onore di Massimo Pallottino* (Rome, 1981), 93–103.

10. See, in this volume, the essay by Dorothy Dvorsky Rohner, 119 ff.

11. Alföldi, *Early Rome and the Latins*, 195 (supra n. 3).

12. Ogilvie, *Early Rome and the Etruscans*, 73 (supra n. 4).

13. A work often cited on the archaeological record of early Rome is Gjerstad's six-volume compilation *Early Rome* (supra n. 8)—only marginally useful as a catalogue and problematic otherwise, as R. E. A. Palmer twenty years ago exposed it to be, due to its founding "on violation of the Latin language, of linguistic rules, of source criticism, of archaeological interpretation, and of logical argument" (R. E. A. Palmer, review of *Early Rome*, v [The Written Sources] and vi [Historical Survey], by E. Gjerstad, *AJA* 79 [1975]: 387). D. Ridgway, "Early Rome and Latium: An Archaeological Introduction," in *Italy before the Romans*, 188 (vol. supra n. 8), asserts that "Palmer's brilliant review of these two volumes is required reading for any archaeologist who still thinks that Gjerstad is primarily an ancient historian. The brutal truth of the matter is that there is nothing to be said in favour of Gjerstad's method in *either* field."

14. In addition to the works mentioned in nn. 8 and 9, other pertinent works are R. Bloch, *The Origins of Rome* (New York, 1960), esp. 85–111; P. Romanelli, "Problemi archeologici e storici di Roma primitivi," *BPI* 64 (1955): 257–60; P. Romanelli, "Certezze e ipotesi sulle origini di Roma," *StudRom* 13 (1965): 156–69; G. Colonna, "Aspetti culturali della Roma primitiva: Il periodo orientalizzante

recente," *ArchClass* 16 (1964): 1–12; G. Devoto, "Le origini tripartite di Roma," *Athenaeum* 31 (1953): 335–43; P. De Francisci, *Primordia Civitatis* (Rome, 1959).

15. See nn. 8 and 9.

16. A. Momigliano, "An Interim Report on the Origins of Rome," *JRS* 53 (1963): 107.

17. A. Ernout and A. Meillet, *Dictionnaire étymologique de la langue latine*, 4th ed. (Paris, 1959), 84.

18. See, for example, G. Wissowa, *Religion und Kultus der Römer*, 2d ed. (Munich, 1912); A. J. Pfiffig, *Religio etrusca* (Graz, Austria, 1975); R. E. A. Palmer, *Roman Religion and Roman Empire: Five Essays* (Philadelphia, 1974); M. Torelli, *Lavinio e Roma: Riti iniziatici e matrimonio tra archeologia e storia* (Rome, 1984); A. Grenier, *Les Religions étrusque et romaine* (Paris, 1948); K. Latte, *Römische Religionsgeschichte* (Munich, 1960); H. J. Rose, "On the Relations between Roman and Etruscan Religion," *SMSR* 4 (1928): 115 ff.

19. On the question of diachronic and synchronic history for early Rome, see Pallottino, "Origins," 199 (supra n. 8). In the same article (204–20) Pallottino summarizes the treatment of early Rome's chronology by modern sources and examines the chronology of archaic Rome in light of archaeological evidence and ancient literary sources. Most important is Pallottino's conclusion that, as regards the Etruscans at Rome, "their presence and their activities in Rome are historical facts that can be checked, belonging as they do, and as we have seen, to a relatively advanced—indeed final—phase in the process of the city's formation." See also Pallottino, "Fatti e legende" (supra n. 9), for additional considerations of the chronology of Etruscan Rome.

20. For example, discussion of the Servian reform by later authors makes reference to aspects of the centuriate assembly which may be more applicable to the institution in the first century B.C. than in the sixth. See Ogilvie, *Commentary*, 168–69, 172–77 (supra n. 2).

21. Ogilvie, *Commentary*, 141–42, 145–46, 229–30 (supra n. 2), reviews the evidence for the location of the *gens* Tarchna at Caere, the problems with the traditional tale propagated by Livy (1.34.) and Dionysius of Halicarnassus (3.47) of a Tarquinian origin and the parentage of Demaratus of Corinth and, finally, other ties of the Etruscan community at Rome and the Tarquin family to Caere. Ogilvie questions how much of the traditional story can be trusted, answering that perhaps no more than the Etruscan origin of Tarquin is authentic. Many have observed that the name Tarquin derives from an Etruscan gentilicium. The name is likely related to Tarchon, the Etruscan hero imputed by Strabo (5.5.2) with the founding of cities in Etruria and the eponym of Tarquinii. Tarchon is a Hellenized transliteration; the proper Etruscan form seems to have been *tarchuna* or *tarchna*. Despite Tarquinii's claim of Tarchon as founder, few Tarchna are attested at Tarquinii. By contrast, the Etruscan nomen Tarchna and its orthographic variants are recorded in inscriptions from three sites in Etruria: Caere, Clusium, and Perusia. By far the largest number of attestations occurs at Caere, where in the Banditaccia necropolis an elegant family tomb, with burials dating from the seventh through the fourth century B.C., provides

epitaphs of thirty-one members of the gens Tarchna. Moreover, an intermediate Latinized form occurs as Tarquenna, and four of the later epitaphs preserve the normalized Latin form of the name as Tarquinius, the nomen of the Etruscan royal family of Rome. See J. F. Hall, "Livy's Tanaquil and the Image of Assertive Etruscan Women in Latin Historical Literature of the Early Empire," *AugAge* 4 (1985): 31–38; Scullard, *Etruscan Cities*, 84–85, 254–56 (supra n. 7); T. Gantz, "The Tarquin Dynasty," *Historia* 24 (1975): 541; R. Werner, *Der Beginn der römischen Republik* (Munich, 1963), 383–87. See also *LE*, 95–96; *RE* IVA, col. 2348 [R. Schachermeyer]; J. F. Hall, "The Municipal Aristocracy of Etruria and Their Participation in Politics at Rome, B.C. 91–A.D. 14," (Ph.D. diss., University of Pennsylvania, 1984), 382–89 (hereinafter cited as "MAE"). Contrary views may be found in J. Heurgon, "Tarquitius Priscus et l'organisation de l'ordre des haruspices sous l'empereur Claude," *Latomus* 12 (1953): 402–17; J. Heurgon, "Tite-Live et les Tarquins," *IL* 7 (1955): 56–64; A. Blakeway, "Demaratus: A Study in Some Aspects of the Earliest Hellenization of Latium and Etruria," *JRS* 25 (1935): 129–49; and Alföldi, *Early Rome and the Latins*, 207 (supra n. 3).

22. R. E. A. Palmer, *The Archaic Community of the Romans* (Cambridge, 1970).

23. Palmer, *Archaic Community*, 1–9, 152–56 (supra n. 22). The most detailed description in an ancient source is D.H. 2.7. See also Liv. 1.13; Cic., *Rep.* 2.8; Fest. 42L; Var., *L.* 5.35, 55, 81, 89, 91. Other pertinent modern treatments are Momigliano, "Interim Report," 108–12 (supra n. 16), and De Francisci, *Primordia Civitatis*, 483–91 (supra n. 14).

24. Palmer, *Archaic Community*, 156–57; also 75–79, 82–84, 130–36, 141–48, 156–75, 195 (supra n. 22).

25. Ibid., 282.

26. D.H. 2.21–23; Palmer, *Archaic Community*, 80–155 (supra n. 22).

27. For explanation of the process of selecting the king when the "auspices returned to the fathers," see Palmer, *Archaic Community*, 184–218 (supra n. 22).

28. D.H. 3.48; Palmer, *Archaic Community*, 94–95, 132, 137–38 (supra n. 22). See also n. 21.

29. Liv. 1.32; Cic., *Rep.* 2.36; R. Thomsen, *King Servius Tullius: A Historical Synthesis* (Copenhagen, 1980), 190–91.

30. Palmer, *Archaic Community*, 94–95 (supra n. 22). Cf. Liv. 1.36.3; D.H. 3.70.5.

31. Palmer, *Archaic Community*, 94; also 170–73 (supra n. 22).

32. Thomsen (*King Servius Tullius*, 57–114 [supra n. 29]) provides the most comprehensive analysis of both ancient and modern discussion about the topic, demonstrating with confidence the Etruscan connections of Servius Tullius. Festus (182L) offers Tibur (in which territory Corniculum was perhaps located) as his place of birth. That city's own Etruscan links make it a possible place of origin for either an Etruscan Servius or an Etruscanized Latin Servius. For the traditional accounts of the Roman annalists, see Liv. 1.39 and D.H. 4.1–3. See also Alföldi, *Early Rome and the*

Latins, 213–15 (supra n. 3). Onomastic arguments which erroneously followed Latin annalists in associating the proper name Servius, presumed to be of Latin derivation, with the Latin common noun *servus*, must be discarded in favor of sounder theory. The Etruscan derivations of both Servius and Tullius are demonstrated by Schulze (*LE*, 231, 246) and more recently by other linguists. See Thomsen, *King Servius Tullius*, 107, nn. 247–50 (supra n. 29).

33. Thomsen, *King Servius Tullius*, 144–211, 231–87 (supra n. 29); Palmer, *Archaic Community*, 93–95, 123–27, 154–55, 203–16 (supra n. 22).

34. Thomsen, *King Servius Tullius*, 74–90, 95–98 (supra n. 29), outlines the evidence for the ties of Servius Tullius with Vulci and the Vibennae brothers and for his activities as the Etruscan Mastarna. See also Alföldi, *Early Rome and the Latins*, 213–23 (supra n. 3); S. Mazzarino, *Dalla monarchia allo stato repubblicano* (Catania, It., 1947), 185–89; R. T. Ridley, "The Enigma of Servius Tullius," *Klio* 57 (1975): 147–77.

35. Liv. 1.41.6. Cf. D.H. 4.5, 8, 12, 30–31, 40; and Cic., *Rep.* 2.36. See Thomsen, *King Servius Tullius*, 107–12 (supra n. 29), for discussion and analysis. From Palmer's observation (*Archaic Community*, 216–17 [supra n. 22]) that the title *mastarna* may indicate a period of service by Servius as Roman *magister populi* under his predecessor, it could reasonably be argued that Servius initially ruled at Rome by virtue of that military office, particularly if the monarchical senate comprised of the leaders of the community's curias refused to authorize the curial grant of imperium prerequisite to inauguration as *rex*. On different grounds, Thomsen makes the suggestion that Servius "had been *magister* at Rome before becoming king" (101). Description of the constitutional powers of curias and of a senate which was comprised of curial leaders in relation to the creation of kings is detailed in Palmer, *Archaic Community*, 205–13 (supra n. 22). On the employment of Etruscan military experts and methods by Roman rulers before Servius, see De Francisci, *Primordia Civitatis*, 646–47 (supra n. 14).

36. Thomsen, *King Servius Tullius*, 162–63 (supra n. 29).

37. The fullest ancient accounts of Servian constitution are found in Liv. 1.42–43, and D.H. 4.15. For commentary on the former, see Ogilvie, *Commentary*, 166–76 (supra n. 2); on the latter, see E. Gabba, "Studi su Dionigi di Alicarnasso, II: Il regno di Servio Tullio," *Athenaeum* 39 (1961): esp. 102–7. Palmer (*Archaic Community*, 152–55, 214–15 [supra n. 22]) discusses the constitutional ramifications of the acts of Servius Tullius regarding the curial system. By contrast, Thomsen (*King Servius Tullius*, 144–211 [supra n. 29]) provides a lengthy account with detailed attention to both ancient and modern sources on the topic of the military aspects of the centuriate reform. Both Palmer (154–55) and Thomsen (126–27) reject the view, which since Mommsen has been considered traditional (see H. Last, "The Servian Reforms," *JRS* 35 [1945]: 30–48), of an extensive creation of tribes—usually at a later date—in favor of the four urban tribes replacing the original three tribes and encompassing the territory of state. On the latter opinion, see esp. E. Gabba, "Considerazioni sulla tradizione letteraria sulle origini della repubblica," in *Les Origines de la république romaine*, Entretiens sur l'antiquité classique, 13

(Vandoeuvres-Geneva, 1967), 133–74; Gabba, "Studi su Dionigi di Alicarnasso," 98–121 (supra n. 37). See also E. Gabba, *Dionysius and the History of Archaic Rome* (Berkeley, Calif., 1991), 152–89. Similarly, Palmer (239–43) and Thomsen (159–63) also rightly reject the arguments of M. P. Nilsson ("The Introduction of Hoplite Tactics at Rome: Its Date and Consequences," *JRS* 19 [1929]: 1–11) to link the reforms to the consular tribunate and assign a post–445 B.C. date. The reorganization of tribes and creation of the centuriate system must remain associated with Servius. The context of Etruscan hoplite formations and tactics implemented at Rome is clearly a phenomenon of the sixth century B.C. and is best associated with Rome's Etruscan rulers, a point Thomsen (159) does not ignore.

38. The role of each curia to provide a hundred foot and ten horse to the tribal army is approximated by the function of the tribes to provide centuries for the centuriate hoplite army. See Palmer, *Archaic Community*, 5–9, 24–25, and esp. 152–54, 215 (supra n. 22); Ogilvie, *Early Rome and the Etruscans*, 53 (supra n. 4); L. R. Taylor, *The Voting Districts of the Roman Republic*, Papers and Monographs of the American Academy in Rome, 20 (Rome, 1960), 7–10 (hereinafter cited as *VDRR*); L. R. Taylor, "The Centuriate Assembly before and after the Reform," *AJPh* 78 (1957): 337–42. See also Thomsen, *King Servius Tullius*, 198–210 (supra n. 29).

39. Palmer is correct in his assessment that "the success of the centuriate reform partly rested upon curtailment of certain curial powers and perhaps the cessation of curial expansion" (*Archaic Community*, 210 [supra n. 22]). From the time when the city was organized into four regions and the Servian tribes were created through the end of the monarchy, Palmer shows the number of curias to have remained at twenty-seven (138). On criteria for enrollment into curias, see ibid., 205. See also R. E. Mitchell, "The Definition of *Patres* and *Plebs*," in *Social Struggles in Archaic Rome*, ed. K. A. Raaflaub (Berkeley, Calif., 1986), 136–37 (vol. hereinafter referred to as *Social Struggles*). See nn. 31 and 35.

40. The soundest analysis of the role of the curias and their leaders in the creation at Rome of a king, or other magistrate with imperium, is Palmer, *Archaic Community*, 206–13 (supra n. 22). On the question of *patrum auctoritas*, in addition to Palmer's discussion (189–209, 256–57, 269–72), see also A. Magdelain, "Auspicia ad Patres Redeunt," in *Hommages à J. Bayet*, Collection Latomus, 70 (Brussels, 1964), 427–73.

41. Palmer's description (*Archaic Community*, 218–19 [supra n. 22]) is apt in its assessment of Rome's constitutional situation after the centuriate revolution: "The military organization, ascribed to Servius Tullius, was intended to supplant only the threefold infantry. Beyond its intended aim the centuriate army went forward to the establishment of a constitution based upon their own organization and led by their own elected annual magistrates. Despite their success at a revolution in government the centuries did not abolish the curias nor were they ever technically free from curiate in electing imperial magistrates. All the Quirites, by curias, consented to the bestowal of *imperium* in accordance with the ancestral custom concerning the bestowal of royal suzerainty. The *Populus Romanus Quiritium* had ceased to be merely infantry. Tradition makes it the first organ of Republican government. In the

event there existed two political organs which may be termed constitutions: the centuriate and curiate. And they were not equal because the centuriate *populus* remained the *populus* of the Quirites and still drew its legal warrant for the public action of its officers from the Quirites of the curiate assembly."

42. See Ogilvie, *Early Rome and the Etruscans*, 71–91 (supra n. 4); Ogilvie, *Commentary*, 195–232 (supra n. 2); Alföldi, *Early Rome and the Latins*, 322–28 (supra n. 3); J. Gagé, *La Chute des Tarquins et les débuts de la République romaine* (Paris, 1976), pass.; Scullard, *Etruscan Cities*, 251–53 (supra n. 7); Gantz, "The Tarquin Dynasty," 539–54 (supra n. 21); Heurgon, "Tite-Live et les Tarquins," 56–64 (supra n. 21).

43. Alföldi, *Early Rome and the Latins*, 76–77, 231–35 (supra n. 3). See also Ogilvie, *Commentary*, 230–31, 247–50 (supra n. 2). Alföldi clearly makes the point that Rome's internal events must be viewed in light of happenings in the larger Etruscan ecumene. This does not necessarily disregard, but rather sets in proper perspective, arguments of an aristocratic reaction against the last Tarquin's domestic policies, particularly as those policies may have related to the continued status of the aristocracy. See J.-C. Richard, "Patricians and Plebeians," in *Social Struggles*, 119–23 (vol. supra n. 39); Mitchell, "The Definition of *Patres* and *Plebs*," 136–37 (supra n. 39); and K. A. Raaflaub, "Stages in the Conflict of Orders," in *Social Struggles*, 208–9 (supra n. 39).

44. Alföldi, *Early Rome and the Latins*, 47–84 (supra n. 3); Ogilvie, *Commentary*, 255–71 (supra n. 2); Scullard, *Etruscan Cities*, 261–66 (supra n. 7). See also n. 3.

45. For consideration as to the dependability of the *fasti*, see A. Degrassi's introductory remarks in *Fasti Consulares et Triumphales* in *InscrIt* 13.1.17–20. A recent summary and discussion of views on this topic is R. T. Ridley, "*Fastenkritik: A Stocktaking,*" *Athenaeum* 58 (1980): 264–98. On the problem of the consular lists for the first three years of the Republic, see Alföldi, *Early Rome and the Latins*, 76–84 (supra n. 3).

46. Alföldi's remarks (*Early Rome and the Latins*, 76 [supra n. 3]) are illustrative in this regard: "There emerges one more remarkable fact. If we disregard the invented consulates of the first years of the Republic . . . we find two Etruscans in charge of Roman affairs at the head of the *fasti:* they are *Sp. Larcius* and with him *T. Herminius.* As the descendants of the Larcii did not continue to play any role in Roman politics and as we find in the *fasti* only one more *Herminius* (consul, 448 B.C.), their existence, as well as that of T. Larcius, dictator four years later, cannot be a fictitious invention. Just after the expulsion of the Tarquins they seem to have been confidants of Porsenna. Perhaps there were also other exponents of Porsenna in Rome: the Etruscan *Volumnii, Aquilii, Manlii* who are all at the head of the Roman state in the next decades can only be explained either by the earlier immigration of these clans from southernmost Etruria or by their more recent arrival from Vulci or Clusium. And also, if the cultural influence of Etruria did not end in the first half of the fifth century, this is not due to a supposed continuity of kingship, but to the ties linking Clusium with Rome." On the Larcii and Herminii, see n. 3. See also *MRR* 1:6–7.

47. Ogilvie, *Commentary*, 234 (supra n. 2).

48. On the consular praetor, see K. A. Raaflaub, "A Comprehensive and Comparative Approach," in *Social Struggles*, 25, n. 59 (vol. supra n. 39); Mazzarino, *Della monarchia*, 86–90 (supra n. 34). On the creation of new curias, see Palmer, *Archaic Community*, 138–39, 205 (supra n. 22).

49. See n. 3.

50. J. Kaimio, "The Ousting of Etruscan by Latin in Etruria," in *Studies in the Romanization of Etruria*, ed. P. Bruun et al., Acta Instituti Romani Finlandiae, 5 (Rome, 1975), 113–15.

51. Ibid.; H. Rix, *Das etruskische Cognomen: Untersuchungen zu System, Morphologie, und Verwendung der Personnamen auf den jüngeren Inschriften Nordetruriens* (Wiesbaden, Ger., 1963).

52. R. Syme, *The Roman Revolution* (Oxford, 1939), 93. This paragraph derives almost entirely from a fuller treatment of the topic in Hall, "MAE," 1–12 (supra n. 21).

53. Contrasting views that Etruscan names disappear from the *fasti* in 487 B.C. are expressed in Raaflaub, "Stages in the Conflict of Orders," 232–33 (supra n. 43), and Scullard, *Etruscan Cities*, 266 (supra n. 7), though Scullard does admit to the "temporary reappearance of some Etruscan names in the Fasti in 461–448."

54. See n. 46. Rather than citing all primary evidence for each magistracy noted below, reference will be made instead to *MRR*, where appropriate citations are collected.

55. Though the chief magistracy of the Roman state in the early Republican period was almost certainly known as the consular praetor, in the matter of identifying the office, it is perhaps best to follow Broughton's example (*MRR*) in the use of the conventional title of consul. See also Palmer, *Archaic Community*, 234 (supra n. 22).

56. On the Etruscan origin of the Larcii, see n. 3. Sp. Larcius was consul of 506 B.C. and very likely a lieutenant of Porsenna from Clusium. See *MRR* 1:6–7; *RE* XII, col. 799 no. 4. A probable brother, T. Larcius, was both consul and dictator in the year 501, reiterating both magistracies in 498. See *MRR* 1:9, 11–12; *RE* XII, col. 797 no. 2. See also Ogilvie, *Commentary*, 279 (supra n. 2).

57. Ogilvie, *Commentary*, 272 (supra n. 2), argues for an Etruscan origin for members of the gens during this early period on the basis of D.S. 16.82.3. Schulze (*LE*, 215) identifies the nomen as Etruscan, relating it to the Etruscan *pust-minas*. P. Postumius Tubertus was consul in 505 B.C. and again in 503, when he celebrated a triumph over the Sabines (see *MRR* 1:7–8; *RE* XXII, cols. 948–49 no. 64). Probably a kinsman, perhaps a brother, A. Postumius Regillensis, dictator of 499 B.C., bears an honorific cognomen. On the accuracy of the traditional date for this dictatorship as well as that of T. Larcius (n. 56), see Ogilvie, *Commentary*, 281–82 (supra n. 2).

58. Schulze (*LE*, 100) suggests that the nomen derives from the Etruscan *vercna* and supplies abundant epigraphic attestation of the gens through southern

Etruria. Ogilvie (*Commentary,* 277 [supra n. 2]) posits that the Verginii came to Rome with Tarquin. For a *stemma* of the Verginii Tricosti, prominent by their consulships in the early Republic, see *RE* VIIIA, col. 1519. Opiter Verginius Tricostus was consul in 502 B.C. See *MRR* 1:8; *RE* VIIIA, col. 1525 no. 17. T. Verginius Tricostus, probably a brother or cousin of the consul of 502, served as consul in 496 B.C. See *MRR* 1:12; *RE* VIIIA, col. 1528 no. 21. Another kinsman, A. Verginius Tricostus Caelimontanus, was consul two years later in 494. The *agnomen* of this branch of the family suggests residence on the Caelian hill, and may associate the gens with those Etruscans who accompanied Mastarna and the Vibennae from Vulci and later occupied that mount. For the consul of 494, see *MRR* 1:13; *RE* VIIIA, col. 1518 no. 11.

59. Ogilvie (*Commentary,* 284 [supra n. 2]) acknowledges Schulze's opinion (*LE,* 380) that the Veturii were Etruscan, as well as the fact that the nomen is linked to the quasi-legendary Etruscan smith Mamurius Veturius (Liv. 1.20), but he nevertheless considers the family to be more likely of Sabine origin. Familial lands were at the mouth of the Tiber, and the name of the Voturia tribe—which included Ostia and coastal environs—derived from the gens. Connections to the lower Tiber would be far more likely for an Etruscan gens and quite surprising for Sabines, who are otherwise unknown in this region where Etruscan presence was strong. Literary, onomastic, and epigraphic evidence go against Ogilvie's opinion in this case. The consul of 499 B.C. was P. Veturius Geminus Cicurinus; see *MRR* 1:10; *RE* VIIIA, col. 1892 no. 16. His brother, T. Veturius Geminus Cicurinus, was consul of 494; see *MRR* 1:13–14; *RE* VIIIA, col. 1893 no. 17. R. Gundel proposes a possible stemma for the Veturii Cicurini in *RE* VIIIA, cols. 1883–84.

60. The Aebutii Helvae are identified on grounds of both nomen and cognomen as Etruscan by Ogilvie (*Commentary,* 284 [supra n. 2]), who further associates the Aebutii Helvae with Clusium on the basis of epigraphic evidence. Schulze (*LE,* 279) also identifies the Aebutii as Etruscan. T. Aebutius Helva, consul of 499 B.C., was in all likelihood yet another of Porsenna's men who remained at Rome and led the new government in its earliest years. See *MRR* 1:10–11; *RE* I, col. 443 no. 15.

61. Ogilvie (*Commentary,* 279 [supra n. 2]) and Schulze (*LE,* 279) identify the family as Etruscan. Postumus Cominius was consul of 501 B.C. See *MRR* 1:9; *RE* IV, cols. 608–9 no. 16.

62. See n. 3 on the Etruscan origin of the Herminii. See also *RE* VIII, col. 833. T. Herminius stands at the top of the legitimate *fasti* along with Sp. Larcius as the first consuls at Rome. Surely, like Larcius, Herminius was a trusted lieutenant of Porsenna. Also like the Larcii, the family remained at Rome, as indicated by consular office in subsequent generations. On the consul of 506 B.C., see *MRR* 1:6–7; *RE* VIII, col. 834 no. 2.

63. Schulze (*LE,* 182–83) provides onomastic and epigraphic evidence to demonstrate an Etruscan origin of the gens Lucretia. While Schulze notes Lucretii at Vulci, the evidence may not be sufficient to categorize the Lucretii among Etruscans who followed Servius Tullius to Rome. In any event, the first member of the gens to attain imperial honors was T. Lucretius Tricipitinus, consul of 504 B.C. Apparently

the same individual is identified as both consul and military tribune for 508. Any office attributed before 506 B.C. is problematic, as indicated in nn. 45 and 46, but it is not impossible that Lucretius functioned in some military capacity under Porsenna during the period in question. See *MRR* 1:5, 7; *RE* XIII, cols. 1690–91 no. 31.

64. Ogilvie (*Commentary*, 275 [supra n. 2]) identifies the Menenii as Etruscan, citing Taylor (*VDRR*, 43–48 [supra n. 38]) for corroboration. Agrippa Menenius is identified as consul of 503 B.C., who was victorious in war against the Sabines and celebrated a triumph in that connection, and who as legate in 493 brought to a conclusion the secession of the plebs. See *MRR* 1:8; *RE* XIV, col. 840–43 no. 12.

65. Ogilvie, *Commentary*, 234 (supra n. 2). Ogilvie is essentially correct in this matter, but it should be realized that at this period it may still be more appropriate to describe Rome as a part of Etruria rather than as subservient to it. Indeed, his other remarks in this context about continued relations between Rome and the Etruscan states suggest as much.

66. Sp. Larcius Flavus was consul in 482 B.C.; see *MRR* 1:23. See also n. 56. Postumus Cominius was consul for the second time in 493; see *MRR* 1:14–15.

67. Lars Herminius was the consul of 448 B.C.; see *MRR* 1:50; *RE* VIII, col. 833 no. 1.

68. The Verginii consuls are Proculus Verginius Tricostus, consul of 486 B.C. (*MRR* 1:20; *RE* VIIIA, cols. 1527–28 no. 19); T. Verginius Tricostus, consul of 479 (*MRR* 1:25; *RE* VIIIA, cols. 1529–30 no. 22); Opiter Verginius Esquilinus, suffect consul of 478 and possibly ordinary consul of 473 (*MRR* 1:25–26, 29; *RE* VIIIA, cols. 1525–27 no. 18); A. Verginius Tricostus Rutilius, consul of 476 (*MRR* 1:27; *RE* VIIIA, col. 1522 no. 12); A. Verginius Tricostus Caelimontanus, consul of 469 (*MRR* 1:31–32; *RE* VIIIA, col. 1522 no. 13); Sp. Verginius Tricostus Caelimontanus, consul of 456 (*MRR* 1:41; *RE* VIIIA, col. 1528 no. 20); T. Verginius Tricostus Caelimontanus, consul of 448 (*MRR* 1:50; *RE* VIIIA, col. 1530 no. 23). For a stemma of familial relationships, see *RE* VIIIA, col. 1519.

69. T. Menenius Agrippa Lanatus was consul of 477 B.C. (*MRR* 1:26–27; *RE* XIV, col. 843 no. 14) and his son, also T. Menenius Agrippa Lanatus, was consul in 452 (*MRR* 1:44–45; *RE* XIV, col. 844 no. 18).

70. Sp. Postumius Albus Regillensis was consul of 466 B.C. (*MRR* 1:33; *RE* XXII, col. 932 no. 52b) and his brother, A. Postumius Albus Regillensis, was consul two years later in 464 (*MRR* 1:34; *RE* XXII, col. 932 no. 52a).

71. T. Veturius Geminus Cicurinus was consul in 462 B.C. (*MRR* 1:35–36; *RE* VIIIA, cols. 1893–94 no. 18) and a cousin, C. Veturius Cicurinus, was consul of 455 (*MRR* 1:42; *RE* VIIIA, col. 1889–90 no. 10).

72. Son of the consul and *magister equitum* of 499 B.C., L. Aebutius Helva was consul in 463 (*MRR* 1:34–35; *RE* I, col. 443 no. 11). T. Lucretius Tricipitinus, probably son of the consul of 504 of the same name, was consul in 462 and *praefectus urbi* in 459 (*MRR* 1:35–36, 39; *RE* XIII, cols. 1687–88 no. 28).

73. A convincing case is made by F. Münzer (*RE* XIV, col. 1149) for the Etruscan origin of the gens Manlia: The Manlii at Rome, divided in three collateral

familial branches—Vulsones, Capitolini, and Torquati—are believed to descend from a common ancestor, the consul of 480 B.C., Cn. Manlius Vulso (*MRR* 1:24–25; *RE* XIV, col. 1157 no. 19), whose cognomen betrays the Volsinian origin of this group of Manlii. See also Hall, "MAE," 312–13 (supra n. 21). The consul of 474, A. Manlius Vulso, is identified by Münzer as the son of the consul of 480 (*RE* XIV, cols. 1157–58, col. 1214 no. 89; see also *MRR* 1:28).

74. The Aquilii are associated by Livy (2.3) as playing a leading role in a conspiracy to return Tarquin to the throne in 509 B.C., from which the inference of Etruscan origin may perhaps be drawn. See Ogilvie, *Commentary*, 242–43 (supra n. 2). On other grounds, J. Gagé (*Huit recherches sur les origines italiques et romaines* [Paris, 1950], 119–23) argues for the Etruscan background of the Aquilii. Perhaps most telling, as with the Manlii, is the cognomen by which the family was known at Rome: Tuscus. C. Aquilius Tuscus was consul in 487 (*MRR* 1:19–20).

75. Schulze (*LE*, 269) identifies the nomen as deriving from the Etruscan *atru*, common at Clusium, whence the family may have come to Rome with Porsenna. See Ogilvie, *Commentary*, 447–48 (supra n. 2). The consul of 454 B.C. was A. Aternius Varus Fontinalis (*MRR* 1:42–43; *RE* II, col. 1923).

76. Schulze (*LE*, 368) asserts the derivation of Romilius from the Etruscan nomen *rumlnas* and attributes to the gens an Etruscan origin. T. Romilius Vaticanus was consul of 455 B.C. (*MRR* 1:42; *RE* IA, col. 1071–72 no. 4).

77. Through onomastic and epigraphic evidence Schulze (*LE*, 231) clearly establishes the Etruscan roots of the gens Sicinia. A consul of 487 B.C., T. Sicinius, with a cognomen of either Tuscus or Sabinus, appears as the first member of the clan at Rome to have attained imperium. See *MRR* 1:19–20; *RE* IIA, col. 2198 no. 13.

78. Hall ("MAE," 382–83 [supra n. 21]) contends that the Etruscan nomen *tarchna* "experienced several stages of transmission into Latin represented by the forms Tarcna (*CIL* XI, 3626, 3629, 3633, 7593), perhaps Tarquenna (Var., *R.* 1.2.27), and finally the normalized Latin gentilicia, Tarquinius and Tarquitius (*LE*, 95–96). That Tarquinius and Tarquitius are merely orthographic variants is asserted by Schulze (*LE*, 95) and Schachermeyer (*RE* IVA, col. 2392 no. 2), as well as by Festus' (363L) explanation that the *scalae Tarquitiae* were so named to avoid the form of the *nomen* made infamous by the Tarquinian kings of Rome." L. Tarquitius Flaccus was magister equitum in 458 B.C. (*MRR* 1:40; *RE* IVA, col. 2392 no. 6).

79. The gens Volumnia derives the Latin form of its name from the Etruscan *velimna*. Both Latin and Etruscan gentilicia are widespread in Etruria, as indicated by epigraphic evidence. See *LE*, 258. Ogilvie (*Commmentary*, 415 [supra n. 2]) identifies the Volumnii as a plebeian Etruscan gens with possible ties to Perusia. See also Münzer for corroboration of Etruscan background in *RE* IXA, col. 873. The first member of the family to acquire imperial honors was the consul of 461 B.C., P. Volumnius Amintinus (*MRR* 1:36–37; *RE* IXA, cols. 877–78 no. 10).

80. Etruscan members of the first board of decemviri included T. Veturius Cicurinus, consul of 462 B.C.; A. Manlius Vulso, consul of 474; T. Romilius Vaticanus, consul of 455; and Sp. Postumius Albus Regillensis, consul of 466. The

second board of decemviri included no Etruscan members. See *MRR* 1:45–47. This exclusion of Etruscans perhaps signaled a deteriorating political harmony which ultimately resulted in a curtailment of Etruscan influence with the establishment of the consular tribunate and reassertion of curiate powers.

81. The Etruscan tribunes were C. Licinius (*RE* XIII, col. 218 no. 11), P. Licinius (*RE* XIII, col. 220 no. 25), and L. Sicinius (*RE* IIA, cols. 2195–96 no. 4).

82. Known Verginii tribunes are attested for the years 461, 460, 459, 458, 457, and 449 B.C. (*MRR* 1:37–41, 48, 89). Known Sicinii tribunes appear in the years 493, 492, 491, and 449 (*MRR* 1:15, 17–18, 48). Known Licinii tribunes are identified for the years 493 (two) and 481 (*MRR* 1:15, 24).

83. Ogilvie (*Commentary*, 529 [supra n. 2]) maintains that the Canuleii and the tribune of 445 B.C. were Etruscan, based on Schulze's (*LE*, 152 n. 4) onomastic arguments and substantial epigraphic evidence linking the Canuleii to Volsinii. See also *RE* III, cols. 1499–1500 no. 2.

84. According to Ogilvie (*Commentary*, 303 [supra n. 2]), the Laetorii were Etruscan, based on the evidence of Schulze (*LE*, 187). C. Laetorius was plebeian tribune for 471 B.C. See *MRR* 1:30; *RE* XII, col. 449 no. 1.

85. Ogilvie (*Commentary*, 382 [supra n. 2]) identifies the Maecilli as Etruscan on epigraphic grounds and the evidence of Schulze (*LE*, 185, 204). Tribunes are recorded for the gens in 471 B.C. by Diodorus Siculus (11.68.8, 416). See *MRR* 1:74.

86. See n. 47.

87. Consular tribunes were M. Manlius Capitolinus (*RE* XIV, col. 1167 no. 50) in 434 B.C.; L. Manlius Capitolinus (*RE* XIV, col. 1167 no. 49) in 422; M. Manlius Vulso (*RE* XIV, cols. 1223–24 no. 96) in 420; A. Manlius Vulso Capitolinus (*RE* XIV, cols. 1224–25 no. 100) in 405, 402, and 397; P. Manlius Vulso (*RE* XIV, col. 1224 no. 97) in 400; Q. Manlius Vulso Capitolinus (*RE* XIV, col. 1224 no. 99) in 399; P. Manlius Capitolinus (*RE* XIV, col. 1174–75 no. 52) in 379 and 367, who also served as *dictator seditionis sedandae et rei publicae gerendae causa* in 368; C. Manlius (*RE* XIV, col. 1162 no. 42) in 379; and A. Manlius Capitolinus (*RE* XIV, cols. 1153–54 no. 9) in 389, 387, 385, 383, and 370. M. Manlius Capitolinus (*RE* XIV, cols. 1167–68 no. 51) was consul of the year 392.

88. A. Postumius Tubertus (*RE* XXII, cols. 945–48 no. 63) was magister equitum in 434 B.C. and dictator in 431. Consular tribunes were Sp. Postumius Albus Regillensis (*RE* XXII, col. 932 no. 52) in 432; M. Postumius Albinus Regillensis (*RE* XXII, col. 932 no. 50) in 426 and 401; P. Postumius Albinus Regillensis (*RE* XXII, col. 932 no. 51) in 414; A. Postumius Albinus Regillensis (*RE* XXII, col. 942 no. 57) in 397 and 381; Sp. Postumius (*RE* XXII, col. 900 no. 22) in 394; L. Postumius Albinus Regillensis (*RE* XXII, col. 942 no. 58) in 389 and 381.

89. H. Lucretius Tricipitinus (*RE* XIII, col. 1687 no. 27) was consul of 429 B.C.; P. Lucretius Tricipitinus (*RE* XIII, col. 1688 no. 29) was consular tribune in 419 and 417; L. Lucretius Tricipitinus (*RE* XIII, cols. 1683–84 no. 20) was suffect consul of 393 and consular tribune in 391, 388, 383, and 381.

90. L. Menenius Agrippa Lanatus (*RE* xiv, col. 844 no. 16) was consul in 440 B.C.; Licinus Menenius Lanatus (*RE* xiv, col. 843 no. 15) was consular tribune in 387, 380, 378, and 376.

91. The five consular tribunes of the Veturii were Sp. Veturius (*RE* viiiA, col. 1891 no. 14) in 417 B.C.; M. Veturius Crassus Cicurinus (*RE* viiiA, col. 1891 no. 13) in 399; C. Veturius (*RE* viiiA, col. 1890 no. 11) in 377 and 369; L. Veturius Crassus Cicurinus (*RE* viiiA, col. 1890 no. 12) in 368.

92. L. Verginius Tricostus (*RE* viiiA, col. 1523 no. 14) was consul of 435 B.C. and consular tribune of 434; L. Verginius Tricostus Esquilinus (*RE* viiiA, col. 1524 no. 15) was consular tribune in 402; L. Verginius Tricostus (*RE* viiiA, col. 1524 no. 16) was consular tribune of 389.

93. P. Licinius Calvus Esquilinus (*RE* xiii, col. 234 no. 43) was consular tribune in 400 and 396 B.C. and magister equitum in 368. The author of the Licinian-Sextian rogations, C. Licinius Stolo (*RE* xiii, cols. 464–70 no. 161) was not only plebeian tribune from 376 to 367 but was also consul in 366 and 364.

94. Palmer, *Archaic Community*, 197–202, 243–302 (supra n. 22). See also Magdelain, "Auspicia," 427–73 (supra n. 40); and Last, "Servian Reforms," 30–48 (supra n. 37).

95. Palmer, *Archaic Community*, 247–53 (supra n. 22).

96. Ibid., 218–43.

97. See n. 93.

98. K. von Fritz, "The Reorganisation of the Roman Government in 366 B.C. and the So-called Licinio-Sextian Laws," *Historia* 1 (1950): 3–44; Palmer, *Archaic Community*, 240–49 (supra n. 22).

99. See nn. 87 and 93.

100. See n. 64.

101. Contrast Richard, "Patricians and Plebeians," 124–25 (supra n. 43).

102. This process and its constituent events are best detailed by W. V. Harris, *Rome in Etruria and Umbria* (Oxford, 1971), 41–146. See also 147–201 for a thorough treatment of the Romanization of Etruscan society during the period from 284 to 91 B.C.

103. Aside from "MAE" (supra n. 21), which deals exclusively with this topic, my published articles on the same theme include: "L. Marcius Phillipus and the Rise of Octavian Caesar," *AugAge* 5 (1986): 37–43; "The *Saeculum Novum* of Augustus and Its Etruscan Antecedents," *ANRW* ii.16.3 (1986): 2564–89; "P. Vergilius Maro: *Vates Etruscus*," *Vergilius* 28 (1982): 44–50.

104. Citizenship was, of course, granted to Italy through the provisions of the *Lex Calpurnia* and *Lex Iulia* of 90 B.C. and the *Lex Plautia Papiria* of 89, of which distinctions in purpose and effect, especially as pertained to Etruria, are discussed by Harris (*Rome in Etruria*, 230–31 [supra n. 102]). Etruscan citizenship seems to have been granted by the *Lex Iulia*. See, in addition to Harris, A. N. Sherwin-White, *The Roman Citizenship* (Oxford, 1939), 132–34.

105. The nomen is patently Etruscan and the gens was well known as Etruscan. See *LE*, 88; Harris, *Rome in Etruria*, 323 (supra n. 102); Taylor, *VDRR*, 180 (supra n. 38); M. Torelli, "Senatori etruschi della tarda reppublica e dell'impero," *DArch* 3 (1969): 325; Hall, "MAE," 334–39 (supra n. 21). The consuls are father and son, M. Perperna being the consul of 130 B.C. and M. Perperna the consul of 92. See *MRR* 1:501–4; 2:17, 54; *RE* XIX, cols. 894–96 nos. 4, 5 [Münzer]. Another son of the elder Perperna, C. Perperna, was praetor before 91. See *MRR* 2:20; *RE* XIX, col. 893 no. 2.

106. On the evidence of V.Max. 4.8.9, which associates the family with the ager Veientanus, Taylor (*VDRR*, 186–87 [supra n. 38]), followed by I. Shatzman (*Senatorial Wealth and Roman Politics*, Collection Latomus, 142 [Brussels, 1975], 240), identifies the Aelii Tuberones as Veientane. Several members of the gens held magisterial office in the second century B.C., including the praetor urbanus of 177 (*MRR* 1:316; *RE* I, col. 535 no. 152), as well as the tribunes of 194, 177, and 132 (*MRR* 1:345, 398, 502; see also *RE* I, col. 535 nos. 153, 154, 155).

107. On the Etruscan origin of the gens, see *LE*, 108, 142, 191. For the placement of the Licinii Sacerdotes in the ager Veientanus, see Hall, "MAE," 301–4 (supra n. 21).

108. The Caeretane origin of the family is demonstrated by R. Syme, "Senators, Tribes, and Towns," *Historia* 13 (1964): 110; and Torelli, "Senatori etruschi," 319 (supra n. 105). See also *LE*, 109. M. Aburius (*MRR* 1:369, 400) was plebeian tribune in 187 B.C. and peregrine praetor in 176. For other Aburii active in politics at Rome, see Hall, "MAE," 177–78 (supra n. 21).

109. Strong epigraphic evidence places the Campatii in Caere; see Torelli, "Senatori etruschi," 320 (supra n. 105); *LE*, 115.

110. On the branch of the gens at Caere, see Torelli, "Senatori etruschi," 321 (supra n. 105); *LE*, 188; E. Badian, "Notes on Roman Senators of the Republic," *Historia* 12 (1963): 133; Hall, "MAE," 270–74 (supra n. 21).

111. E. Rawson, "L. Cornelius Sisenna and the Early First Century," *CQ* 29 (1979): 327–30, posits the Etruscan origin of the Cornelii Sisennae, who, upon their receipt of citizenship through the intervention of the Cornelii Scipiones, moved their gentilicium to cognominal position, replacing it with a new nomen borrowed from their Cornelian patrons. On the role of the family in Roman public affairs and offices filled by Sisennae, see Hall, "MAE," 254–58 (supra n. 21).

112. The senatorial rank of T. Numisius Tarquiniensis (*RE* XVII, col. 1400 no. 10) in 169 B.C. suggests early enfranchisement of a Tarquinian branch of the gens. See Torelli, "Senatori etruschi," 314 (supra n. 105); Harris, *Rome in Etruria*, 327 (supra n. 102); Taylor, *VDRR*, 238 (supra n. 38).

113. Harris (*Rome in Etruria*, 322–23 [supra n. 102]) identifies the Nigidii as of Etruscan origin, probably deriving from Perusia. See also Hall, "MAE," 316–17.

114. The family is linked to Perusia by *CIL* XI, 1944, an inscription dating to the second century B.C. Its pre–Social War enfranchisement is confirmed by the presence of filiation in the nomenclature of C. Vibius Pansa, *triumvir monetalis*

of 90 B.C. See *RRC*, 346–48. See also Harris, *Rome in Etruria*, 249, 324–25 (supra n. 102); Torelli, "Senatori etruschi," 302–3 (supra n. 105); Hall, "MAE," 407–10 (supra n. 21). For more on C. Vibius Pansa and his Etruscan connections, see, in this volume, the essay by Helena Fracchia, 196 ff. and n. 17.

115. Torelli ("Senatori etruschi," 303–4 [supra n. 105]) and Harris (*Rome in Etruria*, 325 [supra n. 102]) agree with the conclusion in various articles of R. Syme—"Personal Names in Annals i–vi," *JRS* 39 (1949): 15; "Ten Tribunes," *JRS* 53 (1963): 59–60; "Missing Persons iii," *Historia* 11 (1962): 152; "Senators, Tribes, and Towns," 125 (supra n. 108)—regarding the Perusine origin and the enfranchisement of the family.

116. Syme (*Roman Revolution*, 200 [supra n. 52]) suggests an Etruscan origin against Münzer's view of an ethnic gentilicium, as advanced in *RE* xvii, col. 927 no. 5. The enfranchisement and Marian connections of the gens is most thoroughly treated in E. Badian, "Caepio and Norbanus," *Historia* 6 (1957): 318–46. See also Hall, "MAE," 318–21 (supra n. 21).

117. The Etruscan origin of the Carrinates and their reception of the franchise before the Social War is explored in Harris, *Rome in Etruria*, 319–21 (supra n. 102). See also Hall, "MAE," 234–37 (supra n. 21).

118. The prominent banking family of the late Republic is linked to Volaterra on the evidence of Cic., *Fam.* 13.5. Hall ("MAE," 263–64 [supra n. 21]) argues that Marian connections are established through the prosecutor Curtius, proscribed with other Marians in 82 B.C.

119. See Harris, *Rome in Etruria*, 202–50 (supra n. 102); Hall, "MAE," 16–57 (supra n. 21). See also A. J. Pfiffig, *Die Ausbreitung des römischen Stadtwesens in Etrurien und die Frage der Unterwerfung der Etrusker* (Florence, 1966); M. Sordi, *I rapporti romano-ceriti e l'origine della civitas sine suffragio* (Rome, 1960).

120. Harris, *Rome in Etruria*, 251–71 (supra n. 102); Hall, "MAE," 66–90 (supra n. 21). See also E. Gabba, "Le origini della guerra sociale e la vita politica romana dopo l'89 a.C.," *Athenaeum* 32 (1954): 41–114, 293–345.

121. Harris, *Rome in Etruria*, 271–94 (supra n. 102); Hall, "MAE," 101–10 (supra n. 21).

122. Torelli, "Senatori etruschi," 285 (supra n. 105).

123. E. Rawson, "Caesar, Etruria, and the *Disciplina Etrusca*," *JRS* 68 (1978): 132–52. E. Badian, *Foreign Clientelae 264–70 B.C.* (Oxford, 1958), 246–48; R. Syme, "Caesar, the Senate, and Italy," *PBSR* 14 (1938): 1–31.

124. Rawson, "Caesar, Etruria," 148–50 (supra n. 123); Harris, *Rome in Etruria*, 296–97 (supra n. 102); D. R. Shackleton-Bailey, "The Roman Nobility in the Second Civil War," *CQ* 10 (1960): 260–67.

125. While there is evidence for only scant ancestral connection of the Iulii Caesares to Etruria, it should be noted that Caesar's father died in 85 B.C. at Pisa, where he was acting as Cinnan legate and had very likely cultivated local ties. For Caesar himself, a direct personal link to Pisa and Etruria is to be found in his first

marriage to Cossutia, daughter of a wealthy Etruscan family of Pisa. See L. R. Taylor, "Caesar's Early Career," *CPh* 36 (1941): 113–32; Badian, "Caepio and Norbanus," 345 (supra n. 116); Hall, "MAE," 258–60 (supra n. 21).

126. On Carrinas (*RE* III, col. 1612 no. 2), see *PIR²*, c 447; Hall, "MAE," 236–37 (supra n. 21). On Norbanus Flaccus (*RE* XVII, col. 930 no. 6, col. 934 no. 9a), see Syme, *Roman Revolution*, 200 (supra n. 52); Hall, "MAE," 318–22 (supra n. 21).

127. T. P. Wiseman, *New Men in the Roman Senate, 139 B.C.–14 A.D.* (Oxford, 1971), 213; *PIR²*, A 960; Hall, "MAE," 190–92 (supra n. 21).

128. Cic., *Fam.* 13.5; Wiseman, *New Men*, 218 (supra n. 127); Hall, "MAE," 263–65 (supra n. 21). See also *RE* IV, col. 1864 no. 6.

129. M. Gelzer (*Caesar: Politician and Statesman* [Cambridge, Mass., 1968], 273) discusses the composition of Caesar's personal staff and describes their function as virtual "cabinet ministers, handling and settling all political business." For Rabirius, see *RE* IA, col. 25 no. 6; Hall, "MAE," 266–68 (supra n. 21).

130. Harris, *Rome in Etruria*, 324–25 (supra n. 102); Hall, "MAE," 409–11 (supra n. 21); *RE* VIIIA, col. 1953 no. 16.

131. Arguments asserting Etruscan provenience for Matius are offered by Shackleton-Bailey, "Roman Nobility," 265 (supra n. 124); Rawson, "Caesar, Etruria," 151 (supra n. 123).

132. Syme, *Roman Revolution*, 132 (supra n. 52); Torelli, "Senatori etruschi," 312 (supra n. 105); Hall, "MAE," 225–26 (supra n. 21); *RE* III, col. 1307 no. 6.

133. On the Etruscan origin of the family, see Hall, "MAE," 293–94 (supra n. 21); contrast Wiseman, *New Men*, 235 (supra n. 127). C. and P. Saserna were legates of Caesar. See Rawson, "Caesar, Etruria," 151 (supra n. 123); *RE* VIII, col. 2513 nos. 22, 24.

134. Torelli, "Senatori etruschi," 228 (supra n. 105); Rawson, "Caesar, Etruria," 151 (supra n. 123); Hall, "MAE," 399–400 (supra n. 21); *RE* VIIIA, col. 820 no. 3.

135. Wiseman, *New Men*, 221 (supra n. 127); Hall, "MAE," 233–34 (supra n. 21); *RE* III, col. 1589.

136. Wiseman, *New Men*, 224 (supra n. 127); Rawson, "Caesar, Etruria," 151 (supra n. 123); Hall, "MAE," 238–42 (supra n. 21); *PIR²*, c 686–87; *RE* III, col. 2004 nos. 2, 4, 5, 7.

137. Wiseman, *New Men*, 229 (supra n. 127); Hall, "MAE," 262–63 (supra n. 21); *RE* IV, col. 1724 no. 1.

138. The role of Spurinna and his connections is ambiguous. The problem is treated in detail by Rawson, "Caesar, Etruria," 143–45 (supra n. 123).

139. See Hall, "MAE," 128–75 (supra n. 21), and the publications listed in n. 103.

140. On Maecenas, other Maecenates, and the Cilnii, see Harris, *Rome in Etruria*, 320–21 (supra n. 102); Badian, *Foreign Clientelae*, 223 (supra n. 123); Hall,

"MAE," 306–12 (supra n. 21); Hall, "L. Marcius Philippus," 37–439 (supra n. 103). Maecenas is treated in detail in the essay, in this volume, by Roger T. Macfarlane, 245 ff. A portrait bust of Maecenas appears as fig. 2 on 246.

141. Hall, "P. Vergilius Maro," 44–50 (supra n. 103); Hall, "MAE," 401–3 (supra n. 21).

142. Hall, "MAE," 349–51 (supra n. 21).

143. On the Ancharii and Ancharia, see Harris, *Rome in Etruria*, 326 (supra n. 102); Torelli, "Senatori etruschi," 323 (supra n. 105); Hall, "MAE," 185–87 (supra n. 21). For Ancharia, mother of Octavia, see *RE* 1, col. 2102 no. 7. For the Appuleii, see Wiseman, *New Men*, 213 (supra n. 127); Hall, "MAE," 190–95 (supra n. 21). For the husband of Octavia, Sex. Appuleius, see *PIR*², A 960.

144. See nn. 129 and 131.

145. Caecina's identity has been variously conjectured by modern commentators; see, for example, Taylor, *VDRR*, 198–99 (supra n. 38). Torelli ("Senatori etruschi," n. 43 [supra n. 105]), offers a restoration of the fragmentary inscriptions *CIL* xi, 6689.54, and *AnnEpigr* (1957): 220 = *NSA* (1955): 123, which suggests the conjecture (Hall, "MAE," 210–13 [supra n. 21]) that he was an A. Caecina Largus, father of A. Caecina Severus, the consul of 1 B.C. (*RE* iii, col. 1241 no. 24; *PIR*², C 106); see also Hall, "MAE," 204–15 (supra n. 21).

146. See n. 126.

147. An alliance between the two may have been struck when both were in Campania following Caesar's death (Cic., *Att.* 14.11.2). Nicolaus of Damascus (*FGrHist*, 90, F 130, 107–9) identifies Pansa as a supporter of Octavian, as is also implied in App., *BC* 3.75–76. See Hall, "MAE," 409–12 (supra n. 21). See also n. 114.

148. On the minting, see *RRC*, 500. See also n. 136.

149. App., *BC* 4.130 records the role of Norbanus at Philippi. See also nn. 116 and 126.

150. M. Sordi ("Ottaviano e l'Etruria nel 44 a.C.," *SE* 40 [1972]: 2–17; see esp. 13–16) advances the argument for a strong Etruscan element in Octavian's army, including a largely Etruscan praetorian cohort, formed after the annihilation of Octavian's first praetorian cohort in fighting at Mutina and the forerunner of the later praetorian guard which, according to Tacitus (*Ann.* 4.5.5), both continued to reflect heavy Etruscan constituency and was organized and first directed by Maecenas, in the opinion of A. Passerini (*Le corti pretorie*, 2d ed. [Rome, 1969]).

151. See n. 135. "Carfulenus was a plebeian tribune in 44, apparently opposed to Antony since he was excluded from the November 28 meeting of the Senate to prevent his casting a veto (Cic., *Phil.* 3.23; *Att.* 15.4.1), and by inference a supporter of Octavian. In fact, his ties to Octavian are made clear by his command of the *legio Martia* as legate of Octavia at Mutina in 43, where Carfulenus perished (Cic., *Fam.* 10.33.4)." Hall, "MAE," 234 (supra n. 21).

152. The gens Vipsania has been assigned various proveniences by scholars; V. Gardthausen (*Augustus und seine Zeit* [Leipzig, 1891], 1:736, 2:409) makes it Etruscan. Onomastic theory points to the Etruscan *visanie* and its orthographic variant *visnie*, both with significant epigraphic attestation, as possible antecedents for the nomen Vipsanius, according to *LE*, 256. Further credence is added to Gardthausen's thesis of the Etruscan origin of the Vipsanii Agrippa by R. E. A. Palmer, "On the Track of the Ignoble," *Athenaeum* 61 (1983): 350, which adduces sufficient circumstantial evidence to argue for deriving M. Agrippa from Pisa, on the basis of the honorific dedications erected to Agrippa's sons and Augustus' grandsons and adopted sons, C. and L. Caesar (*CIL* XI, 1420–21). For Agrippa's role in the rise of Octavian and in the Augustan regime, see Syme, *Roman Revolution*, pass. (supra n. 52); Hall, "MAE," 412–17 (supra n. 21); *RE* IXA, col. 1226–79; *PIR²*, V 457.

153. Hall, "MAE," 128–46 (supra n. 21).

154. Ibid., 192–93 (supra n. 21); *RE* II, col. 258 no. 17; *PIR²*, A 961.

155. Hall, "MAE," 193–94 (supra n. 21); *RE* II, col. 258 no. 4; *PIR²*, A 959.

156. Hall, "MAE," 322–24 (supra n. 21); *RE* XVII, col. 932 no. 9.

157. See n. 145.

158. See Torelli, "Senatori etruschi," 295–96 (supra n. 105) for his relationship to "quidam Caecina Volaterranus," and R. Syme, "The Consuls of A.D. 13," *JRS* 56 (1966): 55–60, for proper identification and nomenclature. See also Hall, "MAE," 216–17 (supra n. 21).

159. Torelli, "Senatori etruschi," 296 (supra n. 105); Hall, "MAE," 215–16 (supra n. 21); *RE* III, col. 1238 no. 8; *PIR²*, C 97.

160. Hall, "MAE," 323–24 (supra n. 21); *RE* XVII, col. 931 no. 8, col. 934 no. 10.

161. Hall, "MAE," 194 (supra n. 21); *RE* II, col. 258 no. 18; *PIR²*, A 962.

162. Hall, "MAE," 289–92 (supra n. 21); *RE* VII, col. 2513 no. 3; *PIR²*, H 24.

163. Hall, "MAE," 182–83 (supra n. 21); *PIR²*, A 157, 274; *RE* I, col. 534 no. 157.

164. On the relation of Strabo and Maecenas, note Syme, *Roman Revolution*, 358 and appendix VI (supra n. 52). For the possibility of family ties between the Aelii Tuberones and the Seii, as suggested by the nomenclature of Strabo's sons Seius Tubero and Aelius Seianus, see the contrastive articles of F. Adams, "The Consular Brothers of Sejanus," *AJPh* 76 (1955): 70–76, and G. V. Sumner, "The Family Connections of L. Aelius Seianus," *Phoenix* 19 (1965): 134–45. See also Hall, "MAE," 365–76 (supra n. 21); *RE* IIA, col. 1125 no. 15.

165. R. E. A. Palmer, "Roman Shrines of Female Chastity from the Caste Struggle to the Papacy of Innocent I," *RSA* 4 (1974): 154–55. The stemma in *PIR*, 487, is very much in error; a corrected and updated genealogy of the Volusii Saturnini is available in F. Coarelli, "I praedia Volusiana e l'albero genealogico dei Volusii Saturnini," in *I Volusii Saturnini: Una famiglia romana della prima età imperiale*,

Archeologia, materiali e problemi, 6 (Bari, It., 1982), 37–44. See *RE* Sup. IX, col. 1857 no. 16, col. 1861 no. 17. See also Hall, "MAE," 430–36 (supra n. 21).

166. Palmer, "Roman Shrines," 155 (supra n. 165); Wiseman, *New Men,* 259 (supra n. 127); Hall, "MAE," 358–60 (supra n. 21); *RE* IA, col. 2023 no. 16.

167. Petronius would have been praetor under Augustus in order to qualify for his A.D. 19 consulate. See Hall, "MAE," 341–45 (supra n. 21). Urgulania's own son, M. Plautius Silvanus, consul of 2 B.C. (*RE* XXI, col. 30 no. 43) was helped to attain consular rank through the friendship of Livia and Urgulania and could, perhaps, because of his maternal lineage, be numbered with those of Etruscan descent who advanced under Augustus; see Torelli, "Senatori etruschi," 329, 336–37 (supra n. 105). For Urgulania, see *RE* Sup. IX, col. 1868. See also Hall, "MAE," 397–98 (supra n. 21).

168. For the long list of extraordinary honors accorded the young princes, see *PIR*², I 216, 222.

169. For a summary of this information, see Hall, "MAE," 155–58 (supra n. 21).

Etruscan and Roman Cortona: New Evidence from the Southeastern Val di Chiana

Helena Fracchia

Despite ample and largely inconclusive discussion about the mythological origins of Cortona in the province of Arezzo, very little is known materially about this Etruscan and then Roman town or its territory.[1] Until very recently, the archaeological evidence for Etruscan Cortona consisted of five large burial tumuli on the hillsides around the modern town (figure 2) and numerous sporadic finds of bronze or pottery, also extramural for the most part. The Università di Perugia, under the direction of M. Torelli, is now conducting excavations in the center of Cortona, and hopefully more evidence will emerge: to date, the remains of a Villanovan hut have been recovered and one of the gates has been dated to circa the fourth century B.C. Other traces of Villanovan frequentation have been found on the hillsides around the present town and in the plain below. At the present time, enough cumulative evidence exists from recent excavations, surveys, older studies, and archives to suggest that the lower slopes of the southeastern Val di Chiana were densely inhabited throughout the Etruscan period, both before and after the establishment of Cortona as an urban center in the fourth century B.C. Taken in combination, the evidence from these sources suggests certain working hypotheses about Etruscan and Roman settlement patterns evident in Cortona, as well as Roman

FIGURE 1. Detail of polychrome mosaic, excavation area 1, Ossaia. *Photo from excavation archive.*

| 191 |

use and reuse of Etruscan monuments, sites, and motifs. The Roman appreciation of and emphasis on various aspects of Etruscan society can be seen across Etruria, although southern Etruria was affected earlier than other areas further from Rome itself. Romanized Etruscans were admitted to the Roman Senate in large numbers under Augustus and then often dedicated architectural or sculptural monuments to their city of origin. Those dedications reflected the Roman status of the benefactor in the new Roman order. Additionally, many of the Etruscan cities were given a mythological Trojan founder, thus linking those cities to the Aeneas-Anchises foundation legend of Rome.

Several years ago Dr. F. Nicosia, archaeological superintendent for Tuscany, excavated—or, more accurately, reinitiated investigations at—the second tumulus of the so-called Sodo at the foot of the Cortona hill, along the Camucia-Arezzo road. During the renewed excavations, this second tumulus turned out to be extremely large and rich in information, although early investigations by A. Minto in the later 1920s and 1930s had been abandoned because nothing had been found: a small portion of the original tumulus plan was recovered.[2]

FIGURE 2. View of Cortona from the site at Ossaia. *Photo from excavation archive.*

The tumulus, although still in the course of excavation, has been the subject of a preliminary presentation by P. Zamarchi Grassi in the exhibition *La Cortona dei principes*.[3] It contains burials dating from the Orientalizing to the Hellenistic periods which show evidence of reuse in Roman times. There is also a monumental stepped altar decorated with sculptures of beasts or monsters embracing men and a parapet consisting of an alternation of three-part molding and large palmettes. The altar sits opposite the area excavated by Minto, is five meters wide by nine meters long, and apparently was used exclusively for cultic activities and not for access to the upper part of the tumulus. The sculptures flanking the steps are badly preserved: the beasts may be lions or sphinxes. One clutches a kneeling warrior who tries to stab the belly of the beast; the other—in worse condition—carries a similar if not exactly parallel scene. The altar faces the present town of Cortona and may have served as the terminus of a funerary procession for the *princeps* buried there. The construction date of this monumental tumulus was most probably in the first half of the sixth century B.C., on the basis of ceramic evidence datable to about 580 B.C. It is at this time not possible to identify the occupant or occupants, nor do we know for how long the "continuum di generazioni" was carried on, to use G. Colonna's phrase;[4] but, since the tumulus evidently was that of a local princeps, its reuse in Roman times may be interpreted as an attempt to "reappropriate" or share that ancient prestige.[5] This sharing of the burial prestige is not unlike other types of religious or legend sharing between the Etruscan *principes* and Rome, dating from as early as the era of Rome's Etruscan kings. For example, augury and haruspicy were the religious responsibility of the Etruscan aristocratic families, and prominent Romans appropriated the titles *augur* and *haruspex* in a clear attempt to share the ancient culture and prestige of the families.[6] An illustration of the persistence of this prestige sharing can be seen in the first coins of Octavian/Augustus, issued in 43 B.C., on which he uses the title *aug(ur)*.[7] Another example is the attempt to share or appropriate legendary origins of Trojan ancestors particularly.[8]

In addition to the architectural magnificence of the tomb, the date, number, and wealth of the various burial chambers provide new, if still largely circumstantial, information about Etruscan Cortona. As stated at the outset, very little is known about the actual Etruscan city.[9] The altar probably did face the city, but the actual physical existence and location of Cortona as an "urban center" in the Archaic period can hardly be established from this slim evidence. In addition, the altar is oriented east-west, with the steps at the front toward the east. It is extremely difficult to believe that the tumulus existed without at least a nuclear habitation nearby, and we should not rule out the possibility of capillary settlements of either small groups of habitations or isolated habitations in the surrounding territory, for which neighboring Chiusi provides ample evidence.[10] A look at the most recent archaeological maps gives a very clear picture of the possible number of small nuclei (figure 3).[11] Most of the sites have not been excavated and are known from the archival evidence, from local informants, or from reconnaissance limited to the immediate site indicated. A major problem in creating a complete archaeological overview of the area is that the southeastern portion of the Val di Chiana directly in front of the Ossaia site once again became a swamp in the seventeenth and eighteenth centuries after the breakdown of the Etruscan drainage system which had functioned for centuries.[12] Obviously, any archaeological evidence in that particular section of the Val di Chiana is hidden under meters of colluvium. Nonetheless, the number of material finds in the area indicates that the occupation of the countryside was well advanced by the sixth century B.C., and the presence of this second and much larger tumulus at the so-called Sodo strongly suggests that there is a habitation nucleus nearby.[13] Several years ago, the presence of an extraurban Etruscan sanctuary of Hellenistic date was postulated south of the tumulus toward the Lago Trasimeno (Trasimene Lake) on the basis of a large quantity of badly destroyed architectural terracottas found there; this would add an element of importance in that period to the lower areas surrounding the town of Cortona. Lastly, the collaborative ongoing excavations and survey being made by the University of Alberta and the Università di Perugia at the Roman villa-*vicus* complex at La Tufa in the Ossaia area between the Trasimene Lake and Cortona have furnished substantial evidence for the Etruscan and Roman settlement pattern in the southeastern Val di Chiana, both

FIGURE 3. Archaeological map of the Cortona region. *Compiled by author.*

during the progressive Romanization of the area and during the Roman period itself.[14]

After two years of excavation, the evidence from Ossaia indicates continuous Roman use of the La Tufa site from the late second or early first century B.C. through the fifth century A.D., with Etruscan sporadic finds datable from the fourth and third centuries B.C. and earlier, and other finds datable to the twelfth and thirteenth centuries A.D. The sprawling site covers an area of approximately three hectares. In order to determine its full extent and its functional and chronological development, several areas have been excavated at some distance from each other and at different altitudes along the terrace which dominates the southeastern Val di Chiana; the immediate area of the entire site has also been surveyed. At this point one of the working hypotheses is that in the late Republican and Augustan periods the original second-century B.C. buildings on the site were incorporated into a villa. In the later second and third centuries A.D., the villa formed the focal point of a vicus, which grew up around these pre-existing structures.

The evidence from the villa complex consists of well-preserved architectural remains, including mosaic floors dating to both the late Republican and the Augustan periods as well as to the later second and third centuries A.D.; several wall paintings; marble sculpture; Italian *terra sigillata*, African red slip, and *terra sigillata chiara medio-adriatica* pottery; and, to date, three stamped bricks. One brick bears the name *C. Vibius* (figure 4); a second carries the name *A. Gelli Potni* (figure 5); while the third displays the name *Caesarum*, referring to Lucius and Gaius Caesar, the grandchildren of Augustus (figure 6).[15] A second *Caesarum* stamped brick from the Cortona area is also known;[16] both stamps provide evidence for a kiln on an imperial property. On the basis of the simple rectangular form of the stamp itself and the letter forms, the name *C. Vibius* most probably refers to the C. Vibius C. F. Pansa Caetronianus who was the consul of 43 B.C. and who died at Forum Gallorum before the battle of Modena. The Vibii family is believed to have bequeathed their property to Lucius and Gaius Caesar.[17] Both *Caesarum* brick stamps support this idea of a legacy. Two generations of the Vibii Pansae family were moneyers, and on the basis of the coin devices that they used there is also some

FIGURE 4. *C. Vibius* brick stamp. *Photo from excavation archive.*

FIGURE 5. *A. Gelli Potni* brick stamp. *Photo from excavation archive.*

FIGURE 6. *Caesarum* brick stamp. *Photo from excavation archive.*

reason to connect them with Terracina[18] as well as now with Cortona: they seem to be of Perusian origin.[19]

Although the Roman period in Cortona is not well known either archaeologically or from written sources, Livy asserts that by 310 B.C. Cortona, along with Perusia and Arretium, had made peace with Rome.[20] At the Ossaia site, the black-glaze pottery that first marks the Roman use of the neighborhood is datable to the later second to first centuries B.C. It is not found in great quantities, and it can probably be assumed that at this point the site was a small farmhouse, quite possibly like that of Poggio Bacherina near Chiusi, which consisted of two rooms around a courtyard and very few finds.[21]

Certainly the statue of the *Arringatore*—the Orator—with the Etruscan name *Aule Meteli* inscribed on its toga hem, which might have been found nearby at Sanguineto,[22] as well as the known existence of Cortona citizen C. Metellius (perhaps a relative of Aule Meteli), a praetor in the Etruscan League, testifies to the continuing importance of the local Etruscan aristocracy during Republican and Augustan times.[23] The continuity, however, seems to be limited to local offices: no Roman senators are known to be from Cortona itself.[24] Despite this absence of senatorial families, the vitality of northern inland Etruria in general is confirmed by the continuity between its ancient, medieval, and modern settlements, of which Cortona provides an excellent example. The presence of an imperial property at Ossaia, near one of the founding cities of the original Etruscan League, is in the spirit of Augustus' reconstruction of the *Lega Etrusca* and in keeping with his general attachment to the area of Arretium—both militarily, due to his successful recruitment of soldiers in the area in 44 B.C., and personally, through his friendship with the Arretine Maecenas. Additionally, the increased admission of families from both Perusia and Arretium into the senatorial rolls during the Augustan age is well documented.[25] It is generally recognized that the connection between the Etruscan aristocratic *gentes* and the Roman aristocracy was strengthened substantially during the Augustan period.[26] Furthermore, Livy tells us that at the end of the fourth century B.C. Arretium and Perusia were practically *capita Etruriae populorum*.[27] Cortona is located right in the border area between these two cities, on the cusp between Umbria and Etruria: it is in this general region where Augustus himself locates the origins of his personal ideology.[28]

On the other hand, whatever political ties and affection Octavian/Augustus may have had for the area and for Maecenas must have been sorely tried during the Perusine wars in the late 40s B.C. As Colonna notes, not only did his friendship with Maecenas suffer after this period but so did the fortunes of Propertius.[29] In fact, curiously, Octavian/Augustus dropped the title of *augur* from his coins after 43 B.C.[30] The reasons for this action are unclear, but could it have been a reaction to the Perusine wars? The Vibii Pansae are believed to have been one of two families from Perusia who obtained Roman citizenship by about 100 B.C.[31] Despite this precocious citizenship and allegiance to Rome, it may be that the bequest of the Vibii Pansae property to the adopted grandchildren of Augustus was not so much an acknowledgment and appreciation of Augustus' political reconstruction of the Etruscan League and his general Etruscan interests as it was an attempt to consolidate the family's standing with the emperor after the Perusine wars. Presumably, the property was bequeathed to the Caesares after 17 B.C., when the young boys were adopted by Augustus. The boys did have an Etruscan connection through their father, Agrippa; but his city was Pisa and not Cortona.

Although the Republican villa at the Ossaia site spread over the two partially artificial terraces on which excavation has begun, the actual nucleus of the early villa is concentrated in the higher terrace (figure 7). Just which architecture pertains to the early phase is still unclear because of the considerable later reuse and evident change in function that occurred in this portion of the villa, but to date several rooms have been uncovered which have black-and-white mosaic floors. The rooms extend over a large distance on this higher terrace. The best preserved mosaic is composed of a black-and-white lozenge pattern (figure 8). A more fragmentary bit of black-and-white checkerboard mosaic has been found nearby (figure 9). Both are related by date and level to another black-and-white *pelta* design mosaic preserved under a nearby house (figure 10). In addition to the abundance of Italian terra sigillata pottery, the *Caesarum* brick stamp was also found in the same area.

FIGURE 7. Overview of upper terrace, excavation area 2. *Photo from excavation archive.*

FIGURE 8. Black-and-white lozenge mosaic, excavation area 2. *Photo from excavation archive.*

FIGURE 9. Black-and-white checkerboard mosaic, excavation area 2. *Photo from excavation archive.*

FIGURE 10. Black-and-white pelta design mosaic under house near excavation site. *Photo from excavation archive.*

A small sculptural head (figure 11), executed in island marble (possibly Parian) in the fully "pathetic" late Hellenistic style and reminiscent (in miniature) of the Sperlonga statues, was found near the lozenge mosaic. The Sperlonga fragments constitute four mythological groups depicting such stories of Greek heroes as Menelaos and Patroklos, Diomedes and Odysseus, other adventures of Odysseus, and Polyphemos. The groups were found in a grotto on the grounds of the villa of Tiberius, although they may have belonged to the previous owner. They reflect the popularity of the mythological cycles pertaining to both the Greek heroes and the Trojan wars. In view of the similarity in style, it is tempting to identify this sculptural head from Ossaia as Odysseus or some other Trojan hero—for example, Dardanos, who has also been associated with Cortona[32]—since Cortona is linked to the Trojan cycle by Vergil and Silius Italicus, both of whom glorified the town and its legendary origins. Vergil himself does not identify Corthyus as Cortona,[33] but Silius Italicus does, and he uses the names interchangeably; going even further, he makes Cortona the headquarters of the hero Tarchon.[34] Theopompus and

FIGURE 11. Late Hellenistic head, marble, excavation area 2. *Photo from excavation archive.*

Lycophron bring Odysseus to Etruria and then to Cortona.[35] According to Theopompus, Odysseus also died and was buried there. It is curious that Cortona, essentially unknown and without any famous senatorial families, should have been emphasized rather than either Perusia, home to a number of senatorial families and families granted citizenship before the Social Wars, or Arretium, birthplace of Maecenas. Both Vergil and Livy praise Etruria and Umbria such that we might expect that at least one of these two major Etruscan cities would have been named.[36] Still, Arretium did not have a legendary past as one of the twelve founding cities of the Etruscan League; and, according to Colonna, Vergil would not have invented a lineage—nor would that have been flattering to Maecenas.[37] Colonna postulates that Vergil wanted to praise Maecenas' region but also wanted to avoid mentioning Perusia because of the recent Perusine wars. Whatever the reasons may be for the distinction given to Cortona, a Trojan hero—possibly Dardanos or Tarchon—was believed to be the town's legendary founder; and the date of the sculpted head found there corresponds to the period of the Augustan restoration of the Etruscan League. If, therefore, the head did represent one of the Trojans, it would be ideologically appropriate. It is worth remarking again that the Vibii Pansae are also known to have had links with the Terracina/Sperlonga area (see p. 198).

Despite the later reuse and concomitant partial destruction of this particular area, a great number of Republican and Augustan coins have been found. Here, too, was found the earliest evidence indicating frequentation or habitation of the site: several Villanovan burnished *impasto* sherds; red-figure and black-glaze pottery; and a stretch of dry wall made of small, nicely worked blocks laid in regular courses of ashlar masonry of uncertain date—most likely the late second to early first century B.C., but possibly earlier since some late red-figure sherds were also found there. Behind the site, an Epigravettian lithic industry has been located.[38] An Etruscan chamber tomb stands on a small projecting hill above the terraces, and A. Neppi Modona reports that a slingstone, a travertine urn, and a sandstone ossuary urn, all with Etruscan inscriptions, were found in the general environs of the Ossaia site; all these finds would be in keeping with an Etruscan cemetery on the hills around the site at Ossaia.[39]

The later villa, of the second to fifth century A.D., is best attested to on the lower terrace (figure 12), although, as mentioned, ample ceramic and some architectural evidence places part of the earlier villa on this terrace too. A splendid polychrome mosaic, consisting of two arms 2 meters wide and about 6.5 meters long meeting in a right angle, indicates the high level of material life enjoyed at this site during the period of urban crisis in Rome. The mosaic consists of large rectangular ruglike decorative groups, mostly geometric in design and executed in white, various tones of blue, yellow, and terra di siena tesserae (figures 1, 13, and 14). This area may have been the corridor of an L-shaped portico which provided an all-encompassing view of the eastern Val di Chiana, from the Trasimene Lake to Mount Cetona and beyond Cortona itself, where there is some evidence of a fair-sized Roman town in the early period. Another piece of marble sculpture was found at the north end of the polychrome mosaic; this piece, also of small size, represents a bejeweled female hand offering a

FIGURE 12. Overview of lower terrace, excavation area 1. *Photo from excavation archive.*

FIGURE 13. Detail of polychrome mosaic, excavation area 1. *Photo from excavation archive.*

FIGURE 14.
Detail of polychrome
mosaic, excavation area 1.
*Photo from excavation
archive.*

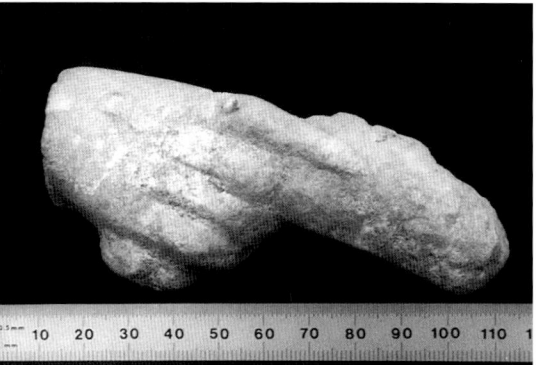

FIGURE 15. Female hand, marble, excavation area 1. *Photo from excavation archive.*

wreath (figure 15). A great many coins datable from the second to fifth centuries A.D. have been found on the lower terrace.

A large wall, buttressed on one side (figure 16), by which this site has been known for centuries, was drawn by a local resident in 1759, when it was preserved to a greater length than it is now. The wall, mostly built in *opus vittatum* but with a small patch of *opus reticulatum* at the base, is covered on the interior side by a thick layer of *cocciopesto*, which probably indicates that it was part of a large cistern, at least in the later period. An aerial photograph of the nearby Villa di Trebbio reveals an immense circular structure on the villa grounds which may possibly be a *nymphaeum;* if so, its location directly downhill from a number of arches that signal the end of the large buttressed wall may be significant. The possible nymphaeum was described in the 1500s as a round temple, by that time already in ruins, with a number of lead pipes in the rubble.

Other remains on the site which can be generally attributed to the later period include the drainage system cut through one of the black-and-white Republican mosaics, the opus vittatum wall laid on top of the lozenge mosaic, and the large sewage system found to the north. Five perfectly preserved *firmalampen,* the most recent of which is dated by its form to the end of the third century A.D. or beginning of the fourth century A.D. (figures 17 and 18), were found in a row beside the tile-lined sewage canal; each lamp had a coin over the central opening.[40] Firmalampen are usually found in burials, but no bones were recovered near the lamp-and-coin deposition. If, during the

FIGURE 16. Drawing of buttressed wall in excavation area 1, executed in 1759, artist unknown.

course of continued excavations in the area, the lamps and coins are found to be associated with burials, it would mean that at least this area of the site ceased to be used by the early to mid–fourth century A.D. Other ceramic material and coins from the fourth to fifth centuries A.D. have been found in the area of the buttressed wall. Neppi Modona also reports that an inscribed amphora handle and an inscription, both dated to the fourth century A.D., came from the area of the Villa di Trebbio.[41]

The placement of the villa at the crossroads of the Perusia-Clusium-Arretium road is no doubt a main factor in the evolution of the site from a villa to a vicus sometime in the later second to early third century A.D., when Roman Cortona may have begun to lose some of its service functions. Most of the Roman remains from Cortona are datable to the early empire and consist of mosaics and cisterns.[42] To the west of the Ossaia site, mosaic fragments, walls, and pottery datable to this later period have been found for half a kilometer toward the valley and for a distance of a kilometer and a half to the south to three kilometers to the north of the site. The numerous locally made *amphorae* and quantities of terra sigillata chiara medio-adriatica characterize the ceramic record of the site datable to this period. The amphorae are made of a dense grayish or pinkish clay with a large quantity of black sand or volcanic inclusion, rather like clay from Cerveteri; the clay is not well worked and the production is rough.

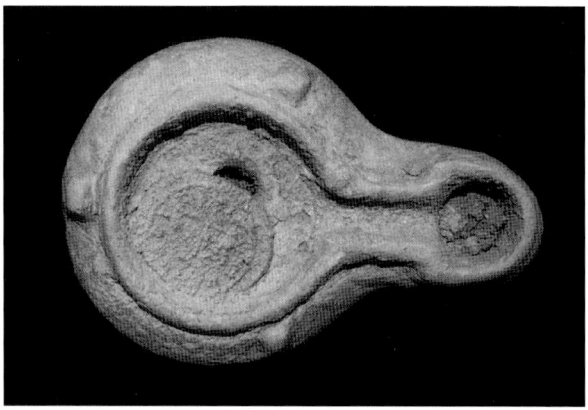

FIGURE 17. Firmalampen with coin. *Photo from excavation archive.*

FIGURE 18. *Fortis* stamp from bottom of firmalampen.
Photo from excavation archive.

The handles are particularly distinctive: they are large, with either a sharp deep valley or groove cut or pressed into the clay. The terra sigillata chiara medio-adriatica pottery is dated tentatively at various sites from the mid–second to the mid–fifth centuries A.D. and is believed to have been made originally in the Ravenna area.[43] To date, it has only been found within a triangular area across Italy from Ravenna to Settefinestre to Urbsiaglia. This type of pottery is distinctive; the favorite shape at Ossaia is a large shallow open bowl 20–25 centimeters in diameter, imitating closely an African red-slip form dated from the second half of the second century A.D. to the first half of the third century A.D.[44] The bowl is slipped in a brownish red or maroon-red paint, and the lower wall of the bowl is covered with brown or orange painted designs of intersecting circles, rays, or curlicues. This pottery, more than anything else, reflects a directional shift in the economic focus of the site during the decades of urban crisis in Rome, in that it reveals a drop in African imports and a commercial reliance on the northeastern Adriatic region for either inspiration or actual importation—just as the northeastern part of Etruria, in a much earlier period (during the fifth and fourth centuries B.C.), seems to have been more closely linked to Spina than to Rome.[45] There is little evidence of crisis in this particular area during the later second and third centuries A.D., although this is still a working hypothesis. Certainly other peripheral regions—for example, Lucania[46]—which were dependent on agriculture and physically distant from large urban centers seem to have suffered much less than previously suspected during the period of crisis that wreaked havoc in Rome.

The idea that the establishment of the early villa reflects the pre-Roman settlement pattern in the area is substantiated, first, by the numerous sporadic Etruscan finds near the early villa and the few red-figure sherds from the excavation;[47] second, by the Etruscan tomb reworked into a chapel on the hillside above the site and the cemetery indicated by Neppi Modona;[48] and last, possibly by the stretch of dry wall found in association with the red-figure and early black-glaze sherds. There are also enough burnished impasto sherds—two with graffiti—to indicate Villanovan frequentation of the area. L. Banti postulates that during the early Archaic period a road from Perusia passed in front of the site and a second road passed behind the mountains (see figure 3).[49] This mountain road may be confirmed by the presence of a Roman pavement found in the higher hills behind Ossaia.[50] The two roads join in a valley that runs east and west behind the Cortona hill. A number of pre-Roman and Roman sites have been located in the Montanare valley, and the density of pre-Roman settlement in particular offers further evidence of another settlement nucleus in the territory of Cortona at a time when there is no documentation for an actual urban center up the hill at the modern town. A similar settlement agglomeration between the second Sodo at Camucia and the apparent Etruscan cemetery/settlement at Ossaia substantiates the importance at an early period of the lower slopes of the Val di Chiana. Just so, the density of Roman settlement in the Montanare valley emphasizes the continued importance of the lower Val di Chiana in the later Roman period, when both the Montanare valley and the site at Ossaia were evidently flourishing, even though there is not much evidence for continued growth in Cortona itself after the early imperial period (cf. pp. 204, 207 in text and n. 42).

The combined recent evidence from the Cortona area, then, allows the postulation of a substantial Etruscan population located on the lower slopes of the Val di Chiana in small agglomerated settlements or isolated establishments scattered over the lower terraces along the northeastern side of the Trasimene Lake; these date from the sixth century B.C. to circa the third century B.C. Many of those same areas later became the sites of Roman establishments. This, of course, may be primarily due to availability of water and accessibility to routes; but given the change in the Republican period of the type of settlement imposed on an Etruscan area, something more is suggested by this repeated use and reuse—as, in fact, the second tumulus of the Sodo was used and reused into late Roman times. As a working hypothesis, it is postulated that the gradual process of Romanization in this area of the Val di Chiana was effected through the intentional reuse and perhaps emphasis of the pre-existing settlement pattern— which, in this area as in many other Etruscan areas, was originally based on small nuclei in the countryside—as well as on the clear development in the later Etruscan period of the more important urban center at Cortona. In the case of Etruscan Cortona, a date for the emergence of that urban center still needs to be established.

Settlement pattern studies have been concentrated in the areas of Etruria closer to Rome and along the coast. Inland Etruria, with the exception of Chiusi (cf. n. 10), has not been so exhaustively considered. It has been easier to identify changes in these patterns in more urbanized situations, through the establishment of a forum or the construction of a characteristically Roman building using typically Roman masonry (such as at Rusellae); but analogous changes can also be seen in the rural or extraurban landscape. Nonetheless, without wanting to make every area equal to every other area of Etruria, it is clear that a Roman reuse of pre-existing important Etruscan locations coupled with visible new Roman buildings and a change in settlement types from small farms to large landholdings reflects the arrival of a new order just as clearly as does the eradication of an Etruscan city and the foundation of a totally new Roman colony in a new location. All these changes are statements of *Romanitas.* That statement was certainly louder and had more impact on the local population if it was made by a Romanized Etruscan family from the same area, such as the Vibii Pansae of Perusia.

N O T E S

The results and thus the hypotheses presented in this essay are based on preliminary data from the ongoing excavations and survey at Ossaia. The excavations will continue until at least 1998. It is a pleasure to acknowledge the financial support for this research provided by the Social Science and Humanities Research Council of Canada in the form of a three-year grant, as well as additional financial support from the Università di Perugia.

Other essays in this volume deal with subjects related to those discussed in this paper. For more on the standing of Etruscan aristocratic families in Roman politics, see the essay by John F. Hall, 149 ff. On claims for ancient origins of Italian cities, see the essays by Steven Bule, 313 ff., and Roger T. Macfarlane, 249. On the Roman use of Etruscan burial tumuli, see the essay by Mark J. Johnson, 232. On the use by Romans of Etruscan art motifs or mythological themes, see the essays by Steven Bule, 308 ff., and Nancy Thomson de Grummond, 358 ff. On the Vibii Pansae family, see the essay by John F. Hall, 165 and n. 114. On *Arringatore*, "the Orator," see the essay by Robert E. A. Palmer, 18, and figure 1 on p. xiv. For more on Maecenas and Propertius, see the essay by Roger T. Macfarlane, 245 ff. Finally, on Tarchon, see the essay by John F. Hall, n. 21.

1. M. Torelli, *Etruria* (Rome, 1982), 301–7.

2. A. Minto, "Il secondo melone del Sodo," *NSA* 7 (1929): 158–67.

3. P. Zamarchi Grassi, ed., *La Cortona dei principes* (Cortona, It., 1992) is the catalogue for the eponymous exhibit, which was open during the summers of 1992 and 1993. The synthesis and brief review of the tomb, its contents, and its architecture presented here is based on this catalogue. Two other articles are useful: F. Nicosia, "Relazione sul Tumulo II del Sodo di Cortona," in *Rendiconti della Pontificia Accademia*, in press; and P. Zamarchi Grassi, "Cortona: Il II melone del Sodo in Rassegna degli scavi e delle scoperte," *SE* 57 (1992): 135.

4. G. Colonna, "Urbanistica e archittetura," in *Rasenna: Storia e civiltà degli Etruschi* (Milan, 1986), 398; vol. hereinafter cited as *Rasenna*.

5. Zamarchi Grassi, "Cortona: Il II melone del Sodo," 135 and nn. 52–54 (supra n. 3).

6. M. Torelli, "Senatori etruschi della tarda repubblica e dell'impero," *DArch* 3 (1969): 335–36.

7. W. H. Gross, "Ways and Roundabout Ways in the Propaganda of an Unpopular Ideology," in *The Age of Augustus*, ed. R. Winkes (Providence, R.I., 1986), 33; *RRC* (Cambridge, 1974), 1:501, no. 493/1.

8. D.H. 1.20.4, 1.28 ff.; G. Colonna, "Virgilio, Cortona, e la leggenda etrusca di Dardano," *ArchClass* 32 (1980): 12.

9. For example, in Via Guelfa, Piazzetta Baldelli, a considerable quantity of mixed material was found, including Archaic impasto pottery, Attic and Etruscan red-figure ware, and gray and black bucchero, as well as loomweights. Some tombs and some walls have also been found, but this is not sufficient evidence upon which to postulate an "urban center" (M. Cappelletti, "Cortona," in *Atlante dei siti archeologici della Toscana*, ed. M. Torelli, M. Menichetti, C. Masseria, and M. Fabbri [Rome, 1992], 400–401, nos. 21.2–28; vol. hereinafter cited as *Atlante*). The scattered mixture of material remains is no different in composition or quantity from that found at any small settlement nucleus.

10. M. Torelli, "La Storia," in *Rasenna*, 44, 49 (vol. supra n. 4).

11. M. Cappelletti, "Perugia," in *Atlante*, 385–405 (vol. supra n. 9).

12. A. Cherici, "Materiali per una carta archeologica del territorio cortonese," in *Cortona: Struttura e storia: Materiali per una conoscenza operante della città e del territorio: Catalogo della mostra* (Cortona, It., 1987), 142–43.

13. P. Bruschetti, "Il Sodo, il tumulo I, l'ambiente," in *La Cortona dei principes*, ed. P. Zamarchi Grassi (Cortona, It., 1992), 183–84.

14. The scientific director of the project is Professor M. Torelli, Istituto di studi comparati delle società antiche, Università degli studi, Perugia. The field directors are Professor H. Fracchia, University of Alberta; and Professor M. Gualtieri, Istituto di studi comparati delle società antiche, Università degli studi, Perugia. The project

has been made possible by the collaboration and permission of Dr. F. Nicosia, Superintendent of Antiquities, Tuscany, and Dr. P. Zamarchi Grassi, also of the superintendency, which body has been gratifyingly generous in support of the project. The Comune of Cortona and its functionaries, particularly Dr. E. Rachini, Cultural Assessor, and Dr. B. Gialluca; the Marchese Bourbon de Petrella, who has permitted excavation in her property, Villa di Trebbio; and Maurizio Loveri, the *anima* of Ossaia, have all helped and supported in innumerable ways and have done much to make the project both possible and a success.

15. An L. Gellius is known from a funerary inscription found nearer to Cortona itself, at a small Roman cemetery in the locality of Lattarino where twenty-four tombs were found. There is no record of the inscriptions from the site other than the one mentioned here (G. F. Gamurrini, "Cortona," *NSA* [1881]: 45).

16. *CIL* xi, 6688, 1.

17. Ibid., vi, 37077. On the tribe, see T. P. Wiseman, "Some Republican Senators and Their Tribes," *CQ* 14 (1964): 131; on the family, see *RE* viiiA, cols. 1948–2000, s.v. "Vibius," esp. nos. 15–17 (cols. 1953–66); on the careers, see *MRR*, 634; in general, see Torelli, "Senatori etruschi," 301–2 (supra n. 6).

The first C. Vibius C. F. Pansa of whom we know was twice military tribune in the early empire and a moneyer in 89–88 B.C. (*CIL* vi, 3542); his son was C. Vibius C. F. Pansa Caetronianus, the moneyer of 48 B.C. and the consul of 43 B.C., who died at Forum Gallorum before the battle of Modena (*CIL* vi, 37077). The next C. Vibius Pansa was the nephew of C. Vibius C. F. Pansa Caetronianus; he held the office of *legatus propraetore* in Vindolicis sometime between 15 B.C. and A.D. 9 (Torelli, "Senatori etruschi," 301–2 [supra n. 6]).

18. *RRC*, 1:465.

19. R. Syme, "Missing Persons ii," *Historia* 7 (1959): 210; Torelli, "Senatori etruschi," 301–2, n. 70 (supra n. 6); W. V. Harris, *Rome in Etruria and Umbria* (Oxford, 1971), 249, 324–25, 328.

20. Liv. 9.37.12.

21. G. Paolucci, informal presentation of work in progress, presented at the Istituto di studi comparati delle società antiche, Università degli studi, Perugia, May 1991.

22. L. Banti, "Contributo alla storia ed alla topographia del territorio Perugino," *SE* 10 (1936): 97–99.

23. Torelli, *Etruria*, 301 (supra n. 1).

24. Torelli, "Senatori etruschi," 330 (supra n. 6).

25. Torelli, *Etruria*, 332 (supra n. 1).

26. Ibid., 336.

27. Liv. 9.37.12.

28. Aug., *Epist.* 32.

29. Colonna, "Virgilio, Cortona, e la leggenda," 13 (supra n. 8).

30. Gross, "Ways and Roundabout Ways," 33 (supra n. 7).

31. Torelli, "Senatori etruschi," 301–2, n. 70 (supra n. 6); Harris, *Rome in Etruria and Umbria*, 249, 324–25 (supra n. 19).

32. Colonna, "Virgilio, Cortona, e la leggenda," 9–10 (supra n. 8).

33. Verg., *A.* 3.170, 7.205.

34. Sil. 4.720, 5.123, 8.472.

35. Theopomp. 1.296, no. 114; Lyc. 805–8.

36. Verg., *G.* 1.498–99, 2.532 ff.; Liv. 9.37.12.

37. Colonna, "Virgilio, Cortona, e la leggenda," 13 (supra n. 8).

38. Cherici, "Carta archeologica," 185 no. 2 (supra n. 12).

39. A. Neppi Modona, *Cortona etrusca e romana nella storia e nell'arte* (Florence, 1925), 25, n. 27; 62, n. 12; 113; 119, n. 6; Gamurrini, "Cortona," 43 (supra n. 15). For Etruscan inscriptions on items found near Ossaia, see *CII* 1061 bis; *CIE* 4663; *CII* 2684 bis.

40. The earliest examples of the lamp type are dated to the second half of the first century A.D., although it has been suggested that they might even begin in the Augustan period. On the basis of the length of the channel and the spout type, the five lamps found at Cortona belong to Buchi type xa and thus should be dated to the later third to early fourth century A.D. The coins, which will obviously allow a closer dating, had not been cleaned at the time this essay was written. For the types, dating, etc., see E. Buchi, *Lucerne del Museo di Aquileia I: Lucerne romane con marchio di fabrica* (Aquileia, It., 1975).

41. *CIL* XI, 1915.

42. Cappelletti, "Cortona," 400 nos. 22.1; 401 nos. 42.1, 24.2, 26.1, 28 (supra n. 9).

43. This class of pottery has proven difficult to date. The date offered here is based exclusively on the copying of the African red-slip form, as all sherds retrieved are from unstratified contexts. The most popular form at the Ossaia site resembles the form 21 of L. Brecciaroli Taborelli ("Contributo alla classificazione di una terra sigillata chiara italica," *Rivista di studi marchiginai* 1 [1978]: 1–38), dated to the first half of the second to the mid–fifth centuries A.D., and form 16 of M. G. Maioli ("Terra sigillata tarda del ravennate," *Rei Cretariae Romanae Fautorum* 16 [1976]: 160–73), dated from the third to the fourth centuries A.D. For the type of pottery see, in addition, G. V. Gentili, "Le ceramiche romane invetriate di Sarsina," in *I problemi della ceramica romana di Ravenna, della Valle Padana e dell'alto Adriatico: Atti del Convegno internazionale . . .* (Bologna, 1972), 1–44; S. Besutti, "Sigillata medio adriatica," in *Settefinistre: Una villa schiavistica nell'Etruria romana*, ed. A. Carandini (Modena, It., 1988), 151.

44. J. W. Hayes, *Late Roman Pottery* (Oxford, 1972), 200–201 form 181.

45. Colonna, "Virgilio, Cortona, e la leggenda," 6 (supra n. 8).

46. M. Gualtieri and H. Fracchia, "Excavation and Survey at Masseria Ciccotti, Oppido Lucano: Interim Report, 1989–92," *EMC* 37 (1993): 313–38.

47. The hypothesis is further supported by the range of material found at Terontola, about 3 km to the south, where finds range through the upper Paleolithic, Neolithic, and Enolithic periods and the Late Bronze Age to the fourth century B.C. and include Etruscan tombs and Roman pottery (Cappelletti, "Perugia," 390–91 nos. 49.1–51 [supra n. 11]). In the other direction, about 3 km to the north at Camucia, in addition to the tumulus discussed at the beginning of this essay (which in itself covers a chronological arc from the Orientalizing to the late Hellenistic periods), several bucchero vases, a sandstone slab with an inscription (*CIE* 442), and other burials scattered within the Camucia area are considered to be Etruscan. Two other burials in the same area are Roman, and one of them is dated to the second century A.D. Two fragments of Roman sculpture were also found in the vicinity of the tomb; both are dated to ca. 50 B.C. (Cappelletti, "Cortona," 403 nos. 40.1–8 [supra n. 9]).

48. Neppi Modona, *Cortona etrusca e romana*, 25, n. 7; 62 (supra n. 39).

49. Banti, "Contributo alla storia," 122, fig. 3 (supra n. 22).

50. G. Donati, *Epigrafia cortonese*, Anno accademico etrusco, 13 (Florence, 1965–67), 100.

The Mausoleum of Augustus:
Etruscan and Other Influences on Its Design

MARK J. JOHNSON

At the time of its construction in the first century B.C. the mausoleum of Augustus in Rome was the most grandiose and impressive Roman tomb in existence (figure 1).[1] Only the later mausoleum of Hadrian would rival it in size and in ostentation. For centuries Augustus' monument remained the most conspicuous structure on its side of the Tiber River in the Campus Martius region of Rome, a witness to the importance of the emperor and his achievements. Yet, surprisingly, it remains a poorly studied monument. Many significant questions about this key example of imperial patronage and Roman funerary architecture remain. One such important issue is that of the origins of its design.

Due to the tumulus form of the building and its location in Italy, most scholars have assumed that its design was derived from Etruscan sources, though such opinions have not been unanimous. In an article published in 1966 R. R. Holloway argued that "the idea that Augustus consciously chose to build an Etruscan tomb is quite impossible."[2] He believed that the design was derived from mounds on the west coast of Asia Minor; these mounds—actually buried villages—were thought to be the tumulus tombs of the princes of Troy and were mentioned as such by Vergil in the *Aeneid*.[3] In Holloway's view Augustus was underscoring the Trojan ancestry, through Aeneas, of the Julii, as he was to do in other monuments and in other ways. J. M. C. Toynbee

---

FIGURE 1. Mausoleum of Augustus, Rome, ca. 28 B.C., exterior from south. *Photo by author.*

| 217 |

and other scholars have been quick to dismiss Holloway's theory and return to the idea of Etruscan derivation.[4] An examination of the problem leads to another conclusion: perhaps there is some truth in both opinions.

According to Suetonius, the mausoleum was built during the sixth consulship of Augustus in 28 B.C., though it is unclear if construction was initiated or completed in that year.[5] In any event, by 23 B.C. work had progressed to the point where the building was ready to receive the burial urn of Marcellus.[6] The site chosen for the mausoleum was the Campus Martius, and some scholars have argued that it was linked with the Horologium Augusti, erected in 10 B.C., and the Ara Pacis Augustae, dedicated in 9 B.C., in a vast complex honoring Augustus. This theory is plausible if one is willing to accept the notion that until that time the northern Campus Martius had been an open field, empty of other buildings with the space between the mausoleum and horologium remaining free. The scarcity of excavations in this region leaves no way to prove or disprove the theory. It also should be remembered that there was a time gap of some eighteen years between the construction of the buildings, which suggests that such an honorific complex was not in the original plans of the emperor.[7] The more important consideration in choosing to construct the mausoleum in the Campus Martius would have been the fact that the Campus was already the site of several tombs of illustrious Romans, including A. Hirtius, C. Vibius Pansa, Sulla, and, of course, Julius Caesar.[8] Not only was Augustus able to secure his place among these tombs of famous Romans, but his own grandiose tomb dominated the area.

The mausoleum stood within a public garden planted with trees, a gift of the emperor to the city. A fence or enclosure of some kind, some 120 meters square, was built to isolate and protect the monument. The *ustrinum*, used for the cremation of the imperial family members, apparently stood to the east of the tomb, possibly fronting on the Via Flaminia.[9]

The mausoleum took the form of a huge conical tumulus, achieved through the construction of five concentric circular walls with intervening spaces and tons of fill material (figure 2). The outer wall, with its original facing of travertine blocks, had a diameter of

FIGURE 2. Mausoleum of Augustus, plan. *Drawing by author after Gatti.*

just over 89 meters or 300 Roman feet. Walls linking the concentric rings created enclosed spaces that would have been filled with earth, leaving a very limited amount of interior space accessible to the visitor. A single entry faces south and gives access to the series of passageways leading to the burial chamber. The first corridor proceeds toward the center of the monument before it gives way to an annular hall. From this, two short passages open to lead the visitor toward the center once again, joining a second annular corridor that encircled the center of the building. Another hall, on axis with the entry corridor, led to the burial chamber. This chamber actually had the form of yet another annular corridor, disposed around a travertine-faced concrete pier some nine meters in diameter. Three small rectangular niches opened into the outer wall to the west, north, and south. In the niches and along the walls were placed urns and statues of Augustus, his family members, and his successors.

The exterior of the building is now partially obscured by the raised surrounding ground level and by the cypress trees planted on its first tier. The first level, about nine meters high at present, has lost most of its original travertine facing. The outer ring is covered with earth sloping slightly toward the center, where it encounters the second ring, faced with *opus reticulatum* and rising to a greater height. The center of the building was destroyed down to its foundation level, so it is now impossible to see how the building was topped, though a safe assumption is that it continued upward in a general conical fashion to a height of perhaps fifty meters.

The exterior of the building can be partially reconstructed on the basis of literary and archaeological evidence. An early description was given by Strabo, who stated that it was a "great mound near the river on a lofty foundation of white marble, thickly covered with evergreen trees to the very summit. Above stands a bronze image of Augustus Caesar; beneath the mound are the tombs of himself and of his relatives and intimates."[10] This account, though brief, makes several important points: that the lower section was faced in a white stone (though actually travertine and not marble); that it took the form of a mound planted with trees; and that this mound was topped by a bronze statue of Augustus. The statue, which must have been colossal to match the scale of the tomb, would have stood on the vertical extension of the cylindrical pier in the center of the building.

Archaeological evidence for reconstructing the exterior is limited. Some clues have been provided by limited finds which, combined with information from Renaissance drawings of the monument, make it clear that the lower, outer wall was topped by a Doric frieze and projecting cornice for a total height of about twelve meters.[11] The entrance was flanked by two Egyptian obelisks, placed slightly in front of the outer wall. Also near the door were the bronze plaques inscribed with Augustus' autobiography, the *Res Gestae*.[12]

Above the outer wall, the reconstruction of the monument becomes quite difficult, if not impossible. The surviving interior walls are of varying heights and are not much help in determining the original exterior appearance of the building. As mentioned, the center of the building was razed to its foundation level; this was due to its conversion into a formal garden in the Renaissance. In the early part of this century it served as a theater—called, appropriately enough, the Augusteo—until it was rescued in the 1920s to 1930s by Mussolini as part of his quest to recapture the ancient glory of Rome. There was, however, precious little for the excavators to find that would help clarify the problem of reconstructing the exterior.

Nevertheless, several attempts to reconstruct the mausoleum have been made. These may be classified into two basic proposals, with several variations (figure 3). The first is that the whole building was

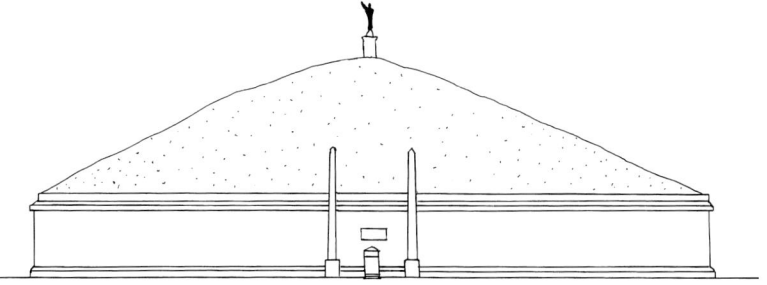

FIGURE 3 *(above and below)*. Mausoleum of Augustus, possible reconstructions. *Drawings by author after Giglioli and Gatti.*

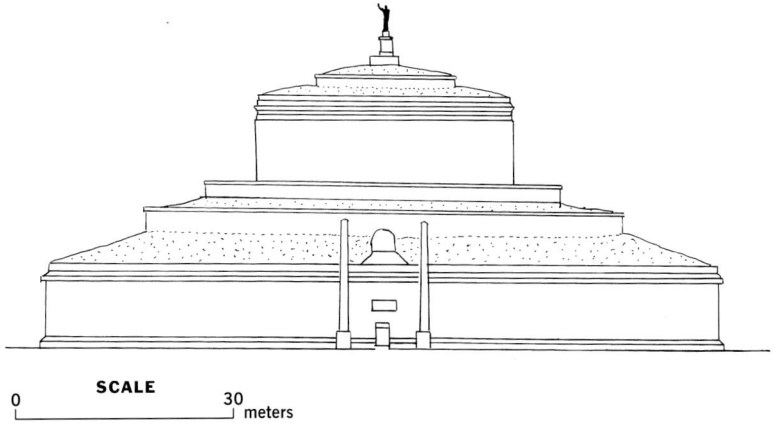

SCALE
0   30
                   meters

covered by an enormous mound which rose from the cornice of the outer wall. Trees and the statue topped the monument. In the second proposal it is accepted that the lower, outer portions of the building were covered with earth and planted with trees, but the suggestion is made that the fourth ring wall rose up above this terrace to create a second, smaller cylinder. This may have been decorated with pilasters and a cornice and topped by a second mound planted with trees before culminating in the statue. Considering the present state of the building and Strabo's limited description, either of the two reconstructions is plausible, though the presence of taller walls toward the center strongly suggests that one or more of them would have been exposed externally. The present state of knowledge renders it impossible to say which theory is closest to the truth.

Whatever its exact form, the monument created for Augustus was an impressive last resting place. In terms of diameter, it would remain forever the largest Roman tomb ever built. Except for its vast size, however, all aspects of its design may be found in other Roman tombs. This is significant, for in order to determine origins of its design it is important to understand its place in Roman funerary architecture.

The mausoleum of Augustus is classified as a tumulus tomb—that is, possessing a circular retaining wall and a mound. Numerous tombs of this type were constructed in the suburbs of Rome during the republic and early empire.[13] A brief look at a few examples will demonstrate how Augustus' tomb relates to the genre.

One of the so-called Tombs of the Horatii on the Via Appia is typical of the numerous tumulus tombs lining the roads outside of the city (figure 4).[14] It is a simple monument much smaller than that of Augustus, has a low retaining wall, and is topped by an earthen mound. There is no burial chamber, which means that the burial was done beneath the ground before the construction of the tumulus. Its dating is uncertain but may be as early as the fifth century B.C.

With a diameter of 41 meters, the tomb known as the "Torrione" on the Via Praenestina is the second largest Roman tumulus tomb after that of Augustus (figure 5).[15] Much of its retaining wall remains standing to a height of almost 9 meters. A masonry-lined passage gives access to a relatively small burial chamber of cruciform shape located

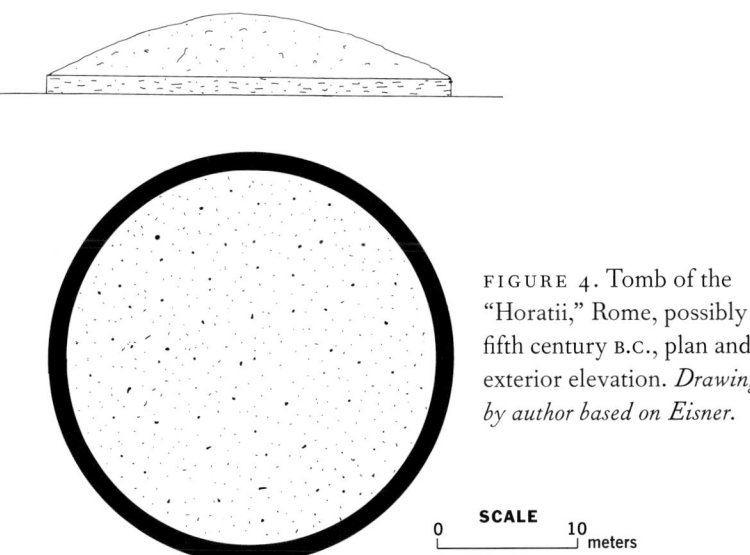

FIGURE 4. Tomb of the "Horatii," Rome, possibly fifth century B.C., plan and exterior elevation. *Drawing by author based on Eisner.*

SCALE

0   10 meters

FIGURE 5. "Torrione," Rome, after 15 B.C., plan. *Drawing by author based on Eisner.*

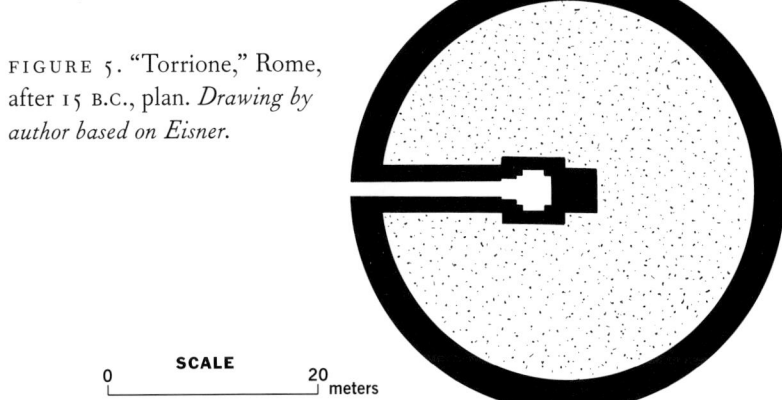

SCALE

0   20 meters

in the center of the monument. A coin found during excavations in the 1930s yielded a date for the tomb to the period after 15 B.C. In stating his case for the "Trojan" origins of the design of the mausoleum of Augustus, Holloway argued that it was the first such monumental tomb in or near Rome and that other similar tombs simply echoed its design. The Torrione does support this opinion, since it dates to the Augustan period but was erected after the emperor's tomb, which therefore may have served as its model. Another important tomb, however, shows that the type was in use in the period prior to that of Augustus' tomb. The so-called Casal Rotondo on the Via Appia has a diameter of over 29 meters and a retaining wall that preserves much of its exterior travertine facing to a height of just under 9 meters (figure 6). It has been convincingly dated to the decade of 40 to 30 B.C.[16]

Apart from general similarities with many Roman tombs, there are certain important features in the mausoleum of Augustus that are also found in other Roman tombs. The so-called Tomb of the Curatii on the Via Appia is a modest tomb with a diameter of 17.5 meters and

FIGURE 6. Tomb known as the Casal Rotondo, Rome, 40–30 B.C., exterior from west. *Photo by author.*

a present tumulus height of about 3 meters (figure 7).[17] Its most noticeable feature is a central pier, 3 meters in diameter, that rises to a height of about 10 meters. It is more than likely that its function was identical to that of the central pier of Augustus' mausoleum: to support a statue.

As noted, the pier in the mausoleum of Augustus is in the center of the annular burial chamber. This arrangement appears in other tombs, notably that in the Vigna Pepoli in Rome, a large tumulus with a diameter of about 38 meters (figure 8).[18] Its retaining wall now stands at 5.5 meters high, though its original tumulus would of course have reached a greater height. A corridor leads to the burial chamber located at the center of the structure. The chamber is of the same form as that in the imperial tomb—an annular corridor encircling a central pier. With a diameter of about 6 meters, it is smaller than that of Augustus' tomb and there are five niches rather than three lining its walls. *Opus reticulatum*, a technique that first appeared in Rome in a datable building in 55 B.C., is used in the interior of the tomb, which means that it may have preceded the imperial mausoleum.

FIGURE 7. Tomb "of the Curatii," Rome, before fourth century B.C., view from the northeast. *Photo by author.*

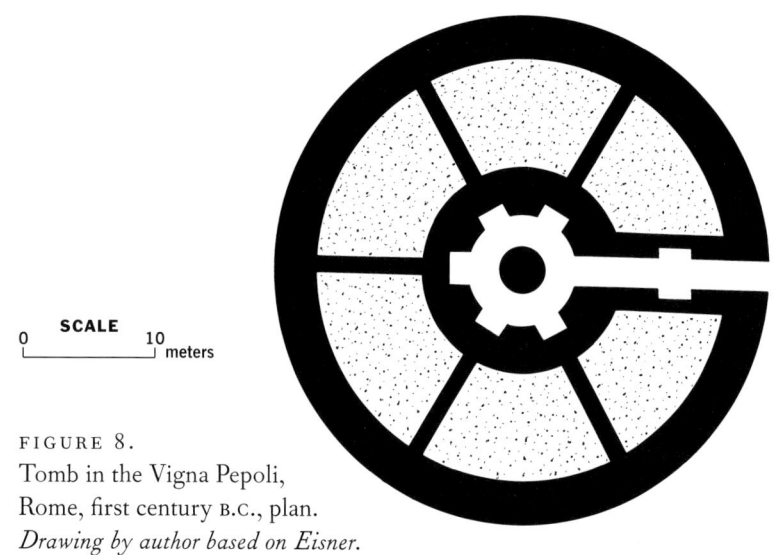

SCALE
0   10
meters

FIGURE 8.
Tomb in the Vigna Pepoli,
Rome, first century B.C., plan.
Drawing by author based on Eisner.

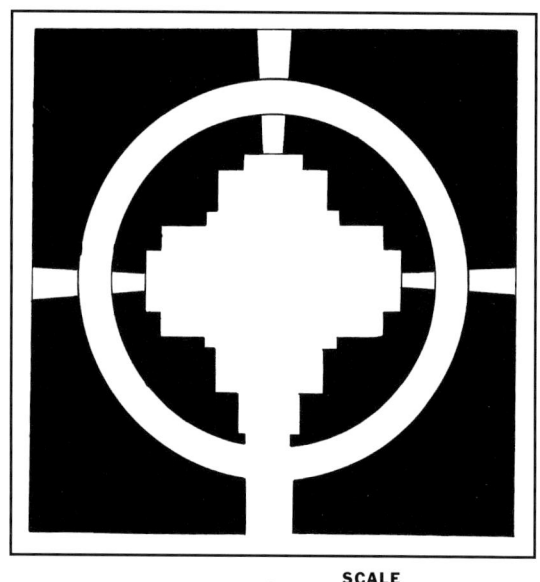

FIGURE 9. Tomb of the Servilii, Rome,
first century B.C., plan. *Drawing by author
after Windfeld-Hansen.*

SCALE
0   5
meters

Another distinctive feature in the mausoleum of Augustus is the annular corridor encircling the burial chamber. This can be seen in the much smaller tomb known as that of the Servilii on the Via Appia of the Augustan period (figure 9).[19] The purpose of such passageways may have been to provide a path for the ritual circumambulation of the burial chamber, though this is uncertain. It is a feature that appears in a relatively small number of Roman tombs.[20]

It is clear from this brief overview that the design of the mausoleum of Augustus could be explained in terms of local Roman funerary architecture. The picture would remain incomplete, however, without an examination of other influences, particularly those from Etruria. The simplest explanation for the appearance of the tumulus type of Roman tomb architecture is that it was derived from Etruscan sources. No one questions that the form of early Roman temples was derived from Etruscan architecture; and it would be incredible to think, in view of this influence, that there would not also be similar influences manifested in other types of buildings, including tombs.

It is well known that the tumulus tomb type was common in Etruria.[21] It appeared there in a very early period and remained in use well into the period of Roman domination. One need only cite the Banditaccia cemetery at Cerveteri, which is comprised largely of tombs of this type of varying sizes, dates, and interior arrangements (figure 10).[22] These tombs were, for the most part, carved out of a tufa ridge, but they imitated built architecture. Each has been given a cylindrical wall or podium, above which rises a tumulus. Passageways are cut into the mounds, giving access to the burial chambers. These chambers take the form of the rooms of domestic architecture and may or may not be located at the center of the tomb.

There are several similar tombs at Populonia dating from as early as the seventh century B.C. that are constructed, rather than carved, buildings, such as the Tomb "dei Carri" (figure 11).[23] It has a cylindrical retaining wall built of an irregular stone masonry. A squarish burial chamber occupies the center of the tomb, with small burial spaces flanking the narrow entry corridor. The whole is covered by an earthen mound. The similarities between these Etruscan tombs and the Roman tumuli are both striking and significant.

FIGURE 10. Tumulus tomb, Banditaccia Cemetery, Cerveteri, sixth century B.C., general view. *Photo by author.*

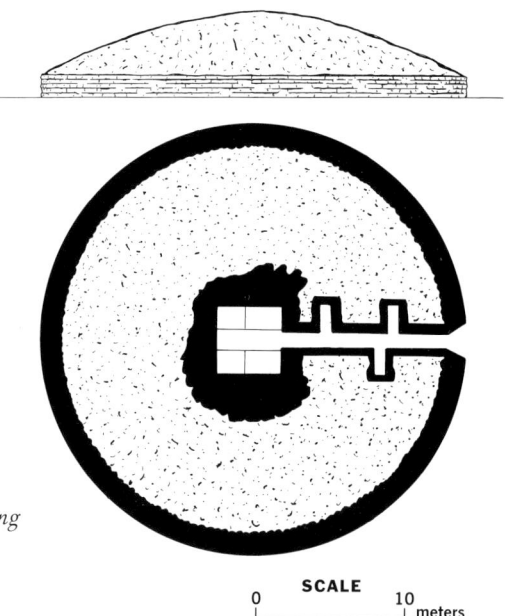

FIGURE 11. Tomb "dei Carri," Populonia, seventh century B.C., plan and elevation. *Drawing by author after Åkerström.*

SCALE

0   10
meters

Also important are the differences, especially in the nature of the burial chambers. The Etruscan tumuli may have more than one chamber, with none of them necessarily being located at the center of the structure. In many of these tombs the form of these chambers is derived from the interior of Etruscan houses, as the builders sought to create a suitable environment for the dead. They are obviously quite different from the interior of the mausoleum of Augustus.[24]

There are, however, some Etruscan tombs which have interiors that prefigure the arrangement of the imperial tomb. Among these may be cited the Montagnola Tomb at Quinto Fiorentino (figure 12) and the *tholos* tomb of Casal Marittimo, which both date to around 600 B.C.[25] Their chambers are constructed of masonry using the corbeling technique. In the center of each is a square pier. The purpose of the pier may have been to help support the masonry ceiling, though technically it would not have been a necessity. Perhaps there was some symbolic meaning attached to a central pier within a circular room—though such meaning, if it existed, is no longer understood. The pier and annular burial chamber of the mausoleum of Augustus

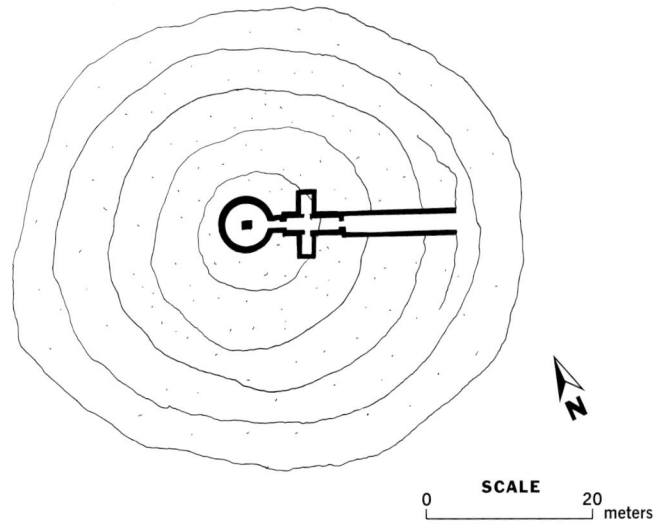

SCALE
0   20
meters

FIGURE 12. Montagnola tomb, Quinto Fiorentino, ca. 600 B.C., plan. *Drawing by author after Boëthius.*

echo this arrangement, though on a larger, more refined scale. This is not to say that the architect of the mausoleum ever saw these particular tombs. It is important to note, though, that Etruscan precedents exist for this aspect of the design of Augustus' tomb.

One other source for the design of the mausoleum has been cited by scholars, this being the tomb of Alexander the Great in Alexandria, Egypt.[26] Not much is known about the tomb, and that only from meager literary sources. Called the "Sema" or "Soma," it was built by the Ptolemaic ruler Philopater within the city walls on the grounds of the palace. All that can be said about its architecture is that it had an enclosure wall and was covered by a structure described by Lucan as "pyramidal."[27] Augustus is known to have visited this tomb, and it has been argued by several scholars that he modeled his own mausoleum after it as part of an attempt to link himself with the Greek hero-ruler.[28] While the proposed ideological links are enticing and should not be ruled out, it is difficult to accept any claims of a formal design relationship between the two monuments. Due to the almost complete lack of knowledge concerning the tomb of Alexander, scholars who argue this thesis are in the awkward position of trying to prove their theory without the benefit of evidence. On the other hand, the same lack of evidence means that there is also no way to disprove the hypothesis.

Another important Hellenistic tomb, that of Mausolus at Halicarnassus, built in the middle of the fourth century B.C., had a limited influence on the monument of Augustus.[29] Specifically, it gave the name "mausoleum," but there is no indication that Augustus was in any way responsible for this designation of his own tomb. Architecturally, the only feature shared by both buildings was an extraordinary monumentality.

Recently, J. Reeder has attempted to broaden the presumed ties with Hellenistic antecedents.[30] She argues that buildings such as the Arsinoeion on Samothrace and the Tholos at Epidauros may have had some role in determining the design of Augustus' mausoleum, particularly in the labyrinth nature of the interior passageways and in the supposed form of the now-lost upper part of the building. Though there may well have been connections between Augustus and these places, as she suggests, her proposal ultimately falls short of convincing in several respects. The design affinities to these Greek buildings are not that close, and it is difficult to argue for a model for the exterior of the mausoleum of Augustus when one cannot be certain of its appearance in any case. More importantly, it may be argued that the functional differences of the buildings ruled out a direct borrowing; no other deities were worshipped at the tomb, and there were no burials made at the temples. Augustus, it appears, was building a tomb and monument for himself and his family, not primarily a place for worship.

Given the affinities with Roman and Etruscan tombs which have been outlined here, it does not appear necessary to look beyond the confines of Italy in order to explain the origins of the design of the mausoleum of Augustus. The primary features of the design of the imperial tomb can all be found in other Roman and Etruscan funerary monuments: the circular plan, retaining wall, tumulus, corridor leading into a relatively small interior space, annular corridor, annular burial chamber, and pier in the middle of that chamber located in the very center of the monument.

There is one question remaining to be answered: Why? Why did Augustus choose this particular form for his own funerary monument? There is a great variety in Roman funerary architecture, and a design could have been chosen from among a number of types such as house tomb, pyramid, temple tomb, cylinder on a square podium, altar tomb, and tower tomb.[31] Yet he chose the simple tumulus type, known for centuries in funerary architecture in Italy. Does this mean that Augustus was looking specifically at Etruscan models for the design of his tomb? Perhaps, though it is more likely that this design was chosen at least in part because it had become a traditional type in aristocratic Roman funerary architecture. For this reason, Augustus had no need to look to the coasts of Asia Minor, Greece, or the capital of Egypt for inspiration. I would like to suggest, however, that there may have been one other source of inspiration for Augustus in choosing the tumulus type.

This other source would be the so-called tomb of Aeneas at Lavinium, modern Practica di Mare. According to the legend, Aeneas disappeared following a battle near the Numicus River, and his body was never found. Dionysius of Halicarnassus records that "the Latins built a hero-shrine to him. . . . It is a small mound, around which have been set out in regular rows trees that are well worth seeing."[32]

Some twenty years ago excavations were done in the area of Lavinium, uncovering a complex of thirteen altars and, nearby, the remains of a small tumulus consisting of a circle of stones some twenty meters in diameter, which served as its foundation (figure 13).[33] The mound had covered a tomb of the seventh century B.C. which was modified by the later construction of a small structure, built of tufa and composed of a *pronaos* and *cella,* though the door between them was actually a false door made of tufa which left the cella inaccessible. These modifications changing the tomb to a *heroon,* or hero shrine, appear to date from the end of the fourth century B.C.

This tumulus has been identified by its excavator as the heroon of Aeneas described by Dionysius, though not all scholars are in agreement on this issue.[34] As the monument to one of the most important figures in Roman legend, it is somewhat underwhelming; but

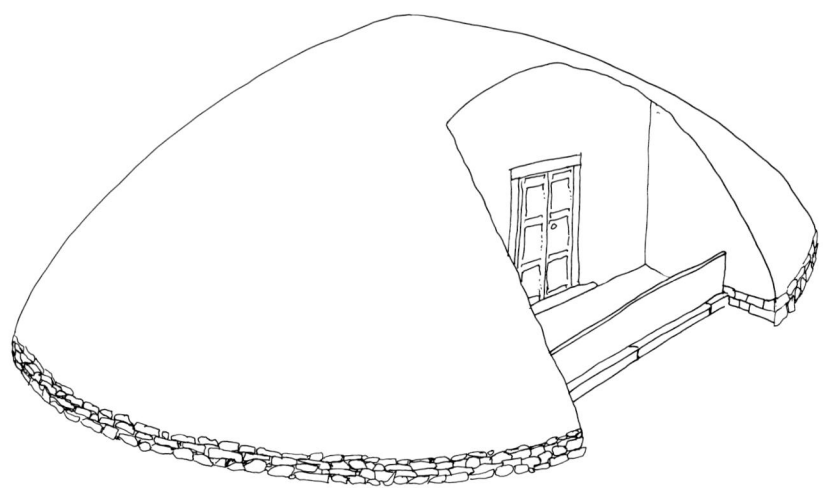

FIGURE 13. "Heroon of Aeneas," Lavinium (Practica di Mare), seventh century B.C., reconstruction. *Drawing by author after Sommella.*

there really is no reason to assume that the Latins of the fourth century B.C.—or even the Romans—would have built anything larger. If the identification of this building should prove to be incorrect, it is fairly certain, based on literary tradition, that another tumulus in the area served as the heroon; and all are similar in size.[35] But which tumulus actually was the venerated shrine is not important for the purposes of this discussion. The key point is that the account of Dionysius remains unchallenged: there was a heroon of Aeneas at Lavinium, and it took the form of a tumulus. Although it is unclear if the tumulus was thought to be the tomb proper of Aeneas or if there was no actual burial, as a heroon its form was that of a tomb, an architectural link commonly found in such buildings. It is also important to recognize that the cult of Aeneas was propagated in the time of Augustus, and it is impossible to believe that Augustus would have been unaware of its presence and practices at Lavinium.[36]

Notwithstanding the small size of the heroon of Aeneas— whichever of the tumuli near Lavinium it might be—there are several important points of comparison between it and the mausoleum of Augustus. Both are located near rivers; both were surrounded by trees; and, most importantly, both are tumuli. There was also a similarity of function. Though the mound may not have contained the burial of Aeneas, it was built near the site of his disappearance or death and it was meant to honor the man and his deeds. As a heroon, it would have also been the site of the cultic worship of Aeneas. The mausoleum of Augustus held the urn of Augustus and therefore had the function of a tomb, but it also commemorated the man and his deeds. In this connection it is worth remembering that the tablets containing the *Res Gestae* were displayed near the entrance of the tomb. A man whose deeds were grand deserved a grandiose tomb. Was his tomb also a hero shrine? A writer of the early third century A.D., Cassius Dio, calls the mausoleum a "heroon."[37] Furthermore, cultic functions at the mausoleum in the first century are documented. Seneca, for example, refers to "the tumulus on which the daily sacrifice to Caesar [i.e., Augustus,] our god, was made."[38]

It is impossible to say if Augustus anticipated his own tomb becoming a heroon. Still, it is clear from other actions that he often sought to link himself with Aeneas. One need only look to monuments such as the Forum of Augustus and the Ara Pacis to see the value he placed on this connection. In his forum he had placed a statue of Aeneas among a group of statues representing his ancestors.[39] Aeneas also figures prominently on a panel of the Ara Pacis, which shows him about to offer a sacrifice upon his arrival in Italy. In the background is depicted a small temple with two statues, identifiable as a shrine and representation of the Penates.[40] Their cult had supposedly been brought to Italy by Aeneas and was revived by Augustus. Significantly, the major center of the cult was at Lavinium, near the heroon of Aeneas.

Although it may be argued that this tumulus or any of the others which might have been the heroon of Aeneas was too small to have served as a model for the mausoleum, one should not be swayed by modern perceptions as to what constituted a "copy" in the ancient world. The emulation of general form and certain details were enough to evoke the intended parallel.[41] As Augustus and his architect went about the process of designing the emperor's tomb, they chose a tumulus design, in part because it was a traditional, conservative, and aristocratic tomb type—long a part of Etruscan and Roman funerary architecture. In this, Toynbee and the others, who have seen an Etruscan derivation of the mausoleum, are correct. The second reason for choosing a tumulus apparently was that, being the type of ruler who never missed an opportunity for political propaganda, Augustus saw another opportunity to link himself with Aeneas by having a similar monument. In this regard, Holloway was partially right: Augustus was looking at a tomb of a prince of Troy; he just did not have to go to Troy to see one.

NOTES

1. On the mausoleum, see A. Bartoli, "L'architettura del mausoleo d'Augusto," *BA*, 2d ser., 7 (1927): 30–46; R. Cordingley and I. Richmond, "The Mausoleum of Augustus," *PBSR* 10 (1927): 191–234; A. M. Colini, "Il mausoleo di Augusto," *Capitolium* 4 (1928–29): 11–22; A. M. Colini and G. Giglioli, "Relazione della prima campagna di scavo nel mausoleo di Augusto, estate-autunno 1926," *BCAR* 54 (1927): 191–234; G. Giglioli, "Il sepolcreto imperiale," *Capitolium* 6 (1930): 532–67; G. Gatti, "Nuove osservazioni sul mausoleo di Augusto," *L'Urbe* 3 (agosto 1938): 1–17; G. Lugli, *I monumenti antichi di Roma e suburbio* (Rome, 1938), 3:194–211; P. Zanker, *The Power of Images in the Age of Augustus* (Ann Arbor, Mich., 1988), 72–77; H. von Hesberg, "Das Mausoleum Augusti," in *Kaiser Augustus und die verlorene Republik* . . . (Berlin, 1988), 245–51; J. C. Reeder, "Typology and Ideology in the Mausoleum of Augustus: Tumulus and Tholos," *ClAnt* 11 (1992): 265–304. H. von Hesberg and S. Panciera, *Das Mausoleum des Augustus: Der Bau und seine Inschriften*, Bayerische Akademie der Wissenschaften, Philosophisch-Historische Klasse, 108 (Munich, 1994) appeared too late for consideration in the present study. I will also deal with the mausoleum at greater length in my book *Roman and Early Christian Imperial Mausolea* (forthcoming).

2. R. R. Holloway, "The Tomb of Augustus and the Princes of Troy," *AJA* 70 (1966): 171–73.

3. Verg., *A.* 3.22, 304, 6.232. They are also mentioned in Hom., *Il.* 2.792–94, 811–15, 7.86–91. See Holloway, "Tomb of Augustus," 173 (supra n. 2).

4. J. M. C. Toynbee, *Death and Burial in the Roman World* (London, 1971), 143; followed by M. Eisner, "Zur Typologie der Mausoleen des Augustus und des Hadrian," *MDAI(R)* 86 (1979): 319–24.

5. Suet., *Aug.* 100. The date for the initiation of construction is usually seen as 28 B.C., after his restoration of the Republic, the celebration of victories in Illyricum and Actium, and the annexation of Egypt. K. Kraft ("Der Sinn des Mausoleum of Augustus," *Historia* 16 [1967]: 186–206, reprinted in his *Gesammelte Aufsätze zur antiken Geschichte und Militärgeschichte* [Darmstadt, 1973], 29–46) argues that the building was begun in the previous decade and that 28 B.C. represents its completion. For a response, see D. Boschung, "Tumulus Iuliorum—Mausoleum Augusti: Ein Beitrag zu seinen Sinnbezügen," *HASB* 6 (1980): 38–41.

6. Verg., *A.* 6.872–75, 882–84; Vell. 2.93.1; D.C. 53.30.4–5. His urn inscription was found in the excavations of Giglioli, "Il sepolcreto imperiale," 534 (supra n. 1).

7. E. Buchner, *Die Sonnenuhr des Augustus* . . . (Mainz am Rhein, 1982), 35, 54; D. Favro, "Reading the Augustan City," in *Narrative and Event in Ancient Art*, ed. P. J. Holliday (Cambridge, 1993), 230–57, esp. 241–44; J. Pollini, "The Gemma Augustea: Ideology, Rhetorical Imagery, and the Creation of a Dynastic Narrative," in ibid., 258–98, esp. 285.

8. F. Castagnoli, "Il Campo Marzio nell'antichità," *Atti della Accademia nazionale dei Lincei*, Memorie delle classe di scienze morali, storiche, e filologiche, 8th ser., vol. 1, fasc. 4 (1946): 91–193, remains the best survey of the ancient topography of the Campus Martius. For its use as an honorific cemetery, see ibid., 94; G. Waurick, "Untersuchungen zur Lage der römischen Kaisergräber in der Zeit von Augustus bis Constantin," *JRGZ(M)* 20 (1973): 107–46, esp. 109–17. For the tombs, see L. Richardson, Jr., *A New Topographical Dictionary of Ancient Rome* (Baltimore, 1992), 356, 358, 360–61, 402. For more on C. Vibius Pansa, see, in this volume, the essays by John F. Hall, 165 and n. 114, and Helena Fracchia, 196 ff. and n. 17.

9. The garden is mentioned by Suetonius (*Aug.* 100) and by Strabo (5.3.8). Its extent is unknown. For the enclosure, see Bartoli, "L'architettura del mausoleo d'Augusto," 44–45 (supra n. 1); for the ustrinum, see Richardson, *New Topographical Dictionary*, 404 (supra n. 8).

10. Strab. 5.3.8.

11. Bartoli, "L'architettura del mausoleo d'Augusto," 30–37 (supra n. 1); P. Virgili, "A proposito del mausoleo di Augusto: Baldassare Peruzzi aveva ragione," *Archeologia laziale* 6 (1984): 209–12. A reconstruction of the frieze is given in von Hesberg, "Das Mausoleum Augusti," 249–50 (supra n. 1).

12. Suet., *Aug.* 101.4. For the text, see P. A. Brunt and J. M. Moore, eds. and trans., *Res Gestae Divi Augusti* (Oxford, 1967). For the obelisks, see C. D'Onofrio, *Gli obelischi di Roma* . . . , 3d ed. (Rome, 1992), 85–87.

13. M. Amand, "La Réapparition de la sépulture sous tumulus dans l'empire romain," *AC* 56 (1987): 162–82; H. von Hesberg, *Römische Grabbauten* (Darmstadt, 1992), 94–113.

14. M. Eisner, *Zur Typologie der Grabbauten im Suburbium Roms* (Mainz am Rhein, 1986), 56–59; the identification of the tomb with the Horatii is tenuous at best.

15. Ibid., 97–100.

16. Ibid., 61–63.

17. Ibid., 54–55. It apparently dated to before the fourth century B.C., as the Via Appia swerves around it.

18. Ibid., 25–27.

19. Ibid., 33–36.

20. See H. Winfield-Hansen, "Les Couloirs annulaires dans l'architecture funéraire antique," *AAAH* 4 (1965): 35–63.

21. A. Akerström, *Studien über die etruskischen Gräber* . . . (Lund, Swed., 1934); M. Demus-Quatember, *Etruskische Grabarchitektur: Typologie und Ursprungsfragen*, Deutsche Beiträge zur Alterumwissenschaft, 11 (Baden-Baden, 1958); A. Boëthius, *Etruscan and Early Roman Architecture*, The Pelican History of Art, 2d ed. rev. (Harmondsworth, Engl., 1978), 94–101.

22. See M. Pallottino, *La necropoli di Cerveteri*, 7th ed. (Rome, 1968); A. Cavoli, *Profilo di una città etrusca: Cerveteri* (Pistoia, It., 1985); and the works cited in the previous note.

23. V. Cecconi and V. Melani, *Profilo di una città etrusca: Populonia* (Pistoia, It., 1981), 22, 79–80.

24. For more on Etruscan tomb architecture, see, in this volume, the essay by Dorothy Dvorsky Rohner, 132 ff.

25. Akerström, *Die etruskischen Gräber*, 163–64 (supra n. 21); Boëthius, *Etruscan and Early Roman Architecture*, 96–97 (supra n. 21); S. Steingräber, *Etrurien: Städte, Heiligtümer, Nekropolen* (Munich, 1981), 54–58, 114–15. Similar central piers are found in the Inghirami Tomb at Volterra and a tomb at Casaglia, for which see ibid., 102–4, 115–16. One of the earliest tombs of this type, the Tomba della Pietrera at Vetulonia, is a large tumulus with a diameter of about 70 meters that dates to the second half of the seventh century B.C.; see ibid., 140–42.

26. P. M. Fraser, *Ptolemaic Alexandria* (Oxford, 1972), 1:14–17, 2:13–18, 30–42; G. Fiaccadori, "The Tomb of Alexander the Great," *PP* 47 (1992): 128–31; R. Bianchi, "The Hunt for Alexander's Tomb," *Archaeology*, July/August 1993, 54–55.

27. Luc. 8.692–99.

28. M.-L. Bernhard, "Topographie d'Alexandrie: Le Tombeau d'Alexandre et le mausolée d'Auguste," *RA*, 6th ser., 47 (1956): 129–56; J.-C. Richard, " 'Mauseoleum': D'Halicarnasse à Rome, puis à Alexandrie," *Latomus* 29 (1970): 370–88; F. Coarelli, "Il Pantheon, l'apoteosi di Augusto, e l'apoteosi di Romolo," in *Città e architettura nella Roma imperiale: Atti del seminario . . .* , Analecta Romana Instituti Danici, Supplementum, 10 (Odense, Denm., 1983), 44; N. Purcell, "Tomb and Suburb," in *Römische Gräberstrassen . . .* , ed. H. von Hesberg and P. Zanker, Bayerische Akademie der Wissenschaften, Philosophisch-Historische Klasse, 96 (Munich, 1987), 27.

29. S. Hornblower, *Mausolus* (Oxford, 1982), 223–74; K. Jeppesen, "What Did the Mausolleion Look Like?" in *Architecture and Society in Hecatomnid Caria: Proceedings of the Uppsala Symposium, 1987*, ed. T. Linders and P. Hellström (Uppsala, Swed., 1989), 15–17; K. Jeppesen, ed., *The Mausolleion at Halikarnassos: Reports of the Danish Archaeological Expedition to Bodrum*, 3 vols. to date (Copenhagen, 1981–). For its influences on the mausoleum of Augustus, see Richard, " 'Mauseoleum' " (supra n. 28).

30. See n. 1 above.

31. Von Hesberg, *Römische Grabbauten*, 55–201 (supra n. 13).

32. D.H. 1.64.5 (E. Cary, ed. and trans., *The Roman Antiquities of Dionysius of Halicarnassus*, Loeb Classical Library, 87–93 [Cambridge, Mass., 1937], 1:212–13). For a helpful account of the various traditions concerning the death, burial, and apotheosis of Aeneas, see J. F. Hall, "The Original Ending of the Aeneas Tale: Cato and the Historiographical Tradition of Aeneas," *Syllecta Classica* 3 (1991): 13–20.

33. For the preliminary excavation reports, see P. Sommella, "Heroon di Enea a Lavinium: Recenti scavi a Pratica di Mare," *RPAA* 44 (1971–72): 47–74; P. Sommella, "Das Heroon des Aeneas und die Topographie des antiken Lavinium," *Gymnasium* 81 (1974): 273–97. The final report has yet to appear. For additional information and interpretations of the site, see Hall, "Original Ending of the Aeneas Tale," 19 (supra n. 32); G. K. Galinski, "The 'Tomb of Aeneas' at Lavinium," *Vergilius* 20 (1974): 2–11; G. K. Galinski, "Aeneas in Latium: Archäologie, Mythos, und Geschichte," in *2000 Jahre Vergil: Ein Symposion*, ed. V. Pöschl, Wolfenbütteler Forschungen, 24 (Wiesbaden, 1983), 37–62, esp. 42–47; R. E. A. Palmer, *Roman Religion and Roman Empire: Five Essays* (Philadelphia, 1974), 120–21; C. F. Giuliani, "Santuario delle tredici are, Heroon di Enea," in *Enea nel Lazio: Archeologia e mito . . .* (Rome, 1981), 169–86; G. Dury-Moyaers, *Enée et Lavinium: A propos des découvertes archéologiques récentes*, Collection Latomus, 174 (Brussels, 1981), 121–27; C. Cogrossi, "Atena Iliaca e il culto degli eroi: L'heròon di Enea a Lavinio e Latino figlio di Odisseo," in *Politica e religione nel primo scontro tra Roma e l'Oriente*, ed. M. Sordi, Contributi dell'Istituto di storia antica, 8 (Milan, 1982), 79–98; F. Zevi, "Il mito di Enea nella documentazione archeologica: Nuove considerazioni," in *L'epos greco in Occidente: Atti del diciannovesimo convegno di studi sulla Magna Grecia . . .* (Taranto, It., 1980), 247–90, esp. 277–90; J. Poucet, "Un Culte d'Enée dans la région lavinate au IVe siècle avant J.-C.?" in *Hommages à Robert Schilling*, ed. H. Zehnacker and G. Hentz (Paris, 1983), 187–201, esp. 190–97.

34. Sommella's identification is accepted by Galinski (" 'Tomb of Aeneas,' " supra n. 33); see also F. Castagnoli, "La leggenda di Enea nel Lazio," *StudRom* 30 (1982): 1–15, esp. 13–14; questions have been raised by M. Pena ("El santuario y la tumba de Eneas," *EClás* 71 [1974]: 1–26) and E. Gruen (*Culture and National Identity in Republican Rome*, Cornell Studies in Classical Philology, 52 [Ithaca, N.Y., 1992], 24–25 with additional references). The most convincing argument in favor of identifying the tumulus with the heroon is given by Castagnoli, who notes the rarity of tumuli which have been converted into heroa. This tumulus fits the account offered by Dionysius.

35. For the veracity of the information offered by Dionysius, see A. Andrén, "Dionysius of Halicarnassus on Roman Monuments," in *Hommages à Léon Herrmann*, Collection Latomus, 44 (Brussels, 1960), 88–104. For other tumuli in the area around Lavinium, see Dury-Moyaers, *Enée et Lavinium*, 123–24 (supra n. 33).

36. On the revival of the cult of Aeneas under Julius Caesar and Augustus, see Palmer, *Roman Religion*, 120–25 (supra n. 33); Hall, "Original Ending of the Aeneas Tale" (supra n. 32); J. F. Hall, "P. Vergilius Maro: *Vates Etruscus*," *Vergilius* 28 (1982): 44–50, esp. 47; J. F. Hall, "The *Saeculum Novum* of Augustus and Its Etruscan Antecedents," *ANRW* II.16.3 (1986): 2564–89, esp. 2585–86; G. K. Galinski, *Aeneas, Sicily, and Rome*, Princeton Monographs in Art and Archaeology, 40 (Princeton, N.J., 1969), 164–69, 190–241.

37. D.C. 56.33.1; J.-C. Richard, "Tombeaux des empereurs et temples des 'divi': Notes sur la signification religieuse des sépultures impériales à Rome," *RHR* 120 (1966): 131.

38. Sen., *De Tranquillitate Animi* 14.9; Richard, "Tombeaux des empereurs," 132 (supra n. 37); D. Pippidi, *Recherches sur le culte impérial,* Institut roumain d'études latines, 2 (Bucharest, 1939), 75. Further examples of cultic practices at this and other imperial tombs will be discussed in my book, as mentioned in n. 1.

39. Zanker, *Power of Images,* 201–3 (supra n. 1); P. Zanker, *Il foro di Augusto* (Rome, 1984), 17–18.

40. E. Simon, *Ara Pacis Augustae* (New York, n.d.), 23–24; Zanker, *Power of Images,* 203–5 (supra n. 1). Other links between Augustus and Aeneas are cited by Hall ("P. Vergilius Maro," 49–50 [supra n. 36]), who points out that Aeneas was honored as founder and ancestor, and by Zanker (*Power of Images,* 205–10 [supra n. 1]).

41. The problem of architectural copying in the Roman world has not, to my knowledge, been the subject of a study. As an example of the differentiation between model and copy in Roman architecture, the Pantheon and its copies may be cited. See K. De Fine Licht, *The Rotunda in Rome: A Study of Hadrian's Pantheon* (Copenhagen, 1968), 221–26; W. L. MacDonald, *The Pantheon: Design, Meaning, and Progeny* (Cambridge, Mass., 1976), 94–104.

Tyrrhena Regum Progenies:
Etruscan Literary Figures
from Horace to Ovid

ROGER T. MACFARLANE

Cassius Etruscus had a poetic style more violent than a river in full flood. Tradition has it that the body of Cassius was burned on a funeral pyre made of bookcases and his own turgid writings. This anecdote occurs in Horace's progammatic tenth *Satire* to illustrate a similar characteristic of Lucilius, Horace's literary model in that collection.

> *[sc. Lucilius] amet scripsisse ducentos*
> *ante cibum versus, totidem cenatus, Etrusci*
> *quale fuit Cassi rapido ferventius amni*
> *ingenium, capsis quem fama est esse librisque*
> *ambustum propriis.*[1]

Horace's anecdote is not flattering. The compounded verb *amburare*, meaning in its roots "to burn around; to scorch,"[2] suggests here that the pyre, its abundance of written fuel notwithstanding, could accomplish only partial cremation of a body as corpulent as that of Cassius.[3] Horace is playing on the theme of Etruscan decadence and excess that had already become topical before his contemporary, Diodorus Siculus, expounded on it.[4]

FIGURE 1. Aeneas carrying Anchises, terracotta, Veii, fourth century B.C., Rome, Museo di Villa Giulia. *Photo courtesy of Soprintendenza Archeologica per l'Etruria Meridionale.*

Cassius Etruscus wrote too much. Horace demanded brevity.[5] This discrepancy is a point of no small consequence for the Augustan critic, who elsewhere in the *Satires* roundly criticizes Lucilius for verbosity.[6] To express his distaste for this overabundant composition, Horace resorts to the metaphor of poetic production as a river: *rapido ferventius amni*. The gist of the metaphor, a stock feature of ancient criticism from Callimachus to Longinus, is not difficult to grasp: just as a flooding river disregards boundaries, so Cassius the Etruscan poet exceeded the bounds of Horatian taste.[7] In subsequent discussion of the faults of Lucilius—and presumably Horace would condemn Cassius Etruscus on the same charges—Horace states that, were Lucilius somehow to be transferred from his own day to Horace's, when poetic refinement was fully developed, Lucilius would learn to bite nervous nails to the quick and erase his work meticulously.[8] But in reality, poets such as Cassius Etruscus were entirely alien to Horace's assiduous craftsmanship, for they strayed beyond the limits of propriety in their composition of two hundred lines before dinner and two hundred more after.[9] However, other than Horace's astringent criticisms, little remains for illuminating the person of the poet Cassius, surnamed the Etruscan.

Porphyrio, the Horatian scholiast whose credibility on such matters is so remarkably poor,[10] confidently identified Cassius Etruscus as Cassius Parmensis. Of this Cassius little is known, though in the sources he is associated with some important poets from Cisalpine Gaul, contemporaries of the Neoterics.[11] Porphyrio mentions that the *Thyestes* of Cassius Parmensis survived to his day, and Horace's epistle to Tibullus soundly infers that Cassius Parmensis had distinguished himself as an author of pastoral or elegiac poetry.[12] But nothing of his writings survives. He was involved in matters of some political importance; most notable is the fact that he was an assassin of Caesar and in the wake of Actium was the last to suffer death.[13] Connecting Cassius Etruscus with Cassius Parmensis cannot, however, be done without making the same mistake that Porphyrio made. For the publication date of the *Satires*—some three years before Actium—makes the correlation chronologically impossible. For that matter, equation of Cassius Etruscus with any other identifiable individual, however desirable it might seem, is tenuous in light of the lack of evidence.

The name Cassius Etruscus has an intriguing taxonomy.[14] The apparently Latin gentilicial with the toponymic cognomen may suggest, on the one hand, that its bearer was a *cliens* of some Cassius—perhaps one of many Etruscans enfranchised after 150 B.C. who assumed their Roman patron's *gentilicium*.[15] Thus, the name could indicate that its owner acquired citizenship at some time during the second century B.C. On the other hand, it does not *necessarily* provide conclusive evidence of any sort, since toponymous gentilicia may in fact only show residence or possession and not genealogy.[16] For that matter, there is no assurance that Cassius was a real person and not merely a satiric fabrication.[17] Consequently, of Cassius Etruscus nothing sure can be said aside from this: he was perhaps too corpulent and he composed more than Horace thought proper. (It could be added, however, that the Roman tendency to restrict literary polemic to antecedents within the same genre suggests that Cassius Etruscus, whoever or whatever he was, wrote satire.) Still, at the very least, Cassius Etruscus serves in this paper as a case study initiating an inquiry into the state of Etruscan letters during the age of Horace, as well as investigation into the identity of several poets of the Augustan age, both canonical and less familiar, who worked before the backdrop of Etruscan political relations within the Augustan regime and whose nomenclature suggests Etruscan connections.[18]

Etruscan written sources, though scarcely extant today, were available in some abundance during the period of Augustus. It is known that the collected writings of Nigidius Figulus, who died in 45 B.C., were numerous, diverse, and certainly at hand.[19] The antiquarian L. Cincius wrote on a range of topics from religious mysteries to consular authority.[20] Vitruvius consulted Etruscan books on the location of temples.[21] Books on haruspicy, such as those by Laris Pulenas of Tarquinia, were worth mentioning on a funerary inscription and, presumably, worth preserving.[22] The famous Zagreb Linen Book survives today, representing countless less fortunate works on Etruscan religious subjects available in antiquity.[23] Ateius Capito, whom Augustus designated as director of the *Ludi Saeculares* in 17 B.C., almost certainly derived much of his scholarly expertise from the study of available Etruscan legal and haruspical sources.[24] In subsequent generations,

Etruscan writings were consulted with apparent ease and frequency at Rome.[25] For instance, the emperor Claudius, the noted scholar of things Etruscan, had unhindered access to original sources. Pliny mentions the survival of Etruscan *fabulae*.[26] And Censorinus in the third century A.D. still knew of Etruscan histories.[27]

How much of this written material was strictly documentary and how much literary is difficult to ascertain. A famous passage in Livy states that Roman schoolboys of the fourth century B.C. were educated at Caere[28] as their later successors would study at Athens. Was it Etruscan literature they studied there, or was their study restricted to the apparent pragmatism of the *Disciplina Etrusca?* Volnius, a tragic poet referred to by Varro, would presumably have written in verse;[29] but was the language of his drama Etruscan or Latin?[30] Lack of proof for the existence of Etruscan literature is frustrating.

The evidence in support of haruspical poetic literature, for instance, is tenuous indeed. It is based on the interpretation of the term *carmen* in association with Etruscan authors. On a pair of Latin *elogia* from Tarquinia recording the careers of two anonymous haruspices,[31] the meager remains of the original texts have elicited a variety of speculative interpretations; however, in each inscription a form of the word *carmen* is clearly preserved. Torelli's collocation of three epigraphic fragments[32] results in this reading of the first *elogium:*

> *fulmine procuravit ostenta suo*
> *carmine et augurales divinationes*
> *complures fecit. Post obitum huius*
> *sub (decem)viros ea discipulina relata est.*[33]

Likewise, although the text of the other *elogium* has been variously augmented, the clearly preserved words of line five stand beyond dispute:

> *et reliquom venerandum discipulinae*
> *antiquae ritum carminibus edidit.*[34]

The term *carmen* in each of these inscriptions suggests to some scholars that the texts written by each of the anonymous haruspices were in verse form.[35] The possibility of that being true is remote, as *carmen* probably ought to be interpreted in this context as sacred formulae, most likely in prose.[36]

As for other forms of literature, the ancient sources are almost utterly silent. They say hardly anything of Etruscan drama,[37] nothing of Etruscan epic, nothing of Etruscan lyric. A lack of lyric in a culture as noted for its famous musicians as was ancient Etruria is odd indeed.[38] In general, the evidence for Etruscan literature is ultimately disappointing. So, while Horace's brief lampoon of Cassius Etruscus is suggestive, it is by no means clear. His dedication of the *Carmina* to the Etruscan Maecenas, however, is very lucid.

Of all that is known of Maecenas (figure 2), the principal literary agent of Augustus, his genealogical descent from kings of Etruria may be the most familiar detail. Horace brackets his collection of *Carmina* with a pair of poems which address Maecenas as *atavis edite regibus* and *Tyrrhena regum progenies*, respectively.[39] The anonymous elegist of the *Appendix Vergiliana* also mentions Maecenas in light of his political significance.

> *regis eras, Etrusce, genus: tu Caesaris almi*
> *dextera, Romanae tu vigil Urbis eras.*[40]

Rome's watchman, of course, assisted in the direction of the Augustan state to no small degree. The role of Maecenas as right-hand man to Augustus was connected, not coincidentally, to his Etruscan heritage, for he was numbered among the group of Octavian's earliest supporters which shared ties through Etruscan ancestry.[41] For the purposes of this paper, the political role of Maecenas, the importance of which is difficult to overstate, is secondary to his literary role.

The indirect influence Maecenas wielded on contemporary poetry is most evident in his patronage of the Augustan poets. He established a literary environment that was conducive to greatness. But his direct involvement, in the form of his own poetry, has survived poorly, being represented by a pittance of fragments.[42] It is also little regarded; both ancient and modern critics have disparaged his multifaceted literary production.[43] This may be undeserved.[44] Recorded among his prose writings are a *Prometheus;* a *Symposium* in which Vergil, Horace, and Messalla Corvinus were interlocutors; and the infamous treatise *De Cultu Suo*, from which Seneca the Younger drew considerable ammunition in his assault on its author's literary excess. In the poetic

FIGURE 2. Bust of Maecenas, marble, Rome, Museo Nuovo nel Palazzio dei Conservatori, inv. 11741. *Photo courtesy of Alinari /Art Resource.*

fragments of Maecenas the literary influence of Lucretius, Horace, Vergil, and especially Catullus is readily apparent.[45] The fragments reveal a metrical eclecticism and strictness rivaled only by Horace: surviving fragments are composed in hendecasyllabic phalaecians, priapeans, iambic trimeters, and dactylic hexameters. No less confined by generic restraints than Horace, Maecenas offered an epigram, a rare galliambic epyllion on the Magna Mater, and poems in other genres. In all, his poetry may have comprised a collection of at least ten books.[46] Even if this detail is based on some error, the variety of his literary output nevertheless maintains impressive dimensions. It was a collection of gems, admirable in its variety, which Augustus mentioned in the conclusion of an intimate verse epistle to Maecenas as preserved by Macrobius:

> *vale, mi ebenum Medulliae,*
> *ebur ex Etruria, lasar Arretinum,*
> *adamas supernas, Tiberinum margaritum,*
> *Cilniorum smaragde, iaspi Iguvinorum,*
> *berulle Porsennae, carbunculum Hadriae,*
> ἵνα συντέμνω πάντα, μάλαγμα *moecharum.*[47]

These reflections, reminiscent of Neoteric[48] poetry, intone the familiar theme of distinguished ancestry. In so doing, the lines suggest a troubling discrepancy between this heritage of Maecenas and his poetic legacy, for among his scattered output nothing stands out as even remotely Etruscan. As literary minister of Augustus he seems, rather, to have composed a variegated literary corpus which one might characterize as entirely Greco-Roman in essence. To press this point too far would require hazardous argument from silence, since most of what he wrote is lost; yet, in itself, the silence of our sources seems telling. His Etruscan ancestry might be expected to have begotten such themes or caused him to employ such words and phrases as might have attracted the attention of scholiasts and other excerptors. This seems not to have been the case; the meager fragments preserve the output of a poet writing largely under Greek literary influence.[49] Ironically, the offspring of Etruscan kings survives now in the learned garb of a Hellenistic scholar-poet.

If, in fact, Maecenas eschewed Etruscan themes in his writings, he was himself oddly exempt from the encouragement his poets received. The poets whom Maecenas assembled under Augustan patronage seem to have been encouraged to write on topics that recalled the ancient splendor of Etruria. This encouragement may be manifest especially in the renewed prestige of the term *vates* among the Augustan poets.[50] The word *vates* had by late Republican times acquired a pejorative meaning equivalent to "fortune-teller" or "soothsayer." In the context of poetic composition, *vates* had been replaced by the transliterated Greek term *poeta*. Maecenas may well have been a key instrument in restoring the term *vates* to its dignified usage.

To a greater or lesser degree, each of the surviving Augustan poets dealt with themes of antique grandeur. The Augustans frequently versified their refusal to treat the grand themes that were being foisted upon them. *Reges et proelia*—wars and panegyric—were among the topics that poets decline in their *recusationes*. The introductory poem of the second book of Propertius suggests that these also included Etruscan topics:

> *nam quotiens Mutinam aut civilia busta Philippos*
> *aut canerem Siculae classica bella fugae,*
> *eversosque focos antiquae gentis Etruscae,*
> *et Ptolemaeei litora capta Phari,*
> *aut canerem Aegyptum et Nilum . . .*
> *te mea Musa illis semper contexeret armis,*
> *et sumpta et posita pace fidele caput.*[51]

Such topics were deemed undesirable for an Augustan poet (writing under the influence of Alexandrian refinement), because the poet who treated them was obliged by the unwieldy nature of his material to exceed the narrow bounds of refinement and taste that his Muse dictated. Expressions of distaste for grand themes are common among the works of the vatic circle assembled by Maecenas.[52]

In this respect, Vergil's *Aeneid* represents one of the great puzzles of Latin literary history.[53] Many have questioned Vergil's motive for renouncing his earlier declarations to avoid writing on grand themes. Both the *Eclogues* and the *Georgics* feature prominent avowals to this effect.[54] Yet, in fact, Vergil did relent and compose the *Aeneid*. Published posthumously in 19 B.C., the *Aeneid* is an epic in which the political interests of supporters of Augustus, as well as Vergil's own genealogical heritage, are beneficially treated. For Vergil himself composes the poem as an Etruscan *vates*, a literal and literary son of Etruria.[55] And the Etruscan interest in Vergil's *Aeneid* is great. This is an important point, because it helps explain the apparent violation of the principles Vergil had set forth in his earlier poems. In the *Aeneid*, according to J. F. Hall, "Vergil consciously constructs his story of Trojan-Etruscan alliance both to reflect the Etruscan support of Augustus and to provide mythological precedent for an Italy in which Trojan (or Roman) and Etruscan labor in tandem, and thus ensure the establishment of an ordered and orderly society."[56] Such a story required a literary vehicle bigger than the bucolic *carmina* and quite unlike the didacticism of his earlier work. Apparently, an obligation to promote Augustanism superseded Vergil's earlier determination to versify smaller themes and resulted in the composition of the *Aeneid*. It may be that the impulse to include Etruscan themes is precisely what produced Vergil's epic.

Horace seems also to have incorporated Etruscan themes into his lyric mode. In form, the *Carmen Saeculare* marks no significant departure from his earlier mode of writing.[57] The genius that had inspired his lyric collection of 23 B.C. was expressed also in the official hymn of the *Ludi Saeculares* of 17 B.C. More than in the Roman odes, in which Horace seems to promote the spirit of Roman nationalism as *Musarum sacerdos*, he adopts in the Secular Hymn a specifically Augustan stance.[58] In addition, certain elements of the Etruscan *saeculum* appear in Horace's poem.[59]

It is generally noticed that Horace paid increased attention to pro-Augustan topics in the *Carmen Saeculare* and *Carmina* 4. To be sure, in the lyric collection of 23 B.C. Horace had addressed politically important issues, but his primary role there could scarcely be seen as that of stalwart advocate. Political influences become more clear and frequent in Horace's later lyrics. This change has formerly been explained as a result of the fall of Maecenas from Augustan grace in the Varro Murena affair of 23 or 22 B.C.[60] But the pro-Etruscan program of the

Carmen Saeculare might as easily be explained as Horace's compliance with his patron's suggestions.

A similar tendency toward Etruscan themes may also be seen in the later work of Propertius, premier elegist among the poets of Maecenas. The *Monobiblos* of Propertius attracted the attention of Maecenas, as had Horace's early works, and earned him a spot among the group of poets enlisted for the promotion of Augustan Rome's new image.[61] Under the patronage of Maecenas, Propertius published Books Two and Three of his elegiac corpus between 26 and 20 B.C. Then, in 16 B.C., he released the enigmatic fourth book.[62] This collection of unusual poems displays in its most refined state the elegist's craft; the material, however, on which Propertius works that craft seems almost entirely resistant to natural poesis. Book 4 becomes a struggle for elegiac propriety. In the opening poem, for instance, Propertius cites the names of the original three Roman tribes. The order in which the elegiac poet arranges the names of the three tribes—Tities, Ramnes, Luceres—may be ultimately attributable to Ennius.[63] For an elegist to incorporate the work of the father of Latin hexameter poetry into his own poem is surprise enough; but it is especially surprising to see the group of authors who list the tribes in this order: Ennius, Varro, Cicero, Livy, Propertius, Plutarch, Festus, and Servius. A crowd of historians and antiquarians makes strange company indeed for an elegist to keep.[64] Book 4 continues with similar surprises: the erotic tale of Tarpeia's infatuation with Tatius, 4.4, bears little resemblance to the related accounts by historians; in 4.6 the elegist provides an elaborate treatment of the Battle of Actium; 4.9 deals with the establishment of the Ara Maxima and the cult of Hercules Invictus. The poet himself states in the introductory poem that he is prepared to sing new topics: *sacra diesque canam et cognomina prisca locorum.*[65] The remainder of the book continues to demonstrate the new direction of the poet's elegy.

Among the more startling items in Book 4, the second poem—the great Vertumnus elegy—is particularly appropriate in a discussion of Etruscan themes in the Roman poets. In 4.2 Propertius successfully presents a highly refined elegiac poem of over sixty lines on a "most unlikely antiquarian subject,"[66] the statue of the Etruscan god Vertumnus which stood in Rome at the top of the Vicus Tuscus. The poem is a monologue, addressed to an unnamed passerby. "Why marvel," Vertumnus begins, "at the many shapes in my one substance?" (1). He then enjoins the reader to "learn the ancestral tokens of the god Vertumnus.[67] A Tuscan, I am sprung from Tuscans" (2–3). Drawn out by *evocatio* from Volsinii, a town where he was the chief god,[68] Vertumnus took up his place on the Velabrum, next to the Forum Romanum, where once the Tiber used to bend.[69] Perhaps it would be more appropriate to say "turn," because in the subsequent lines the god makes puns on the sound *ver-* and the meaning of his name.

> *at postquam ille suis tantum concessit alumnis,*
>   *Vertumnus* ver*so dicor ab amne deus.*
> *seu, quia* vert*entis fructum praecepimus anni,*
>   *Vertumni rursus credidit esse sacrum.*
> *prima mihi* var*iat liventibus uva racemis,*
>   *et coma lactenti spicea fruge* tume*t.*[70]

The punning aside, Vertumnus proceeds to describe his multifaceted nature: his ability to alter his shape to suit any situation. A girl, a man, a reaper, a pleader; Phoebus, Iacchus, Faunus;[71] a fowler, a fisher, a peddler, or a shepherd—Vertumnus changes his nature whenever the inhabitants of the neighborhood change his clothing. Thus, he says, his country's native language named him from his mutability. The speaking statue observes how Rome welcomed both him and the Etruscans whence he came. He recollects fondly the thrashing Titus Tatius and his Sabines took at the hands of Romulus and the Etruscans; and he overlooks the eventual reconciliation among the three groups. Vertumnus concludes with a prayer to *diuum Sator*, the begetter of the gods, that Rome may prosper and that future generations of Romans may continue to pass before his feet.

The topic Propertius chose in this poem is, as stated above, puzzling. Perhaps knowing more about the duties and characteristics of Vertumnus would help. Failing more accurate information on Vertumnus, it is at least important to note that Propertius leads off his collection of poems on state themes with one about the chief Etruscan god.[72] The poem apparently comes as a response to an invitation from the *Princeps* to address state themes—specifically, themes that pertained to the Roman assumption of Etruscan properties, both divine and real. This last book of Propertius bears, as does Horace's later lyric, the clear signs of a commissioned work of poetry.[73] It is worth recalling J. Griffin's sarcastic beratement of *Carmina* 4 as exactly the kind of poetry Augustus intended Augustan poetry to be.[74] Perhaps.

Written during a more fully developed period of the general influence of Augustus, the fourth elegiac book reflects the impulse of Propertius to compose elegy on state themes. This impulse, notably, marks the novelty of the book with an Etruscan theme. The elegist's reaction to his patron's enhanced influence is not unlike that of Vergil, who composed the national epic, or that of Horace, who composed a national anthem, the *Carmen Saeculare*, on Etruscan themes. Each of these compositions suggests a development in Augustan policy on literature that occurred as the personal influence of Augustus became more firmly established, sometime after 23 B.C. Ironically, the poets seemed to become motivated to write in a way Maecenas was neither able nor willing to impose—either upon his protégés or upon himself—before this time.

Apart from the principal poets of the circle Maecenas assembled are some lesser-known individuals mentioned in Ovid's final poem, the posthumous *Epistle from Pontus* 4.16. As poetry, this work is unmoving: it is not the final emotional appeal for restitution that one might expect in its exiled author's last work, but rather a resignation.[75] But in its fifty-two lines, this tantalizing literary historical document lists thirty rivals of Ovid who have become popular at Rome during his exile at the end of the Augustan Age, withholding much useful information on most of them. Ten of the thirty, says H. B. Evans, are virtually unknown.[76] The fact that three of these ten have Etruscan nomenclature leads to certain conclusions about Etruscan literature at the end of the Augustan Age.[77]

The first of Ovid's Etruscan unknowns—actually, two are mentioned—are the Prisci in line 10.[78] Ovid compares either Priscus to the subtle Numa:

> *quique dedit Latio carmen regale Severus,*
> *et cum subtili Priscus uterque Numa.*[79]

Various references in later sources suggest the identification of at least one of these Prisci as a Tarquitius Priscus. The gentilicial name Tarquitius is related to the name of Rome's Etruscan monarchs, the Tarquinii.[80] His dates are unknown. Macrobius refers on two occasions to the *Ostentaria*, a work on Etruscan haruspicy transcribed by Tarquitius Priscus.[81] Of the fragments preserved, both are in prose, though one ends with a trimeter clausula.[82] E. Bormann's theory — based on his reading of *CIL* XI, 7566, *carminibus edidit* — that Tarquitius Priscus wrote in *senarii* and other short verses (e.g., *epodes?*) is perhaps incorrect;[83] however, in favor of Bormann's thesis two facts ought to be considered: first, the context of Ovid's listing, which suggests an author of works in verse; and second, the polemic address of *Catalepton* 5.3–4. The anonymous author of that poem inveighs against Selius, Tarquitius, and Varro as an extravagant generation of scholars (*scholasticorum natio madens pingui*). Of these three, only Varro, who wrote learned Menippean verse, may be identified with certainty; Selius remains obscure.[84] However, since the gist of *Catalepton* 5 clearly has to do with poetry (cf. *formosi*, 7; *Camenae*, 11–12) and since literary invective generally deals with rivals in its own genre, the natural conclusion is that the Tarquitius of *Catalepton* 5 was a poet also. If he may be connected to the Priscus of Ovid's farewell, then the two Prisci (*Priscus uterque*) may be identified as father and son—the father addressed in the pseudo-Vergilian poem,[85] the son mentioned as Ovid's rival a generation later in the letter from exile. Unfortunately, Ovid says far too little of his rivals to allow more than speculative identification.

The next of Ovid's unknown Etruscan poets is called Tuscus, author of a *Phyllis*. The work was almost certainly an erotic elegy with possible reference to Vergilian pastoral: *quique sua nomen Phyllide Tuscus habet*.[86] O. Hennig identified this poet as Clodius Tuscus *grammaticus*, the compiler of a farmer's almanac, which Tuscus is said to have offered Ovid as a *calendarium* for the *Fasti*.[87] The anonymous scholia on the almanac are used by Servius in the *Aeneid* commentary.[88] Granted, Tuscus was not so rare a *cognomen* as to make the identification of Ovid's Tuscus certain.[89] Nevertheless, the three poetic tasks attributed to this Tuscus seem similar enough to those of Clodius Tuscus to encourage the view that they were the same individual.

The third Etruscan mentioned among Ovid's rivals is a tragic poet named Turranius: *Musaque Turrani tragicis innixa coturnis.*[90] This man's *nomen* is derived ultimately from a transliteration of Τυρρηνιός—the Greek adjective meaning Etruscan.[91] The name is sometimes confused with the better known names of Thoranius or Toranius,[92] but there is no need to question the integrity of the text on this passage.[93] He may possibly be identified as Turranius Gracilis, a source for Pliny's *Natural History* on topics such as mermen, sea creatures, and cereals of Baetica and Africa.[94] Pliny gives no dates for him but says that he was born in Spain, near the Promontory of Mellaria (3.3).

Another possibility is to identify Ovid's tragic poet as C. Turranius, the first *praefectus annonae*, an appointee of Augustus who still held the position in the reign of Claudius.[95] Given this man's responsibility in the distribution of grain, he may well be the son or grandson of C. Turranius, the praetor of 44 B.C.[96] The family had longstanding possession of land in Italy.[97] The fact that the elder Turranius is grouped in the company of L. Marcius Philippus and Sp. Oppius in the *Philippics* (3.25) probably throws some light on this "very obscure" and "dim figure."[98] The association among prominent Etruscan supporters of Octavian easily justifies the Augustan appointment to an eminent political office. If this identification is valid, Turranius would hardly have been the first politician-poet.

To be sure, much of this is conjectural; whether these particular identifications of Ovid's unknowns are correct is difficult to say. Sure verification aside, they do show that at the time of Ovid's death in A.D. 17 poets of Etruscan descent were active in Roman literary circles. Each of those mentioned in Ovid's list by his Etruscan name is associated with a particular type of poetry. Most telling is that each of these poets writes in a genre that is soundly within the established Greek and Roman literary traditions: the *Phyllis* of Tuscus, the tragic muse of Turranius, and the *regale carmen* of Priscus (if he is Tarquitius Priscus). Like Maecenas, none appears to stray from the beaten path of Greco-Roman literature.

Among the next generation of Roman poets comes A. Persius Flaccus, the Stoic satirist under Nero, whose Etruscan nomenclature and heritage are sure.[99] Ancient biographies give Volterrae as his birthplace. His note on the absurdity of those who make too much importance of their diluted regal ancestry may have an autobiographical tone.

> *an deceat pulmonem rumpere ventis*
> *stemmate quod Tusco ramum millesime ducis?*[100]

Persius holds, of course, a significant position between Horace and Juvenal, the notable surviving masters of the most thoroughly Roman genre. Except for this one moment, Persius may just as well have come from Apulia or Aquinum. In his writings, nothing stands out as particularly Etruscan in character. What was true of Maecenas, *atavis editus regibus*, is equally true of Persius: neither made as much of his Etruscan ancestry as others anticipated he should.

Whether the writings of literary Etruscans served as pyre fuel, as in the reputed case of Cassius Etruscus, or whether they suffered destruction through more natural and gradual but nevertheless thorough means, it is certain that very little evidence of Etruscan literature has survived from antiquity. There are abundant references in Roman texts to various aspects of the *Disciplina Etrusca*, for Roman scholars had ready access to pertinent writings in regard to it. However, scholars at Rome are silent on matters of Etruscan literature. They make no mention of Etruscan writings in canonical genres adapted from Greek. The circle of poets assembled by Maecenas seem to have been encouraged to write about Etruscan topics, but they were unable to do so. Perhaps their inability was due to a lack of material; for when they eventually came to treat such themes, though never in more than a limited way, the results were cast in forms that were already tried and true in Greek literature. Even Maecenas himself produced abundantly in genres imported to Latium from Greece.

The Augustan poets produced what material they did on Etruscan themes in agreement, it seems, with their patron's vision of developing a national literature with themes of greatness that survived the decline of ancient Etruria and the coming of Rome. The mature works of

Vergil, Horace, and Propertius illuminate this vision. The experiment was not long-lived. And by the time Augustus died, the vision was gone. As Ovid marked the end of the age in exile, his rivals included men with Etruscan background writing solidly within the parameters of Greek genres. Unmindful, as was Persius, of their Etruscan ancestry, these poets offered little expectation of an Etruscan literary revival.

NOTES

1. "... [sc. Lucilius] loves to have written two hundred lines before a meal and as many after dining; so, more violent than a swift river was the talent of Cassius Etruscus who, according to the story, was cremated upon his own bookcases and texts" (Hor., *S.* 1.10.60–64).

2. A. Kiessling and R. Heinze, eds., *Q. Horatius Flaccus: Satiren*, 9th ed. (Dublin, 1967), 171; C. T. Lewis and C. Short, *A Latin Dictionary* (Oxford, 1879), s.v. "amburare," groups this passage with others under the definition, "Of those whom the lightning had struck, but not killed: Sen., *Ag.* 537," etc.; contrast to *OLD*, s.v. "amburare," 3.b: "to cremate (a corpse)": Cic., *Sest.* 143 (that of Clodius); *Mil.* 86 (that of Oetaean Hercules). Of this latter set, the second passage must be taken as a rhetorical understatement for Kiessling and Heinze's thesis to hold. However, Horace's use of Phaethon's scorching (*Carm.* 4.11.25) may be most telling: cf. Ov., *Met.* 2.310–13, 326, where the bolt of Ovid's Helios makes by no means only partial contact with Phaethon.

3. Ps.-Acr., *Ad Hor. Sat.* 1.10.63–64: *Capsis quem fama est esse librisque ambustum propriis. Aspere, quasi tam verbosa aut tam multa scripserit, ut, cum non videre[n]tur legi digna, illis ipsis mortuus exustus sit* ("[When Horace writes] *Capsis quem fama est esse librisque ambustum propriis,* [he means] 'roughly', as if [Cassius] wrote such lengthy and such abundant works, that, since they seemed unworthy of reading, his body was cremated upon those very works themselves"). For the pyre stuffed with papyrus, Kiessling and Heinze refer to Mart. 8.44.14, 10.97.1.

4. D.S. 5.40.3–5: "Etruria's abundance has led its inhabitants of late to an effete lifestyle, καθόλου δὲ τὴν μὲν ἐκ παλαιῶν χρόνων παρ' αὐτοῖς ζηλουμένην ἀλκὴν ἀποβεβλήκασιν ἐν πότοις δὲ καί ῥᾳθυμίαις ἀνάνροις βιοῦντες οὐκ ἀλόγως τὴν τῶν πατέρων δόξαν ἐν τοῖς πολέμοις ἀποβεβλήκασι" ("... on the whole they have forfeited the prowess that has been among them an object of emulation from ancient times and by living a life of drunkenness and effeminate sloth they have forfeited, not unfittingly, their ancestral glory in war"). Cf. 8.18.1 on the Sybarites' affinity with Tyrrhenian luxuriance, which surpassed that of all other *barbaroi;* and Catul. 39.11.

5. Hor., *S.* 1.10.9–10: *est brevitate opus, ut currat sententia, neu se // impediat verbis lassas onerantibus auris* ("Brevity is needed, so that the thought may be quick and not hinder ears wearying under burdensome words").

6. Ibid., 1.4.6–13.

7. Call., *Ap.* 108–12; [Longinus,] *Subl.* 33.5 (against Archilochus). In Horace the clearest statement is in *S.* 1.1.59–60; cf. 1.10.36–37 (of Varro Atacinus?), 50–51 (of Lucilius); *Carm.* 4.2.5–24, 27–32 (of Pindaric versus Horatian lyric style).

8. Hor., *S.* 1.10.68–72.

9. Cf. Plutarch's assessment of Cicero's prolixity: five hundred lines in one night (*Cic.* 40).

10. Porph., *Ad Hor. Sat.* 1.10.61–62: *Cassi Etrusci Parmensis dicit, cuius tragoedia haec est Thyestes exstat* ("He means Cassius Etruscus of Parma, whose tragedy, i.e. the *Thyestes*, is extant"). On the accuracy of his judgment, see, for instance, R. G. M. Nisbet and M. Hubbard, *A Commentary on Horace Odes, Book 1* (Oxford, 1970), xlvii–li, which disparages the "uneven standard," "conspicuous deficiencies," and "lack of common sense" that invalidate the reliability of Horace's scholiasts.

11. E. Rawson, *Intellectual Life in the Late Roman Republic* (Baltimore, 1985), 35, n. 86.

12. Hor., *Ep.* 1.4.

13. Vell. 2.87.3.

14. The Latin *gentilicium* "Cassius" seems oddly paired with this cognomen when matched to such instances from epigraphic sources as Sex. Largenna Etruscus, L. Tarquitius Etruscus, or L. Plexina Etruscus; cf. W. Schulze, *Zur Geschichte lateinischer Eigennamen*, 2d ed., Akademie der Wissenschaften, Göttingen, Philologisch-Historische Klasse, Abhandlungen, n.f., Bd. 5, Nr. 5 (Berlin, 1966), 89, n. 3 (Schulze groups the name under "Lateinische gentilnamen," 423). For other apparently cognominal instances of "Etruscus," see *CIL* XI, 1606, 1609 (Gellio C. F. Sca Etrusco Decurioni Flor[entiae]), 2080 (L. Turio Etrusco), 2461 (L. Titi T. F. Etrusci), 3370 (cf. 7566), 4385 (a certain]ruscu[mentioned with T. Braetius Rufus).

15. W. V. Harris, *Rome in Etruria and Umbria* (Oxford, 1971), 208–10, evaluates H. R. W. Rix's study in nomenclature (*Das etruskische Cognomen: Untersuchungen zu System, Morphologie, und Verwendung der Personnamen auf den jüngeren Inschriften Nordetruriens* (Wiesbaden, Ger., 1963).

16. R. E. A. Palmer, *The Archaic Community of the Romans* (Cambridge, 1970), 134; cf. R. Syme, "Senators, Tribes, and Towns," *Historia* 13 (1964): 105–9. J. F. Hall ("The Municipal Aristocracy of Etruria and Their Participation in Politics at Rome, B.C. 91–A.D. 14" [Ph.D. diss., University of Pennsylvania, 1984], 8–9 [hereinafter cited as "MAE"]) advises that since a person with Etruscan nomenclature may have descended only indirectly from Etruscan emigrés to other parts of the Italian peninsula, one must produce onomastic, epigraphic, and literary documentation before asserting that a given individual is or is not Etruscan.

17. N. Rudd (*The Satires of Horace* [Cambridge, 1966], 132–59), in discussing names in the *Satires*, lists six categories: (a) Horace's contemporaries, (b) the dead, (c) Lucilian characters, (d and e) typical characters, and (f) cryptonyms. Rudd groups Cassius Etruscus among the dead.

18. See also, in this volume, the essay by John F. Hall, 167 ff.

19. Hall, "MAE," Appendix 61.2 (supra n. 16).

20. *RE* III, cols. 2555–56 [G. Wissowa]; J. Heurgon, "L. Cincius et la loi du *clavus annalis*," *Athenaeum* 42 (1964): 432–37; Rawson, *Intellectual Life*, 247–48 (supra n. 11).

21. Vitr. 1.7.1.

22. Laris Pulenas, a Tarquinian dignitary, wrote books on haruspicy (*CIE* 5430: *ʒix neθsrac acasce*), which he mentions before his civic duties in Tarquinia and before his priesthoods. Cf. M. Pallottino, *Etruscologia*, 6th ed. (Milan, 1977), 403–4; but see also the vastly different interpretation of S. S. Bilbija, *The Mummy of Zagreb and Other Etruscan, Lydian, Lycian Written Monuments* (Chicago, 1989), 94–95. For more on Laris Pulenas, see, in this volume, the essay by Nancy Thomson de Grummond, 359 and figure 4 on p. 339.

23. Pallottino, *Etruscologia*, 198–99, 223–24 (supra n. 22).

24. Tac., *Ann.* 3.70.4: *humani divinique iuris sciens;* Macrobius (7.13.11) refers especially to Ateius Capito's authority in matters of divine law. See J. F. Hall, "The *Saeculum Novum* of Augustus and Its Etruscan Antecedents," *ANRW* II.16.3 (1986): 2586–88, on Ateius Capito's introduction of Etruscan ritual elements into the Secular Games of Augustus in 17 B.C.

25. Cf. Plu., *Quaest. Conv.* 8.7–8.

26. Plin., *Nat. Hist.* 36.93.

27. Cens. 17.6.

28. Liv. 9.36.

29. Var., *L.* 5.55.

30. K. O. Müller (cited in *RE* IXA, cols. 766–67, s.v. "Volnius" [W. Strzelecki]) posited that Volnius wrote in order to preserve his language. If in fact he was writing contemporaneously with Varro, as the tense of Varro's verb suggests, a composition in Etruscan may only have served an antiquarian interest.

31. *CIL* XI, 3370 = *ILS* 2924; *CIL* XI, 7566; M. Torelli, *Elogia tarquiniensia*, Studi e materiali di etruscologia e antichità italiche, 15 (Florence, 1975), 105–19. Torelli, who speculates much on the membership of the two individuals to the haruspical college at Tarquinia, calls them Anonimi I and II; J. Heurgon ("Tarquitius Priscus et l'organisation de l'ordre des haruspices sous l'empereur Claude," *Latomus* 12 [1953]: 402–17) less timidly follows E. Bormann ("Etruskisches aus römischer Zeit," *Archäologisch-epigraphische Mitteilungen aus Österreich-Ungarn* 11 [1887]: 94 ff.) in his identification of the haruspex of the former fragment as Tarquitius Priscus.

32. Torelli, *Elogia tarquiniensia*, 105–16 and pl. 8 (supra n. 31). Torelli combines (1) an epigraphic fragment published by Bormann in 1869 ("Etruskisches aus römischer Zeit," pass. [supra n. 31]) = *CIL* XI, 7566, together with (2) a fragmentary inscription published by P. Romanelli ("Tarquinia: Scavi e ricerche nell'area della città," *NSA* 73 [1948]: 260–61) and (3) a small inscribed triangular stone recorded in his log by L. Marchese but now lost (see Torelli's pl. 17 for Marchese's

sketch). From these three disparate stones Torelli recovers a portion of the "Fasti Tarquiniensi dell'ordo LX haruspicum." Torelli's text varies greatly from Bormann's and, if correct, dashes the use of the texts to identify Tarquitius Priscus.

33. "In his *carmen*, he concerned himself with things shown by lightning, and he made numerous augural prophecies. After the death of this man that knowledge was conveyed to the decemvirs" (*CIL* XI, 7566, according to Torelli).

34. " . . . and he produced the remaining venerable rite of the ancient *disciplina* in his *carmina*" (*CIL* XI, 3370.4–5, according to Bormann).

35. For example, T. J. Cornell, reviewing Torelli's *Elogia tarquiniensia* in *JRS* 68 (1978): 168, adduces Lucretius (6.381) and Censorinus (4.13) to support his view that Etruscan sacred books were written in meter (*carmina*). Lydus (*Ost.* 54) and Isidorus Hispalensis (*Orig.* 8.9.35) may also suggest versified originals.

36. Cf. C. Bailey, ed. and trans., *Titi Lucreti Cari De Rerum Natura Libri Sex* (Oxford, 1947), 3:1612 (from Lucr. 6.381): *Tyrrhena . . . carmina* he translates as "Tyrrhenian *prophecies*" (my emphasis), *carmen* being the "regular word for a religious formula or prescription"); see also Rawson, *Intellectual Life*, 27 (supra n. 11).

37. On Etruscan theater, see, in this volume, the essay by Robert L. Maxwell, 267 ff.

38. E. Richardson, *The Etruscans: Their Art and Civilization* (Chicago, 1976), 225. On Etruscan music in general, see, in this volume, the essay by Harrison Powley, 287 ff.

39. Hor., *Carm.* 1.1.1 ("born from ancient kings"), 3.29.1 ("Tyrrhenian offspring of kings"). Cf. *S.* 1.6.1–2; Prop. 3.9.1; etc. These frequent contemporary recollections of the regal ancestry of Maecenas are curious. In Horace especially, they punctuate in a memorable way the poems in which Horace himself declares his dedication to the lesser genres. For instance, *Carm.* 1.1 opens with the broad invocation of Maecenas, descended from Etruscan kings, and closes with the poet's contentment to achieve much in little verses of lyric poetry. This is essentially true of the statement in 3.29 as well, in that Horace equates low birth with freedom from affairs of state and the leisure to write lyric. One wonders if Maecenas is being ribbed for negligence to fulfill his regal birthright by engaging grand themes.

40. "You were, Etruscan, the race of a king: you were Great Caesar's right hand, the sentinel of the City of Rome" (*Eleg. Maec.* 13–14).

41. Hall, "MAE," Appendix 58.5 (supra n. 16); J. F. Hall, "L. Marcius Philippus and the Rise of Octavian Caesar," *AugAge* 5 (1986): 37–43.

42. For the collected fragments of writings by Maecenas, see W. Morel, ed., *Fragmenta Poetarum Latinorum*, 2d ed. (Leipzig, 1927); P. Lunderstedt, *De Maecenatis Fragmentis*, Commentarii Philologici Ienenses, 9.1 (Jena, Ger., 1911); J.-M. André, "Mécène écrivain," *ANRW* II.30.3 (1983): 1765–87; and now, E. Courtney, ed., *The Fragmentary Latin Poets* (Oxford, 1993), 276–81. Cf. *RE* XIV, cols. 207–29, s.v. "Maecenas (6)" [A. Kappelmacher].

43. Criticism of Maecenas for his literary style came from all sides: from Augustus himself, who parodied without mercy his friend's *myrobraches cincinni* ("myrrh-scented, curly-haired dandies"; Suet., *Aug.* 86.3) to Seneca the Younger, whose invective seems not to have been so good-natured (*Ep.* 19.9, 92.35, 114.4).

44. E. Norden, *Die antike Kunstprosa vom VI. Jahrhundert v. Chr. bis in die Zeit der Renaissance*, 7th ed. (Darmstadt, 1974), 1:292–94, was among the first to see the style of Maecenas as a manifestation of Asianism.

45. André, "Mécène écrivain," 1783 (supra n. 42).

46. From "Book 10" the grammarian Charisius cites a usage by Maecenas of the word *catinus* in the masculine gender: *catinus masculino genere dicitur, ut Maecenas in X . . . ait: ingeritur fumans calido cum farre catinus* (Courtney, *Fragmentary Latin Poets*, 1 [supra n. 42] = Lunderstedt, *De Maecenatis Fragmentis*, 7 [supra n. 42]). Assuming accurate transmission of text, this statement suggests that Maecenas wrote some work (an epic) of at least ten books; or, possibly, Charisius cites some anthology of which Maecenas is either sole or joint author.

47. Macrob., *Sat.* 2.4.12: "Farewell, my Medullian ebony, / my ivory from Etruria, my Arretine lasar, / my Adriatic diamond, my Tiberine pearl, / my emerald of the Cilnii, my jasper of the Iguvini, / my beryl of Prosenna, my carbuncle of Hadria— / *to circumscribe them all*— / my *emollient* of adulterers." Though Macrobius states that Augustus wrote these lines, Kappelmacher (*RE* xiv, col. 228 [supra n. 42]) believes that Augustus was referring to verses Maecenas had once written himself: "Die Verse stammen aus einem langeren Gedicht des M." ("The verses stem from a longer poem of M[aecenas]").

48. Kappelmacher (ibid.) observes that in the Macrobius passage "Zugrunde liegt hellenistische Poesie" (". . . lies the foundation of Hellenistic poetry").

49. J. K. Newman, *Augustus and the New Poetry*, Collection Latomus, 88 (Brussels, 1967), 35–36.

50. J. K. Newman, *The Concept of Vates in Augustan Poetry*, Collection Latomus, 89 (Brussels, 1967) is indispensable; cf. Newman, *Augustus and the New Poetry*, chap. 4, "The Concept of Vates," 99–128 (supra n. 49).

51. Prop. 2.1.27–36: "For as often as I was about to sing Mutina, or the civil funerals of Philippi, or the naval wars of the Sicilian flight, and sing the overturned hearths of the ancient Etruscan race, and the captured shores of Ptolemaean Pharos, and Egypt and the Nile . . . my Muse had ever connected you [Maecenas] among those battles, a trusted head when treaties were sealed or broken."

52. E.g., Hor., *Carm.* 2.20, 4.2, 4.15; *Epod.* 2.1.250–59; Prop. 3.3, 3.4., 4.1.

53. Cf. R. F. Thomas, "From *Recusatio* to Commitment: The Evolution of the Virgilian Programme," *Papers of the Leeds Latin Seminar* 5 (1986): 61–73.

54. E.g., Verg., *Ecl.* 6.1–9; *G.* 4.559–66. The significance of the *sphragis* to the *Georgics* is set within its literary historical framework with especial succinctness by R. Scodel and R. F. Thomas, "Virgil and the Euphrates," *AJPh* 105 (1984): 339. R. Coleman (ed., *Vergil: Eclogues* [Cambridge, 1977], 175–76), commenting on

Ecl. 6.3, notes the substantial difference between Vergil's contribution to the epic genre and, say, that of Furius Bibaculus in his epic aggrandizement of his contemporary Julius Caesar; if the *Aeneid* does promote the political agenda of its sponsors, then in its deft use of allegory it seems to surpass its literary antecedents.

55. J. F. Hall, "P. Vergilius Maro: *Vates Etruscus*," *Vergilius* 28 (1982): 44–50. On Mantua as an Etruscan place name, see C. de Simone, "Il nome etrusco del poleonimo *Mantua*," *SE* 58 (1992): 197–200.

56. Ibid., 48; cf. J. F. Hall, "Vergil, Augustus, and the Etruscans: Factional Politics and the Amorality of Empire," paper presented at the NEH Symposium on Vergil and the Morality of Empire, University of Colorado, Boulder, 25 April 1986, 9–10; manuscript copy in my possession.

57. In Book 4 Horace violates the metrical precept of Sapphics—that each hendecasyllable contain a caesura between the fifth and sixth syllables (a precept he apparently had imposed against Lesbian and Catullan precedent upon the metre)— with much greater frequency than in the collection of 23 B.C. In this matter, the *Carmen Saeculare* foreshadows the style of Book 4, where also the caesura is less rigidly applied.

58. For *Musarum sacerdos*, see Hor., *Carm.* 3.1.2–4. For the Augustan stance, see G. K. Galinsky, "Sol and the Carmen Saeculare," *Latomus* 26 (1967): 620; J. Griffin, "Caesar Qui Cogere Posset," in *Caesar Augustus: Seven Aspects*, ed. F. Millar and E. Segal (Oxford, 1984), 205–6.

59. See Hall, "*Saeculum Novum*," 2582–88 (supra n. 24).

60. The "fall from grace" theory began with R. Syme, *The Roman Revolution* (Oxford, 1939), 340–42, 409, and has been followed almost universally. Tac., *Ann.* 3.30.3–4, the key piece of ancient evidence implicating Maecenas in the conspiracy of Varro Murena, has been scrutinized recently by P. White, "Maecenas' Retirement," *CPh* 86 (1991): 130–38, who asserts that the fidelity and loyalty Maecenas manifested toward Augustus were never compromised; cf. P. White, *Promised Verse: Poets in the Society of Augustan Rome* (Cambridge, Mass., 1994), 95–108. G. Williams, who earlier supported Syme's theory of disgrace, has recently recanted his opinion in "Did Maecenas 'Fall from Favor'? Augustus' Literary Patronage," in *Between Republic and Empire: Interpretations of Augustus and His Principate*, ed. K. Raaflaub and M. Toher (Berkeley and Los Angeles, 1990), 258–75.

61. Propertius clearly is not of Etruscan descent. For his Umbrian heritage, see Prop. 1.22.9–10, 4.1.121–34.

62. M. Hubbard (*Propertius* [London, 1974], 117) reflects the common opinion that the commissioning by Augustus of Book 4 effected artistically restrained and, therefore, flawed poetry. Against this view, see J. P. Sullivan, *Propertius: A Critical Discussion* (Cambridge, 1976), 40 and 138 ff., in which the whole book is regarded as a *recusatio*. H. E. Pillinger ("Some Callimachean Influences on Propertius Book 4," *HSCP* 73 [1969]: 171–99) justifies the book's paradoxical nature as the poet's indentification with Callimachus, master of the *poikilia* (variegated) style; J. P. Hallet ("Book IV: Propertius' Recusatio to Augustus and Augustan Ideals" [Ph.D. diss.,

Harvard University, 1971]) asserts that the second elegy is aetiological. Notice, however, that Propertius selects the Etruscan god of metamorphosis; hence, is there an underlying criticism of Rome's treatment of an old ally?

63. Palmer, *Archaic Community*, 7 (supra n. 16).

64. Further, inclusion of Propertius among this group conflicts with that Alexandrian penchant for focused refinement of expression that the Augustan poets adapted and Propertius himself exemplifies. By contrast, the others in the list were all extremely prolific. Incredibly, the antiquarian-polymath Marcus Terentius Varro, for example, is said to have published nearly five hundred books by his seventy-seventh year (Gel. 3.10.17) and some six hundred books during his lifetime (cf. G. B. Conte, *Latin Literature: A History* [Baltimore, 1994], 210–20); Livy's great history of Rome from its foundation to 9 B.C. filled 142 books, of which only a portion has survived to our time; and Cicero, whose prose works have survived in considerable abundance, was also noted for his ability to produce voluminous amounts of poetry (supra n. 9).

65. Prop. 4.1.69: "I shall sing of rites, of calendars, and of ancient place names."

66. Pillinger, "Callimachean Influences," 179 (supra n. 62).

67. L. Richardson, ed., *Sexti Properti Elegiae I–IV* (Norman, Okla., 1977), on Prop. 4.2.21–22, cites three forms of the name as manifest in Etruria: Vertumnus (Vortumnus), masculine; Veldumnius, masculine; and Voltumna, feminine, on which see Liv. 4.23, 25, 61, and 5.17.

68. Varro (*L.* 5.46) calls Vertumnus the *deus Etruriae princeps* (cf. discussion of E. Richardson, *Etruscans*, 232 [supra n. 38]). Among poets dependent upon this treatment by Propertius are Ovid (*Met.* 14.623–771 [Pomona and Vortumnus]), Porphyrio (*Ad Hor. Epod.* 1.20.1), and [Tibullus] (3.8.13); cf. Hor., *S.* 2.7.14. A statuette in Florence (Museo Archeologico, inv. 72725) is "often if erroneously" identified as Vertumnus, according to O. Brendel, *Etruscan Art* (Harmondsworth, Engl., 1978), 297–98.

69. M. C. J. Putnam, "The Shrine of Vortumnus," *AJA* 71 (1967): 177–79; E. Nash, *Pictorial Dictionary of Ancient Rome*, 2d ed. (London, 1968), s.v. "vicus Tuscus"; L. Richardson, Jr., *A New Topographical Dictionary of Ancient Rome* (Baltimore, 1992), s.v. "signum Vortumni."

70. Prop. 4.2.9–14. As translated by W. G. Shepherd (*Propertius: The Poems* [Harmondsworth, Engl., 1985]), it reads: "But after he ceded so much to his foster-children, / I was called god *Ver*tumnus from streams re*ver*ted. / Or else because I received the anni*ver*sary first-fruits, / He supposed Vertumnus' rites to come by re*ver*sion. / For me the first grape changes hue in a purpling bunch, / and bristly corn-ears swell with milky grain" (Shepherd's italics).

71. Surely the corrected text of the codex Laurentianus (F4Δ in the sigla for E. A. Barber, ed., *Sexti Properti Carmina*, 2d ed. [Oxford, 1960]) must be read, and not *fautor* as Barber prints; cf. Richardson, *Sexti Properti Elegiae*, 426 (supra n. 67). Cf. H. C. Parker, "*Romani Numen Soli:* Faunus in Ovid's *Fasti*," *TAPhA* 123 (1993): 200, n. 2.

72. [Tib.] 3.8.13 places Vertumnus on Olympus: *talis in aeterno felix Vertumnus Olympo / mille habet ornatus, mille decenter habet* ("Thus, blessed Vertumnus on eternal Olympus / has a thousand adornments, and has them fittingly").

73. Hubbard, *Propertius*, 117 (supra n. 62).

74. Griffin, "Caesar Qui Cogere Posset," 206 (supra n. 58).

75. The poem does take on considerable pathos in comparison with *Am.* 1.15, the *sphragis* in which Ovid stands abreast of Homer, Hesiod, Aratus, Lucretius, Gallus, Vergil, and others.

76. H. B. Evans, *Publica Carmina: Ovid's Books from Exile* (Lincoln, Neb., 1983), 6. The seven of Evans's virtual unknowns not discussed in this paper are (with line number) an epic poet, Camerinus (19); a Vergilian imitator, *velivolique maris vates* (21) [perhaps Germanicus, cf. Ov., *Pont.* 4.5.42]; a composer of historical epic, *qui acies Libycas Romanaque proelia dixit* (23); the versatile Marius (24); Trinacrius, a Sicilian tragic author of a *Perseus* (25); Lupus, a tragedian (26); and Rufus, a writer of Pindaric lyrics (28).

77. The same hazards of using onomastic evidence to prove ethnic identity apply as mentioned above in n. 16.

78. O. Hennig (*De P. Ovidii Nasonis Sodalibus* [Bratislava, Czech., 1898], 18) suggests that they were epic poets but concludes that nothing is known; with the latter point Evans (*Publica Carmina*, 6 [supra n. 76]) concurs.

79. Ov., *Pont.* 4.16.9–10: " . . . and the Severus who gave the regal *carmen* to Latium and each Priscus with subtle Numa . . ."

80. Fest. 363. Cf. *RE* IVA, cols. 2392–94, s.v. "Tarquitius Priscus (7)" [W. Kroll]; Hall, "MAE," Appendix 87.6 (supra n. 16); Harris, *Etruria and Umbria*, 23, 27 (supra n. 15).

81. Macr. 3.7.2 (on Verg., *Ecl.* 4.43) on the portentous coloration of sacrificial victims, and 3.20.3 on numinous trees. Cf. Lact., *Div. Inst.* 1.10.2; Ammian. 25.2.7; Lyd., *Ost.* 2.5.7.

82. Macr. 3.7.2: *genus progeniem propagat in claritate laetioremque efficit* ("The race sets forth its offspring illustriously and makes them more fortunate").

83. *RE* IVA, col. 2394, s.v. "Tarquitius Priscus (7)" (supra n. 80).

84. P. and C. Selius are mentioned by Cicero (*Ac.* 2.11) as having come recently to Rome on an embassy.

85. The problems of dating any poem in the *Appendix Vergiliana* are well known. There is no agreement on the date of any of the fifteen constituent poems of the *Catalepton*, much less the whole. Opinions on authenticity also vary considerably. Thus, while nobody seems to think that all the poems are really by Vergil, the subject matter of *Cat.* 5 and 8 is considered by some to indicate sure forgery (e.g., H. R. Fairclough, "The Poems of the Appendix Vergiliana," *TAPhA* 53 [1922]: 5–34; J. C. Bramble, "Minor Figures," in *Cambridge History of Classical Literature* [Cambridge, 1982–85], 2:472); others treat those poems as authentic (e.g., R. E. H. Westendorp Boerma, "L'Enigme de l'appendix Vergiliana," in *Vergiliana*, ed. H. Bardon and

R. Verdière [Leiden, 1971], 414–20; cf. Conte, *Latin Literature*, 432 [supra n. 64]). Although there is general consensus that most of the poems of the *Appendix Vergiliana* were written in the early first century A.D., the triple reference to Selius, Tarquitius, and Varro may recommend Westendorp Boerma's dating of *Cat.* 5 to the period of Vergil's youth, while caution still seems to discourage attributing the authorship of the poem to Vergil himself.

86. Ov., *Pont.* 4.16.20: ". . . and the Tuscus who has a name from his *Phyllis* . . ." The love of Phyllis for Demophoön was a popular story in Alexandrian erotic tradition; cf. Call. 556 Pf.; Verg., *Ecl.* 5.10–11; *Culex* 131–33; etc.

87. Lyd., *Ost.* 59 f.; Wissowa (*RE* IV, col. 104, s.v. "Clodius Tuscus [61]") is diffident of the identification of Clodius Tuscus with the Tuscus of Ovid (*Pont.* 4.16) as made in R. Merkel, ed., *P. Ovidius Naso Fastorum Libri Sex* (1841; reprint, Hildesheim, Ger., 1971), lxvi.

88. Servius refers to his source by full name only once, at *A.* 12.657; but he refers to Clodius *scriba commentariorum* at *A.* 1.52, 176, 2.229.

89. For Tuscus as a cognomen that would become fashionable among the *boni viri et locupletes* of Spain during the Flavians and Antonines, see R. Syme, "Spaniards at Tivoli," *AncSoc* 13–14 (1982–83): 249, 259 = *Roman Papers* 4:94, 114; and R. Syme, "Spanish Pomponii: A Study in Nomenclature," *Gerión* 1 (1983): 255 = *Roman Papers* 4:255, n. 36, in which Syme cites I. Kajanto, *The Latin Cognomina* (Helsinki, 1965), 188, showing that 23 of 48 epigraphic instances of Tuscus come in Spain.

90. Ov., *Pont.* 4.16.29: " . . . and Turranius' Muse leaning upon the tragic buskins . . ."

91. M. Leumann, *Lateinische Laut- und Formenlehre*, fasc. 2 of *Lateinische Grammatik* by M. Leumann, J. B. Hofmann, and A. Szantyr, 5th ed. (1926–28; reprint, Munich, 1977), 139; Schulze, *Eigennamen*, 420 (supra n. 14): "*h* ist früh geschwunden" ("*h* disappeared early"). Cf. Nigid. in Gel. 13.6.3 and Arrius in Catul. 84.

92. Hennig, *De P. Ovidii Nasonis Sodalibus*, 55–56 (supra n. 78). Kroll (*RE* VIIA, col. 1140) indicates that *De Orthographia*, often ascribed to Apuleius, in which a *Helena* by a Turranius is mentioned, may not be authentic—in which case less is known about the Turranii than former scholars thought.

93. *RE* VIIA, cols. 1439–44 [var.] identifies fourteen males and one female bearing the gentilicium Turranius.

94. Plin., *Nat. Hist.* 3.3, 9.11, 18.75.

95. *RE* VIIA, cols. 1441–44, s.v. "Turranius (5)" [E. Stein]; Tac., *Ann.* 1.7. R. Syme ("Pliny the Procurator," *HSCP* 73 [1969]: 220 = *Roman Papers* 2:759) regards Pliny's Turranius Gracilis and the Augustan praefect as the same person.

96. *RE* VIIA, cols. 1440–41, s.v. "Turranius (4)" [F. Münzer]; cf. *MRR* 3.207, s.v. "C. Toranius."

97. Cic., *Agr.* 3.3. A textual emendation by J. N. Madvig's edition (cf. A. C. Clark, ed., *M. Tulii Ciceronis Orationes,* Oxford Classical Texts [Oxford, 1901–11], 4:173) includes the Turranii among the *possessores* of Sullan land allotments whom Cicero claims to have pleased by his resistance to the land law of Rullus. Cf. Cic., *Fam.* 13.4, to Q. Valerius Orca, a recently appointed land commissioner encouraged in this epistle to protect the interests of the Volterrans.

98. Syme, *Roman Revolution,* 91 (supra n. 60); R. Syme, "Caesar, the Senate, and Italy," *PBSR* 14 (1938): 16, n. 15 = *Roman Papers* 1:104, n. 5.

99. Probus (*Vita Persi* 1) gives Persius the Etruscan praenomen Aules: *Aules Persius Flaccus natus est . . . in Etruria Volaterris, eques Romanus* ("Aules Persius Flaccus was born at Volaterrae in Etruria, a Roman citizen of the equestrian class").

100. Pers. 3.27–28: "Or is it appropriate to burst your lungs with pride because you draw your roots over a thousand generations from an Etruscan stock?" For the absurdly diluted genealogy, see R. A. Harvey, *A Commentary on Persius,* Mnemosyne Supplement, 64 (Leiden, 1981), 85; cf. Mart. 5.35.4; Suet., *Gal.* 2.

Quia Ister Tusco Verbo Ludio Vocabatur: The Etruscan Contribution to the Development of Roman Theater

Robert L. Maxwell

In 364 B.C., according to Livy, plague struck Rome. A *lectisternium* was declared in the hopes of appeasing the gods, but the scourge was not alleviated. Influenced by superstition, says Livy, the Romans instituted *ludi scaenici* (literally, "scenic games"), a new thing to a warlike race—in the hopes that this would appease the gods.[1] Livy does not comment on the efficacy of this remedy, but presumably it worked. Livy calls the *ludi scaenici* a *peregrina res*—a foreign importation— and he specifically indicates one set of foreigners: the Etruscans. He says that players brought in from Etruria danced gracefully in the Etruscan fashion—*more Tusco*. He says that they did not sing, but rather danced to the pipes; however, he does indicate that the spoken word was a part of the act, for he notes that their peformance was so popular that it was taken up by the young men, the *iuuentus,* who in imitation of these Etruscan performers would hurl rude (in both senses) comic verses at each other, presumably before an audience of some kind. The Romans adopted the word *histrio* for these actors from the Etruscan term *ister,* which Livy translates *ludio,* or player: *Quia ister Tusco verbo ludio vocabatur.*[2]

| 267 |

Thus Livy accounted for the origins of Roman drama. Horace, in his account of dramatic origins,[3] makes no mention of Etruscans, emphasizing rather the Greek contribution—although a connection can be made between Horace's mention of Fescennine verses and the probability that they originated in the Etruscan town of Fescennium.[4] Vergil's brief account leaves the Etruscans out as well.[5] Livy does make one other reference to Etruscan letters, in which he mentions a man who was raised and educated on *etruscis litteris* and was fluent in the Etruscan tongue. He claims that in an earlier age boys were educated on Etruscan literature just as in his own day they were brought up on Greek.[6] What was this Etruscan literature? Could it have included drama, as the Greek did? Livy says nothing more, although Varro offers a tantalizing bit of information when he mentions in passing that the name for the Roman tribes Titienses, Ramnenses, and Lucernes might be Etruscan, citing as his authority one Volnius, who wrote Etruscan tragedies—*qui tragoedias Tuscas scripsit.*[7] This Volnius is otherwise unknown, and it is unclear from Varro whether these tragedies were Etruscan in origin, whether they were simply written in the Etruscan tongue, or both.

Livy's account of the plague and the imported Etruscan players is corroborated (if not simply copied) by two other Roman authors, Valerius Maximus and Cluvius Rufus. Valerius Maximus describes the plague, stating that the Romans were recalled from their normal warlike activities because of it. Like Livy, he emphasizes the religious superstition of the people and says they decided to compose songs to the gods. Never a people to resort to half measures, they decided to be more elaborate, and the young men (*iuuentus*) added to these songs crude dances and gestures; this (the crudeness?) caused them to fetch a *ludius* (stage player) from Etruria. His agility (*pernicitas*) was after the old style of the Cretans and Lydians, says Valerius, from whom the Etruscans descend. This *ludius* so charmed the Romans with his delightful and novel performance that—since the Etruscan word for *ludius* was *hister*—the name *histrio* was thenceforth used instead of *scaenicus* (actor).[8]

The account given by Cluvius Rufus of the same event is rather different from those offered by Livy and Valerius. Cited by Plutarch in his essay on "Why the Romans call the Dionysiac artists *histriones*," Cluvius states that the reason the Romans called in Etruscan actors was that the plague had killed all the native stage actors. Therefore the Romans invited many excellent artists (τεχνίτας) from Etruria (ἐκ *Τυρρηνίας*); the most famous of these was named Hister; and so, from then on, all actors were called *histriones*.[9]

The accounts of Livy and Valerius are so close that it seems likely that they were at least following the same source; the version offered by Cluvius Rufus differs somewhat from the other two. But they do seem to agree on one point: that the Romans of the fourth century B.C. admired the Etruscan acting community and were able to draw on it to supply their own dramatic needs. In this they are further corroborated by the account in Tacitus of the introduction of a Greek-style stage contest in A.D. 60 (the same contest at which Nero modestly accepted the prize for lyre playing). After briefly recounting the history of theater building at Rome, Tacitus decries the fact that under Nero conditions had degenerated to such a point that nobles were being forced to appear on the stage. He contrasts this with the older custom of importing actors from Etruria, implying that this was a general practice and not just a one-time event as recorded by Livy, Valerius, and Cluvius Rufus.[10]

These are the major literary sources for Etruscan activities in Roman drama. The sources are tantalizingly parsimonious in detail, but they do establish that the Romans themselves believed that the Etruscans had influenced their drama. The archaeological record yields further information, particularly through Etruscan tomb paintings. In Tarquinia is a tomb dating to the early sixth century B.C. which has been named the Tomb of the Augurs.[11] On the back wall is a depiction of mourning, and on either side are scenes of gymnastic contests. In addition, on each of the side walls is a masked figure wearing a distinctive costume; on the left wall he is labeled *Phersu* (figures 1–3). His name has been posited by many twentieth-century scholars as the etymological ancestor—or at least a cognate—of the Latin *persona*, or mask.[12] Here, then, is further evidence of Etruscan influence on the Roman vocabulary of drama; but there is more apparent from these paintings than just that. Both J. Heurgon and M. Bieber

FIGURE 2. Tomb of the Augurs, Tarquinia, general view, showing location of Phersu detailed in figure 1 (left wall). *Photo courtesy of Hirmer Verlag München.*

examine the costume of Phersu and that of a similar figure in the Tomb of the Pulcinella, pointing out the similarity of these costumes to that of the much later Harlequin.[13] The figure in the Tomb of the Pulcinella is posed and dressed in exactly the same manner as the Phersu of the left wall of the Tomb of the Augurs, except that he poses in the mirror image of Phersu and his costume is in a checkerboard pattern.[14] The Phersu figure is also found in the Tomb of the Olympic Games, wearing the same checkerboard costume.[15]

This short, multicolored, checkered dress corresponds to the ancient costume known as the *centunculus,* worn by the mimes, as Apuleius informs us.[16] Mimes were known for their colorful costumes; Ovid, for example, comments on the *cultu versicolore* ("multicolored costuming") at the *Floralia,* one of the original venues of mime at Rome.[17] A description of this costume appears in the *Codex Theodosianus,* where mime actresses are forbidden from wearing gems, embroidered silks, and gilded or purple-dyed cloth, implying that

FIGURE 3. Tomb of the Augurs, right wall. Phersu figure is at far right. *Photo courtesy of Hirmer Verlag München.*

previously they had worn such. They were permitted, however, to continue wearing checkered and many-colored silks (*scutlatis et uariis coloribus sericis*) and gold without gems.[18] *Scutlata serica* was silk woven in a diamond or lozenge pattern. It is easy to see why most modern scholars connect this with the Harlequin of the Italian commedia dell'arte, since Harlequin wore just such a checkered costume. And here a similar figure appears in a sixth-century B.C. Etruscan tomb. Could the Etruscans have known mime?

Mime was a widespread phenomenon, reaching every corner of the Greek and Roman world and possibly beyond. A study of Greco-Roman documents mentioning mime actors shows large numbers of them on the Italian peninsula mainly around Rome, but also as far away as Spain, Germany, Upper Egypt, and Persia.[19] Mime is thought to have originated in Sicily in the sixth or fifth century B.C.—certainly within the realm of possibility for a connection to have existed between it and the scenes depicted in the Tomb of the Augurs. The term *mime* designated a very broad and fluid category of popular theater, and mime actors provided a wide range of entertainment, from low farce to sophisticated drama. The grammarian Diomedes provided one of the only ancient definitions of this form of entertainment:

> Mime is the imitation of some sort of speech and movement
> without reverence, or the imitation of wanton deeds and words with
> insolence; it was defined by the Greeks thus: mime is imitation of

life (μίμησις βίου), comprising both things which are allowed and those which are not permitted. It is called mime from μιμεῖσθαι, as though it alone imitated, although other poems do the same thing.[20]

A few of the descriptions of mime performances which survive are detailed enough to give a good idea of what went on in the acting area (which was not always a stage). A performance which took place in the second century B.C. is described both in Diodorus Siculus and Athenaeus.[21] During a feast put on by Antiochus IV Epiphanes (175–164 B.C.), mimes appeared as part of the entertainment. At the climax of their performance, the king was brought in wrapped up, apparently à la Cleopatra. When the instruments sounded a note, he leaped up, naked, and danced and joked with the mime actors. This entertaining performance appears to have been plotless, consisting of dance numbers and banter among the artists.

A very famous mime, performed in A.D. 41 at Rome before the emperor Caligula, was the *Laureolus* of the mimographer Catullus. A number of authors describe different scenes from this mime. According to Josephus, the climax of the play was a scene where Laureolus, the leader of a robber band, is caught and crucified. Suetonius describes a scene which must have preceded this one in which the principal actor leaps from a crumbling building, followed by the secondary actors (his robber band? pursuing soldiers?). Both Suetonius and Josephus are impressed by the artificial blood used; by the end, according to Suetonius, the stage was flowing with gore (*cruore scaena abundauit*).[22] Juvenal names the actor who played Laureolus as one Lentulus who, he says, did such a good job that he should have been put on a real cross (*iudice me dignus uera cruce*). The scholiast obligingly (if prosaically) adds that Juvenal was only being sarcastic and that of course a fake cross was used (*deprehensus in falso cruce fixus est*), but Martial informs us that at a later performance of the same mime the victim was not so fortunate: a slave or criminal (presumably a double for the principal actor) was actually crucified on stage (*non falsa pendens in cruce Laureolus*).[23]

A papyrus fragment dating from the second century A.D. contains substantial portions of the scripts of two mimes. One is a farce concerning the adventures and rescue of Charition, a young Greek woman who has been captured by Indian natives. She is about to be sacrificed when her brother arrives with a rescue party and effects her escape by attacking the natives and then making them drunk. An interesting aspect of this play is that the natives speak their own language, a made-up stage language. If such a play had been put on in turn-of-the-century vaudeville, the actors would no doubt have been costumed in blackface and grass skirts, ranting mumbo-jumbo; this appears to be exactly the sort of low humor envisaged in the Charition mime.[24]

The rest of the papyrus is another matter. This fragment contains the lines of a female lead who plays the part of an adulteress. She has fallen in love with one of her slaves, but he rebuffs her advances, since he loves a slave girl. The adulteress orders the slave lovers killed; they escape but are captured and executed. Later in the play she has her husband poisoned as well. The play reaches a climax when the dead bodies are brought onstage; there, to the surprise of all, they revive and denounce the adulteress, ensuring that she and her henchman get their just deserts.[25]

A mosaic floor decoration has recently been discovered in Spain which probably depicts a mime performance of the fourth century A.D. The work features a "Nilotic" scene measuring approximately three square meters and containing an ibis, a crocodile, the god of the River Nile, and a hippopotamus. This section is surrounded by four apses, the two surviving of which are depicted in figure 4. The apses are decorated by figures of pygmies and cranes; each pygmy is accompanied by a line of dialogue. In apse 1, the pygmy to the left is being attacked by an animal, a crane. He says, *Su(m) Cerbios, (H)e(m) fili Gerio, uale!* ("I am Cervius—Ah, my son Geryon, farewell!") His son, a second pygmy, is rescuing him: *Subduc te, Pater!* ("Get out of here, Father!") A woman, also running to his aid, is labeled on the right *Uxor Mastale* (Mastale, wife)—no doubt the spouse of the first pygmy. She says, *Ai misera! Decollata so(m)!* ("Woe is me, wretch that I am! I've been beheaded [or, I've lost my head]!") The second apse apparently shows a slightly later scene. It shows three pygmies framed by two palm trees; the first pygmy, obviously straining, is dragging away the body of the crane by a rope tied around its neck. He says, *Et tu, ere, suma!*

("Take it, master, you too!") The second curses the crane: *(H)e(m)*, *importuna!* ("You perverse thing!") The third, trying to push the crane along, says, *Timio ne uecti(m) franga(m)!* ("I'm afraid I'm going to break my crowbar!")[26]

This gives some idea of the sorts of things that could go on in mime. The crude, violent, and vulgar were at home there, as well as the romantic and exotic. Mime entertainment was also often mixed with other sorts of entertainment, such as athletic contests and horse races; this is known from literary sources, but it is also confirmed by documentary sources: a circus program from Oxyrhynchus dating to

FIGURE 4. Mosaic, from Puente Genil, Spain, fourth century A.D. *Drawing by Mary Ann Addy Maxwell.*

the sixth century A.D. shows mime acts interspersed with six chariot races, singing trapeze artists, a gazelle-and-dogs act (possibly a hunt), and an athletic competition.[27]

All this leads directly back to the Tomb of the Augurs (figure 5), which, it will be recalled, depicts various athletic events in addition to the two Phersu figures, the left one of whom so resembles Harlequin. Examination of the Phersu on the right wall of the tomb shows him doing something very odd. He is holding in his right hand a rope which is tangled around the legs and arms of a man whose head is covered by a hood and who wears only a loincloth. This unfortunate is being attacked by a dog. Presumably the man is unable to defend himself effectively because of the ropes and hood, although he is provided with a stick. This scene recurs in the painting already mentioned from the Tomb of the Olympic Games, contemporary with the Tomb of the Augurs.[28] As already observed, mime performances might include such violent scenes as animals attacking the actors and Laureolus being crucified onstage; in addition, they often provided

FIGURE 5. Tomb of the Augurs, right wall, right end. Phersu figure (second from left) is same as that shown at far right in figure 3. *Photo from G. Q. Giglioli, L'arte etrusca (Milan, 1935).*

comic diversion at athletic contests. Of course, other violent forms of entertainment maintained a long-standing and notorious presence in Italy. Nevertheless, the context of the two figures within the ensemble of the painting, as well as the costume of Phersu, suggest that this represents a performance closely related to mime.

Another sixth-century tomb from Tarquinia, the Tomb of the Olympic Games, has wall paintings pertinent to this subject (figure 6, a general view of the tomb, and figure 7). On the central wall, beginning with the right, is a seated man. This has plausibly been interpreted to be the deceased watching the activities of the other figures, who are entertainers.[29] If this is so, this set of murals may easily be interpreted as separate scenes in a variety show going from right to left all the way around the room, beginning with the seated man. The first, moving toward the left, is a woman performing a balancing act; a candelabrum is poised on her head, onto which a youth is throwing rings. There is a piper who may be playing at the same time, or he may be the next act. If the latter, he may be connected with the youth who stands behind him and seems to be commenting, or perhaps pantomiming with his hands. Behind him are two boys who could be performing but seem more likely to be spectators, perhaps the children of the deceased. Around the corner (figure 8) is a man, apparently in the act of defecating. He is accompanied by an inscription which reads *aranθ heracanasa*, which as far as I know has not been interpreted. I cannot imagine why such a scene would be in someone's tomb in such a context unless this, too, were part of an act. As demonstrated, mime descended to the crudest sort of entertainment; and although I am not aware of an ancient "defecation mime," this type of scatological humor—bathroom jokes and so forth—could certainly arise in the context of a mime performance and, in fact, has arisen in at least one modern act with close parallels to ancient mime. In the early twentieth century the French cabaret artist Joseph Pujol became famous under the stage name Le Pétomane (The Tooter) for his gas-passing performances at the Moulin Rouge, which included "playing" tunes, imitating animals, and blowing out candles.[30]

Next in sequence is an old man leading a boy (figure 9). If this is indeed a dramatic scene, they bring to mind the stock characters of

FIGURE 6. Tomb of the Olympic Games, necropolis of the Monterozzi, Tarquinia, early sixth century B.C., general view. *Photo courtesy of Hirmer Verlag München.*

FIGURE 7. Tomb of the Olympic Games, central wall. *Photo from M. Moretti,* New Monuments of Etruscan Painting *(The Pennsylvania State University Press, 1970), pp. 22–23. Copyright 1970 by The Pennsylvania State University. Reproduced by permission of the publisher.*

FIGURE 8. Tomb of the Olympic Games, left wall. *Photo from M. Moretti, New Monuments of Etruscan Painting (The Pennsylvania State University Press, 1970), pp. 26–28. Copyright 1970 by The Pennsylvania State University. Reproduced by permission of the publisher.*

New Comedy, the *paedagogos* (sort of a male governess) and his ward. But the slave and his young master appear not only in New Comedy but also in mime, as is demonstrated by two artistic representations, the first an Athenian terracotta lamp from the late third century B.C. (figure 10) on which three actors, identified as *mimologoi*—mime players—in a playlet called *The Mother-in-Law*, are depicted. The middle figure is the slave, a bald man with enormous ears who appears to be being beaten by the young master on the left. An old man, probably the stock character of the aged master, is departing.[31] A parallel scene appears on the wall between the orchestra and the *proscenium* of the theater at Sabratha, in North Africa, dating from the second century A.D. (figure 11). This wall is covered with scenes from drama, one of which depicts a mime of a youth in the act of beating his slave, possibly egged on by the woman on the right. These two slaves apparently play the character *stupidus*, or fool, in mime (both are wearing the standard costume for the role). Although the old man in the Tomb of the Giocolieri (figure 9) does not appear to correspond exactly to this type, he would fit into the mime context.

Continuing to the left (figure 8) is a nude youth carrying a staff, striding or running away. He may be participating in a race of some sort, since athletic contests often took place at the same show as mime performances. Ahead of him is another nude youth, who may be a servant or retainer for the man around the corner (not shown) holding a saddled horse by the bridle, another indication of a possible athletic competition.

FIGURE 9. Detail of old man leading youth, Tomb of the Olympic Games, left wall. *Photo from M. Moretti*, New Monuments of Etruscan Painting *(The Pennsylvania State University Press, 1970), pl. 21. Copyright 1970 by The Pennsylvania State University. Reproduced by permission of the publisher.*

FIGURE 10. Athenian lamp, terracotta, late third century B.C. *Drawing by Mary Ann Addy Maxwell.*

FIGURE 11. Relief showing mime, from theater at Sabratha, North Africa, second century A.D. *Drawing by Mary Ann Addy Maxwell.*

FIGURE 12. Tomb of the Olympic Games, right wall. *Photo from M. Moretti, New Monuments of Etruscan Painting (The Pennsylvania State University Press, 1970), pp. 26–28. Copyright 1970 by The Pennsylvania State University. Reproduced by permission of the publisher.*

On the right wall, continuing to the left around the room, is a dance scene (figure 12). The central player may be playing the pipes, to which the women on either side of him are dancing (figures 13 and 14). These dancers appear to be using the same sort of gestures as the youth beside the piper on the central wall (figures 6 and 7) and may also be doing pantomime of some sort. In any case, a dance, for which the Etruscans were so famous, appears to be the finale of this performance.

What did the Etruscans contribute to Roman drama? There was a strong native tradition, as the evidence of literary sources shows, that the Romans received at least some of their drama from Etruria; and, as has been seen, the Etruscan town of Fescennium is explicitly linked with the branch of Roman popular theater known as Fescinnine verses. A much more prominent genre in Roman popular theater was, however, mime. This genre, like farce or burlesque, included crude "low" humor, violent acts, and variety numbers and was often included as a part of athletic contests; and, as shown in this essay, paintings in at least two Etruscan tombs depict figures performing just such actions in just such contexts. This is convincing evidence that the Etruscans performed and participated in mime before the Romans did. It is usually thought that mime—a genre which eventually eclipsed all other Roman dramatic forms—came to Rome via the Greek world, where it originated. Given the early existence of mime in Etruria, though, it seems entirely possible that the Romans, as with so many other aspects of their culture, received mime through an Etruscan filter.

FIGURE 13. Tomb of the Olympic Games, right wall, detail of dancer at center. *Photo from M. Moretti*, New Monuments of Etruscan Painting *(The Pennsylvania State University Press, 1970), pl. 20. Copyright 1970 by The Pennsylvania State University. Reproduced by permission of the publisher.*

FIGURE 14. Tomb of the Olympic Games, right wall, detail of dancer at left side. *Photo from M. Moretti,* New Monuments of Etruscan Painting *(The Pennsylvania State University Press, 1970), p. 25. Copyright 1970 by The Pennsylvania State University. Reproduced by permission of the publisher.*

NOTES

1. Liv. 7.2.1–3.

2. "Because *ister* is the Etruscan word for *ludio*." Ibid., 7.2.3–6.

3. Hor., *Ep.* 2.1.139–63.

4. See, e.g., J. Heurgon, *La Vie quotidienne chez les Etrusques* (Paris, 1961), 298. See also G. E. Duckworth, *The Nature of Roman Comedy: A Study in Popular Entertainment* (Princeton, N.J., 1952), 7–8. See also, in this volume, the essay by Harrison Powley, 290.

5. Verg., *G.* 2.381 ff.

6. Liv. 9.36.3.

7. Var., *L.* 5.55.

8. V.Max. 2.4.4.

9. Plu., *QR* 107. There were other ancient etymologies for *histrio* unrelated to the Etruscans. Paulus' excerpts of Festus inform us that *histriones* were so called because they came from Histria (Paul., *Fest.* 101). Isidore of Seville believes that the word either comes from the fact that this "type" (*genus*) comes from Histria, or because they tell complicated tales with stories (*historiis*), as if the word was *historiones* (*Orig.* 18.48).

10. Tac., *Ann.* 14.20–21.

11. See M. Sprenger and G. Bartoloni, *The Etruscans: Their History, Art, and Architecture* (New York, 1983), pls. 79–80.

12. M. Bieber, *The History of the Greek and Roman Theater*, 2d ed. (Princeton, N.J., 1961), 147; Heurgon, *La Vie quotidienne*, 264 (supra n. 4); A. Hus, *Les Etrusques et leur déstin* (Paris, 1980), 214; H. Rheinfelder, *Das Wort "persona": Geschichte seiner bedeutungen mit besonderer Berücksichtigung des französischen und italienischen Mittelalters*, Beihefte zur Zeitschrift für romanische Philologie, Heft 77 (Halle, Ger., 1928), 24–25; cf. *OLD*, 1356, s.v. "persona," which appears to accept this etymology as well.

There is one ancient etymology of the word *persona*. Gavius Bassus (in *De Origine Vocabulorum*, quoted in Gel. 5.7.1) claims that it comes from *persono*, "to sound through." He explains that as the head and the face are shut in on all sides by the *persona*, the mask, only one passage is left for the voice; this is a narrow and restricted passage *through* which the voice must *sound*, thus magnifying the voice. However, the *o* in *persona* is long; that of *persono* is short; Gavius Bassus therefore feels it necessary to explain this away, rather lamely—it is *propter vocabuli formam* ("because of the formation of the word"). The tenth-century manuscript "Commentum Einsidlense in Donati Artem Minorem" (112, 172 in H. Keil, *Grammatici Latini* [1857; reprint, Hildesheim, Ger., 1961], 8:202, 248–49) also traces the ancestry of *persona* to *persono*. See discussion of this etymology in Rheinfelder, *Das Wort "persona,"* 25–26 (supra this n.).

13. Heurgon, *La Vie quotidienne*, 264 (supra n. 4); Bieber, *Greek and Roman Theater*, 147 (supra n. 12).

14. See Bieber, *Greek and Roman Theater*, fig. 543 (supra n. 12).

15. M. Moretti, *New Monuments of Etruscan Painting* (University Park, Penn., 1970), 118.

16. Apul., *Apol.* 13.19. On the costuming of mimes, see R. L. Maxwell, "The Documentary Evidence for Ancient Mime" (Ph.D. diss., University of Toronto, 1993), 7–10.

17. Ov., *Fast.* 5.355–56. See also Duckworth, *Nature of Roman Comedy*, 13–14 (supra n. 4). Unfortunately, very little more is known about the *Floralia*.

18. *Cod. Theod.* 15.7.11 (21 Sept. 393).

19. Maxwell, "Documentary Evidence," 65–66 (supra n. 16). H. Reich's magisterial study (*Der Mimus . . .* [Berlin, 1903], esp. teil 2) finds traces of mime as far away as India and sees its descendants in the jongleurs and fools of the Middle Ages.

20. My translation; the original reads: *Mimus est sermonis cuiuslibet [imitatio et] motus sine reuerentia, uel factorum et [dictorum] turpium cum lasciuia imitatio; a Graecis ita definitus: μῖμός ἐστιν μίμησις βίου τά τε συγκεχωρημένα καὶ ἀσυγχώρητα περιέχων. Mimus dictus παρὰ τὸ μιμεῖσθαι, quasi solus imitetur, cum et alia poemata idem faciant* (Keil, *Grammatici Latini*, 1:491 [supra n. 12]).

21. D.S. 31.16.3; Ath. 195, 439.

22. J., *AJ* 19 [13].94; Suet., *Cal.* 57.

23. Juv. 8.187–89; Mart., *Sp.* 7.

24. *POxy* 413$^{r, v4}$.

25. *POxy* 413^{VI-3}.

26. A. Daviault, J. Lancha, and L. A. López Palomo, *Un mosaico con inscripciones: Une Mosaïque à inscriptions: Puente Genil (Cordoba)*, Publications de la Casa de Velazquez, Série études et documents, 3 (Madrid, 1987); my translations.

27. *POxy* 2707.

28. Moretti, *New Monuments*, 118 (supra n. 15).

29. Ibid., 17.

30. On Pujol, see J. Nohain and F. Caradec, *Le Pétomane, 1857–1945: Sa vie, son oeuvre* (Paris, 1967).

31. C. Watzinger, "Mimologen," *MDAI(A)* 26 (1901): 1–8 and pl. 1.

The Musical Legacy of the Etruscans

Harrison Powley

Since the Renaissance, scholars have attempted to understand the significance of music in the ancient world. Although some ancient music survives in notations that can be melodically and even rhythmically interpreted, its nature, so intriguingly described by many early Greek writers, eludes us today.[1] Musicologists, working closely with archaeologists and historians of many disciplines, attempt to comprehend the religious, social, and political implications of this music. They work not only with the extant notated fragments of music, but also with literary and archaeological sources. Comparative studies of contemporary musical practices suggest the sound and function of ancient music, and several scholars have even tried to reconstruct its sound.[2] The study of music in the Etruscan culture, however, must rely entirely upon archaeological evidence and the references to possible Etruscan musical practices as described in Greek and Roman literary sources. The absence of Etrurian literary sources and notated musical fragments precludes all but the broadest speculations and conclusions. Even comparisons to present-day Mediterranean folk music are clouded by time and successive cultural invasions. This essay is a sampling of several literary and iconographical documents for Etruscan musical characteristics.[3] From these may be reconstructed all that can be surmised from present evidence about Etruscan musical practices.

FIGURE 1. Tomb of the Leopards, necropolis of the Monterozzi, Tarquinia, ca. 470 B.C. Musicians on right wall. *Photo courtesy of Hirmer Fotoarchiv, München.*

| 287 |

The splendid surviving tomb paintings, bas-reliefs, and *repoussé* illustrate the pervasive quality of music in Etruscan society. Convivial banquet scenes swarm with musicians—most often players of reed pipes and string instruments (figure 1)—who entertain the reclining guests with irreclaimable melodies and rhythms.[4] Religious rites and processions carved in stone echo to the sound of instrumentalists.[5] Greek dramatists and historians attribute the invention of bronze and brass instruments to the Etruscans.[6] Roman historians frequently report the sound of the assimilated Etruscan *lituus, cornu,* and *tuba* in Roman legions.[7]

Still, literary documents reveal little about the character of ancient music, and this is particularly true of the references to music in Roman sources.[8] The hypothesis that ancient musical styles were generally homogeneous is difficult to refute, based on the limited surviving documents. Moreover, it is too simple to assume that Etruscan and later Roman musical styles on the Italian peninsula differed little from their Greek counterparts. References to Greek musicians abound in Roman documents. It is tempting to speculate further: if the Etruscans did originate in Asia Minor, as Herodotus claimed, the intersection of their musical styles with those of the Greeks could be deduced because the music of the Greeks was itself heavily influenced by the music of that region.[9] In fact, the names of several Greek modes (*harmoniai*) derive from Asia Minor: Phrygian, Lydian, Syntonolydian, and Mixolydian, for example. If these cultures have common roots, then similarities might be expected in their music. Related musical dialects might also explain why Greek musical styles were so readily adapted by the Romans.

While Roman civilization imposed its imperial stamp on many diverse peoples, the conquered in return infused many conventions into the culture of their rulers. For example, Greek influence appears in late Republican Rome in terms of literature, art, and culture. Because Etruscans ruled Rome in its formative urbanizing period, Etruscan culture forms a strong and basic component of Roman society.[10] Since no Etruscan writing on music theory survives today, a profitable beginning point for discussion may be to explore the Greek philosophical view of music and its acculturation by Rome. This exploration will necessarily be brief, for, while further speculation about musical correspondences—either practical or theoretical—between the Greeks and the Etruscans because of possible ancestral links is a tempting topic, it is also tantalizingly complex and beyond the scope of this essay.

Both Plato and Aristotle discuss music in the context of education. In the *Republic*, Plato addresses how citizens should be instructed. He considers education to be a moral process that is carefully molded to the citizen's roles in society. Education in music should ultimately lead the child to the virtuous life.[11] Aristotle expands on the concept that music can imitate goodness and thus lead the soul to virtue; in this context music is a vital element in education. After discussing whether music should be a part of education, Aristotle explores the influence and impact of rhythm and melody upon the individual. Music, he asserts, has the power to generate particular effects on the ethical character of the soul.[12] This philosophic legacy also affects many other discussions of music in Greek literature. Special treatises of a more theoretical and technical nature, beginning with the Pythagorean tradition and refined by music theoreticians from Aristoxenus to Aristides Quintilianus, form a sophisticated body of literature that has fascinated scholars since the Renaissance.[13]

To the more practical and mundane Roman, music assumed a different stance; it played a less prominent role in the education of Roman youth. To fathom the Etruscan view of music is nearly impossible, but the *Saturnalia* of Macrobius, written in the early fifth century A.D. as a manual for the education of youth, recalls several interesting Etruscan customs.[14] Macrobius implies that there had been a change in the social value of music in Roman society after the second Punic War (218–201 B.C.).[15] Prior to this time the youth of Roman aristocratic families followed the longstanding custom—dating back perhaps to the time of Rome's Etruscan kings—of being educated at the Etruscan metropolis of Caere, where, presumably, they received some orientation in Etruscan music.[16]

After mentioning the dancing of a man or a woman at a banquet (a scene commonly depicted in Etruscan tomb painting), Macrobius says that you will find that youths of good family, and indeed sons of senators, used to attend the dancing school and there learn to dance with castanets. There is the further fact, though I do not press it, that even Roman matrons saw nothing unbecoming in dancing, but the most respectable of them went in for it, provided only that it was not taken so seriously as to make professional excellence the aim.[17]

Macrobius then paraphrases from Sallust's *Bellum Catilinae* a commentary on Sempronia, a Roman matron of late Republican date, who perhaps played the lyre and danced too expertly for her social position.[18]

Macrobius next considers whether it is inappropriate for well-born youths to dance and make music.[19] Even politicians are not immune from his censure. He notes that the elder Cato berates the Roman senator Caelius, calling him "Fessinnius," meaning cheeky or insolent, because he behaved in a manner unbefitting his office in that he danced, sang, and told off-color tales.[20] The name *Fessinnius* is etymologically related to the southern Etruscan town, Fescennium, and to the term *fascinum* (the evil eye, witchcraft, or an enchanting). The *fescennini versus* were vulgar wedding songs, perhaps used to deter the spells of witchcraft. The performance of related songs at harvest festivals by masqueraders may have played a role in the development of Roman drama.[21]

Macrobius' summary of Roman attitudes about music is echoed by many earlier authors. Rarely do the writers explore the philosophical or moral aspects of music; instead, they often merely restate or summarize positions taken by Plato and Aristotle. For example, Cicero's discussion of music in his *Laws* is his most philosophic save for his summary of the music of the spheres in his *Somnium Scipionis*, the conclusion to his *De Republica*.[22]

> For I agree with Plato [*R.* 4.424d] that nothing gains an influence so easily over youthful and impressionable minds as the various notes of song, the greatness of whose power both for good and evil can hardly be set forth in words. For it arouses the languid, and calms the excited; now it restrains our desires, now gives them free rein. Many Greek States considered it important to retain their old tunes; but when their songs became less manly, their character turned to effeminacy at the same time, perhaps because they were

corrupted by the sweetness and debilitating seductiveness of the new music, as some believe, or perhaps when other vices had first caused a relaxation of the strictness of their lives, and their ears and their hearts had already undergone a change, room was offered for a change in their music as well. For this reason the man who was by far the wisest and by far the most learned whom Greece has produced was very much afraid of such a degeneration. For he says there can be no change in the laws of music without a resulting change in the laws of the State [Pl. *R.* 4.424c].[23]

Surprisingly, the moralist Seneca has little to say about music. In his letter to Lucilius "On Gathering Ideas," however, Seneca describes some musical practices of the early Empire as a prelude to his plea to live a rich yet balanced life.

> Do you not see how many voices there are in a chorus? Yet out of the many only one voice results. In that chorus one voice takes the tenor, another the bass, another the baritone. There are women, too, as well as men, and the flute [*tibia*] is mingled with them. In that chorus the voices of the individual singers are hidden; what we hear is the voices of all together. To be sure, I am referring to the chorus which the old-time philosophers knew; in our present-day exhibitions [*commissio*, an entertainment or a concert] we have a larger number of singers than there used to be spectators in the theaters of old. All the aisles are filled with rows of singers; brass instruments surround the auditorium; the stage resounds with flutes and instruments of every description; and yet from the discordant sounds a harmony [*concentus*] is produced.
>
> I would have my mind of such a quality as this; it should be equipped with many arts, many precepts, and patterns of conduct taken from many epochs of history; but all should blend harmoniously into one.[24]

Quintilian contends that a knowledge of the philosophical significance of music was essential to the orator. In Book 1 of his *Institutio Oratoria*, an extended passage asserts that for the orator a knowledge of basic music theory is requisite to understanding the Greek philosophers. The orator should also value practical skills in music because they help train his voice to read the lyric poets.

Quintilian alludes to ancient, possibly Etruscan, musical customs in discussing music at banquets.

> Even at banquets of our own forefathers it was the custom to intro-
> duce the pipe [*tibiae*] and lyre [*fides*], and even the hymn of the
> Salii has its tune. These practices were instituted by King Numa and
> clearly prove that not even those whom we regard as rude warriors,
> neglected the study of music, as least in so far as the resources of
> that age allowed.[25]

In his ninth book, Quintilian returns to musical matters, especially as they relate to rhetorical gesture and technique.

> For in the first place nothing can penetrate to the emotions that
> stumbles [*sic*] at the portals of the ear, and secondly man is naturally
> attracted by harmonious sounds. Otherwise it would not be the case
> that musical instruments, in spite of the fact that their sounds are
> inarticulate, still succeed in exciting a variety of different emotions
> in the hearer. In the sacred games different methods are employed to
> excite and calm the soul, different melodies are required for the war-
> song and the entreaty sung by the supplicant on bended knee, while
> the war-note of the trumpet that leads the army forth to battle has
> no resemblance to the call that sounds retreat. It was the undoubted
> custom of the Pythagoreans, when they woke from slumber, to
> rouse their souls with the music of the lyre [*lyra*], that they might be
> more alert for action, and before they retired to rest, to soothe their
> minds by melodies from the same instrument, in order that all rest-
> lessness of thought might be lulled to orderly repose.[26]

The Roman historian Livy recounts in his ninth book the disrup-
tion of an old religious custom in the year 311 B.C. The passage bolsters
the archaeological evidence of Etruscan *tibicines* participating in religious ceremonies.

> The flute players [*tibicines*], angry at having been forbidden by the
> last censors to hold their feast, according to old custom, in the tem-
> ple of Jupiter, went off to Tibur in a body, so that there was no one
> in the City to pipe at sacrifices. Troubled by the religious aspect of
> the case, the senate dispatched representatives to the Tiburtines,
> requesting them to use their best endeavours to restore them to
> Rome. The Tiburtines courteously undertook to do so; and sending
> for the pipers to their senate-house, urged them to return. When

they found it impossible to persuade them, they employed a ruse, not ill-adapted to the nature of the men. On a holiday various citizens invited parties of pipers to their houses, on the pretext of celebrating the feast with music. There they plied them with wine, which people of that profession are generally greedy of, until they got them stupefied. In this condition they threw them, fast asleep, into wagons and carried them away to Rome; nor did the pipers perceive what had taken place until daylight found them—still suffering from the debauch—in the wagons, which had been left standing in the Forum. The people then flocked about them and prevailed with them to remain. They were permitted three days every year to roam the City in festal robes, making music and enjoying the licence that is now customary, and to such as should play at sacrifices was given the privilege of banqueting in the temple.[27]

Present knowledge of Etruscan music, however, stems more clearly from archaeological evidence found in their tombs. The colorful wall paintings, sculptured reliefs, and decorated vases depict musicians and dancers of both sexes in diverse ensembles. Apparently, Etruscan music functioned significantly both in the public and private spheres. Scenes of funerary rituals, marriages, banquets, athletic contests, hunting, and domestic activities illustrate the importance of music in the Etruscan culture.[28]

With some notable exceptions, the musical instruments used by the Etruscans are commonly found among other Mediterranean peoples of antiquity. The differing combinations of instruments show rich and colorful musical traditions. Derivatives of many of these instruments appear to be still used in eastern Mediterranean folk music.[29] Inasmuch as the Etruscans excelled in metallurgy, many ancient authors attributed the invention of wind instruments made of bronze to them. The cornu, lituus, and tuba (the Latin names for these instruments) are unique to the Etruscan *instrumentarium* and were adopted by the Roman military as signal instruments. Unlike the Greeks, who preferred string instruments, the Etruscans valued wind instruments, especially the double reedpipes (*tibiae* in Latin, *auloi* in Greek). The Etruscans also played the small transverse flute and panpipes (*syrinx*). The tomb paintings portray string instruments, mainly the Greek *kithara* and lyra. Percussion instruments, chiefly the *tympanum* and *crotalum*, often accompany dancers.

The string instruments most frequently depicted are the kithara and lyra.[30] One of the most important string instruments of antiquity, the kithara (figure 2) has seven or more equal-length strings stretched between a yoke attached across two vertical arms that protrude from a wooden sound chest.[31] Different pitches are obtained from various string tensions and thicknesses. The kithara is larger and more powerful than the lyra, and its sound chest is either rectangular or rounded in a cradlelike shape. The performer normally stands to play the instrument, which is secured to the left wrist with a strap. The right hand plucks the strings with a plectrum.[32]

The lyra (figure 3) is found in Mesopotamia as early as 3000 B.C. It is similar to the kithara but differs in that it has a tortoise shell for a sound chest. It also has seven or more strings. Iconographic evidence often shows the lyra player in a sitting position with the left hand on the strings and the right holding the plectrum. With the left hand the performer might pluck several strings simultaneously or in rapid arpeggiolike patterns, dampen the strings, or stop the strings to produce different pitches.[33]

The unique contribution of Etruscan metallurgy, including the ability to bend a metal tube, led to the development and refinement of several important wind instruments: the cornu, lituus, and tuba. Of Etruscan origin, the cornu (figure 4) was a long bronze or brass tube curved to resemble the letter G. Its circumference was about 3 meters, and a wooden bar extending across the instrument gave support and served as a grip. It had a detachable mouthpiece and often a flared bell. The cornu was used with the lituus and tuba in state processions and funerals. The Romans used it as a rhythmical signal instrument in the military and in the arena at gladiatorial contests.[34]

Also of Etruscan origin, the lituus (figure 5) was a long bronze or brass tube curved at the end to resemble the letter J. It is similar in shape to the ritual staff carried by Etruscan priests and augurs, which is probably why it bears the same name. Several examples of this instrument survive, including one 1.5 meters long that was discovered in 1827 at Caere and is now in the Museo Etrusco-Gregoriano at the Vatican. This

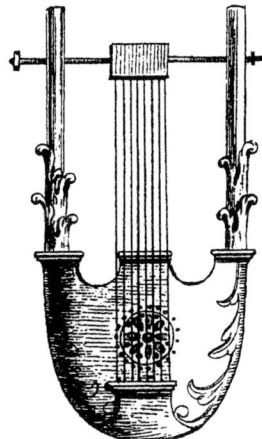

FIGURE 2. Kithara. *Drawing adapted from F. Blanchinus,* De Tribus Generibus Instrumentorum Musicae Veterum Organice *(Rome, 1742).*

FIGURE 3. Lyra. *Drawing adapted from F. Blanchinus,* De Tribus Generibus Instrumentorum Musicae Veterum Organice *(Rome, 1742).*

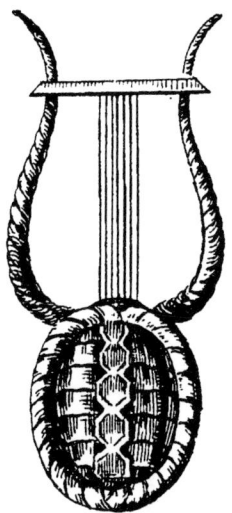

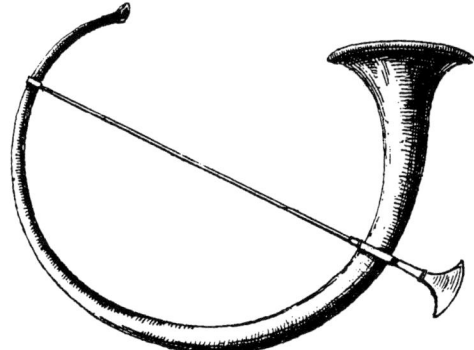

FIGURE 4. Cornu. *Drawing adapted from F. Blanchinus,* De Tribus Generibus Instrumentorum Musicae Veterum Organice *(Rome, 1742).*

lituus had a detachable mouthpiece and could play a natural scale of six notes. Often portrayed on sarcophagi, the lituus was used in Etruscan and Roman funeral processions with other brass instruments and in marriage ceremonies with the tibiae, the cornu, and string instruments.[35]

The tuba (figure 6), a long, straight, trumpetlike instrument made of bronze, brass, and sometimes iron or ivory, was 1.2 to 1.5 meters in length, with a flared bell. The detachable mouthpiece was of horn or ivory. The instrument was common to many ancient peoples but seems to have been particularly important in the Etruscan culture. The tuba, often in company with other brass instruments, was used in state and religious processions and at funerals. It also functioned as a military signal instrument.[36]

Other wind instruments are quite common in Etruscan iconographical depictions: tibia, transverse flute, and syrinx. The Latin tibia (figure 7) is the same instrument as the Greek aulos. A reed pipe, later made of bone, wood, or ivory, it could be played singly but was more commonly played simultaneously with another pipe, as a pair (tibiae or auloi). Tibiae varied widely in length, but about 50 centimeters was typical. Early representations of the paired tibiae show pipes of equal lengths, but later evidence points to dissimilar lengths. Often the end of the pipe had a conical bell extension that amplified the sound. Over the years scholars have differed as to whether the pipes used single or double reeds; current thought supports a single-reed theory. Speculation also surrounds the possibility of polyphony coming from the two pipes being played simultaneously. Most likely the resultant sound was a unisonlike texture, not unlike that made in multiple-pipe playing in folk music today.[37] The tibiae permeated Etruscan musical culture. Professional players performed at such wide-ranging activities as banquets, boxing matches, marriage ceremonies, funeral rituals, food preparations, disciplining of slaves, and hunting parties.[38] Ovid wrote that the tibiae sang in the temples, in the games, and at mournful funeral rites.[39] These activities are all depicted in the various tomb paintings. The tibiae also found use in theatrical presentations.[40]

The second of the common Etruscan wind instruments, the flute, was known in Mesopotamia and Egypt as early as the second millennium B.C. From Perusia at the end of the second century B.C., a relief

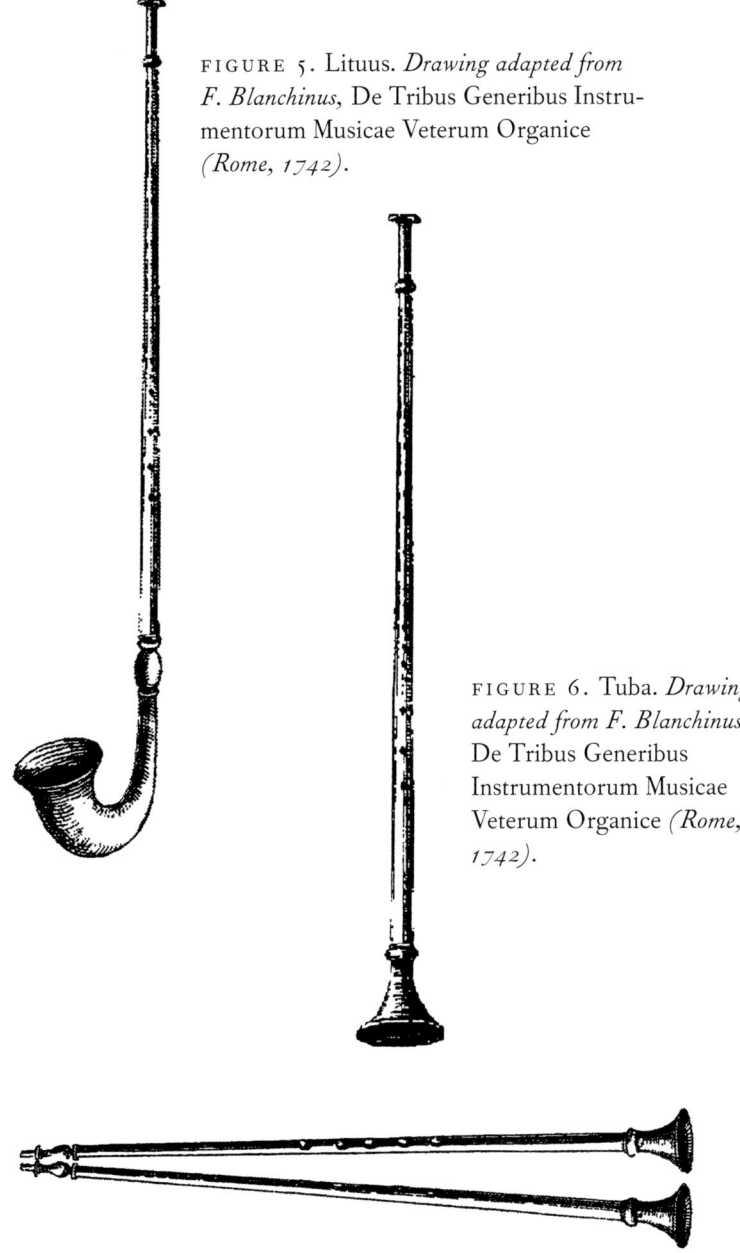

FIGURE 5. Lituus. *Drawing adapted from F. Blanchinus*, De Tribus Generibus Instrumentorum Musicae Veterum Organice *(Rome, 1742).*

FIGURE 6. Tuba. *Drawing adapted from F. Blanchinus*, De Tribus Generibus Instrumentorum Musicae Veterum Organice *(Rome, 1742).*

FIGURE 7. Tibiae. *Drawing adapted from F. Blanchinus*, De Tribus Generibus Instrumentorum Musicae Veterum Organice *(Rome, 1742).*

on a funeral urn shows an early representation of a transverse flute with eight holes.[41] The third wind instrument, the syrinx or Greek panpipes (figure 8) consisted of a row of hollow pipes made of cane, wood, clay, or bronze; the player blew across their tops to produce music. The number of pipes ranged from five to thirteen.[42] The pipes could be of variable or equal lengths; if equal, changes in pitch were made by filling the pipes with wax. Iconographical evidence indicates that Etruscan panpipes had a winglike shape.[43]

Dancers are most often portrayed playing simple rhythm instruments and hand drums. Holding a crotalum in each hand, dancers are common figures in Etruscan tomb paintings of banquets (figure 9). Crotala were made of two pieces of wood, bone, or metal probably tied together by leather; these castanetlike instruments were held by moving fingers and the thumb and served to accentuate the rhythmic patterns of the dance. Many Mediterranean peoples used the crotala, probably the most common percussion instrument of antiquity.[44]

The tympanum (figure 10), a single- or double-sided hand drum with a rim made of metal or wood, was about 30 centimeters in diameter. Usually held in the left hand and struck with the fingers of the right, the tympanum of antiquity is associated with the orgiastic cults of Dionysius and Cybele.[45] It is often pictured with tibiae and dancers.[46]

Iconographical and literary evidence make it plain that music played a significant role in Etruscan society. The religious, social, and political uses of music are clear, but in the absence of written music from that period its sound cannot be determined with any accuracy today. Although a few fragments of ancient Greek music and even cuneiform tablets of ancient Near Eastern music exist, there are no extant remnants of Etruscan or Roman music. Of the many instruments used by the Etruscans, only several of the metal instruments survive. Recently, however, "a sunken Etruscan ship has been discovered that contained a box filled with reedless double pipes [tibiae]."[47] When these are studied, perhaps another lacuna in the history of ancient music will be filled.

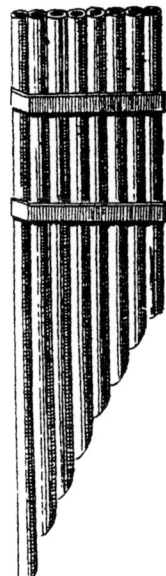

FIGURE 8. Syrinx. *Drawing adapted from F. Blanchinus,* De Tribus Generibus Instrumentorum Musicae Veterum Organice *(Rome, 1742).*

FIGURE 9. Crotala. *Drawing adapted from F. Blanchinus,* De Tribus Generibus Instrumentorum Musicae Veterum Organice *(Rome, 1742).*

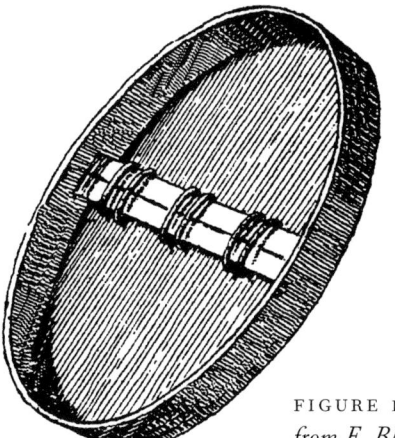

FIGURE 10. Tympanum. *Drawing adapted from F. Blanchinus,* De Tribus Generibus Instrumentorum Musicae Veterum Organice *(Rome, 1742).*

NOTES

1. For a general overview of ancient music and musical instruments, see the appropriate articles in S. Sadie, ed., *The New Grove Dictionary of Music and Musicians*, 20 vols. (London, 1980) (hereinafter cited as *NGDMM*) and S. Sadie, ed., *The New Grove Dictionary of Musical Instruments*, 3 vols. (London, 1984) (hereinafter cited as *NGDMI*). See esp. "Etruria," in *NGDMM*, 6:287–91 [G. Fleischhauer]. T. J. Mathiesen's *A Bibliography of Sources for the Study of Ancient Greek Music*, Music Indexes and Bibliographies, 10 (Hackensack, N.J., 1974) provides a comprehensive introduction and summary of the sources. Still useful is I. Henderson's "Ancient Greek Music," in *Ancient and Oriental Music*, ed. E. Wellesz, vol. 1 of *The New Oxford History of Music*, ed. G. Abraham (London, 1957). A good survey of the Greek literary sources referring to music is A. Barker's *The Musician and His Art*, vol. 1 of his *Greek Musical Writings* (Cambridge, 1984).

2. The earliest notated fragments of ancient music (ca. 1400 B.C.) are cuneiform tablets that contain a fragment of an Ugaritic hymn to Nikal, wife of the moon god. See the recording and analytical liner notes by A. D. Kilmer and R. L. Crocker, *Sounds from Silence* (Berkeley, Calif., 1976). G. Paniagua (*Musique de la Grèce antique*, Atrium Musicae de Madrid, Harmonia Mundi, HM 1015) reconstructs the major fragments (preserved on papyrus or stone) of ancient Greek music.

3. Ethnomusicologist D. Olsen discusses the difficulties of interpreting "musically related artifacts and/or iconography" in "The Ethnomusicology of Archaeology: A Model for the Musical/Cultural Study of Ancient Material Culture," *Selected Reports in Ethnomusicology* 8 (1990): 175–97. His model for understanding music in ancient cultures consists of a synthesis of evidence derived from archaeomusicological, iconological, historiographic, and ethnological processes. He specifically addresses evidence provided by Etruscan tomb paintings and Roman statuary.

4. For example, see the many photographs in M. Moretti, *New Monuments of Etruscan Painting* (University Park, Penn., 1970), especially those from the Tomba dei Giocolieri, Tomba Cardarelli, Tomba della Nave, Tomb no. 3226, Tomba del Guerriero, Tomb no. 2327, and Tomb no. 3242. Illustrations of musicians from the main tombs near Tarquinia (Tomba delle Leonesse, Tomba del Citaredo, Tomba dei Leopardi, and the Tomba del Triclinio) are reproduced in many sources, including M. Pallottino, *Etruscan Painting* (Geneva, 1952), and M. Sprenger and G. Bartoloni, *The Etruscans: Their History, Art, and Architecture* (New York, 1983). G. Fleischhauer, *Etrurien und Rom*, Musikgeschichte in Bildern, Bd. 2 Lfg. 5 (Leipzig, [1965]), 5–45, discusses iconographical and cultural aspects of Etruscan musical life.

5. For example, see Fleischhauer, *Etrurien und Rom*, 40–43 (supra n. 4).

6. See, for example, A., *Eu.* 2.567; S., *Aj.* 1.17; scholium to E., *Ph.* 1.1377; D.S. 5.40.1; Ath. 4.184a; and Poll. 4.85.

7. The most extensive study of Roman musical customs is G. Wille, *Musica Romana: Die Bedeutung der Musik im Leben der Römer* (Amsterdam, 1967); see

esp. the discussion of Etruscan musical influences on Rome (562–72). The Latin names for musical instruments are used in this essay.

8. For example, a summary description of references to music in the writings of Cicero is given by P. R. Coleman-Norton, "Cicero Musicus," *Journal of the American Musicological Society* 1.2 (1948): 3–22.

9. Hdt. 1.94.

10. H. H. Scullard, *The Etruscan Cities and Rome* (Ithaca, N.Y., 1967), 243–66. See also, in this volume, the essay by John F. Hall, 150 ff.

11. Pl., *R.* 3.399a–c. In his *Leges* (7.812c–b), written just before his death, Plato turns again to music and virtue.

12. Arist., *Pol.* 1339b–1340a. See also Pl., *R.* 3.395, 401–2; *Lg.* 2.659c–e.

13. See the exemplary edition of Aristides Quintilianus by T. J. Mathiesen, trans., *On Music in Three Books*, Music Theory Translation Series, ed. C. V. Palisca (New Haven, Conn., 1983). For a thorough discussion of the revival of ancient Greek theory in the Renaissance, see C. V. Palisca, *Humanism in Italian Renaissance Musical Thought* (New Haven, Conn., 1985).

14. Macr., *Sat.* 1.6.7–10 (on the toga and bulla), 1.15.14–15, 3.7.2.

15. Ibid., 3.14.4–5. On the change from Etruscan to Greek play performances, see, in this volume, the essay by Robert L. Maxwell, 268 f.

16. Liv. 9.36.

17. Macr., *Sat.* 3.14.4–5.

18. "Now among these women was Sempronia, who had often committed many crimes of masculine daring. In birth and beauty, in her husband also and children, she was abundantly favoured by fortune; well read in the literature of Greece and Rome, able to play the lyre ["psallere," to play on a cithara, lyre, or stringed instrument] and dance more skillfully than an honest woman need, and having many other accomplishments which minister to voluptuousness. But there was nothing which she held so cheap as modesty and chastity; you could not easily say whether she was less sparing of her money or her honour; her desires were so ardent that she sought men more often than she was sought by them. Even before the time of the conspiracy she had often broken her word, repudiated her debts, been privy to murder; poverty and extravagance combined had driven her headlong. Nevertheless, she was a woman of no mean endowments; she could write mean verses, bandy jests, and use language which was modest, or tender, or wanton; in fine, she possessed a high degree of wit and charm" (Sal., *Cat.* 25.1–5 [J. C. Rolfe, trans., *The War with Catiline*, Loeb Classical Library, 117 (1921; reprint, London and Cambridge, Mass., 1960), 43, 45]).

19. "However, we certainly know that the sons and—though I am shocked to say so—the unmarried daughters, too, of noble families regarded the practice of dancing as one of their necessary accomplishments, our evidence being the speech of Scipio Africanus Aemilianus [185/4–127 B.C.] against the judiciary law of Tiberius Gracchus. And this is what he says: 'They are taught disreputable tricks. In the company of effeminate fellows, and carrying zither and lute, they go to a school for actors, and there they learn to sing songs which our ancestors regarded as disgraceful

in young people of good family. Girls and boys of good family go, I say, to a dancing school and mix with such effeminate persons. When someone told me this I could not bring myself to believe that men of noble birth taught their children such lessons. But when I was taken to the dancing school, I saw, upon my word, more than fifty boys and girls in that school and among them—and this more than anything else made me grieve for the State—a boy still wearing the amulet of a freeborn child, the son of a candidate for public office, a boy less than twelve years old, dancing with castanets a dance which it would have been improper for a shameless little slave to dance.' You see how Africanus lamented the fact that he had seen the son of a candidate for office dancing with castanets—the son of a man whom hopes and plans to win office could not deter, even at a time when it was his duty to protect himself and his family from any breath of scandal, from doing a thing which, clearly, was not regarded as disgraceful. And, besides, there are earlier complaints that most of the nobility indulged in this shameful conduct" (Macr., *Sat.* 3.14.6–8 [P. V. Davies, trans., *The Saturnalia* (New York, 1969), 232–33]). For more on the wearing of the amulet, see, in this volume, the essay by Robert E. A. Palmer, 17 ff.

20. "Thus it is certainly true that Marcus Cato calls a not undistinguished senator, Caelius by name, a loafer and a lampoonist, and goes on to charge him, in these words, with performing a step dance: 'Getting off his gelding, the fellow performs a step dance and pours out a flood of cheap patter.' And elsewhere he says of the same man: 'What is more, he sings when so disposed, sometimes recites Greek verses, cracks jokes, varying the tone of his voice and performing a step dance.' There you have Cato's own words, and, as you see, he regards even singing as something incompatible with dignity in a man. And yet others were so far from reckoning it an act to be ashamed of that the renowned Lucius Sulla is said to have been a very accomplished singer" (Ibid., 3.14.9–10 [233]).

21. *OCD*, 434 no. 35, s.v. "Fescennini (versus)" [W. Beare]. See also Wille, *Musica Romana*, 24 (supra n. 7). See also, in this volume, the essay by Robert L. Maxwell, 268.

22. Cic., *Rep.* 6.18.18–19.

23. Cic., *Leg.* 2.25.38–39 (C. W. Keyes, trans., *De Legibus*, Loeb Classical Library, 27 [1928; reprint, London and Cambridge, Mass., 1948], 417, 419).

24. Sen., *Ep.* 84.9–10 (R. M. Gummere, trans., *Ad Lucilium Epistulae Morales*, Loeb Classical Library, 123 [1920; reprint, London and New York, 1930], 281, 283).

25. Quint., *Inst.* 1.10.20 (H. E. Butler, trans., *Institutio Oratoria*, Loeb Classical Library, 105 [1920; reprint, London and Cambridge, Mass., 1953], 169). It is speculated that the Salii, an ancient association of priests of Mars, instituted by Numa (715–673 B.C.) may have Etruscan links. See J. F. Hall, "Mars and Anna Perenna: March Gods and the Etruscan New Year in Archaic Rome," in *By Study and Also by Faith: Essays in Honor of Hugh W. Nibley . . .*, ed. J. M. Lundquist and S. D. Ricks (Salt Lake City, Utah, 1990), 1:643–58.

26. Quint., *Inst.* 9.4.10–13 (Butler, *Institutio Oratia*, 511, 513 [supra n. 25]). For Etruscan association with the secular games, see J. F. Hall, "The *Saeculum Novum* of Augustus and Its Etruscan Antecedents," *ANRW* 11.16.3 (1986): 2564–89.

27. Liv. 9.30.5–10 (B. O. Foster, trans., *Ab Urbe Condita*, Loeb Classical Library, 63 [1926; reprint, London and Cambridge, Mass., 1948], 279, 281). Foster (280 n. 1) adds at the end of the quoted passage that "the story of the secession of the flute-players is found also in Ovid, *Fast.* vi. 651 ff., and Plutarch, *Questiones Romanae*, 55. The three days (the so-called 'lesser Quinquartus') were June 13th, 14th, 15th, and were a festival peculiar to the guild of pipers."

28. See Fleischhauer, *Etrurien und Rom*, pls. 1–20 (supra n. 4), for the most comprehensive collection and discussion of Etruscan musical instruments.

29. However, Olsen ("Ethnomusicology of Archaeology," 179 [supra n. 3]) cautions against the assumption that modern instruments may be direct descendants of ancient ones.

30. For an extensive discussion of the kithara and lyra, see M. Maas and J. M. Snyder, *Stringed Instruments of Ancient Greece* (New Haven, Conn., 1989).

31. Figures 2–10 are adapted from F. Blanchinus, *De Tribus Generibus Instrumentorum Musicae Veterum Organice* (Rome, 1742).

32. "Kithara (1)," in *NGDMI*, 2:440–42 [J. W. McKinnon and R. Anderson].

33. "Lyre (2)", in *NGDMI*, 2:582–84 [McKinnon].

34. "Cornu," in *NGDMI*, 1:504 [McKinnon].

35. "Lituus," in *NGDMI*, 2:532–33 [McKinnon]. See also Fleischhauer, *Etrurien und Rom*, pls. 15, 18–19 (supra n. 4). The Vatican Museums' surviving lituus is item number 14 in case H of room 3. On the ritual staff by the same name, see, in this volume, the essay by Nancy Thomson de Grummond, 361 f.

36. "Tuba (ii)," in *NGDMI*, 3:668–69 [McKinnon].

37. "Tibia," in *NGDMI*, 3:581–82 [McKinnon and Anderson].

38. On the pugilists, see Fleischhauer, *Etrurien und Rom*, 30 pl. 7 (supra n. 4).

39. Ov., *Fast.* 6.653.

40. "Tibia," in *NGDMI*, 3:581–82 [McKinnon and Anderson].

41. See Fleischhauer, *Etrurien und Rom*, 44 pl. 20 (supra n. 4).

42. "Syrinx," in *NGDMI*, 3:489–90 [McKinnon and Anderson]. Ovid recounts the myth of Pan and the nymph Syrinx in his *Metamorphoses*. As Pan attempts to seize Syrinx, she flees to a river where she is aided by other nymphs who, in order to conceal her, transform her into a handful of marsh reeds. As Pan stands sighing, the wind blows across the reeds, making a plaintive sound. Pan then picks some reeds and fashions the instrument which preserves the nymph's name (Ov., *Met.* 1.689–721).

43. Fleischhauer, *Etrurien und Rom*, 36 pl. 12 (supra n. 4).

44. "Crotalum," in *NGDMI*, 2:518 [McKinnon and Anderson].

45. Sal., *Cat.* 63.2.19ff.

46. McKinnon and Anderson, "Tympanum," in *NGDMI*, 3:686.

47. Olsen, "Ethnomusicology of Archaeology," 184 (supra n. 3).

POST-ROMAN
ITALY

Etruscan Echoes in
Italian Renaissance Art

STEVEN BULE

In terms of human artistic expression, the period of time separating
Renaissance Italy from the Etruscan "Golden Age" is a long one—
more than 1,800 years. What makes it remarkable, however, is that
even after nearly two millennia the spirit of Etruscan culture was very
much alive in the Renaissance. And that same spirit is still alive in central Italy today, as Nancy Thomson de Grummond discusses in her
essay included in this volume. Those who have spent time in this
region know how pervasive the spirit of antiquity can be. The desire
of modern Tuscans to be linked with this past civilization is very much
a part of Dr. de Grummond's thesis, and her reference to how the
modern Sienese view their Palio is also quite revealing in this regard.[1]

Furthermore, a few miles northeast of Pisa, in the medieval city
of Lucca, excavations of the past few years beneath a section of the
sixteenth-century city walls suggest an Etruscan presence in that city
dating to the sixth century B.C., considerably earlier than previously
thought—to the delight of natives of that area. This new data could
extend the limits traditionally established for Etruria at that date
in that part of Tuscany. With all this in mind, it may be that the sub-
title of the Vatican Etruscan exhibit which stimulated these essays—
"Legacy of a Lost Civilization"—is actually misleading.[2] Rather than

FIGURE 1. Ambrogio Lorenzetti, detail from *Allegory of Good Government*,
1338–40, Siena, Palazzo pubblico. *Photo by author.*

| 307 |

being lost, it seems that, in a very real sense, ancient Etruria is alive and well and has been for some time.

In presenting some personal observations regarding the influence of ancient Etruria on art produced in Renaissance Italy, this essay is essentially simple in its intentions. It does not pretend to present definitive or comprehensive examples to illustrate the effect of a specific Etruscan work on a Renaissance work, although specific Renaissance works are examined for possible general Etruscan roots. Without question, there are many examples which illustrate the influence of the Etruscans on the Renaissance, and there may be better ones than those selected for discussion here. Many published studies, in fact, have addressed this topic, some in more detail than others.[3] In addition, some of the comparisons and observations presented here may stretch the point beyond what can readily be proven. The purpose of this essay, however, is to stimulate and celebrate; and with this end in mind, some subjective speculation may not be out of place.

It is wise to proceed cautiously when considering the influence of one group upon another. An example of the difficulties involved in establishing specific connections is the overzealousness of art historians and critics of the nineteenth century that led to some extreme views on this very topic—for instance, J. Ruskin's statement concerning fourteenth- and fifteenth-century Italian artists: "Giotto was a pure Etruscan-Greek; . . . converted indeed to worship S. Francis instead of Heracles. . . . Ghiberti, Donatello, Fra Angelico, Botticelli all made works which were absolutely pure Etruscan, merely changing subjects."[4] It is very difficult to see much of what he might have viewed as being "pure Etruscan" in works by these masters, although one can more or less understand what he meant regarding the spirit of antique revival in the art of these masters. The extent to which some of these historians and critics have gone to establish connections between the Etruscans and the Renaissance is illustrated by the citation of the well-known Etruscan silhouetted profile of the so-called Velcha Woman (Tomb of Orcus I, Tarquinia) as the source for Leonardo da Vinci's portrait of Ginevra de Benci (National Gallery, Washington, D.C.), which also emphasizes a face silhouetted against a dark background. In their eagerness to make this farfetched connection, these critics (mercifully left nameless here) inexplicably overlooked Leonardo's obvious indebtedness to earlier fifteenth-century northern European portraits. It is this sort of methodology (or, rather, lack of it) that could lead one to conclude that the Etruscans invented the profile! So much for the accuracy and objectivity of nineteenth-century romanticism; but at least it demonstrates the advisability of exercising scholarly caution in proposing connections between the two cultures. Still, notwithstanding the difficulties involved, it may be possible to see past these obstacles and recognize that, however it was transmitted over the centuries, a major inspiration of Renaissance art was the art of the Etruscans. In order to set these observations in context, however, some brief discussion is needed regarding the historical significance of ancient Etruria during the Renaissance. In this case, three basic challenges need mentioning: first, as stated, the distance in time between ancient Etruria and the Renaissance is huge; second, the influence of the intervening Roman culture and its effects on the Renaissance, including the so-called Etruscanization of Rome and Romanization of Etruria, is a significant factor; and third, the Middle Ages had a strong impact on the Renaissance's understanding of antiquity.

When students are asked to define the Renaissance, one of the first definitions offered is usually "the revival of antiquity" or "the revival of classicism." This view is, of course, excessively simplistic and is certainly overused in survey courses; yet it is nonetheless one of the key ideas regarding what the Renaissance was and even how it saw itself. It must be remembered, however, that this revival took place at different times and to different degrees during the late fourteenth and early fifteenth centuries in Italy. The difference between the Florentine and Venetian revivals of antiquity and classicism illustrates this point and has been the focus of numerous studies.[5] However, one fundamental and often overlooked reason for this difference is that, unlike their Tuscan counterparts, the Venetians did not have an Etruscan foundation or heritage; and this seems to have played a significant role in how Tuscans in general, and specifically Florentines, viewed the antique past—*their* antique past. It is clear that Renaissance Tuscans were quite aware of the Etruscans and recognized them as distant ancestors. Documented references to the Etruscans and their art in Renaissance sources are not as rare as one might think, although they are not always easily located in primary and secondary sources, nor do they tend to be as detailed as one would hope. However, many of these references are fascinating in a number of ways and indicate that Tuscans of the Renaissance certainly knew of and admired this ancient culture.

One of the best known and most detailed surviving Renaissance accounts of the discovery of an Etruscan work of art is that of Giorgio Vasari, written in 1554, in which he tells of the discovery of the Chimera of Arezzo, now in Florence.[6]

> In our time, that is in 1554, when trenches, fortifications, and ramparts are being made at Arezzo, there was found a bronze sculpture made as the Chimera. . . . In this sculpture, one can recognize the perfecting of that art which took place in antiquity among the Etruscans. [That it belongs to this culture] can be seen in its Etruscan style. . . . And this sculpture, because of its beauty and antiquity, has been placed by Duke Cosimo in the hall of the new rooms of his palace.[7]

Vasari obviously had some knowledge of the Etruscans, their art, and even their manner of writing—which, as he stated in this same account, no one understood. His concept of a distinct and recognizable Etruscan "style" is very interesting, as is the indication that works of antiquity—in this case an Etruscan bronze—were highly prized for aesthetic and antiquarian reasons and were collected by those who could afford them "because of [their] beauty and antiquity," to use Vasari's words. The Chimera attracted a great deal of attention and quickly became quite well known throughout Europe.

Over a century before Vasari, in 1420, Lorenzo Ghiberti, creator of the Gates of Paradise in Florence, observed in regard to the Etruscans: "I believe that, at that time more than any other, the art of painting flourished in Etruria—and even more importantly than it ever did in Greece."[8] Though details are lacking in this observation, it would appear that Ghiberti had seen paintings (frescoes) on the interior of one or perhaps more Etruscan tombs and obviously held their art in high esteem. Like Vasari, Ghiberti seems to have had at his disposal enough of a variety of ancient art to distinguish Etruscan styles from those of Greece and Rome (and of other cultures?) and to make an aesthetic judgment based on visual comparison.

That there was a concern during the Renaissance for the ancient Etruscan past is evident. Yet a caveat must be presented: people of the Renaissance did not enjoy the accumulated knowledge of history available to today's art historians, and both the objects collected and ideas about them frequently lacked any kind of context. In fact, it is clear that during the Renaissance there was considerable confusion of antique art with early medieval art. The use and reuse of antique works throughout the Middle Ages, especially in churches for altars, holy water basins, columns, and pulpits, was random and incorrect and often created problems for the Renaissance perception of antiquity.[9] The loss and destruction of works over the centuries—both prior to and after the Renaissance—has, of course, also taken a heavy toll on the current ability of scholars to see specific connections between antiquity and the Renaissance.

Notwithstanding the lack of historical perspective, the admiration for and collecting of antique artifacts were vital aspects of the "revival of antiquity" during the fifteenth century. This passion was so intense for Lorenzo de' Medici that, when Florence took control of the marble-rich region near Carrara, "il Magnifico" ordered that all objects found in ruins there should go directly to him; this mandate seems to have included gems, coins, and statuettes.[10] A sculptor from nearby Lucca, named Matteo Civitali, however, was not so willing to comply. A letter from Antonio Ivani to Donato Acciaioli written in 1474 reads:

> Shortly before Lorenzo's return with me, a certain Matteo, a sculptor in marble, had bought from its rustic discoverer [a farmer] a bronze Hercules of half a cubit, and a gem of carnelian, sculpted with a head, very lifelike in its delineation. This marble sculptor obstinately insists on keeping it. If we find other things which are worthy your interest, they will be passed to you, to be handed on to Lorenzo.[11]

The small bronze Hercules figure mentioned may well have been Etruscan. This reference not only suggests Lucca's proud independence from Florence but might also be viewed as an example of how the esteem in which antique items were held could overpower even the deference usually commanded by the wealthy and powerful—a sort of "finders keepers, losers weepers" scenario. Other instances of Renaissance masters who collected and, on occasion, restored antique models are plentiful.[12]

Despite this great interest in antique artifacts, the question remains as to how much of antiquity was actually available for examination during the early Renaissance. Significantly, an early surviving account of the opening of an Etruscan tomb in the mid–fifteenth century is fairly bland, with no real surprise or excitement indicated.[13] Was this just another of many tomb discoveries? Was the unearthing of antiquities and tombs so common that the writer was used to this type of discovery? With the growth of cities in the fourteenth century, the finding of ancient artifacts increased significantly, especially where towns expanded into former Roman and Etruscan sites. The need to drain swamp land and clear areas inhabited anciently resulted in many new discoveries. One account of excavation for the construction of a drainage channel reported "tombs, and notable urns bearing Etruscan writing, small bronze statuettes, precious stones, and a variety of coins and other antiquities, some found in the town, others in the surrounding fields."[14] During another sixteenth-century dig near Florence, two hundred Etruscan bronze statuettes were reported to have been uncovered in one day, and over five hundred after just a few days.[15] This account and others support R. Bianchi Bandinelli's early observations (1925) regarding the presence of Chiusian urns in Florence, as well as their influence on Florentine art in the late sixteenth century.[16]

In 1546, Cardinal Farnese, acting in behalf of Pope Paul III (Farnese), sequestered "sei mila libbre di metallo . . . di oggetti e frammenti antichi" from Corneto (Tarquinia) for the decoration of San Giovanni in Laterano, Rome.[17] Later, in 1573 and 1599, additional excavations near Tarquinia produced statues of stone and gold, as well as metal items, needed to pay for the decoration of columns and capitals for the Lateran church.[18] We have no clear idea as to what type of objects were taken, but it is very likely that Etruscan items (of metal, stone, and gold) would be included in this papal plunder of an ancient Etruscan town.

Though space limitations do not permit a more thorough listing here, it is quite clear from these accounts that a considerable number of artifacts from antiquity, including Etruscan items, was available during the Renaissance. Similar finds undoubtedly occurred widely during the Quattrocento and earlier. Certainly, Tarquinia and Volterra were the sites of vast Etruscan finds during this period.[19] In 1489, Cornelio Benigno went to Viterbo with a papal brief to visit a "marble sepulchre" called "Nicodemio," only to find that he was too late: the artifacts were all gone and the gold had already been sold for proceeds to repair the city wall.[20]

From these few surviving documentary references, there seems to be little doubt—in spite of the lack of hard evidence and the barriers of time, intervening influences, and cultural misunderstanding—that a great amount of Etruscan art was recognized, collected, and studied during the Renaissance. This degree of interest would also seem to indicate that the Etruscan spirit had been simmering in Tuscany through all the intervening ages; while often difficult to isolate, it was there nevertheless and, as pointed out so well by Dr. de Grummond, continues to be a vital source of pride and influence there today.

One of the great pastimes of Renaissance humanist scholars was attempting to establish the antique origins of their cities and towns. This was especially the case in Florence. In 1415, the great humanist Leonardo Bruni, a native of Arezzo, was granted Florentine citizenship. The following year, he completed the first book of his monumental *History of the Florentine People*. A copy of this book is depicted under Bruni's crossed arms in the reclined marble effigy from his tomb in Santa Croce, Florence (figure 2), carved by Bernardo Rossellino and his workshop before 1450.[21] Not only did Bruni show his gratitude to the city by praising its founders' republican virtues, but he went into some detail to establish the city's Etruscan roots. Bruni provided a similar cultural genealogy for the city of Mantua, thereby linking the Gonzaga dynasty with the fathers of Florence. He encouraged the citizens of Mantua to take pride in the fact that their city was three centuries older than Rome.[22]

This interest in suggesting cultural ties to and origins in the antique past is found in Masolino's well-known panel of the late 1420s depicting *Pope Liberius Founding the Basilica of Sta. Maria Maggiore*, now in the Capodimonte Museum at Naples (figure 3).[23] The fourth-century Pope Liberius is shown furrowing the contour of the new church with his hoe, snow having miraculously fallen to indicate the basilica's outline. His features, however, are those of the then-contemporary pope, Martin V (1417–1431).[24] The allusion here is clearly to the legend of the founding of ancient Rome and to Martin's widely publicized role as a new Romulus. In the distance, a colored pyramid rises over the onlookers. Beside it stands an open gate, and a shallow mound completes the scene. The lines of perspective draw attention to these distant details, which must have held some iconographical meaning.

FIGURE 2.
Bernardo Rossellino and workshop, detail of Tomb of Leonardo Bruni, ca. 1449, Florence, Church of Santa Croce.
Photo by author.

FIGURE 3. Masolino, *Pope Liberius Founding the Basilica of Santa Maria Maggiore*, ca. 1423, Naples, Capodimonte Museum. *Photo by author.*

The pyramid depicted here seems to refer to the Meta Romuli, one of the two large pyramids found in Rome which bore the names of Romulus and Remus and which were principal attractions for medieval visitors to Rome.[25] Romulus and Remus, of course, were held to be the founders of Rome, a sacred city; but they were also considered precursors of the two great apostles associated with Rome, Peter and Paul. Thus, in the Masolino panel, Martin is seen establishing a new Rome—a spiritual Rome—following centuries of decay and neglect, just as Romulus had founded the physical city and Peter had established the first spiritual Rome. One contemporary source, in fact, referred to Martin as a *tertius Romulus*.[26] This connection between the physical city and the new spiritual city had been made by various popes throughout the early Christian period. The propagandistic function of this panel at the time of Martin and its application to the political situation in Rome during the early fifteenth century is clear.

This tradition carried over into the early Middle Ages, as evidenced in Romanesque paintings representing Christ's crucifixion framed between two huge pyramidlike constructions, also a graphic reference to the two pyramids symbolizing the tombs of the founders of Rome. Giotto used this same motif in his Stefaneschi Altarpiece, in which the scene of the crucifixion of St. Peter depicts the cross between the two pyramids. It would seem, therefore, that the Masolino panel is derived from an earlier type, in both detail and iconographic intention.

Perhaps in no instance is the aggressive attempt to link one's clan and native city to the ancient past more evident than in the history of the Medici family of Florence in the early sixteenth century. The Medici and their supporters were forced to leave Florence in 1494, two years after the death of Lorenzo "il Magnifico," during the turmoil which characterized the height of Girolamo Savonarola's popularity and influence. A briefly revived republican form of government followed (1502–12), during which the exiled Medici were maneuvering behind the scenes to reenter Florence and assume their position of leadership. Finally, in 1513, the family succeeded in returning to power; and with the election of Cardinal Giovanni de' Medici to the papacy as Leo X, a new period of Medici influence and power was assured. As P. Jacks has observed, "The fascination with Etruscan

civilization served increasingly to exalt the roots of the Medici family"
and to apologize, in a sense, for the "wide infusion of Florentines
at the papal court."²⁷ Leo X made very overt attempts to legitimize
the family's claim to power by emphasizing Medici and Florentine
Etruscan roots through carefully orchestrated references to Romulus,
Remus, Numa, and Aeneas and by the use of a rich, seemingly well-
known and well-understood iconography.

Like the Florentines, the rival Sienese to the south made a con-
certed effort early in the fifteenth century to establish the ancient origins of their city and its descendancy from Remus.²⁸ Unlike Florence,
however, Siena had no prominent ruins at that time to confirm ancient
roots. The city fathers, therefore, promoted an official mythology
intended to establish roots that were even older and deeper than those
of Florence. A now-lost fresco, created in 1410 for the Palazzo Pubblico
and showing a view of Rome, and Jacopo della Quercia's symbolic
Fonte Gaia, which alluded to the divine genealogy of the city's
founders and included images of Romulus and Remus (or Senius and
Ascanius) suckling from the She-Wolf, were carefully planned and
strategically located civic commissions intended to make connections
that were otherwise difficult to confirm.

The image of the She-Wolf, however, was not new to fifteenth-
century Siena. This is evident in Ambrogio Lorenzetti's famous fresco
of the *Allegory of Good Government*, dating from 1338–40 and produced for Siena's Palazzo Pubblico. On one wall the artist has depicted
an enthroned figure of the Commune of Siena, who holds an orb and a
scepter (figure 1). At his feet is a detail of the *Lupa* suckling Senius and
Ascanius—descendants of Remus, the legendary founder of Siena.
Above and to the side of the enthroned allegorical civic figure are the
Virtues who guide the Commune, as well as a reclining figure representing Peace. On the wall depicting the effects of good government
on city and country life, Lorenzetti's painting of the city gate (perhaps
the Porta Romana), through which pass rich and poor alike, includes a
representation of the wolf and twins as they were probably placed on
the actual city gate. To further solidify this iconography, the elders of
the city had an ancient Roman column transported from a distant city,
placed it at the entrance of the Palazzo Pubblico, and had a bronze

sculpture of the She-Wolf *(Lupa Nutrix)* with the twins placed on its top. Numerous stone and bronze images of She-Wolves suckling Romulus and Remus were to be found throughout the city, appearing on the façade of the cathedral as well as on various civic structures. It seems that by the 1430s the She-Wolf, based on the famous Capitoline Wolf, had become the city's "official" symbol.[29]

For the Florentines, Siena's attempt to trace its roots to the ancient past was seen merely as a pretentious and deceptive ploy, and they refuted Siena's propaganda aggressively. With the election of Sienese native Enea Silvio Piccolomini as Pope Pius II in 1458, the issue over Siena's origins was rekindled. Although the historical evidence was shaky at best, Pius' writings and orations indicate that he felt obligated to support the notion of Siena's ancient beginnings.[30] It is also noteworthy that Pius II took his given name "Aeneas"—*Enea* in Italian—seriously and saw himself as a new Aeneas when planning a crusade in 1460 to combat the advancing Turks. This governmental preoccupation with links to the classical past, both in Siena and Florence, does a great deal to explain why Etruscan art was so well known and influential during the Renaissance and even before; art as a medium of propaganda to achieve political ends has an extremely long and colorful history.

Perhaps the most well-known and often-cited example of the influence of Etruscan art on a work from the late Middle Ages (proto-Renaissance) is the *Annunciation* relief from Nicola Pisano's remarkable marble pulpit in the Baptistery of Pisa, dated 1260 (figure 4).[31] Regardless of the Byzantine sources which Pisano may have known (i.e., illuminated manuscripts and mosaics of the Nativity), there can be little question as to the ultimate source for the reclining figure of the Virgin Mary. The obvious "classicizing" influences and tendencies in the drapery type and folds, the hairstyle, and the spirit of quiet and calm recall any number of Etruscan terracotta sarcophagi and smaller urns with figures of reclining women (figure 5).

Of a later date (1335–40), yet also seemingly dependent on an Etruscan prototype, is the figure of Eve from Ambrogio Lorenzetti's *Maestà* in the Abbey of San Galgano in Monte Siepi (figure 6). The blonde figure, languidly stretching out to her right and supporting

FIGURE 4. Nicola Pisano, *Annunciation* relief from Baptistery Pulpit, 1260, Pisa, Baptistery. *Photo courtesy of Scala/Art Resource.*

FIGURE 5. Sacrophagus of Lartie Seianti, from Chuisi, ca. 150 B.C., British Museum, inv. D756. *Photo courtesy of British Museum.*

herself on her right arm, demonstrates an awkward twist of the lower torso and bend of the left leg at the knee. Especially problematic in this figure is the odd transition in the waist and hip area to suggest the twisting movement of the upper body moving in one direction and the lower body moving in the opposite direction. In addition to a similarity of pose, a similar awkwardness in the depiction of torsion is also evident in the Etruscan models, as shown.

Similarly, Michelangelo's expressive figures of *Night*, *Day*, *Dawn*, and *Dusk* from the New Sacristy, San Lorenzo, Florence (figures 7 and 8)—each resting atop a sarcophagus—recall, though they may not directly reflect, Etruscan funerary figures. The chapel's use of sculptural and architectural funerary symbols which include rams' skulls, small masks, garlands, vases, candelabra, and false doorways might also be seen as ultimately deriving from Etruscan sources. We know that Michelangelo had visited some Etruscan tombs;[32] and, as stated above, numerous terracotta and bronze figurines (perhaps of reclined warriors) were also well known during this time.

FIGURE 6. Ambrogio Lorenzetti, detail of Eve from *Maestà*, 1335–40, Monte Siepi, Abbey of San Galgano. *Photo by author.*

FIGURE 7. Michelangelo, detail of Tomb of Lorenzo de' Medici showing figure of *Dawn*, 1520s, Florence, New Sacristy of San Lorenzo. *Photo courtesy of Alinari/Art Resource.*

FIGURE 8. Michelangelo, detail of Tomb of Lorenzo de' Medici showing figure of *Dusk*, 1520s, Florence, New Sacristy of San Lorenzo. *Photo courtesy of Alinari/Art Resource.*

A parallel with the Etruscan reclined figure motif might also be seen in a few of Michelangelo's figures on the Sistine Ceiling. The figure of the reclined Noah from *The Drunkenness of Noah* and the pairs of "bronze nudes" located in the four corners before the spandrels (now quite visible, thanks to the recent restoration of the fresco; figure 9) appear to derive from this same tradition, though Michelangelo's figures are certainly inspired by dynamic Hellenistic movement and emotionalism.

That Michelangelo drew from Hellenistic Greek sources such as the Belvedere Torso and the *Laocoön* for the figure of the reclined Adam (figure 10) from the Sistine *Creation of Adam* is certain, and studies correctly make this connection by comparing the powerful anatomies of each. Overlooked, to my mind, however, are possible subtle Etruscan origins for Adam, including the reclined banqueter from the Tomb of the Lionesses which, in reverse, assumes a similar pose to that of Adam with outstretched arm (figure 11). While the significant differences between these two figures cannot be ignored, I am convinced that the influence of Etruscan art on Michelangelo was much more than we have heretofore considered and is worthy of further investigation.[33]

The most curious statue of the early Florentine Renaissance, on many levels, is Donatello's bronze *David,* now in the Bargello Museum in Florence (figure 12). This work has been singled out in textbooks as the first large-scale, free-standing nude figure since antiquity. In addition to this bit of historical trivia, much has been written regarding the figure's peculiar psychology, nudity, and sinuous pose. However, David's posture may not reflect the classical contrapposto which many have taken for granted.[34] When viewed from slightly off-center, the figure does not reflect a classical sense of stasis but appears to be moving subtly forward and upward, as if the transfer of weight is taking place rather awkwardly. M. Greenhalgh has correctly observed that Donatello may have seen Etruscan figures from candelabra and censers (figure 13) which include a similar sinuous curvilinearity and lack of classical stasis.[35]

Etruscan images of women holding babies in their arms might also be considered the original sources for many early medieval and

FIGURE 9. Michelangelo, detail of Sistine Chapel ceiling showing "bronze" nude, ca. 1511, Vatican City. *Photo courtesy of Alinari/Art Resource.*

FIGURE 10. Michelangelo, detail of Adam from the *Creation of Adam*, ca. 1511, Vatican City, Sistine Chapel. *Photo courtesy of Alinari/Art Resource.*

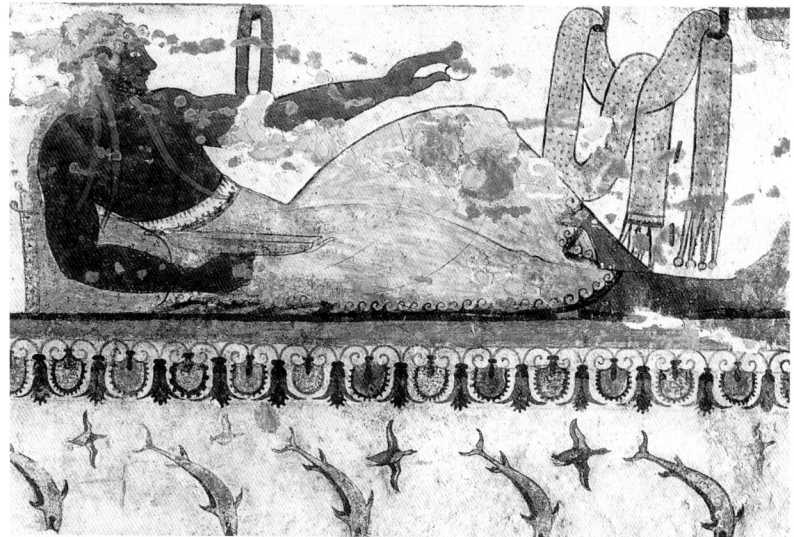

FIGURE 11. Banqueter from Tomb of the Lionesses, Tarquinia, ca. 520–510 B.C. Reversed here for comparison purposes. *Photo courtesy of Alinari/Art Resource.*

FIGURE 12 *(above left)*. Donatello, *David*, ca. 1430s, Florence, Bargello Museum. *Photo courtesy of Alinari/Art Resource.*

FIGURE 13 *(above right)*. Statue of Etruscan warrior or god, bronze, mid–fifth century B.C., Paris, Bibliothèque Nationale, Cabinet des Médailles. *Photo by author.*

Renaissance paintings and statues of the Madonna and Child. One example, Donatello's bronze *Madonna and Child* from the Church of the Santo, Padua, provides an interesting comparison (figure 14). The most immediate sources for this frontally oriented figure are, without question, Byzantine madonnas and their later medieval derivatives[36]— but these representations show the Child fully clothed. Depictions such as Donatello's of the Madonna holding a nude Child increased in frequency and popularity during the proto-Renaissance and were quite common by the fifteenth century. Michelangelo's *Bruges Madonna* and Raphael's variations of this theme, done in the first decade of the sixteenth century, also follow this type.

Recent studies have attempted to explain the rise in depictions of the nude Christ Child within the context of Renaissance humanistic and theologic developments. The evolution from the fully clothed Child in the Byzantine and medieval periods to the nude Child in the Renaissance is a relatively logical and simple one. However, the origins of this type may be older than the Christian period. As has been pointed out by L. Vagnetti, Etruscan terracotta figures of a crowned goddess holding a nude child in front of her survive from the area of Veii.[37] Similar examples survive from other sites (figure 15).

The prototypes typically cited for Michelangelo's Vatican *Pietà* (figure 16) include French and German late Gothic sculpted images of an emaciated dead son lying on the lap of the grieving mother. It has been suggested by many scholars that Michelangelo's use of this non-Italian theme was the result of the work having been commissioned by a French cardinal for his own tomb. In addition to late Gothic sculpture, late fifteenth-century Italian paintings of this theme have also been cited as possible models, including (but not limited to) works by Cosimè Tura, Ercole de' Roberti, and Giovanni Bellini. Indeed, there can be no doubt that Michelangelo was aware of these works due to his travels to Bologna, Ferrara, and Venice after his "exile" from Florence in 1494. However, curiously missing from this list of prototypes are Etruscan works, such as the *Mater Matuta* (figure 17). The monumental bulk and quiet reserve of the Etruscan statuettes bear, in many ways, an even more striking and provocative comparison to

FIGURE 14 *(above left)*. Donatello, *Madonna and Child*, late 1440s, Padua, Church of the Santo. *Photo by author.*

FIGURE 15 *(above right)*. Statue of Etruscan woman, terracotta, sixth century B.C., Marzabotto, Museo Civico. *Photo by author.*

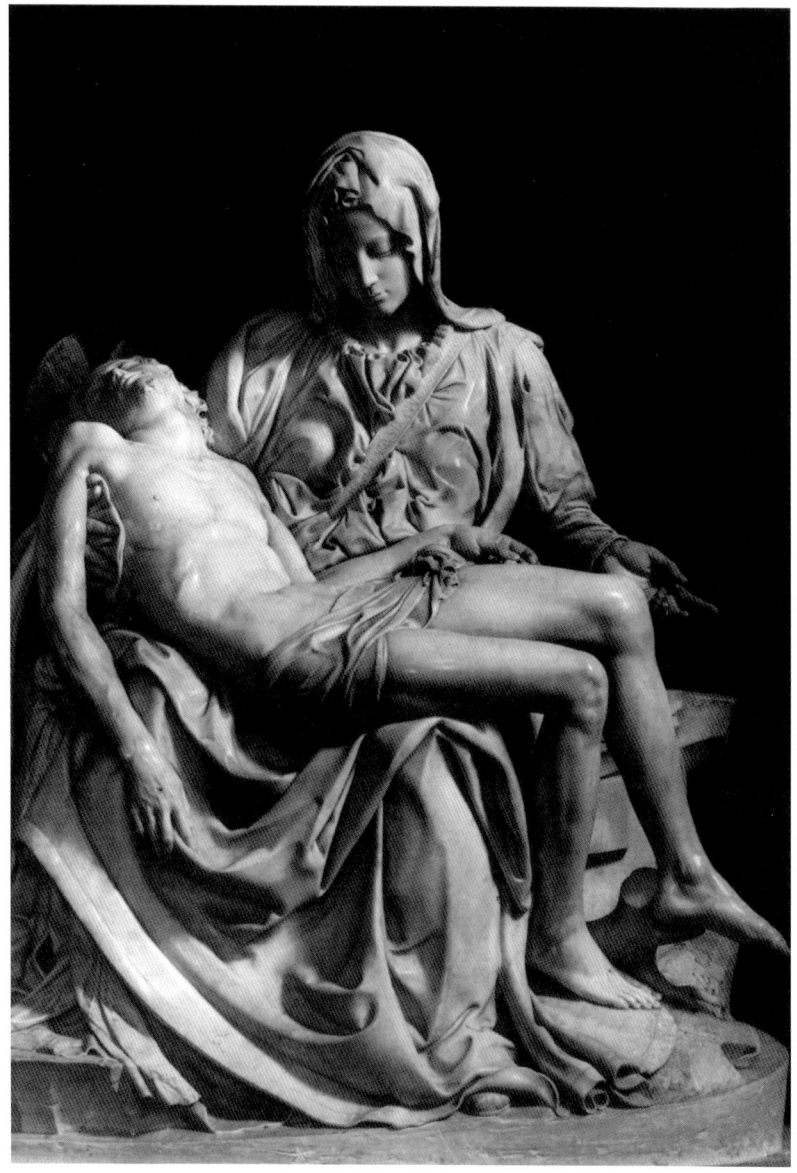

FIGURE 16. Michelangelo, *Pietà*, 1498–1500, Vatican City, St. Peter's Basilica. *Photo by author.*

FIGURE 17. Cinerary urn, "Mater Matuta," pietra fetida, from Pacchiarotti property, La Pedata, Chianciano, ca. 400 B.C., Florence, Museo Archeologico. *Photo by author.*

Michelangelo's masterpiece than do the frequently cited Gothic and fifteenth-century sculptures.[38]

Scholars have also commented on the numerous "antique" elements present in Donatello's spectacular Cantoria, originally executed for the Florence cathedral and now housed in the Museo dell'Opera del Duomo in Florence (figure 18). Located beneath the frieze of dancing putti is an anthemion frieze decorated with full-faced framed heads and palmettes. Though Donatello has drawn on a variety of sources in designing his elaborate choir loft, for this particular frieze he appears to have altered Greek and Etruscan antefix motifs of gorgons.[39] For the dancing and musical putti frieze, he may have drawn from urn reliefs, Arretine ware, and Greek vases depicting dancers—the latter perhaps known to him from Etruscan tombs—as well as Etruscan wall frescoes of dancing figures such as those in the Tomb of the Lionesses at Tarquinia. Although documentary references are lacking to confirm the connections, the visual evidence for these possible sources is quite compelling.

FIGURE 18. Donatello, *Cantoria*, mid-1430s, Florence, Museo dell'Opera del Duomo. *Photo courtesy of Alinari/Art Resource.*

The prevalence of antique/classical motifs and ideas in Italian art beginning about 1250 is so visible a development that it is easy to take this "revival" for granted and consequently oversimplify its presence and significance. The unfortunate result is that the influence of ancient Etruria on the art and consciousness of the Renaissance has been, even among "specialists" in the field, generally forgotten, unfairly de-emphasized, or only casually mentioned in a passing footnote (although there are notable exceptions). From the few surviving documentary and plentiful visual sources, however, it is clear that Renaissance Tuscany was keenly aware of ancient Etruria and seriously considered itself the direct descendant of that culture. Notwithstanding the importance of the Middle Ages, Byzantium, and the Greco-Roman cultures for the formation of the Italian Renaissance, a pivotal and powerful influence that deserves more mention than it typically receives is that of the Etruscans. Manifested in the art they left behind, the voice of their influence echoes vibrantly through the Renaissance and reverberates strongly down the years to the Italy of today.

NOTES

1. See, in this volume, the essay by Nancy Thomson de Grummond, 337 ff.

2. Congratulations are due to Professor John F. Hall for having organized this conference and for gathering together students of things Etruscan. It was an honor to be a part of the celebration of Etruscan culture; and for those who teach at Brigham Young University it was equally exciting to inaugurate the university's new Museum of Art with the exhibit from Vatican City. I speak for many in expressing gratitude to the museum's director, James Mason, for his vision of bringing fine art to Utah Valley and his many efforts to realize that vision.

3. The bibliography regarding the legacy of the Etruscans is actually quite extensive. A very informative recent essay, with a detailed bibliography, is N. T. de Grummond's "Rediscovery," in *Etruscan Life and Afterlife: A Handbook of Etruscan Studies*, ed. L. Bonfante (Detroit, 1986), 18–46. A random sampling of older studies includes P. Ducati, *Etruria antica*, 2 vols. (Turin, 1925); C. C. Van Essen, "Elementi etruschi nel rinascimento toscano," *SE* 13 (1939): 497–99; A. Chastel, "L'Etruscan revival du xve siècle," *RA*, 3d ser., 1 (1959): 165–80; R. Weiss, *The Renaissance Discovery of Classical Antiquity* (Oxford, 1969); and S. Valtieri, "Il 'revival' etrusco nel rinascimento toscano," *L'architettura* 17 (1971): 546–54.

4. J. Ruskin, "Mornings in Florence," in *The Works of John Ruskin*, ed. E. T. Cook and A. Wedderburn (London, 1903–12), 23:342.

5. For general studies on the classical revival in Renaissance Italy, see P. Burke, *Culture and Society in Renaissance Italy, 1420–1540* (London, 1972); J. Hale, ed., *Renaissance Venice* (London, 1973); B. Marx, *Venezia—Altera Roma? Ipotesi sull'umanesimo veneziano*, Quaderni (Centro tedesco di studi veneziani), 10 (Venice, 1978); S. Bertelli, N. Rubinstein, and C. H. Smyth, *Florence and Venice, Comparisons and Relations: Acts of Two Conferences at Villa I Tatti in 1976–77* (Florence, 1979–80); P. P. Bober and R. Rubinstein, *Renaissance Artists and Antique Sculpture: A Handbook of Sources* (London, 1986).

6. M. Pallottino, "Vasari e la Chimera," *Prospettiva* 8 (1976): 4–6; reprinted in *Immagini inedite e alternative di arte antica*, vol. 3 of his *Saggi di antichità* (Rome, 1979), 1167–70; my translation.

7. G. Vasari, *Le vite de' più eccellenti pittori, scultori e architettori . . .* , ed. G. Milanesi (Florence, 1878–85), 1:221–22. The English translation is taken from de Grummond, "Rediscovery," 29 (supra n. 3).

8. L. Ghiberti, *I commentari*, ed. O. Morisani (Naples, 1947), 2:8; my translation.

9. Numerous studies have been published about the use of *spolia*. See D. Kinney, "Spolia from the Baths of Caracalla in S. Maria in Trastevere," *ABull* 68 (1986): 379–97; D. Kinney, "Mirabilia Urbis Romae," in *The Classics of the Middle Ages*, ed. A. S. Bernardo and S. Levin (Binghamton, N.Y., 1990), 207–21. Two older but useful studies include I. Ragusa, "The Re-Use and Public Exhibition of Roman Sarcophagi during the Middle Ages and Renaissance" (master's thesis, New York University, 1951); K. Fittschen, "Der Herakles-Sarcophag in S. Maria sopra Minerva in Rom: Eine Arbeit der Renaissance?" *Bollettino della Commissione archeologica comunale* 82 (1970–71): 63–69.

10. C. Klapisch-Zuber, *Les Maîtres du marbre: Carrare 1300–1600* (Paris, 1969), 81. For a detailed study on the vast Medici collection of antiquities, see N. Dacos et al., *Il tesoro di Lorenzo il Magnifico . . .* (Florence, 1973).

11. G. Sforza, *Gli studi archeologici sulla Lunigiana e i suoi scavi dal 1442 al 1800* (Modena, It., 1895), 17–18.

12. A very useful and detailed resource for this issue is provided by S. B. Wilk, *Fifteenth-Century Central Italian Sculpture: An Annotated Bibliography* (Boston, 1986), esp. 73–77. For a fascinating study related to one artist's reworking of antique pieces, see D. Pincus, "Tullio Lombardo as a Restorer of Antiquities: An Aspect of Fifteenth-Century Venetian Antiquarianism," *Arte veneta* 33 (1979): 29–42.

13. This find and its description are discussed by J. R. Spencer, "Volterra, 1466," *ABull* 48 (1966): 95.

14. This document, preserved in the Biblioteca Comunale, Siena, is quoted in M. Greenhalgh, *Donatello and His Sources* (New York, 1982), 8.

15. A. M. Fortuna and F. Giovannoni, *Il lago degli idoli: Testimonianze etrusche in Falterona* (Florence, 1975).

16. R. Bianchi Bandinelli, "Clusium: Ricerche archeologiche e topografiche su Chiusi e il suo territorio in età etrusca," *MonAL* 30 (1925): 209–584, esp. 220 ff.

17. "... six thousand pounds of metal ... of antique objects and fragments" (M. Pallottino, "Tarquinia," *MonAL* 36 [1937]: 1–620, esp. 20–21). Greenhalgh (*Donatello and His Sources*, 21 [supra n. 14]) incorrectly reported this amount as "six thousand pounds weight of gold," and I unfortunately used this source carelessly for my paper presented at the Provo conference. Closer examination of Pallottino's article showed that the weight amount cited was correct (although the sixteenth-century Roman pound was less than our modern pound), but Greenhalgh somehow confused the word "metallo" for "gold." The amount of metal plundered is still staggering, but the distinction between "metallo" and "gold" is a significant one.

18. Archivio di Stato di Roma, Atti del camarlingato, 1572–73, cap. 112; R. A. Lanciani, *Storia degli scavi di Roma e notizie intorno le collezioni romane di antichità* (Rome, 1913), 4:193.

19. L. Alberti, *Descrittione di tutta l'Italia*, rev. ed. (Venice, 1588), 252–53. The author here recounts that statues, altars, urns, and carved stones were "always being found."

20. L. Urlichs, "Viaggio in Etruria," *Bollettino dell'Istituto di correspondenza archeologica* 65 (1839): 65–75.

21. For Bruni's humanism and use of the classical past, see D. J. Wilcox, *The Development of Florentine Humanist Historiography in the Fifteenth Century*, Harvard Historical Studies, 82 (Cambridge, Mass., 1969). The Bruni tomb and its history and iconography are discussed by A. M. Schulz, *The Sculpture of Bernardo Rossellino and His Workshop* (Princeton, N.J., 1977), 34 f.

22. L. Bruni, *The Humanism of Leonardo Bruni: Selected Texts*, trans. G. Griffiths, J. Hankins, and D. Thompson (Binghamton, N.Y., 1987), 181.

23. For a recent and thorough treatment of Masolino, see P. L. Roberts, *Masolino da Panicale*, Clarendon Studies in the History of Art (New York, 1993).

24. This connection is made by M. Meiss, "The Altered Program of the Santa Maria Maggiore Altarpiece," in *Studien zur Toskanischen Kunst: Festschrift für Ludwig Heinrich Heydenreich . . .* , ed. W. Lotz and L. L. Möller (Munich, 1964), 170; and A. Braham, "The Emperor Sigismund and the Santa Maria Maggiore Altarpiece," *The Burlington Magazine* 122 (1988): 108.

25. Detailed discussion on this and other monuments from ancient Rome, and their survival throughout the centuries, is included in L. Richardson, Jr., *A New Topographical Dictionary of Ancient Rome* (Baltimore, 1992), esp. 252–53 for the *Meta Romuli*.

26. In a sermon delivered in Rome, Agapito de' Rustici made the following reference to Martin V: "From these events we can understand how, just as Camillus . . . who rebuilt Rome . . . is likened to a 'second Romulus,' so you, who restored the squalid and nearly extinct city with marvelous prudence, ought to be called the 'third Romulus'" (as edited and quoted in M. Lehnerdt, "Cencio und Agapito de' Rustici," *Zeitschrift für vergleichende Litteraturgeschichte* 13 [1899]: 166; my translation).

27. P. J. Jacks, *The Antiquarian and the Myth of Antiquity: The Origins of Rome in Renaissance Thought* (New York, 1993), 181 f.

28. For a detailed account of the history of Siena at this time, see D. L. Hicks, "The Sienese State in the Renaissance," in *From the Renaissance to the Counter-Reformation: Essays in Honor of Garrett Mattingly*, ed. C. H. Carter (New York, 1965), 75–94; J. Hook, *Siena: A City and Its History* (London, 1979); M. Ascheri, "Siena nel rinascimento: Dal governo di 'popolo' al governo nobilare," in *I ceti dirigenti nella Toscana del Quattrocento: Atti del V et VI convegno, Firenze, 10–11 dicembre 1982, 2–3 dicembre 1983* (Florence, 1987), 405–30.

29. The use of this image and its symbolism in Quattrocento Siena is summarized by R. Munman, "Urbano da Cortona: Corrections and Observations," in *Verrocchio and Late Quattrocento Italian Sculpture*, ed. S. Bule, A. P. Darr, and F. Superbi Gioffredi (Florence, 1992), 225–42. See also R. Munman, *Sienese Renaissance Tomb Monuments* (Philadelphia, 1993).

Regarding the Capitoline Wolf, the work was restored during the mid–fifteenth century, and the bronze figures of Romulus and Remus, attributed by some to Antonio Pollaiuolo, appear to have been added around 1480. It is pictured on the dust jacket of this volume.

30. F. A. Gragg, trans., *The Commentaries of Pius II* (Northampton, Engl., 1940), 135 f. Also Jacks, *The Antiquarian and the Myth of Antiquity*, 122 f. (supra n. 27).

31. M. Seidel, "Studien zur Antikenrezeption Nicola Pisanos," *Mitteilungen des Kunsthistorischen Institutes im Florenz* 19 (1975): 307 ff.

32. For Michelangelo and the Tomba dell'Orco, see A. Hekler, "Michelangelo und die Antike," *Wiener Jahrbuch* 7 (1930): 201–23, esp. 212 f.

33. An additional connection between Michelangelo and the Etruscans has been made by L. Bonfante and N. T. de Grummond ("Wounded Souls: Etruscan Ghosts and Michelangelo's 'Slaves,'" *ARID* 17–18 [1989]: 99–116).

Although preliminary findings have yet to be published, the recent cleaning of Michelangelo's *Last Judgment* in the Sistine Chapel reveals fascinating iconographic and visual motifs that seem (to me and to other observers in informal consultation) clearly indebted to Etruscan sources, especially in reference to religious practices and iconography. Studies on these and related issues will certainly be forthcoming.

34. Notable exceptions to this view are M. Lisner, "Gedanken vor frühen Standbildern des Donatello," in *Kunstgeschichtliche Studien für Kurt Bauch zum 70. Geburtstag von seinen Schülern*, ed. M. Lisner and R. Becksmann (Berlin, 1967), 77–92, esp. 84; and J. Pope-Hennessy, *Italian Renaissance Sculpture* (London, 1971), 11–12.

35. Greenhalgh, *Donatello and His Sources*, 170 (supra n. 14). M. Trachtenberg ("An Antique Model for Donatello's Marble David," *ABull* 50 [1968]: 268–69) attempts to link Donatello's early marble *David* (ca. 1410, now in the Bargello in Florence) to a specific Etruscan figure; however, this is not altogether successful.

36. Including well-known panel paintings by Duccio and Margaritone da Arezzo.

37. L. Vagnetti, *Il deposito votivo di Campetti a Veio* ..., Studi e materiali di etruscologia e antichità italiche, 9 (Florence, 1971).

38. L. Bonfante has previously discussed the Italic *kourotrophos*, a woman suckling (or holding) a child (or children), and links this image to a prehistoric Mediterranean mother-goddess tradition. See her "Iconografia delle madri: Etruria e Italia antica," in *Le Donne in Etruria*, ed. A. Rallo (Rome, 1989). My thanks go to Shirley J. Schwarz for bringing this study to my attention.

39. N. Dacos, "Présents américains à la Renaissance: L'Assimilation de l'éxotisme," *Gazette des beaux arts* 73 (1969): 57–64.

Etruscan Italy Today

Nancy Thomson de Grummond

In recent years there has been a great deal of interest in the Etruscan presence in modern Italy. Particularly remarkable is the curiosity about Etruscan anthropology and the possible survival of ethnic and genetic characteristics. Questions about this subject have been pointed especially toward the inhabitants of Murlo, the small town close to Siena where well-known excavations of Etruscan remains have been conducted by an American team since the 1960s on the hilltop called Poggio Civitate.[1] The modern inhabitants of Siena themselves take great pride in their Etruscan heritage and have already made the claim that the early representations of horseracing at Poggio Civitate (figure 2) show a spectacle that prefigures their own famous civic celebration, the horserace known as the Palio.

Lately Murlo has been in the news more than ever as a kind of special case study for Etruscan survival. It is a relatively isolated and stable community in an area that has a well-established and significant Etruscan background. It has been pointed out that some of the inhabitants of Murlo today bear a strong physical resemblance to Etruscan individuals as they appear represented in art, as may be seen in the image of one of the thirty-five inhabitants of the tiny traditional and historic center of Murlo (figure 3). His Etruscan counterpart may be seen in the head of a gentleman represented on a sarcophagus from

FIGURE 1. Roofs, Florence. Roof tiles such as these, so common in modern Italy, are laid in a manner almost identical to that first used for Etruscan tiles. They speak eloquently of how Italy is still Etruscan today. *Photo by author.*

FIGURE 2. Horse race on plaque, terracotta, Poggio Civitate, Murlo, sixth century B.C. *Photo courtesy of Erik Nielsen.*

FIGURE 3. Inhabitant of Murlo. Comparison with the Etruscan men shown in figures 4 and 26 reveals obvious similarities in such details of facial structure as cheekbones, eye sockets, nose shape, and age lines. *Photo copyright Giulio Andreini—Italia. Dal reportage "Gente etrusca"—Murlo (Siena).*

FIGURE 4. Sarcophagus of the magistrate Laris Pulenas, from Tarquinia, second century B.C., Tarquinia, Museo Nazionale. *Photo courtesy of Jaca Books. Grateful acknowledgment is made to Iwanami Shoten, Publishers, Tokyo, for permission to reproduce this photograph.*

Tarquinia (figure 4), one of many such figures depicted reclining on ash urns and sarcophagi in both southern and northern Etruria.[2]

Thus far, few conclusions have been drawn from anthropological studies, although several suggestions have been made. The Etruscan Foundation, based at the castle of Spannocchia near Siena, has been conducting research of this kind. It has been followed by the ambitious project of A. Piazza of the department of genetics of the University of Torino, who took blood samples from 150 individuals in the area of Murlo and is relating these to a pattern he has observed in Italy, in which certain genetic markers seem to characterize the population of Tuscany, showing a blood typology distinct from presumed Celtic strains in northern Italy and Greek ones in southern Italy. And at the University of Florence, a team led by anthropologist J. Moggi Cecchi has examined the skeletal remains of forty-seven Etruscan specimens and has noted that the dentition shows a recurring anomaly in the incisors—a concavity on the interior surface—which also may be found in significant percentages in the Tuscan population of the nineteenth century as sampled in burials from Florence. He has traced this anomaly further, in specimens from ancient Metapontum in southern Italy, and pronounces it a characterisic of the indigeneous peoples of Italy.[3]

This essay will not deal any further with these intriguing anthropological problems, for which, in any case, it may be some years before we have meaningful results. Instead, I wish to focus on certain other aspects of the Etruscan presence in Italy today which I have had occasion to observe personally in and around the area of Siena.

Murlo is located approximately forty-five kilometers south of Siena and about one hour's drive south of Cetamura of the Chianti area, the site where I work each year (see figure 1 on p. 2).[4] The experiment at Murlo interests me especially because I have often mused about Etruscan survival in the Chianti, as well as in the area a little further north, around Florence, where an important Etruscan city once flourished at present-day Fiesole. My school, Florida State University, has a study center in Florence; and on the occasions when I have been assigned to teach there I have been able to make further observations relevant to this theme. In this essay I wish to concentrate especially on this zone of Italy in northern Etruria and share some of my perceptions

FIGURE 5. View of hill of Cetamura. *Photo by author.*

that there are many elements of landscape, architecture, religion, and customs of daily life that preserve the old Etruscan ways. For those who have spent much time in the region known as Toscana or Tuscany—a name that means, literally, the land of the Etruscans—many of my observations will probably be familiar and will not seem profound. I make no claims of proven connections, but what I hope to do is bring together a body of material that, when combined, will present a coherent image deserving of the label "Etruscan Italy Today."

First is the landscape. At Cetamura itself (figure 5), a hilltop that is too high and too cold for the famous viticulture of the Chianti region, botanists assert that the site preserves a forest ecology that goes back to antiquity, featuring oaks, chestnuts, and an undergrowth of Mediterranean broom plant—certainly all plants that were well known in classical antiquity. These combine to convey a feeling of what it would have been like for an Etruscan traveling through the forests and up and down the hills among the small Etruscan settlements of the Chianti.

Of course, on adjacent lower hills there are everywhere the vineyards that create the great Chianti wines (figure 6). It is clear that the grapevine was abundant in ancient Etruria: grape pips have been

FIGURE 6. Vineyards in Chianti. *Photo by author.*

excavated at a farm of the sixth century B.C. at Podere Tartuchino in the Albegna River valley of southern Etruria; literary references indicate that Clusium (modern Chiusi; see figure 1 on p. 2) was already growing an appealing wine by the fourth century B.C.; and in the first century A.D. the Roman writer Pliny the Elder noted established grapes and vintages of Etruria at Arezzo and Florence.[5] But proof that wine-drinking in Etruria was quite widespread—to the extent that one cannot imagine the beverage to be solely an import—is proven by the countless representations of the Etruscans in their cups, and by the variety and number of vessels associated with the serving and drinking of wine that have been excavated at numerous sites of northern and southern Etruria.[6]

In addition to grapes, olives are widely planted in the Chianti (figure 7), as in many parts of Tuscany today, providing the famous olive oil that is an important part of the economy. The Etruscans certainly knew the olive by the sixth century B.C., as is proven by the discovery of olive pits in a tomb at Cerveteri—fittingly called the Tomb of the Olives—dating to circa 575 B.C. The Roman author Cato the Elder, writing in the second century B.C., refers as a matter of course to large-scale cultivation of the olive in Italy, suggesting that olive

FIGURE 7. Olive groves in Chianti. *Photo by author.*

orchards had a well-established tradition by this time.[7] Bordering
many of these orchards, vineyards, and other fields is another type of
vegetation that was fairly typical of the landscape of Etruria, judging
from its appearance in Etruscan and Roman painting and sculpture:
the tall needle cypress trees that seem to have been used in ancient
Italy for the marking of boundaries, as they are today.[8]

Besides the landscape, I have been struck also by the way in
which the architecture of Tuscany seems to preserve some of the same
building methods and elements first introduced into the area by the
Etruscans. To begin with something of a rarity, there has survived in
Vetulonia—an important Etruscan site in antiquity but a tiny isolated
town today—a remarkable small hut (figure 8). Its unpretentious features take on considerable significance when compared with an item
in the Vatican Museum's exhibit "The Etruscans: Legacy of a Lost
Civilization" (figure 9): a burial urn dating to the Iron Age (eighth
century B.C.) in the shape of a hut with oval plan.[9] Experts believe that
the pitched roof on the urn probably reflects a thatched covering in
actual examples from the Iron Age period. The hut at Vetulonia is of
twentieth-century date, but it evidently was built with a ground plan

FIGURE 8. Hut in Vetulonia. *Photo by author.*

FIGURE 9. Ash urn in hut shape, from Castel Gandolfo, first half of ninth century B.C., Vatican, Museo Gregoriano Etrusco, inv. 15396. *Photo courtesy of Monumenti Musei e Gallerie Pontificie.*

(the oval) and a roofing (the thatching) that have a continuous tradition going back some 2,800 years.

While this hut is indeed a rarity, the style of architecture used in the Chianti area today is widespread and common in Tuscany and seems to reflect Etruscan techniques of design and construction in common usage from the Archaic period in the sixth century B.C. down through the Hellenistic period of the third and second century B.C. Some of the elements of this style continued in Roman times and were passed on through medieval and Renaissance architecture to the modern era. In the little town of Gaiole in the heart of the Chianti district (figure 10), where the vineyards grow right up to the houses, this style is evident. Nearby, at a farmhouse called Borro al Fumo (figure 11), many details of the same kind of architecture are clearly visible.[10] The red tile roof features a system that is well known in Etruscan architecture, with the earliest examples in Italy going back to at least the third quarter of the seventh century B.C.—precisely at Murlo. A proposed reconstruction of the roof of the porchlike Southeast Building at Poggio Civitate (figure 12) shows the relationship of the rectangular pan-shaped tiles and the curved cover tiles that go over the gaps

FIGURE 10. Gaiole-in-Chianti. *Photo by author.*

FIGURE 11. Borro al Fumo. *Photo by author.*

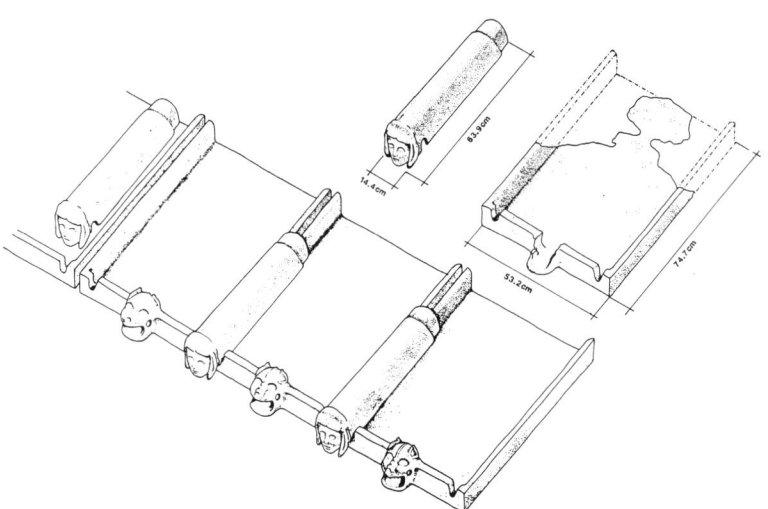

FIGURE 12. Reconstruction of roof at Poggio Civitate dating from seventh century B.C. *Drawing by E. Simmons; courtesy of Erik Nielsen.*

between them. In addition, there is a reconstruction in the Murlo museum of actual tiles from the roof of the great Upper Building at Poggio Civitate, also of early date.[11]

Another well-known reconstruction was made at Acquarossa in central Italy; the same was done at Marzabotto near Bologna.[12] And in fact, practically every Etruscan habitation site must deal with this material. Cetamura has yielded more rooftiles, both in terms of count and weight, than any other kind of manmade material. The reason for this is clear, since most buildings were covered with such tiles and the tiles tend to wear out and need replacement about every twenty or twenty-five years. The Greeks, who used a similar system, began to do so around the same time as the Etruscans or perhaps earlier;[13] but it is the widespread practice in ancient Etruria that explains the presence of such roofs all over Tuscany in modern times. Medieval and Renaissance Florence used this system; and today Florence and Fiesole, along with numerous other cities of modern Italy, are still roofed with red tiles, as may be seen by views from the window of my apartment in Florence in 1993 (figures 1 and 13). In these two details, the tiles are arranged almost identically to the way they were at Murlo in the seventh century B.C.

FIGURE 13. Roof, Florence. *Photo by author.*

FIGURE 14. Interior of roof, Borro al Fumo. *Photo by author.*

FIGURE 15. Construction of roof, Montespertoli. *Photo courtesy of Mario Galassi.*

The traditional way of doing the underside of such roofs is also Etruscan (figure 14), as may be seen at Borro al Fumo. This is a method that survives in rural areas, where the technology is still passed on from generation to generation. Across a central ridgepole were laid poles or rafters; the pan tiles were then often laid directly over these and could be seen from inside the house. Just recently, in the hills above Florence at Montespertoli, a medieval tower was restored as a home.[14] The owner and his assistants knew exactly how to build the Etruscan-style frame to support the tiles (figure 15). The ancient way of laying the beams inside the house is preserved in various tombs at Cerveteri, such as the Tomb of the Ship, from the Archaic period; and it also occurs in painted tombs at Tarquinia, from the Archaic and later, such as in the fascinating Tomb of the Hunter, where the entire system was painted on the walls and ceiling. In this case the framework does not support the usual rooftiles, but instead a hunter's canvas tent.[15]

The walls of many Chianti houses (figures 10 and 11) are identical in their masonry to the walls of buildings at Cetamura. The only difference is in the mortar, which is superior today. Workmen can frequently be seen in the region (figure 16) using this technique of laying the irregular stones with a fine vertical face. In comparison, some unmortared masonry at Cetamura (figure 17) uses a fairly similar pattern of laying the stones. This is the basement of a Hellenistic building, Structure B, associated with water management.

Then there are the pavements. The kind of irregular polygonal flagstone pavement excavated in Structure C at Cetamura (figure 18), a Hellenistic building of uncertain usage, survives not only in the countryside but in the very heart of Florence. One of the two main squares of the city, the Piazza della Signoria, which still has much of its medieval look, also has a pavement of an older style which is absolutely in the Etruscan tradition (figures 19 and 20). Many of the streets in Florence still have this older style of polygonal paving as well.

And finally come the doors. As can be seen in the painted, Archaic-period Tomb of the Augurs from Tarquinia (figure 2 on p. 270), the Etruscans used grand paneled doors that often had large and conspicuous nail heads. These doors are imposing, perhaps because they are conceived of as doors to the underworld. Another example of the door

FIGURE 16. Modern masonry technique, Chianti. *Photo by author.*

to the underworld occurs on an ash urn of a type found at Chiusi and rendered here in a line drawing (figure 21).[16] The carving is a little crude but indicates clearly enough that such paneled doors with studs could also have the shape of an arch. Nail heads have been found at Cetamura, made of bronze, perhaps of the very kind that created these studs in the door; they are actually caps that were fitted over the iron nail shafts. These must have studded some of the more imposing portals of Cetamura, and in Florence they may be seen still in a number of places. Many doors show the use of the paneling and are lined with the handsome studs. The door of a Florentine palazzo in Borgo Santa Croce (figure 22) is astonishingly like the door in the ash urn from Chiusi.

I turn now from the architecture and landscape of Tuscany to customs of daily life. At Cetamura was found an inscription with the name of one of the inhabitants of the settlement: reading from right to left in Etruscan style, *Lausini* (figure 23). It serves to remind us that

FIGURE 17. Structure B, Cetamura. *Photo by author.*

FIGURE 18. Structure C, Cetamura. *Photo by author.*

FIGURE 19. Piazza della Signoria, Florence. *Photo by author.*

FIGURE 20. Pavement, Piazza della Signoria, Florence. *Photo by author.*

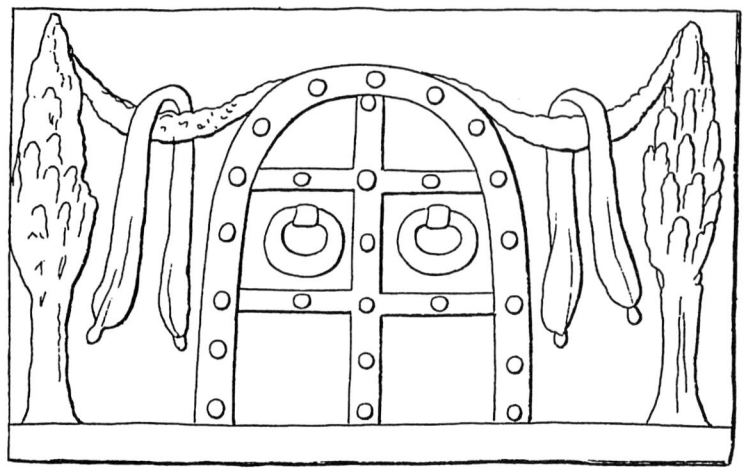

FIGURE 21. Door to the Underworld, ash urn, Chiusi. *Drawing from Brunn and Körte.*

the Etruscans were the first native inhabitants of Italy to use the alphabet, having learned it from the Greeks and Phoenicians, and that they then taught it to the Romans when the Etruscans ruled Rome in the sixth century B.C. Proof that the Romans learned it from the Etruscans and not from the Greeks lies in several points, but for the sake of brevity I will mention only that the first letters for the Romans were not alpha, beta, and gamma but A, B, and C, because the Etruscans did not use the gamma, pronouncing it instead as an unvoiced consonant: a "hard" C.[17]

Other potsherds from Cetamura (figure 24) show what are traditionally but erroneously called Roman numerals. P. Keyser has convincingly demonstrated that these number forms were in fact invented by the Etruscans and, like the alphabet, were then taught to the Romans.[18] When one reads letters and sees numerals on signs about Italy today, rarely is it considered that the Etruscans were the first to use these letters and numbers in Italy. Though they now read from left to right as the Romans arranged them, it must be acknowledged that the presence of these elements constitutes a survival of Etruscan practice. The numerals are of course quite common, and it is almost

FIGURE 22. Door, Palazzo Spinelli, Borgo Santa Croce, Florence. *Photo by author.*

FIGURE 23. Bowl with graffito *Lausini,* Cetamura, third to second century B.C. *Photo by author.*

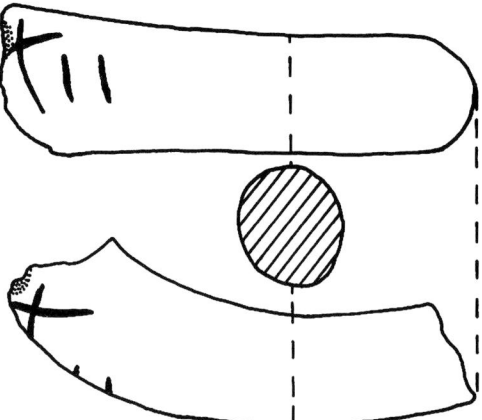

FIGURE 24. Graffito
with numeral, Ceta-
mura, third to second
century B.C. *Drawing
courtesy of author.*

unnecessary to refer to the clock tower in the Piazza della Signoria
in Florence, with its "Roman" numerals (figure 19). These occur likewise in the other main square of Florence, the Piazza della Repubblica,
where an inscription over the main archway records the year—
MDCCCXCV—in which the piazza was renovated. Monuments of
famous men that stand in public squares in Italy normally record the
date in Etruscan numerals. A statue in the Piazza dell'Indipendenza in
Florence, for example, shows the Baron Bettino Ricasoli, the inventor
of the recipe for Chianti wine that is most widely used today, with the
date of MDCCCXCVII (figure 25).

It is especially in the conservative world of religion and superstition that survivals occur, and this is what I will stress for the remainder of this essay. First I wish to discuss briefly a gesture that pertains
to concepts of evil, used in antiquity by the Etruscans and still to be
seen to this day in Italy. I refer to that notorious and offensive gesture,
the horned hand, or *mano cornuta*, which Italians make today in several
contexts.[19] The gesture is just as powerful today as it was in antiquity
or in the Middle Ages and is still used to ward off evil, or to turn evil
back onto someone who is trying to project evil. The belief persists
that there are people who have the evil eye and can harm another person or that person's belongings or children with just a look, and that
the best way to turn their evil back on them is to hold up the hand in

FIGURE 25. Statue of Baron Ricasoli, Piazza dell'Indipendenza, Florence, 1897. *Photo by author.*

FIGURE 26. Ash urn, terracotta, "The Old Couple," from Volterra, second to first century B.C., Volterra, Museo Etrusco Guarnacci. The husband's left hand (shown resting on an offering bowl in the lower right corner of the picture) forms the mano cornuta. *Photo courtesy of Jaca Books. Grateful acknowledgment is made to Iwanami Shoten, Publishers, Tokyo, for permission to reproduce this photograph.*

FIGURE 27. Charu, Tomb of the Aninas, Tarquinia, second century B.C. *Photo courtesy of Jaca Books. Grateful acknowledgment is made to Iwanami Shoten, Publishers, Tokyo, for permission to reproduce this photograph.*

the mano cornuta. The Etruscans used this gesture in their funerary art to protect the grave, as may be seen on an ash urn from Volterra (figure 26).[20] The gesture also has a strongly sexual connotation, so that when the hand is placed erect the whole configuration stands for the female presenting her genitalia. Thus in the Tomb of the Lionesses at Tarquinia, with its provocative erotic dance, the female holds up her hand as an invitation to her partner.[21] This context helps to explain how the horned hand also came to be used as the symbol of a man whose wife was cuckolding him and why this gesture is especially insulting to Italian men today.

Continuing with the theme of evil, it is sometimes suggested that Etruscan demons provided the inspiration for medieval and Renaissance depictions of the devils who torment sinners in hell.[22] A useful comparison in this regard is an image of that prince of Etruscan demons, Charu or Charun (figure 27), as he appears in the Hellenistic Tomb of the Aninas Family at Tarquinia.[23] His name sounds like that of the Greek underworld ferryman, Charon, but his function and power are actually quite different. The important thing about Charu is that he carries not an oar, like Charon, but a hammer. And, as is clear from the relief on the sarcophagus of the magistrate Laris Pulenas from Tarquinia, second century B.C. (figure 4), with that hammer he does not necessarily do friendly things. Charon uses his oar to row one across the waters of the underworld, but Charu evidently uses his hammer to make sure that one is dead. Here not one but two Charus deliver the blow to poor Laris Pulenas. This role appears to survive in the Roman demon Dis Pater, a figure who participated in the Roman gladiatorial games; his job was to come out at the conclusion of a gladiatorial contest, approach the defeated gladiator, and—just to make sure that he was dead—deliver a blow to the head as the crowd, no doubt, cheered wildly.[24]

The motif of the demon with the hammer was perpetuated in a splendid fourteenth-century Last Judgment in the Duomo at San Gimignano near Siena by the artist Taddeo di Bartolo (figure 28). In the middle of this scene is a gleeful devil disemboweling a sinner, while over toward the left is a familiar figure, a demon descendant of Charu who does his job with a great mallet.[25] The hammer of Charu lives on, not only in scenes of the Last Judgment, but also in a most curious survival within the confines of the Vatican, and in relation to the chief priest of the Catholic religion, the pope. There is a very direct reference to the fatal blow of the hammer of Charu in a ritual that is performed at the death of a pope. When the pontiff is thought to have breathed his last, he is approached by the papal *camerlengo*, the chamberlain, with a little silver hammer. The chamberlain taps the pope on the head three times and calls his name. When the pope does not answer, it is official: he is dead and a new leader for the church must be chosen.[26] The symbol of the hammer to indicate the finality of death is almost certainly a survival from Etruscan as well as Roman times.

Finally, there is another instrument of church ritual that may go back to the Etruscans—the crozier, a rod of power carried by bishops and by the pope as bishop of Rome. The crozier is commonly used by modern-day bishops of both the Roman Catholic and Anglican faiths, and the conservative nature of the instrument is suggested by a twelfth-century image of a bishop showing the wand in use at that

FIGURE 28. Taddeo di Bartolo, detail of demons from fresco *The Last Judgment*, San Gemignano, 1396. *Photo courtesy of Fratelli-Fontanelli–Fotografia.*

time (figure 29).[27] The staff has a curved end on it that looks a great deal like the Etruscan priest's wand that was passed on to the Romans and known as the *lituus*.[28] An actual example, measuring fourteen inches in length and dating to around 580 B.C., was found in a tomb at Cerveteri.[29] And to see an Etruscan lituus in use, one need only return to Murlo, coming full circle, to look at another one of the relief types from the Upper Building of the sixth century B.C., which shows a

FIGURE 29. Image from tomb of Bishop Ulger, Angers, 1131. *Drawing from Kirsch and Luksch.*

FIGURE 30. Relief with seated figure with lituus, terracotta, Poggio Civitate, Murlo, sixth century B.C. *Photo courtesy of Erik Nielsen.*

series of seated figures, with one at the very forefront—perhaps a deity, perhaps a priest—who holds the special wand (figure 30).

Vineyards, olive groves, cypress trees, red tile roofs, polygonal pavements, irregular masonry walls, and paneled doors fitted with studs—these are the elements of landscape and architecture that recall the Etruscans in Italy. Among the customs of daily life and afterlife are the survival of numbers and letters, the gesture of the mano cornuta, the hammer, and the crozier. Until physical anthropology demonstrates scientifically through genetic evidence that direct descendants of the Etruscans live on, these are seemingly our best indications of how Italy is still Etruscan today.

NOTES

1. On Murlo, see most recently K. M. Phillips, Jr., *In the Hills of Tuscany: Recent Excavations at the Etruscan Site of Poggio Civitate (Murlo, Siena)* (Philadelphia, 1993), with annotated bibliography on the site by I. E. M. Edlund-Berry, 105–40; R. D. De Puma and J. P. Small, eds., *Murlo and the Etruscans: Art and Society in Ancient Etruria*, Wisconsin Studies in Classics (Madison, 1994). I wish to express my sincere appreciation to Erik Nielsen for sharing his views on Murlo and providing me with appropriate illustrations and to Ingrid Edlund-Berry for supplying me with crucial materials for this study. I am grateful to Larissa Bonfante for her good advice and help with the bibliography.

2. On the sarcophagus from Tarquinia, belonging to Laris Pulenas and dating to the second century B.C., see M. Sprenger and G. Bartoloni, *Etruschi: L'arte* (Milan, 1981), 152 and pls. 250–51.

3. See J. Moggi Cecchi, "Shedding Light on Etruscan Origins: Mitochondrial DNA Studies Launched," *Amici di Spannocchia* 13 (1993): 5; A. Steiner, "Gli Etruschi tra noi," *Archeo* 8.12 (December 1993): 54–61; C. S. Lee et al., "The Genes Tell the Whole Story," *Newsweek*, 26 July 1993, 50; G. M. Pace, "Vivono a Firenze i nipotini di Porsenna," *La repubblica*, 22 September 1992. For a much earlier attempt to link the modern Tuscans to the ancient Etruscans, see M. Cappieri, "La Composition ethnique de la population italienne: L'Ethnic étrusque," *Bulletin et mémoires de la Société d'anthropologie de Paris*, ser. 13, 5 (1978): 299–319. I thank Karena Brown for this reference. For the ever-expanding bibliography on Etruscan anthropology, see M. J. Becker, "Human Skeletons from Tarquinia," *SE* 58 (1993): esp. 235–38.

4. On Cetamura, see most recently N. T. de Grummond, P. Rowe, R. Marrinan, and G. Doran, "Excavations at Cetamura del Chianti, 1987–91," with an appendix on "The Geological Context of Cetamura del Chianti," by J. K. Osmond, *Etruscan Studies* 1 (1994): 84–122.

5. Plin., *Nat. Hist.* 15.25, 36.

6. On the cultivation of grapes in Etruria, see M. Cristofani, *The Etruscans: A New Investigation* (New York, 1979), 51; N. J. Spivey and S. Stoddart, *Etruscan Italy* (London, 1990), 68. For a general treatment of Etruscan feasting with references to the consumption of wine, see J. P. Small, "Eat, Drink, and Be Merry: The Etruscan Banquet," in De Puma and Small, *Murlo and the Etruscans*, 85–94, rich in bibliography (vol. supra n. 1).

7. Cato, *Agr.* 10. On the cultivation of the olive, see Cristofani, *Etruscans: A New Investigation*, 51–52 (supra n. 6); and Spivey and Stoddart, *Etruscan Italy*, 68 (supra n. 6).

8. On the cypress in ancient art and literature and its presence in many parts of the ancient world, including Etruria, see *RE* VIII, cols. 1909–38.

9. F. Buranelli, *The Etruscans: Legacy of a Lost Civilization: From the Vatican Museums*, trans. N. T. de Grummond (Memphis, Tenn., 1992), 41.

10. I wish to thank Dr. and Mrs. J. Woodruff Ewell and Charles Ewell for permitting examination and photography of the architecture of their home, Borro al Fumo, at Lecchi-in-Chianti.

11. See E. Nielsen, "Some Preliminary Thoughts on New and Old Terracottas," *ORom* 16.5 (1987): 92–119, esp. fig. 82 (see fig. 12 on p. 347). Professor Nielsen advises me that interpretation of the details of the roofing system are ongoing. For the basic relationship of pan tiles and cover tiles I am discussing here, no alteration in view is foreseen. On the reconstruction in the Murlo museum, see the description in *The Etruscan Museum of Poggio Civitate* (Florence, 1988), 46, and Steiner, "Gli etruschi tra noi," 59 illus. (supra n. 3). For descriptions and illustrations of individual tiles, see S. Stopponi, ed., *Case e palazzi d'Etruria* (Milan, 1985), 99–100.

12. On Acquarossa, see esp. C. E. Ostenberg, *Case etrusche di Acquarossa* (Rome, 1975), 103. On Marzabotto, see G. A. Mansuelli, *Guida alla città etrusca e al Museo di Marzabotto* (Bologna, 1982), 51 and figs. 41–42.

13. Terracotta rooftiles had already appeared during the Bronze Age in Greece, but they did not have a continuous tradition with the system used in the seventh century B.C.; see O. Wikander, "Ancient Roof Tiles: Use and Function," *OAth* 17.15 (1988): 203–5.

14. I wish to thank Mario Galassi for discussing his restoration project and for kindly sharing with me his slides of his home at Montespertoli.

15. On the Tomb of the Hunter, See S. Steingräber, *Catalogo ragionato della pittura etrusca*, trans. P. Baglione and D. Rescaldini (Milan, 1984), 301–2 and pl. 52.

16. On the ash urn, see H. Brunn and G. Körte, *I rilievi delle urne etrusche* (Berlin, 1870–1916), 3:121–22 and pl. 101.2.

17. On the bowl from Cetamura inscribed with the name *Lausini*, see N. T. de Grummond and H. Rix, "Ager Saenensis: Cetamura in Chianti," in "Rivista di epigrafia etrusca," *SE* 52 (1984): 276–77. On the alphabet as transmitted by the Etruscans, see G. Bonfante and L. Bonfante, *The Etruscan Language: An Introduction* (Manchester, Engl., 1983), 42–46, 63, 65; M. Cristofani, "Sull'origine e la diffusione dell'alfabeto etrusco," *ANRW* 1.2 (1972): 466–89.

18. P. Keyser, "The Origin of the Latin Numerals 1 to 1000," *AJA* 92 (1988): 529–46.

19. On the mano cornuta, see F. Elworthy, *The Evil Eye: The Origins and Practices of Superstition* (New York, 1958), 260–67.

20. On the ash urn from Volterra, see Sprenger and Bartoloni, *Etruschi: L'arte*, 162 and pls. 286–87 (supra n. 2).

21. On the Tomb of the Lionesses, see Steingräber, *Catalogo ragionato*, 322 (supra n. 15).

22. See esp. F. Weege, *Etruskische Maleri* (Halle, Ger., 1921), 49–54. Cf. N. T. de Grummond, "Rediscovery," in *Etruscan Life and Afterlife: A Handbook of Etruscan Studies*, ed. L. Bonfante (Detroit, 1986), 23.

23. On Charu, see F. De Ruyt, *Charun: Démon étrusque de la mort*, Etudes de philologie, d'archéologie, et d'histoire anciennes, 1 (Rome, 1934); I. Krauskopf, *Todesdämonen und Totengötter im vorhellenistischen Etrurien: Kontinuität und Wandel* (Florence, 1987).

24. On Dis Pater, see De Ruyt, *Charun: Démon étrusque*, 191, 246 (supra n. 24). For a jolly reconstruction of Dis Pater in the arena, see P. Connolly, *Pompeii* (London, 1979), 73. I thank Lisa Pieraccini for bringing this to my attention.

25. On Taddeo di Bartolo, see S. Symeonides, *Taddeo di Bartolo*, Accademia sienese degli intronati, 7 (Siena, It., 1965), 38–39, 156–57, 233, and pls. LXXVI–LXXVII. The date of 1393 seems to have been written on the frescoes; the reading is now disputed by some.

26. See C. Hollis, ed., *The Papacy: An Illustrated History from St. Peter to Paul VI* (New York, 1964), 265.

27. The image is that of Bishop Ulger of Angers (d. 1131), as published by J. P. Kirsch and V. Luksch, *Illustriete Geschichte der katholischen Kirche* (Munich, 1903–5), 292.

28. On the history of the lituus and its predecessors and successors, see F. Focke, "Szepter und Krummstab: Eine symbolgeschichtliche Untersuchung," *Festgabe für Alois Fuchs* ... (Paderborn, Ger., 1950), esp. 362–87 for the relationship between lituus and crozier. He notes that the latest references to the activity of augurs refer to the fourth century A.D., while the earliest description of the bishop with the wand (not necessarily curved) belongs to the end of the sixth or early seventh century. I am most grateful to Jerzy Linderski for supplying this reference.

29. Cristofani, *Etruscans: A New Investigation*, 99 (supra n. 6).

Chronology of Etruscan Italy

49	Caesar's restoration of rights to disenfranchised
44	Assassination of Caesar
43	Octavian's refuge in Etruria
41	Perusine War
31	Battle of Actium
27	Establishment of Augustan Principate
17	*Ludi saeculares* and *saeculum aureum novum* of Augustus

A.D.

14	Death of Augustus

List of Technical Terms

AGNOMEN: third of a Roman's three names, indicating branch of family

AMPHORA: large to very large Greek or Roman pottery vase with handles, used for transportation and storage of wine, grain, and other food items

ARYBALLOS: small vase used to hold ointments and perfumes

ASHLAR MASONRY: courses of hewn or squared stone masonry

AUTOCHTHONOUS: indigenous, originating in the homeland

BRICK STAMPS: names impressed on bricks used in Roman building construction indicating place of manufacture and consul at the time; very useful in exact dating of sites

BUCCHERO: black pottery of Etruscan manufacture with burnished surface, giving a metallic effect

BULLA: bubble-shaped locket of gold worn by Roman and Etruscan boys of free birth

CALENDARIUM: account book

CARMEN: nearly any ordered vocal form in Latin, from prophecies to poetry to music without lyrics

CELLA (pl. CELLAE): room in temple or tomb

CENTUNCULUS: patchwork or cloth of many colors; traditional costume of mimes

CHARITIDES: divinities representing virtues especially valued in marriage

CHIARO,-A: light in color

CHTHONIAN: having underworld connotations

CISTA: wooden box used for storing sacred implements

CLAUSULA: tradition used by Athenian, Hellenistic, and stylish Latin prose writers of employing certain sets of rhythmic patterns, especially to end sentences

CLIENS: freeman under protection of a Roman citizen

COCCIOPESTO: nonporous plaster with stones or shells embedded in it

COGNOMEN: second of a Roman's three names, indicating clan

COMMISSIO: an entertainment or concert

CONCENTUS: harmony

CORBELING: building technique in which each of a succession of masonry courses projects out beyond the one below it

CORNU: curved wind instrument of Etruscan origin, often with flared bell

CROTALUM (pl. CROTALA): castanet-like instrument made of two flat clapper pieces tied together at one end

CROZIER: symbolic staff of Anglican and Roman Catholic bishops, including the pope

CURIA: unit into which Roman people were divided under the monarchy for religious and political purposes

CURIO (pl. CURIONES): presiding officer of curia (q.v.)

DACTYLIC HEXAMETER: meter standard in epic poetry in both Greece and Rome, as well as Roman satire and some Latin lyric

DITHYRAMB: a kind of lyric poetry or choric hymn sung to flute accompaniment

DIOSKOUROI: twin sons of Leda named Castor (fathered by her husband, Tyndareos) and Pollux (fathered by Zeus) who were allowed by Zeus to share Pollux's immortality after Castor's death; known in Etruscan as Tinas Cliniar

DISPLUVIUM: roof structure to channel water runoff

DOMI NOBILES: aristocrats of Italian municipalities

ELOGIUM (pl. ELOGIA): usually funerary inscription(s)

EPIGRAVETTIAN: of the late Upper Paleolithic period

EPODE: in Greek, the shorter line of a two-line unit of poetry; in Latin, a form of lyric verse employing such two-line units

EPONYM: one for whom something is named

EVOCATIO: formal Roman religious practice of courting deities of enemy cities to abandon shrines in that city in exchange for new dwellings in Rome

EXERGUE: semicircular or triangular space between main scene and lower or upper border of reverse of decorated mirror; contains inset scene or design apart from, but possibly related to, main scene

FASTI: calendars or chronological listings

FIBULA: pin, brooch, clasp, or buckle

FIDES: lyre

FIDICENES: string instruments

FIRMALAMPEN: oil lamps of fired clay

GALLIAMBIC EPYLLION: miniature epic verse form in variant metre that originated in Hellenistic Greek poetry and was transposed to Latin

GENUS (pl. GENERA): kind(s)

GENS (pl. GENTES): clan(s)

GENTILICUM (pl. GENTILICIA): generally, pertaining to the clan; specifically, nomen gentilicium, or that part of Roman proper name indicating the extended family (or gens) of its bearer; somewhat similar to modern surname; see also cognomen

HARMONIAI: Greek modes in music

HENDECASYLLABIC PHALAECIAN: eleven-syllabic verse, often of light content, named after Greek poet Phalaecus

HEROON: shrine to a hero, often similar in form to a tomb

HEXAMETER: poetic line consisting of six rhythmic units of syllables

HISTRIO (pl. HISTRIONES): Latin term for actor(s)

IAMBIC TRIMETER: six-syllabic meter used in Greek tragedy and Roman drama, lyric, and other poetic genres

IMPASTO: red unpainted Etruscan pottery fired at a low temperature

IMPERIUM: ruling authority by which a Roman magistrate exercised his office

ISTER: Etruscan term for theatrical performers; source of Latin *histrio*

IUUENTUS: young people in the prime of life

KITHARA: string instrument similar to lyra (q.v.), but larger and built with wooden sound box

KOLPOS: pouchlike folds of peplos above girdle of wearer

KOMOS: revelry

KOTHON: drinking vessel

KRATER: large, round-bodied, wide-mouthed vase used for mixing wine and water

KYLIX: wide-mouthed, shallow pottery drinking cup with handles and often stem

LAR (pl. LARES): protector god(s) for boundaries and crossroads

LARUA (pl. LARUAE): evil spirit(s) threatening boys in particular

LECTISTERNIUM: ritual feast honoring the gods, whose images were placed on couches at the table

LEKYTHOS: medium single-handled pottery vessel used for storage of cosmetic oils and for funerary purposes

LITHIC: manufactured of stone

LITUUS: wand used by Etruscan priests; also, an Etruscan wind instrument consisting of a long tube curved at the end

LUDI SCAENICI: literally, "scenic games"; a dramatic presentation

LUDIUS: stage player

LYRA: lyre; string instrument with seven or more strings and a tortoise shell as sound box

MAGISTER EQUITUM: cavalry commander in Rome's monarchical army, or second-in-command to dictator in republican army

MAGISTER POPULI: commander of Rome's monarchical army

MANO CORNUTA: hand gesture of a fist with index and little finger extended to represent horns; used in Italy mostly in connection with evil, eroticism, or insult

MEDIO-ADRIATICO: middle Adriatic

MEGARON HOUSE: Mycenean-style house with porch and outer room leading to inner room where hearth is

MIMOLOGOS (pl. MIMOLOGOI): reciter(s) of mimes

NOMEN: gentilicium, gentilicial or clan name

NYMPHAEUM: decorative pool, often with statuary of nymphs

OLPE: leather oil flask

OPUS RETICULATUM: wall masonry incorporating triangular blocks set in a diamond pattern; used from first century B.C. to first century A.D.

OPUS VITTATUM: wall masonry of stones or bricks set in the interlocking pattern common in modern brickwork

PAGANI: residents of rural districts of Rome

PATRUM AUCTORITAS: right of curiones (q.v.) to preapprove legislation for consideration

PELIKE: Greek storage jar similar to amphora, but smaller and always flat-based

PELTA: shield-shaped design

PEPLOS: sleeveless dress formed from rectangle of material folded at top to create flounce, wrapped around wearer, and fastened at shoulders with pins

PERNICITAS: agility

PERSONA: Latin term for mask

PHRYGIAN CAP: headgear associated with Trojans

PITHOS: large Greek storage jar with flat base, ovoid body, and fairly small flaring mouth

PORTICO: colonnade or porch

PRAEBIA: obsolete Latin term for remedy

PRAEFECTUS URBI: appointed city supervisor of Rome

PRIAPEAN: fifteen-syllabic lyric line derived from Greek Aeolian verse and named for the Italic god Priapus

PRINCEPS: senior senator; leading Roman politician

PRONAOS: porch or space preceding interior of classical building

PROTOCORINTHIAN: earliest Corinthian pottery

PYXIS: pottery cosmetic box or jar

RECUSATIO: refusal

REPOUSSÉ: process of beating metal on wooden mold to give shape and design

ROGATION: legislation; specifically, putting legislation to the vote

SCAENICUS: Latin term for actor; superseded by Latin term *histrio*

SCHOLIA (pl. SCHOLIAE): commentary on the writings of one classical writer by another

SCUTLATA SERICA: silk woven in diamond or lozenge pattern

SENARIUS (pl. SENARII): Latin metrical line nearly equivalent to Greek iambic trimeter (q.v.) and thus considered appropriate for speeches in Roman dramatic texts

SIGILLATA: adorned with small figures

SILEN: hybrid man with goat's ears and bushy tail; consort of Dionysius; satyr

SLIP: liquid clay applied to surface of pottery as finishing element

SPOLIA: pieces of ancient and classical art reused in medieval buildings and churches

STAMPIGLIATO: stamped; decorative designs impressed into clay

STEMMA: familial connections depicted in a pedigree tree

STEPHANE: metal circlet used as headband

SYMPOSIUM: banquet

SYRINX: Greek panpipes; a row of from five to thirteen hollow pipes of varying pitches

TABERNA (pl. TABERNAE): place of commerce, such as a shop, with living quarters behind and above it

TANG: squared or pointed projection from disk of mirror by which it attaches to handle

TERRA DI SIENA: earth-tone shade of brown

TERRA SIGILLATA CHIARA: mid-Adriatic pottery made of dark striated clay medio-adriatica

TESSERAE: small bits of stone, glass, or tiles used in mosaic work

THOLOS: circular, beehive-shaped tomb

TIBIA (pl. TIBIAE): flute or pipe, played singly or in pairs; Etruscan equivalent to Greek auloi

TIBICINES: musicians who play flute or reed instruments

TONDO: circular picture field, usually referring to rounded interior of kylix

TORQUE: collar or neck chain

TRIMETER: poetic line consisting of three rhythmic units of syllables

TUBA: a long, straight, trumpetlike instrument with flared bell

TUFA: porous rock formed as deposit of streams

TUMULUS (pl. TUMULI): burial mound

TYMPANUM: a single- or double-sided hand drum

USTRINUM: walled enclosure used for cremation in ancient Rome

VATES: prophet or poet

VICUS: village, hamlet

VILLANOVAN: Iron Age Italian culture first excavated at Villanova

VOLUTE: decorated with spirals

Bibliography

Compiled by J. F. Hall
with the assistance of
Sally Turner Johnson, Emily Sewell, and Trevor Luke

This list does not include all the items cited in the notes, though most of those which directly relate to Etruscan Italy have been retained. As far as reasonably possible, full bibliographic information of each source is given here, including information which may not appear in the notes. Primary sources are omitted, except where the notation of a particular edition is important. Abbreviation format for journals, as given in the List of Abbreviations, is used where possible. Standard reference works appearing with full bibliographic information in the List of Abbreviations are not listed again here, unless more specific information needs to be offered on individual volumes of a series such as *CSE*.

For the purposes of alphabetization, all particles are consistently treated as the first element or elements of the surname (e.g., G. Devoto, R. D. De Puma, and J. de la Genière are all listed under D). The written works of an individual author are listed in chronological order, with edited works immediately following in a separate listing, also chronologically arranged. In cases where several essays by different authors published in the same anthology are listed, they appear separately under the authors' names with a short-form citation to the full anthology. This is followed by the notation *supra* (above) or *infra* (below), directing the reader toward the place in the bibliography where the anthology is cited in full, under its editor's name. When only one essay from an anthology appears—or more than one essay by the same author—bibliographic information for the anthology is given in full in the essay entry.

Adams, F. "The Consular Brothers of Sejanus." *AJPh* 76 (1955): 70–76.
Akerström, A. *Studien über die etruskischen Gräber unter besonderer Berücksichtigung der Entwicklung des Kammergrabbes.* Lund, Swed., 1934.
Alföldi, A. *Early Rome and the Latins.* Ann Arbor, Mich., 1965.
———. *Römische Frühgeschichte: Kritik und Forschung seit 1964.* Heidelberg, 1976.
Allegro, N. "Louteria a rilievo da Himera." *Secondo quaterno imerese (Studi e materiali dell'Istituto di archeologia dell' Università di Palermo)* 3 (1982): 122.
Amand, M. "La Réapparition de la sépulture sous tumulus dans l'empire romain." *AC* 56 (1987): 162–82.
Ampolo, C. "La storiografia su Roma arcaica e i documenti." In *Tria corda: Scritti in onore di A. Momigliano.* Edited by E. Gabba. Como, It., 1983.
———. "La grande Roma dei Tarquinii rivisitata." In *Alle origini di Roma.* Edited by E. Campanile. Pisa, 1988.

Amyx, D. *Corinthian Vase-Painting in the Archaic Period.* Berkeley, Calif., 1988.

Anderson, L. H. "Relief Pithoi from the Archaic Period of Greek Art." Ph.D. diss., University of Michigan–Ann Arbor, 1977.

André, J.-M. "Mécène écrivain." *ANRW* 11.30.3 (1983): 1765–87.

Andrén, A. "Dionysius of Halicarnassus on Roman Monuments." In *Hommages à Léon Herrmann.* Collection Latomus, 44. Brussels, 1960.

Anzidei, A. P., A. M. Bietti Sestieri, et al. *Roma e il Lazio dall'età della pietra alla formazione della città: I dati archeologici.* Rome, 1985.

Atti: Secondo congresso internazionale etrusco, Firenze, 26 maggio–2 giugno 1985. Supplemento di *SE.* 3 vols. Rome, 1989.

Badian, E. "Caepio and Norbanus." *Historia* 6 (1957): 318–46.

———. *Foreign Clientelae 264–70 B.C.* Oxford, 1958.

———. "Notes on Roman Senators of the Republic." *Historia* 12 (1963): 129–43.

———. "The Early Historians." In *Latin Historians.* Edited by T. A. Dorey. London, 1966.

Bailey, C., ed. and trans. *Titi Lucreti Cari De Rerum Natura Libri Sex.* 3 vols. Oxford, 1947.

Banti, L. "Contributo alla storia ed alla topografia del territorio Perugino." *SE* 10 (1936): 97–99.

Barber, E. A., ed. *Sexti Properti Carmina.* 2d ed. Oxford, 1960.

Barker, A. *The Musician and His Art.* Vol. 1 of *Greek Musical Writings* by A. Barker. Cambridge Readings in the Literature of Music. Cambridge, 1984.

Barker, G. "The Conditions of Cultural and Economic Growth in the Bronze Age of Central Italy." *PPS* 38 (1972): 70–208.

Bartoli, A. "L'architettura del mausoleo d'Augusto." *BA,* 2d ser., 7 (1927): 30–46.

Bartoloni, G. *La cultura villanoviana: All'inizio della storia etrusca.* Rome, 1989.

Baur, P. V. C. *Centaurs in Ancient Art: The Archaic Period.* Berlin, 1912.

Beazley, J. D. "The World of the Etruscan Mirror." *JHS* 69 (1949): 1–17.

———. *Etruscan Vase Painting.* New York, 1976.

———. *The Development of Attic Black-Figure.* Berkeley, Calif., 1986.

Becker, M. J. "Human Skeletons from Tarquinia." *SE* 58 (1993): 211–48.

Benson, J. L. *Horse, Bird, and Man: The Origins of Greek Paintings.* Amherst, Mass., 1970.

Berggren, E., and K. Berggren. *Excavations in Area B, 1957–60.* Vol. 2, fasc. 2, of *San Giovenale: Results of Excavations Conducted by the Swedish Institute of Classical Studies at Rome and the Soprintendenza alle antichità dell'Etruria meridionale.* Skrifter Utgivna av Svenska Institutet Rom, 4°, 26. Stockholm, 1981.

Bernhard, M.-L. "Topographie d'Alexandrie: Le Tombeau d'Alexandre et le mausolée d'Auguste." *RA,* 6th ser., 47 (1956): 129–56.

Besutti, S. "Sigillata medio adriatica." In *Settefinestre: Una villa schiavistica nell'Etruria romana.* Edited by A. Carandini. Modena, It., 1988.

Bianchi, R. "The Hunt for Alexander's Tomb." *Archaeology,* July/August 1993, 54–55.

Bianchi Bandinelli, R. "Clusium: Ricerche archeologiche e topografiche su Chiusi e il suo territorio in età etrusca." *MonAL* 30 (1925): 209–584.

————. "Problems of Pictorial and Architectural Space." In R. Bianchi Bandinelli, *Rome, the Center of Power: 500 B.C. to A.D. 200*, translated by P. Green. New York, 1970.

Bieber, M. *The History of the Greek and Roman Theater.* 2d ed. Princeton, N.J., 1961.

Bietti Sestieri, A. M. "The Metal Industry of Continental Italy, 13th–11th Century B.C., and Its Connections with the Aegean." *PPS* 39 (1973): 383–424.

————. "Produzione e scambio nell'Italia protostorica: Alcune ipotesi sul ruolo dell'industria metallurgica nell'Etruria mineraria all fine dell'età del bronzo." In *L'Etruria mineraria* (infra).

————. "La cultura di villaggio." In Cristofani, M., ed., *Civiltà degli Etruschi* (infra).

————. *The Iron Age Community of Osteria dell'Osa: A Study of Sociopolitical Development in Central Tyrrhenian Italy.* Cambridge, 1992.

Bietti Sestieri, A. M., et al. *Roma e il Lazio dall'età della pietra alla formazione della città.* Rome, 1985.

Bilbija, S. S. *The Mummy of Zagreb and Other Etruscan, Lydian, Lycian Written Monuments.* Chicago, 1989.

Blanchinus, F. *De Tribus Generibus Instrumentorum Musicae Veterum Organice.* Rome, 1742.

Blakeway, A. "Demaratus: A Study in Some Aspects of the Earliest Hellenization of Latium and Etruria." *JRS* 25 (1935): 129–49.

Bloch, R. *The Origins of Rome.* New York, 1960.

Boardman, J. "Herakles in Extremis." *Studien zur Mythologie und Vasenmalerei: Festschrift für Konrad Schauenburg zum 65. Geburtstag am 16. April 1986.* Mainz am Rhein, 1986.

Bober, P. P., and R. Rubinstein. *Renaissance Artists and Antique Sculpture: A Handbook of Sources.* London, 1986.

Boëthius, A. *Etruscan and Early Roman Architecture.* The Pelican History of Art. 2d ed., rev. Harmondsworth, Engl., 1978.

Boëthius, A., et al. *Etruscan Culture, Land, and People: Archeological Research and Studies Conducted in San Giovenale and Its Environs by Members of the Swedish Institute in Rome.* Translated by N. G. Sahlin. New York and Malmö, Swed., 1962.

Boitani, F., M. Cataldi, and M. Pasquinucci. *Etruscan Cities.* Edited by F. Coarelli. Translated by C. Atthill et al. London, 1975.

Bonfante, G., and L. Bonfante. *The Etruscan Language: An Introduction.* Manchester, Engl., 1983.

Bonfante, L. *Etruscan Dress.* Baltimore, 1975.

————. "An Etruscan Mirror with 'Spiky Garland' in the Getty Museum." *GMusJ* 8 (1980): 147–54.

————. "Daily Life and Afterlife." In de Grummond, N. T., ed., *A Guide to Etruscan Mirrors* (infra).

————. "Human Sacrifice on an Etruscan Funerary Urn." *AJA* 88 (1984): 531–39.

————. "Daily Life and Afterlife." In Bonfante, L., ed., *Etruscan Life and Afterlife* (infra).

———. "Iconographia delle madri: Etruria e Italia antica." In *Le Donne in Etruria*. Edited by A. Rallo. Rome, 1989.

———, ed. *Etruscan Life and Afterlife: a Handbook of Etruscan Studies*. Detroit, 1986.

Bonfante, L., and N. T. de Grummond. "Wounded Souls: Etruscan Ghosts and Michelangelo's 'Slaves.'" *ARID* 17–18 (1989): 99–116.

Bonghi Jovino, M. "Gli scavi nell'abitato di Tarquinia e la scoperta dei 'bronzi' in un preliminare inquadramento." In Bonghi Jovino, M., and C. Chiaramonte Trère, eds., *Tarquinia: Ricerche, scavi, e prospettive* (infra).

Bonghi Jovino, M., and C. Chiaramonte Trère, eds. *Tarquinia: Ricerche, scavi, e prospettive: Atti del Convegno internazionale di studi La Lombardia per gli Etruschi, Milano, 24–25 giugno 1986*. Milan, 1987.

Boriskovskaya, S. P. "Etruscan Relief Pithoi from Caere." *Wissenschaftliche Zeitschrift der Universität Rostock* 19 (1970): 567 ff.

Bormann, E. "Etruskisches aus römischer Zeit." *Archäologisch-epigraphische Mitteilungen aus Österreich-Ungarn* 11 (1887): 94 ff.

Boschung, D. "Tumulus Iuliorum—Mausoleum Augusti: Ein Beitrag zu seinen Sinnbezügen." *HASB* 6 (1980): 38–41.

Bottini, A. "Elena in Occidente: Una tomba dalla chora di Metaponto." *BA* 73 (1988): 1–20.

Bramble, J. C. "Minor Figures." In *Cambridge History of Classical Literature*. 2 vols. Cambridge, 1982–85.

Brecciaroli Taborelli, L. "Contributo alla classificazione di una terra sigillata chiara italica." *Rivista di studi marchigiai* 1 (1978): 1–38.

Brendel, O. *Etruscan Art*. Harmondsworth, Engl., 1978.

Brilliant, R. "Roman Architecture." In *Roman Art from the Republic to Constantine*. London, 1974.

Brommer, F. *Denkmalerlisten zur griechischen Heldensage*. 4 vols. Marburg, Ger., 1976.

Brown, F. E. *Roman Architecture*. New York, 1982.

Brunn, H., and G. Körte. *I rilievi delle urne etrusche*. 3 vols. Berlin, 1870–1916.

Brunt, P. A., and J. M. Moore, eds. *Res Gestae Divi Augusti*. Oxford, 1967.

Bruschetti, P. "Il Sodo, il tumulo 1, l'ambiente." In *La Cortona dei Principes*. Edited by P. Zamarchi Grassi. Cortona, It., 1987.

Buchi, E. *Lucerne del Museo di Aquileia I: Lucerne romane con marchio di fabrica*. Aquileia, It., 1975.

Buchner, E. *Die Sonnenuhr des Augustus: Nachdruck aus RM 1976 und Nachtrag über die Ausgrabung 1980/1981*. Mainz am Rhein, 1982.

Buranelli, F. *The Etruscans: Legacy of a Lost Civilization: From the Vatican Museums*. Translated by N. T. de Grummond. Memphis, Tenn., 1992.

Burns, A. "Hippodamus and the Planned City." *Historia* 25 (1976): 414–28.

Camp, J. M. *The Athenian Agora: Excavations in the Heart of Classical Athens*. London, 1986.

Cappelletti, M. "Cortona" and "Perugia." In *Atlante dei siti archeologici della Toscana*. Edited by M. Torelli, M. Menichetti, C. Masseria, and M. Fabbri. Rome, 1992.

Cappieri, M. "La Composition ethnique de la population italienne: L'Ethnic étrusque." *Bulletin et mémoires de la Société d'anthropologie de Paris*, ser. 13, 5 (1978): 299–319.

Carancini, G. L. "I ripostigli dell'età del bronzo finale." In Istituto italiano di preistoria e protostoria, ed., *Il bronzo finale in Italia* (infra).

Carpiceci, A. C. *Pompeii Nowadays and 2000 Years Ago.* Edition Il Turismo. Florence, 1977.

Carpino, A. "Etruscan Relief Mirrors: Origins, Functions, and Cultural Significance." Ph.D. diss., University of Iowa, 1993.

Castagnoli, F. "Il Campo Marzio nell'antichità." *Atti dell'Accademia nazionale dei Lincei*, Memorie delle classe di scienze morali, storiche, e filologiche. 8th ser., vol. 1, fasc. 4 (1946): 93–193.

———. "La leggenda di Enea nel Lazio." *StudRom* 30 (1982): 1–15.

Cateni, G. *Volterra: Museo Guarnacci.* Pisa, 1988.

Cavoli, A. *Profilo di una città etrusca: Cerveteri.* Pistoia, It., 1985.

Cecconi, V., and V. Melani. *Profilo di una città etrusca: Populonia.* Pistoia, It., 1981.

Chapouthier, F. "Léda devant l'oeuf de Némésis." *BCH* 66–69 (1942–43): 1–21.

Chastel, A. "L'Etruscan revival du xve siècle." *RA*, 3d ser., 1 (1959): 165–80.

Cherici, A. "Materiali per una carta archeologica del territorio cortonese." In *Cortona: Struttura e storia: Materiali per una conoscenza operante della città e del territorio: Catalogo della mostra.* Cortona, It., 1987.

Clairmont, C. *Das Parisurteil in der antiken Kunst.* Zürich, 1951.

Coarelli, F. "I praedia Volusiana e l'albero genealogico dei Volusii Saturnini." In *I Volusii Saturnini: Una famiglia romana della prima età imperiale.* Archeologia materiali e problemi. Rome, 1982.

———. "Il Pantheon, l'apoteosi di Augusto, e l'apoteosi di Romolo." In *Città e architettura nella Roma imperiale: Atti del seminario del 27 ottobre 1981 nel 25 anniversario dell'Accademia di Danimarca.* Analecta Romana Instituti Danici. Supplementum, 10. Odense, Den., 1983.

———. *Guida archeologica di Roma.* Edited by A. Mondadori. Milan, 1984.

———, ed. *Etruscan Cities.* Translated by C. Atthill et al. London, 1975.

Cogrossi, C. "Atena Iliaca e il culto degli eroi: L'heròon di Enea a Lavinio e Latino figlio di Odisseo." In *Politica e religione nel primo scontro tra Roma e l'Oriente.* Edited by M. Sordi. Contributi dell'Istituto di storia antica, 8. Milan, 1982.

Coleman, R., ed. *Vergil: Eclogues.* Cambridge, 1977.

Coleman-Norton, P. R. "Cicero Musicus." *Journal of the American Musicological Society* 1.2 (1948): 3–22.

Colini, A. M. "Il mausoleo di Augusto." *Capitolium* 4 (1928–29): 11–22.

Colini, A. M., and G. Giglioli. "Relazione della prima campagna di scavo nel mausoleo di Augusto, estate-autunno 1926." *BCAR* 54 (1927): 191–234.

Collon, D. *First Impressions: Cylinder Seals in the Ancient Near East.* London, 1987.

Colonna, G. "S. Omobono: La ceramica etrusca dipinta." *BCAR* 77 (1962): 125–53.

———. "Aspetti culturali della Roma primitiva: Il periodo orientalizzante recente." *ArchClass* 16 (1964): 1–12.

———. "Preistoria e protostoria di Roma e del Lazio." In *Popoli e civiltà dell'Italia antica*. Vol. 2. Rome, 1974.

———. "Caere." In "Rivista di epigrafia etrusca." Column edited by M. Cristofani. *SE* 46 (1978): 348–52.

———. "Virgilio, Cortona, e la leggenda etrusca di Dardano." *ArchClass* 32 (1980): 12.

———. "Caere." In "Rivista di epigrafia etrusca." Column edited by M. Cristofani. *SE* 52 (1984): 317–18.

———. "Urbanistica e archittetura." In *Rasenna: Storia e civiltà degli Etruschi*. Milan, 1986.

Comstock, M., and C. Vermeule. *Greek, Etruscan, and Roman Bronzes in the Museum of Fine Arts, Boston*. Greenwich, Conn., 1971.

Connolly, P. *Pompeii*. London, 1979.

Conte, G. B. *Latin Literature: A History*. Baltimore, 1994.

Cook, A. B. *Zeus: A Study in Ancient Religion*. 3 vols. in 5. Cambridge, 1914–40.

Cordingley, R., and Richmond, I. "The Mausoleum of Augustus." *PBSR* 10 (1927): 191–234.

Cornell, T. J. Review of *Elogia tarquiniensia*, by M. Torelli. *JRS* 68 (1978): 168.

———. "The Value of the Literary Tradition Concerning Archaic Rome." In Raaflaub, K. A., ed., *Social Struggles in Archaic Rome* (infra).

Courby, F. *Les Vases grecs à reliefs*. Paris, 1922.

Courtney, E., ed. *The Fragmentary Latin Poets*. Oxford, 1993.

Cristofani, M. "Sull'origine e la diffusione dell'alfabeto etrusco." *ANRW* 1.2 (1972): 466–89.

———. *The Etruscans: A New Investigation*. New York, 1979.

———. "Il popolamento." In *Gli Etruschi in Maremma: Popolamento e attività produttive*. Edited by M. Cristofani. Milan, 1981.

———. *Dizionario della civiltà etrusca*. Archeologia (Florence, Italy). Florence, 1985.

———. *I bronzi degli Etruschi*. Novara, It., 1985.

———. "L'area urbana." In *Caere 1: Il parco archeologico*. Edited by M. Cristofani. Rome, 1988.

———, ed. *Civiltà degli Etruschi*. Milan, 1985.

———, ed. *Caere 1: Il parco archeologico*. Rome, 1988.

———, ed. *Caere 3.1–2: Lo scarico arcaico della vigna parrochiale*. Rome, 1992–93.

Cuomo di Caprio, N. *La ceramica in archeologia: Antiche tecniche di lavorazione e moderni metodi d'indagine*. Rome, 1985.

Curri, C. B. "Un cilindretto etrusco di Roselle." In *Studi di antichità in onore di Guglielmo Maetzke*. 3 vols. Rome, 1984.

Curtius, L. "Neue hermeneutische Miscellen." *AA* 63–64 (1948–49): 47–64.

Dacos, N. "Présents américains à la Renaissance: L'Assimilation de l'éxotisme." *Gazette des beaux arts* 73 (1969): 57–64.

Dacos, N., et al. *Il tesoro di Lorenzo il Magnifico . . . Catalogo della Mostra: Palazzo Medici Riccardi*. 2 vols. Florence, 1973.

Daviault, A., J. Lancha, and L. A. López Palomo. *Un mosaico con inscripciones: Une Mosaïque à inscriptions: Puente Genil (Cordoba)*. Publications de la Casa de Velazquez, Série études et documents, 3. Madrid, 1987.

Dawkins, R. M., ed. *The Sanctuary of Artemis Orthia at Sparta: Excavated and Described by Members of the British School at Athens, 1906–1910.* Society for the Promotion of Hellenic Studies Supplementary Papers, 5. London, 1929.

de Albentiis, E. *La casa dei romani.* Milan, 1990.

De Fine Licht, K. *The Rotunda in Rome: A Study of Hadrian's Pantheon.* Copenhagen, 1968.

De Francisci, P. *Primordia Civitatis.* Rome, 1959.

Degrassi, A., ed. *Fasti Consulares et Triumphales.* In *InscrIt* 13.1.17–20.

de Grummond, N. T. *Etruscan Dress.* Baltimore, 1975.

———. "Rediscovery." In Bonfante, L., ed., *Etruscan Life and Afterlife* (supra).

———. "Mythology, Iconography, Religion." In Roncalli, F., and L. Bonfante, *Antichità dall'Umbria a New York* (infra).

———, ed. *A Guide to Etruscan Mirrors.* Tallahassee, Fla., 1982.

de la Genière, J. "A propos d'un vase grec." *MMAI* 63 (1908): 31–56.

del Chiaro, M. A. *Etruscan Art from West Coast Collections.* Santa Barbara, Calif., 1967.

———. "Etruscan Vases at San Simeon." *California Studies in Classical Antiquity* 4 (1971): 115–23.

———. *Etruscan Red-Figured Vase-Painting at Caere.* Berkeley, Calif., 1974.

Demus-Quatember, M. *Etruskische Grabarchitektur: Typologie und Ursprungsfragen.* Deutsche Beiträge zur Alterumwissenschaft, 11. Baden-Baden, 1958.

De Puma, R. D. *Etruscan and Villanovan Pottery: A Catalogue of Italian Ceramics from Midwestern Collections.* Iowa City, Iowa, 1971.

———. "The Dioskouroi on Four Etruscan Mirrors in Midwestern Collections." *SE* 41 (1973): 159–70.

———. "Greek Gods and Heroes on Etruscan Mirrors." In de Grummond, N. T., ed., *A Guide to Etruscan Mirrors* (supra).

———. *Etruscan Tomb Groups: Ancient Pottery and Bronzes in Chicago's Field Museum of Natural History.* Mainz am Rhein, 1986.

———. "Mirrors." In Roncalli, F., and L. Bonfante, eds., *Antichità dall'Umbria a New York* (infra).

———. *CSE* USA 2: Boston and Cambridge. Ames, Iowa, 1993.

De Puma, R. D., and J. P. Small, eds. *Murlo and the Etruscans: Art and Society in Ancient Etruria.* Wisconsin Studies in Classics. Madison, 1994.

De Rita, D., and L. Versino. "Geologia e geomorfologia." In *Sorgenti della Nova: Una communità protostorica e il suo territorio nell'Etruria meridionale: Università degli studi, Braccio est della Crociera, Cortile d'onore, Milano, 1981.* Edited by N. Negroni Catacchio et al. Mostre dell'Università all'Antica ca' granda. Rome, 1981.

De Ruyt, F. *Charun: Démon étrusque de la mort.* Etudes de philologie, d'archéologie, et d'histoire anciennes, 1. Rome, 1934.

de Simone, C. "Gli Etruschi a Roma: Evidenza linguistica e problemi metodologici." In *Gli Etruschi e Roma: Atti dell'incontro di studio in onore di Massimo Pallottino.* Rome, 1981.

———. "Il nome etrusco del poleonimo *Mantua*." *SE* 57 (1992): 197–200.

Devoto, G. "Le origini tripartite di Roma." *Athenaeum* 31 (1953): 335–43.

di Gennaro, F. "Organizzazione del territorio nell'Etruria meridionale protostorica: Applicazione di un modello grafico." *DArch*, 2d ser., 4 (1982): 103–12.

———. *Forme di insediamento tra Tevere e Fiora dal bronzo finale al principio dell'età del ferro.* Biblioteca di *SE* (Istituto di studi etruschi e italici), 14. Florence, 1986.

———. "Il popolamento dell'Etruria meridionale e le caratteristiche degli insediamenti tra l'età del bronzo e l'età del ferro." In *Etruria meridionale: Conoscenza, conservazione, fruizione: Atti del convegno Viterbo, 29/30 novembre–1 dicembre 1985.* Rome, 1988.

Dinsmoor, W. B. *The Architecture of Ancient Greece: An Account of Its Historic Development.* New York, 1975.

Dobbins, J. J. "Problems of Chronology, Decoration, and Urban Design in the Forum at Pompeii." *AJA* 98 (1994): 629–94.

Dohrn, T. *Die etruskische Kunst im Zeitalter der griechischen Klassik: Die Interimsperiode.* Mainz am Rhein, 1982.

Donati, G. *Epigrafia cortonese.* Anno accademico etrusco, 13. Florence, 1965–67.

D'Onofrio, C. *Gli obelischi di Roma: Storia e urbanistica di una città dall'età antica al XX secolo.* Collana di studi e testi per la storia della città di Roma. 3d ed. Rome, 1992.

Doran, G., N. T. de Grummond, P. Rowe, and R. Marrinan. "Excavations at Cetamura del Chianti, 1987–91." *Etruscan Studies* 1 (1994): 84–122.

Ducati, P. *Etruria antica.* 2 vols. Turin, 1925.

Duckworth, G. E. *The Nature of Roman Comedy: A Study in Popular Entertainment.* Princeton, N.J., 1952.

Dury-Moyaers, G. *Enée et Lavinium: A propos des découvertes archéologiques récentes.* Collection Latomus, 174. Brussels, 1981.

Eisner, M. "Zur Typologie der Mausoleen des Augustus und des Hadrian." *MDAI(R)* 86 (1979): 319–24.

———. *Zur Typologie der Grabbauten im Suburbium Roms.* Mitteilungen des Deutschen Archäologischen Instituts, Römische Abteilung, 26. Mainz am Rhein, 1986.

Elworthy, F. T. *The Evil Eye: The Origins and Practices of Superstition.* New York, 1958.

Ernout, A., and A. Meillet. *Dictionnaire étymologique de la langue latine.* 4th ed. Paris, 1959.

Evans, A. *The Palace of Minos: A Comparative Account of the Successive Stages of Early Cretan Civilization as Illustrated by the Discoveries at Knossos.* 4 vols. London, 1935.

Evans, H. B. *Publica Carmina: Ovid's Books from Exile.* Lincoln, Neb., 1983.

Fairclough, H. R. "The Poems of the Appendix Vergiliana." *TAPhA* 53 (1922): 5–34.

Falconi Amorelli, M. T. "Tomba villanoviana con bronzetto nuragico." *AC* 18 (1966): 1–15.

Favro, D. "Reading the Augustan City." In Holliday, P. J., ed., *Narrative and Event in Ancient Art* (infra).

Feytmans, D. "Les Pithoi à reliefs de l'île de Rhodes." *BCH* 74 (1950): 135–80.

Fiaccadori, G. "The Tomb of Alexander the Great." *PP* 47 (1992): 128–31.

Fischer-Graf, U. "Spiegelwerkstätten in Vulci." *Archaeologische Forschungen* 8 (1980): 3–42.

Fittschen, K. *Untersuchungen zum Beginn der Sagendarstellungen bei den Griechen.* Berlin, 1969.

———. "Der Herakles-Sarcophag in S. Maria in Rom: Eine Arbeit der Renaissance?" *BCAR* 82 (1970–71): 63–69.

Fleischhauer, G. *Etrurien und Rom.* Musikgeschichte in Bildern, Bd. 2, Lfg. 5. Leipzig, 1965.

———. "Etruria." In Sadie, S., *The New Grove Dictionary of Music and Musicians* (infra).

Focke, F. "Szepter und Krummstab: Eine symbolgeschichtliche Untersuchung." *Festgabe für Alois Fuchs zum 70. Geburtstag am 19. Juni 1947.* Paderborn, Ger., 1950.

Foerst, G. *Die Gravierungen der präenestinische Cisten.* Rome, 1978.

Fortuna, A. M., and F. Giovannoni. *Il lago degli idoli: Testimonianze etrusche in Falterona.* Florence, 1975.

Fraccaro, P. "La storia romana arcaica." *RIL* 85 (1952): 85–118.

Fraser, P. M. *Ptolemaic Alexandria.* 3 vols. Oxford, 1972.

Frederiksen, M. "The Etruscans in Campania." In Ridgway, D., and F. R. Ridgway, *Italy before the Romans* (infra).

Frier, B. W. *Libri Annales Pontificium Maximorum: The Origins of the Annalistic Tradition.* Papers and Monographs of the American Academy at Rome, 27. Rome, 1975.

Fugazzola Delpino, M. A. "Problematica protovillanoviana." *Origini* 10 (1976): 245–332.

———. "The Proto-Villanovan: A Survey." In Ridgway, D., and F. R. Ridgway, *Italy before the Romans* (infra).

———. *Gli Etruschi di Tarquinia.* Edited by M. Bonghi Jovino. Modena, It., 1986.

Fugazzola Delpino, M. A., and F. Delpino. "Il bronzo finale nel Lazio settentrionale." In Istituto italiano di preistoria e protostoria, ed., *Il bronzo finale in Italia* (infra).

Furtwängler, A. *Die antiken Gemmen: Geschichte der Steinscheidekunst im klassischen Altertum.* 3 vols. Leipzig and Berlin, 1900.

Gabba, E. "Le origini della guerra sociale e la vita politica romana dopo l'89 a.C." *Athenaeum* 32 (1954): 41–114, 293–345.

———. "Studi su Dionigi di Alicarnasso, II: Il regno di Servio Tullio." *Athenaeum* 39 (1961): 98–121.

———. "Considerazioni sulla tradizione letteraria sulle origini della repubblica." In *Les Origines de la république romaine,* Entretiens sur l'antiquité classique, 13. Vandoeuvres-Geneva, 1967.

———. *Dionysius and the History of Archaic Rome.* Berkeley, Calif., 1991.

Gagé, J. *Huit recherches sur les origines italiques et romaines.* Paris, 1950.

———. *La Chute des Tarquins et les débuts de la République romaine.* Paris, 1976.

Galinski, G. K. "Sol and the Carmen Saeculare." *Latomus* 26 (1967): 619–33.

———. *Aeneas, Sicily, and Rome.* Princeton Monographs in Art and Archaeology, 40. Princeton, N.J., 1969.

———. "The 'Tomb of Aeneas' at Lavinium." *Vergilius* 20 (1974): 2–11.

———. "Aeneas in Latium: Archäologie, Mythos, und Geschichte." In *2000 Jahre Vergil: Ein Symposion*. Edited by V. Pöschl. Wolfenbütteler Forschungen, 24. Wiesbaden, 1983.

Gamurrini, G. F. "Cortona." *NSA* (1881): 45.

Gantz, T. "The Tarquin Dynasty." *Historia* 24 (1975): 539–54.

Gardthausen, V. *Augustus und seine Zeit*. 2 vols. Leipzig, 1891.

Gatti, G. "Nuove osservazioni sul mausoleo di Augusto." *L'Urbe* 3 (agosto 1938): 1–17.

Gelzer, M. *Caesar: Politician and Statesman*. Cambridge, Mass., 1968.

Gentili, G. V. "Le ceramiche romane invetriate di Sarsina." In *I problemi della ceramica romana di Ravenna, della Valle Padana e dell'alto adriatico: Atti del Convegno internazionale, Ravenna, 10–12 maggio 1969*. Bologna, 1972.

Giglioli, G. "Il sepolcreto imperiale." *Capitolium* 6 (1930): 532–67.

Giuliani, C. F. "Santuario delle tredici are, Heroon di Enea." In *Enea nel Lazio: Archeologia e mito: Bimillenario Virgiliano: Roma, 22 settembre–31 dicembre 1981, Campidoglio, Palazzo dei Conservatori*. Rome, 1981.

Gjerstad, E. *Early Rome*. 6 vols. Lund, Swed., 1953–73.

Goette, H. R. "Die Bulla." *BJ* 186 (1986): 133–64.

Greenhalgh, M. *Donatello and His Sources*. New York, 1982.

Grenier, A. *Les Religions étrusque et romaine*. Paris, 1948.

Griffin, J. "Caesar Qui Cogere Posset." In *Caesar Augustus: Seven Aspects*. Edited by F. Millar and E. Segal. Oxford, 1984.

Grimal, P. *Roman Cities*. Translated and edited by G. M. Woloch. Wisconsin Studies in Classics. Madison, 1983.

Gross, W. H. "Ways and Roundabout Ways in the Propaganda of an Unpopular Ideology." In *The Age of Augustus*. Edited by R. Winkes. Louvain-la-Neuve, Fr., and Providence, R.I., 1986.

Gruen, E. *Culture and National Identity in Republican Rome*. Cornell Studies in Classical Philology, 52. Ithaca, N.Y., 1992.

Gualtieri, M., and H. Fracchia. "Excavation and Survey at Masseria Ciccotti, Oppido Lucano: Interim Report, 1989–92." *EMC* 37 (1993): 313–38.

Hall, J. F. "P. Vergilius Maro: *Vates Etruscus*." *Vergilius* 28 (1982): 44–50.

———. "The Municipal Aristocracy of Etruria and Their Participation in Politics at Rome, B.C. 91–A.D. 14." Ph.D. diss. University of Pennsylvania, 1984.

———. "Livy's Tanaquil and the Image of Assertive Etruscan Women in Latin Historical Literature of the Early Empire." *AugAge* 4 (1985): 31–38.

———. "L. Marcius Phillipus and the Rise of Octavian Caesar." *AugAge* 5 (1986): 37–43.

———. "The *Saeculum Novum* of Augustus and Its Etruscan Antecedents." *ANRW* II.16.3 (1986): 2564–89.

———. "Vergil, Augustus, and the Etruscans: Factional Politics and the Amorality of Empire." Paper presented at the NEH Symposium on Vergil and the Morality of Empire, University of Colorado, Boulder, 25 April 1986.

———. "Mars and Anna Perenna: March Gods and the Etruscan New Year in Archaic Rome." In *By Study and Also by Faith: Essays in Honor of Hugh W. Nibley on the*

Occasion of His Eightieth Birthday, 27 March 1990. Edited by J. M. Lundquist and S. D. Ricks. 2 vols. Salt Lake City, Utah, 1990.

―――. "The Original Ending of the Aeneas Tale: Cato and the Historiographical Tradition of Aeneas." *Syllecta Classica* 3 (1991): 13–20.

Hallet, J. P. "Book IV: Propertius' Recusatio to Augustus and Augustan Ideals." Ph.D. diss. Harvard University, 1971.

Hannestad, L. *The Paris Painter: An Etruscan Vase-painter.* Translated by M. Moltesen. Historisk-filosofiske meddelelser, 47.2. Copenhagen, 1974.

Harris, W. V. *Rome in Etruria and Umbria.* Oxford, 1971.

Harrison, J. "The Judgment of Paris: Two Unpublished Vases in the Graeco-Etruscan Museum at Florence." *JHS* 7 (1886): 196–219.

Harvey, R. A. *A Commentary on Persius.* Mnemosyne Supplement, 64. Leiden, 1981.

Hayes, J. W. *Late Roman Pottery.* Oxford, 1972.

Haynes, S. *Civiltà archaica Vulci.* London, 1975.

―――. "Ein etruskisches Parisurteil." *RhM* 83 (1976): 227–31.

―――. *Etruscan Bronzes.* London, 1985.

Hekler, A. "Michelangelo und die Antike." *Wiener Jahrbuch* 7 (1930): 201–23.

Helbig, W. *Führer durch die öffentlichen Sammlungen Klassischer Altertümer in Rom: Die Päpstlichen Sammlungen im Vatikan und Lateran.* Vol. 4, 4th ed. Tübingen, Ger., 1963.

Henderson, I. "Ancient Greek Music." In *Ancient and Oriental Music.* Edited by E. Wellesz. Vol. 1 of G. Abraham, ed. *The New Oxford History of Music.* London, 1957.

Hennig, O. *De P. Ovidii Nasonis Sodalibus.* Bratislava, Czech., 1898.

Herbig, R. "Die Kranzspiegelgruppe." *SE* 24 (1955–56): 183–205.

Heres, G. *CSE* DDR 1. 2 vols. East Berlin, 1986.

Heurgon, J. "La Vocation étruscologique de l'empereur Claude." *CRAI* (1953): 92–97.

―――. "Tarquitius Priscus et l'organisation de l'ordre des haruspices sous l'empereur Claude." *Latomus* 12 (1953): 402–17.

―――. "Tite-Live et les Tarquins." *IL* 7 (1955): 56–64.

―――. *La Vie quotidienne chez les Etrusques.* Paris, 1961.

―――. "L. Cincius et la loi du *clavus annalis.*" *Athenaeum* 42 (1964): 432–37.

Hicks, D. L. "The Sienese State in the Renaissance." In *From the Renaissance to the Counter-Reformation: Essays in Honor of Garrett Mattingly.* Edited by C. H. Carter. New York, 1965.

Höckmann, U. *CSE* BRD 1. 3 vols. Munich, 1987.

―――. "Die Datierung der hellenistisch-etruskischen Griffspiegel des 2. Jahrhunderts v. Chr." *JDAI* 102 (1987): 247–89.

―――. "Zur Datierung der sogennanten Kranzspiegel." In *Atti: Secondo congresso internazionale etrusco* (supra).

Holliday, P. J., ed. *Narrative and Event in Ancient Art.* Cambridge Studies in New Art History and Criticism. Cambridge, 1993.

Hollis, C., ed. *The Papacy: An Illustrated History from St. Peter to Paul VI.* New York, 1964.

Holloway, R. R. "The Tomb of Augustus and the Princes of Troy." *AJA* 70 (1966): 171–73.

Hook, J. *Siena: A City and Its History.* London, 1979.

Hornblower, S. *Mausolus.* Oxford, 1982.

Hubbard, M. *Propertius.* London, 1974.

Hus, A. *Les Etrusques et leur déstin.* Paris, 1980.

Istituto italiano di preistoria e protostoria, ed. *Il bronzo finale in Italia: Atti della XXI riunione scientifica, Firenze, 21–23 ottobre 1977, in memoria di Ferrante Rittatore Vonwiller.* Florence, 1979.

Jacks, P. J. *The Antiquarian and the Myth of Antiquity: The Origins of Rome in Renaissance Thought.* New York, 1993.

Jacobsthal, P., and A. Langsdorf. *Die bronze Schnabelkannen.* Berlin, 1929.

Jeppesen, K., ed. *The Mausolleion at Halikarnassos: Reports of the Danish Archaeological Expedition to Bodrum.* Jutland Archeological Society Publications. 3 vols. to date. Copenhagen, 1981– .

———. "What Did the Mausolleion Look Like?" In *Architecture and Society in Hecatomnid Caria: Proceedings of the Uppsala Symposium, 1987.* Edited by T. Linders and P. Hellström. Uppsala, Swed., 1989.

Jolivet, V. "Aspects du théâtre comique en Etrurie préromaine et romaine: A propos d'un vase étrusque à figures rouges du Musée du Louvre." *RA* (1983): 13–50.

Jones, H. S. *A Catalogue . . . Sculptures of the Palazzi dei Conservatori.* Oxford, 1926.

Jucker, I. "Ein etruskischer Spiegel mit Parisurteil." *MH* 39 (1982): 5–14.

Jung, F. *Die Sagen von den Argonauten, von Theben und Troia in der klassischen und hellenistischen Kunst.* Munich, 1989.

Kaimio, J. "The Ousting of Etruscan by Latin in Etruria." In *Studies in the Romanization of Etruria.* Edited by Patrick Bruun et al. Acta Instituti Romani Finlandiae, 5. Rome, 1975.

Kajanto, I. *The Latin Cognomina.* Helsinki, 1965.

Keil, H. *Grammatici Latini.* 1857. Reprint, Hildesheim, Ger., 1961.

Keyser, P. "The Origin of the Latin Numerals 1 to 1000." *AJA* 92 (1988): 529–46.

Kinney, D. "Spolia from the Baths of Caracalla in S. Maria in Trastevere." *ABull* 68 (1986): 379–97.

———. "Mirabilia Urbis Romae." In *The Classics in the Middle Ages.* Edited by A. S. Bernardo and S. Levin. Binghamton, N.Y., 1990.

Kirsch, J. P., and V. Luksch. *Illustriete Geschichte de katholischen Kirche.* Munich, 1903–5.

Klapisch-Zuber, C. *Les Maîtres du marbre: Carrare, 1300–1600.* Paris, 1969.

Kraft, K. "Der Sinn des Mausoleum of Augustus." *Historia* 16 (1967): 186–206. Reprinted in K. Kraft, *Gesammelte Aufsätze zur antiken Geschichte und Militärgeschichte.* Darmstadt, 1973.

Krauskopf, I. *Der Thebanische Sagenkreis und andere griechische Sagen in der etruskischen Kunst.* Mainz am Rhein, 1974.

———. *Todesdämonen und Totengötter im vorhellenistischen Etrurien: Kontinuität und Wandel.* Florence, 1987.

La civiltà arcaica di Vulci e la sua espansione: Atti del X convegno di Studi etruschi e italici: Grosseto, Roselle, Vulci, 29 maggio–2 giugno 1975. Florence, 1977.

Lambrechts, R. *Les Miroirs étrusques et prénestins des Musées Royaux d'Art et d'Histoire à Bruxelles.* Brussels, 1978.

Lanciani, R. A. *Storia degli scavi di Roma e notizie intorno le collezioni romane di antichità.* 6 vols. Rome, 1902–16.

Last, H. "The Servian Reforms." *JRS* 35 (1945): 30–48.

Latte, K. *Römische Religionsgeschichte.* Munich, 1960.

Lehnerdt, M. "Cencio und Agapito de' Rustici." *Zeitschrift für vergleichende Litteraturgeschichte* 13 (1899): 166–74.

L'Etruria mineraria: Atti dei XII convegno di Studi etruschi e italici. Florence, 1981.

Leumann, M. *Lateinische Laut- und Formenlehre.* Fasc. 2 of *Lateinische Grammatik,* by M. Leumann, J. B. Hofmann, and A. Szantyr. 5th ed. 1926–28. Reprint, Munich, 1977.

Levi, D. "Early Hellenic Pottery of Crete." *Hesperia* 14 (1945): 1–32.

Lewis, C. T., and C. Short. *A Latin Dictionary.* Oxford, 1879.

Liepmann, U. *CSE* BRD 2. Munich, 1988.

Lisner, M. "Gedanken vor frühen Standbildern des Donatello." In *Kunstgeschichtliche Studien für Kurt Bauch zum 70. Geburtstag von seinen Schülern.* Edited by M. Lisner and R. Becksmann. Berlin, 1967.

Lord, L. E. "The Judgment of Paris on Etruscan Mirrors." *AJA* 41 (1937): 602–6.

Lugli, G. *I monumenti antichi di Roma e suburbio.* 3 vols. Rome, 1938.

Lunderstedt, P. *De Maecenatis Fragmentis.* Commentarii Philologici Ienenses, 9.1. Jena, Ger., 1911.

MacDonald, W. L. *The Pantheon: Design, Meaning, and Progeny.* Cambridge, Mass., 1976.

Madvig, J., ed. *M. Tulii Ciceronis Orationes Selectae Duodecim.* Hauniae, 1858.

Magdelain, A. "Auspicia ad Patres Redeunt." In *Hommages à J. Bayet.* Collection Latomus, 70. Brussels, 1964.

Maioli, M. G. "Terra sigillata tarda del ravennate." *Rei Cretariae Romanae Fautorum* 16 (1976): 160–73.

Mandel, O. *Philoctetes and the Fall of Troy: Plays, Documents, Iconography, Interpretations Including Versions by Sophocles, André Gide, Oscar Mandel, and Heiner Müller.* Lincoln, Neb., 1981.

Mansuelli, G. A. "Materiali per un supplemento al 'Corpus' degli specchi etruschi figurati." *SE* 17 (1943): 487–521.

———. *Guida alla città etrusca e al Museo di Marzabotto.* Bologna, 1983.

Martelli, M. "La cultura artistica." In *Gli etruschi: Una nuova immagine.* Edited by M. Cristofani. Florence, 1984.

———. *Le ceramiche degli Etruschi: La pittura vascolare.* Novara, It., 1987.

Marx, B. *Venezia—Altera Roma? Ipotesi sull'umanesimo veneziano.* Quaderni (Centro tedesco di studi Veneziani), 10. Venice, 1978.

Mathiesen, T. J. *A Bibliography of Sources for the Study of Ancient Greek Music.* Music Indexes and Bibliographies, 10. Hackensack, N.J., 1974.

Maxwell, R. L. "The Documentary Evidence for Ancient Mime." Ph.D. diss., University of Toronto, 1993.

Mazzarino, S. *Dalla monarchia allo stato repubblicano.* Catania, It., 1947.

McKinnon, J. W. "Cornu," "Lituus," "Lyre (2)," and "Tuba." In Sadie, S., ed., *The New Grove Dictionary of Musical Instruments* (infra).

McKinnon, J. W., and Anderson, R. "Crotalum," "Kithara (1)," "Syrinx," "Tibia," and "Tympanum." In Sadie, S., ed., *The New Grove Dictionary of Musical Instruments* (infra).

Meiss, M. "The Altered Program of the Santa Maria Maggiore Altarpiece." In *Studien zur Toskanischen Kunst: Festschrift für Ludwig Heinrich Heydenreich zum 23. März 1963.* Edited by W. Lotz and L. L. Möller. Munich, 1964.

Melani, V. *Profilo di una città etrusca: Populonia.* Pistoia, It., 1981.

Merkel, R., ed. *P. Ovidius Naso Fastorum Libri Sex.* 1841. Reprint, Hildesheim, Ger., 1971.

Messerschmidt, F. "Disiecta Membra: Masken und Schauspieler Terrakoten in Gräber von Vulci und Tarquinia." *MDAI(R)* 46 (1931): 44–80.

Meyer, J. C. *Pre-Republican Rome: An Analysis of the Cultural and Chronological Relations 1000–500 B.C.* Odense, Den., 1983.

Milani, L. A. *Il mito di Filottete nella letteratura classica e nell'arte figurata.* Florence, 1879.

Mingazzini, P. *Vasi della collezione Castellani: Catalogo.* Rome, 1930.

Minto, A. "Il Secondo Melone del Sodo." *NSA* 7 (1929): 158–67.

Mitchell, R. E. "The Definition of *Patres* and *Plebs.*" In Raaflaub, K. A., ed., *Social Struggles in Archaic Rome* (infra).

Moggi Cecchi, J. "Shedding Light on Etruscan Origins: Mitochondrial DNA Studies Launched." *Amici di Spannocchia* 13 (1993): 5.

Momigliano, A. "An Interim Report on the Origins of Rome." *JRS* 53 (1963): 95–121.

Morel, W., ed. *Fragmenta Poetarum Latinorum.* 2d ed. Leipzig, 1927.

Moret, J.-M. "Le Jugement de Paris en Grande-Grèce: Mythe et actualité politique: A propos du lébès paestan d'une collection privée." *AK* 21.2 (1978): 76–98.

Moretti, M. *New Monuments of Etruscan Painting.* University Park, Penn., 1970.

Müller-Karpe, H. *Vom Anfang Roms.* Heidelberg, 1959.

———. *Zur Stadtwerdung Roms.* Heidelberg, 1962.

Munman, R. "Urbano da Cortona: Corrections and Observations." In *Verrocchio and Late Quattrocento Italian Sculpture.* Edited by S. Bule, A. P. Darr, and F. S. Gioffredi. Florence, 1992.

———. *Sienese Renaissance Tomb Monuments.* Memoirs of the American Philosophical Society, 205. Philadelphia, 1993.

Nardi, G. "Bracieri" and "Dolii." In *Caere 3.2: Lo scarico arcaico della vigna parrochiale.* Edited by M. Cristofani. Rome, 1993.

Nash, E. *Pictorial Dictionary of Ancient Rome.* 2d ed. London, 1968.

Negroni Catacchio, N. "Il bronzo finale nella valle del fiume Fiora." In Istituto italiano di preistoria e protostoria, ed., *Il bronzo finale in Italia* (supra).

———. "Ritrovamenti dell'età del bronzo sul colle di Talamonaccio (Orbetello-Grosseto)." *RSP* 34 (1979): 261.

————. "Rapporto tra l'area alto-adriatica e quella medio-tirrenica durante il bronzo finale." *Padusa* 20 (1984): 515–17.

————. "La fase di transizione bronzo-ferro in Etruria alla luce degli scavi di Tarquinia." In Bonghi Jovino, M., and C. Chiaramonte Trère, eds., *Tarquinia: Ricerche, scavi, e prospettive* (supra).

————. "L'abitato del bronzo finale di Sorgenti della Nova: Possibilità di confronti con i modelli abitativi dei centri villanoviani." In *Atti: Secondo congresso internazionale etrusco* (supra).

Negroni Catacchio, N., et al. *Sorgenti della Nova: Una comunità protostorica e il suo territorio nell'Etruria meridionale: Arezzo, Museo archeologico, dicembre 1982– gennaio 1983: Grosseto, Museo archeologico e d'arte della Maremma, aprile–maggio 1983*. Rome, 1982.

Neppi Modona, A. *Cortona etrusca e romana nella storia e nell'arte*. 2d ed. Florence, 1977.

Newman, J. K. *The Concept of Vates in Augustan Poetry*. Collection Latomus, 89. Brussels, 1967.

————. *Augustus and the New Poetry*. Collection Latomus, 88. Brussels, 1967.

Nicholls, R. V. *CSE* Great Britain 2, Cambridge: Corpus Christi College, the Fitzwilliam Museum, the Museum of Archeology and Anthropology, the Museum of Classical Archeology. Cambridge, 1993.

Nicosia, F. "Relazione sul Tumulo II del Sodo di Cortona." In *Rendiconti della Pontificia Accademia*. In press.

Nielsen, E. "Some Preliminary Thoughts on New and Old Terracottas." *ORom* 16.5 (1987): 92–119.

Nilsson, M. P. "The Introduction of Hoplite Tactics at Rome: Its Date and Consequences." *JRS* 19 (1929): 1–11.

Nisbet, R. G. M., and M. Hubbard. *A Commentary on Horace Odes, Book 1*. Oxford, 1970.

Norden, E. *Die antike Kunstprosa vom 6. Jahrhundert v. Chr. bis in die Zeit der Renaissance*. 7th ed. 2 vols. Darmstadt, 1974.

Ogilvie, R. M. "Livy, Licinius Macer, and the *Libri Lintei*." *JRS* 48 (1958): 40–46.

————. *A Commentary on Livy, Books 1–5*. Oxford, 1965.

————. *Early Rome and the Etruscans*. Glasgow, 1976.

Olsen, D. "The Ethnomusicology of Archaeology: A Model for the Musical/ Cultural Study of Ancient Material Cultural." *Selected Reports in Ethnomusicology* 8 (1990): 175–97.

Ostenberg, C. E. *Case etrusche di Acquarossa*. Rome, 1975.

Owens, J. E. *The City in the Greek and Roman World*. London, 1991.

Pairault, F.-H. *Recherches sur quelques séries d'urnes de Volterra à représentations mythologiques*. Collection de l'Ecole française de Rome, 12. Rome, 1972.

Pallottino, M. "Tarquinia." *MonAL* 36 (1937): 1–620.

————. *L'origine degli Etruschi*. Rome, 1947.

————. *Etruscan Painting*. Geneva, 1952.

————. "Fatti e legende (moderne) sulla più antica storia di Roma." *SE* 31 (1963): 3–37.

——. *La necropoli di Cerveteri*. 7th ed. Rome, 1968.

——. *Etruscologia*. 6th ed. Milan, 1977.

——. *The Etruscans*. Rev. ed. Translated by J. Cremona. Edited by D. Ridgway. Harmondsworth, Engl., 1978.

——. "Vasari e la Chimera." *Prospettiva* 8 (1976): 4–6. Reprinted in Pallottino, M., *Immagini inedite e alternative di arte antica*. Vol. 3 of *Saggi di antichità*. Rome, 1979.

——. "The Origins of Rome: A Survey of Recent Discoveries and Discussion." In Ridgway, D., and F. R. Ridgway, *Italy before the Romans* (infra).

——. "Prospettive attuali del problema delle origini etrusche." In *Atti: Secondo congresso internazionale etrusco* (supra).

——. *A History of Earliest Italy*. Translated by M. Ryle and K. Soper. Jerome Lectures, 17th ser. Ann Arbor, Mich., 1991.

Palmer, R. E. A. *The Archaic Community of the Romans*. Cambridge, 1970.

——. *Roman Religion and Roman Empire: Five Essays*. Philadelphia, 1974.

——. "Roman Shrines of Female Chastity from the Caste Struggle to the Papacy of Innocent I." *RSA* 4 (1974): 113–59.

——. Review of *Early Rome*, V (The Written Sources) and VI (Historical Survey), by E. Gjerstad. *AJA* 79 (1975): 387.

——. "On the Track of the Ignoble." *Athenaeum* 61 (1983): 343–61.

Paniagua, G. *Musique de la Grèce antique*. Atrium Musicae de Madrid, Harmonia Mundi. HM 1015.

Pareti, L. *La tomba Regolini-Galassi del Museo Gregoriano Etrusco e la civiltà dell'Italia centrale nel sec. VII A. C.* Monumenti vaticani di archeologia e d'arte, 8. Rome, 1947.

Parker, H. C. "*Romani Numen Soli:* Faunus in Ovid's *Fasti*." *TAPhA* 123 (1993): 200–217.

Passerini, A. *Le corti pretorie*. 2d ed. Rome, 1969.

Pellegrini, E. "Nuovi dati su due ripostigli dell'età del bronzo finale del Grossetano: Piano del Tallone e 'tra Manciano e Samprugnano.'" *BPI* 83 (1981–82): 341–60.

Pena, M. "Il santuario y la tumba de Eneas." *EClás* 71 (1974): 1–26.

Peroni, R. *Ripostigli del età dei metalli 1. Ripostigli del massiccio della Tolfa*. Inventaria archeologica, Italia, 1. Florence, 1961.

——. *Ripostigli del età dei metalli 2. Ripostigli del grossetano*. Inventaria archeologica, Italia, 2. Florence, 1961.

——. "Interventi." In *La civiltà arcaica di Vulci* (supra).

——, ed. *Il bronzo finale in Italia: Archeologia, materiali, e problemi 1*. Bari, It., 1980.

——. "Presenze micenée e forme socioeconomiche nell'Italia protostorica." In *Magna Grecia e mondo miceneo: Atti del XXII convegno di studi sulla Magna Grecia, Taranto, 7–11 ottobre 1982*. Edited by G. Pugliese Caratelli. Taranto, It., 1983.

Peroni, R., and F. di Gennaro. "Aspetti regionali dello sviluppo dell'insediamento protostorico nell'Italia centro-meridionale alla luce dei dati archeologici e ambientali." *DArch*, 3rd ser., 4 (1986): 194–98.

Peroni, R., and N. Negroni Catacchio. "Ultime pagine di Ferrante Rittatore Von-willer sul 'protovillanoviano.'" In Istituto italiano di preistoria e protostoria, ed., *Il bronzo finale in Italia* (supra).

Pfiffig, A. J. *Die Ausbreitung des römischen Stadtwesens in Etrurien und die Frage der Unterwerfung der Etrusker.* Florence, 1966.

————. *Religio etrusca.* Graz, Austria, 1975.

Pfister-Roesgen, G. *Die etruskischen Spiegel des 5. Jhs. v. Chr.* Frankfurt am Main, 1975.

Phillips, K. M., Jr. *In the Hills of Tuscany: Recent Excavations at the Etruscan Site of Poggio Civitate (Murlo, Siena).* Philadelphia, 1993.

Pillinger, H. E. "Some Callimachean Influences on Propertius Book 4." *HSCP* 73 (1969): 171–99.

Pincus, D. "Tullio Lombardo as a Restorer of Antiquities: An Aspect of Fifteenth-Century Venetian Antiquarianism." *Arte veneta* 33 (1979): 29–42.

Pippidi, D. *Recherches sur le culte impérial.* Institut roumain d'études latines, 2. Bucharest, 1939.

Poggiani Keller, R., and P. Figura. "I tumuli e l'abitato di Crostoletto di Lamone (prov. di Viterbo): Nuovi risultati e precisazioni." In Istituto italiano di preistoria e protostoria, ed., *Il bronzo finale in Italia* (supra).

Pollini, J. "The Gemma Augustea: Ideology, Rhetorical Imagery, and the Creation of a Dynastic Narrative." In Holliday, P. J., ed., *Narrative and Event in Ancient Art* (supra).

Pope-Hennessy, J. *Italian Renaissance Sculpture.* London, 1971.

Pottier, E. "Les Vases archaïques à reliefs." *BCH* 12 (1888): 491–510.

Poucet, J. "Un Culte d'Énée dans la région lavinate au ive siècle avant J.-C.?" In *Hommages à Robert Schilling.* Edited by H. Zehnacker and G. Hentz. Paris, 1983.

Poultney, J. W. *The Bronze Tables of Iguvium.* American Philological Association Monograph. Baltimore, 1959.

Prayon, F. "Architecture." In Bonfante, L., ed., *Etruscan Life and Afterlife* (supra).

Proietti, G., et al. *Cerveteri.* Rome, 1986.

Purcell, N. "Tomb and Suburb." In *Römische Gräberstrassen: Selbstdarstellung, Status, Standard: Kolloquium in München vom 28. bis 30. Oktober 1985.* Edited by H. von Hesberg and P. Zanker. Bayerische Akademie der Wissenschaften. Philosophisch-Historische Klasse, 96. Munich, 1987.

Putnam, M. C. J. "The Shrine of Vortumnus." *AJA* 71 (1967): 177–79.

Quilici, L. *Roma primitiva e le origini della civiltà laziale.* Rome, 1979.

Raaflaub, K. A. "A Comprehensive and Comparative Approach" and "Stages in the Conflict of Orders." In Raaflaub, K. A., ed., *Social Struggles in Archaic Rome* (infra).

————, ed. *Social Struggles in Archaic Rome: New Perspectives on the Conflict of Orders.* Berkeley, Calif., 1986.

Raddatz, K. "Eisenzeitliche Fundstellen von Vulci: Versuch einer archäologischen Landesaufnahme im sudichen Etrurien." *Praehistorische Zeitschrift* 58 (1983): 211–53.

Ragusa, I. "The Re-Use and Public Exhibition of Roman Sarcophagi during the Middle Ages and Renaissance." Master's thesis. New York University, 1951.

Rasmussen, T. "Corinth and the Orientalising Phenomenon." In *Looking at Greek Vases*. Edited by T. Rasmussen and N. Spivey. Cambridge, 1991.

Rawson, E. "The First Latin Annalists." *Latomus* 35 (1976): 689–717.

———. "Caesar, Etruria, and the *Disciplina Etrusca*." *JRS* 68 (1978): 132–52.

———. "L. Cornelius Sisenna and the Early First Century." *CQ* 29 (1979): 327–46.

———. *Intellectual Life in the Late Roman Republic*. Baltimore, 1985.

Rebuffat-Emmanuel, D. *Le Miroir étrusque: D'après la collection du Cabinet des Médailles*. Collection de l'Ecole française de Rome, 20. Rome, 1973.

———. *CSE* France 1, Louvre 1. Rome, 1988.

Reeder, J. C. "Typology and Ideology in the Mausoleum of Augustus: Tumulus and Tholos." *ClAnt* 11 (1992): 265–304.

Reich, H. *Der Mimus: Ein litterar-entwicklungsgeschichtlicher Versuch*. Band 1, teil 1 and 2. Berlin, 1903.

Reinhardt, K. *Das Parisurteil*. Frankfurt, 1938.

Renard, M. "Miroir étrusque inédit de la Collection P. Desneux." In *Hommages à Waldemar Deonna*. Collection Latomus, 28. Brussels, 1957.

Rheinfelder, H. *Das Wort "persona": Geschichte seiner bedeutungen mit besonderer Berücksichtigung des französischen und italienischen Mittelalters*. Beihefte zur Zeitschrift für romanische Philologie, Heft 77. Halle, Ger., 1928.

Rich, J., and A. Wallace-Hadrill, eds. *City and Country in the Ancient World*. Leicester-Nottingham Studies in Ancient Society, 2. London and New York, 1991.

Richard, J.-C. "Tombeaux des empereurs et temples des 'divi': Notes sur la signification religieuse des sépultures impériales à Rome." *RHR* 120 (1966): 127–42.

———. "'Mausoleum': D'Halicarnasse à Rome, puis à Alexandrie." *Latomus* 29 (1970): 370–88.

———. "Patricians and Plebeians." In Raaflaub, K. A., ed., *Social Struggles in Archaic Rome* (supra).

Richardson, E. *The Etruscans: Their Art and Civilization*. Chicago, 1976.

Richardson, L., ed. *Sexti Properti Elegiae I–IV*. Norman, Okla., 1977.

Richardson, L., Jr. *A New Topographical Dictionary of Ancient Rome*. Baltimore, 1992.

Richter, G. M. A. *Engraved Gems of the Greeks, Etruscans, and Romans*. 2 vols. London, 1968–71.

Ridgway, D. "Early Rome and Latium: An Archaeological Introduction." In Ridgway, D., and F. R. Ridgway, eds., *Italy before the Romans* (infra).

Ridgway, D., and F. R. Ridgway, eds. *Italy before the Romans: The Iron Age, Orientalizing, and Etruscan Periods*. London, 1979.

Ridley, R. T. "The Enigma of Servius Tullius." *Klio* 57 (1975): 147–77.

———. "*Fastenkritik*: A Stocktaking." *Athenaeum* 58 (1980): 264–98.

Rittatore Vonwiller, F. "La cultura protovillanoviana." In *Popoli e civiltà dell'Italia antica*. Vol. 4. Rome, 1975.

———. "Preistoria e protostoria della valle del fiume Fiora." In *La civiltà arcaica di Vulci* (supra).

Rix, H. R. W. *Das etruskische Cognomen: Untersuchungen zu System, Morphologie, und Verwendung der Personnamen auf den jüngeren Inschriften Nordetruriens.* Wiesbaden, 1963.

Roberts, P. L. *Masolino da Panicale.* Clarendon Studies in the History of Art. New York, 1993.

Romanelli, P. "Tarquinia: Scavi e ricerche nell'area della città." *NSA* 73 (1948): 260–61.

———. "Problemi archeologici e storici di Roma primitivi." *BPI* 64 (1955): 257–60.

———. "Certezze e ipotesi sulle origini di Roma." *StudRom* 13 (1965): 156–69.

Roncalli, F. *Le lastre dipinte da Cerveteri.* Florence, 1905.

Roncalli, F., and L. Bonfante, eds. *Antichità dall'Umbria a New York.* Perugia, It., 1991.

Rose, H. J. "On the Relations between Roman and Etruscan Religion." *SMSR* 4 (1928): 115 ff.

———. *A Handbook of Greek Mythology: Including Its Extension to Rome.* New York, 1959.

Rudd, N. *The Satires of Horace.* Cambridge, 1966.

Ruskin, J. "Mornings in Florence." In *The Works of John Ruskin.* Edited by E. T. Cook and A. Wedderburn. 39 vols. London, 1903–12.

Ryberg, I. S. *An Archaeological Record of Rome from the Seventh to the Second Century B.C.* London and Philadelphia, 1940.

Sadie, S., ed. *The New Grove Dictionary of Music and Musicians.* 20 vols. London, 1980.

———, ed. *The New Grove Dictionary of Musical Instruments.* 3 vols. London, 1984.

Säflünd, G. *Etruscan Imagery: Symbol and Meaning.* Studies in Mediterranean Archeology and Literature, 118. Jonsered, Swed., 1993.

Salskov Roberts, H. *CSE* Denmark 1. Odense, 1982.

———. "Later Etruscan Mirrors: Evidence for Dating from Recent Excavations." *ARID* 12 (1983): 31–54.

Saronio, P. "Nuovi scavi nella città etrusca di Misano a Marzabotto." *SE* 33 (1965): 391.

Sassatelli, G. *CSE* Italia 1. Rome, 1982.

Scheffer, C. *Cooking and Cooking Stands in Italy 1400–400 B.C.* Vol. 2, pt. 1, of *Acquarossa: Results of Excavations Conducted by the Swedish Institute of Classical Studies at Rome and the Soprintendenza alle antichità dell'Etruria meridionale.* Skrifter Utgivna av Svenska Institutet Rom, 4°, 38. Stockholm, 1981.

Schefold, K. *Myth and Legend in Early Greek Art.* New York, 1966.

———. *Die Göttersage in der klassischen und hellenistischen Kunst.* Munich, 1981.

Schefold, K., and F. Jung. *Die Sagen von den Argonauten, von Theben und Troia in der klassischen und hellenistischen Kunst.* Munich, 1989.

Scheibler, I. *The Archaic Cemetery.* Translated by S. C. D. Slenczka. German Archaeological Institute, Athens. Kerameikos Book, 3. Athens, 1973.

Schulz, A. M. *The Sculpture of Bernardo Rossellino and His Workshop.* Princeton, N.J., 1977.

Scodel, R., and R. F. Thomas. "Virgil and the Euphrates." *AJPh* 105 (1984): 339.

Scullard, H. H. *The Etruscan Cities and Rome*. Ithaca, N.Y., 1967.

Sear, F. *Roman Architecture*. Ithaca, N.Y., 1982.

Séchan, L. *Etudes sur la tragédie grecque dans ses rapports avec la céramique*. Paris, 1926.

Seidel, M. "Studien zur Antikenrezeption Nicola Pisanos." *Mitteilungen des Kunsthistorischen Institutes im Florenz* 19 (1975): 307 ff.

Serra Ridgway, F. R. "Impasto ceretano stampigliato: Gli esemplari del British Museum: Origini e affinità." In *Italian Iron Age Artefacts in the British Museum: Papers of the Sixth British Museum Classical Colloquium*. Edited by J. Swaddling. Oxford, 1986.

Sforza, G. *Gli studi archeologici sulla Lunigiana e i suoi scavi dal 1442 al 1800*. Modena, It., 1895.

Sgubini Moretti, A. M. *Dizionario della civiltà etrusca*. Florence, 1985.

Shackleton-Bailey, D. R. "The Roman Nobility in the Second Civil War." *CQ* 10 (1960): 253–67.

Shatzman, I. *Senatorial Wealth and Roman Politics*. Collection Latomus, 142. Brussels, 1975.

Shepherd, W. G. *Propertius: The Poems*. Harmondsworth, Engl., 1985.

Sherwin-White, A. N. *The Roman Citizenship*. Oxford, 1939.

Sichtermann, H. *Griechische Vasen in UnterItalien: Aus der Sammlung Jatta in Ruvo*. Deutsches Archäologisches Institut, 3/4. Tübingen, Ger., 1966.

Simon, E. *Ara Pacis Augustae*. New York, n.d.

———. "Etruskischer Griffspiegel mit dem Urteil des Paris." *AA* (1985): 299–306.

Small, J. P. "Eat, Drink, and Be Merry." In De Puma, R. D., and J. P. Small, eds., *Murlo and the Etruscans* (supra).

Soffredi, A. "L'abitato all'aperto dell'età del bronzo di Scarceta (Manciano-Grosseto)." In *La civiltà arcaica di Vulci* (supra).

Sommella, P. "Heroon di Enea a Lavinium: Recenti scavi a Pratica di Mare." *RPAA* 44 (1971–72): 47–74.

———. "Das Heroon des Aeneas und die Topographie des antiken Lavinium." *Gymnasium* 81 (1974): 273–97.

Sordi, M. *I rapporti romano-ceriti e l'origine della civitas sine suffragio*. Rome, 1960.

———. "Ottaviano e l'Etruria nel 44 a.C." *SE* 40 (1972): 2–17.

Spencer, J. R. "Volterra, 1466." *ABull* 48 (1966): 95–96.

Spivey, N. J., and S. Stoddart. *Etruscan Italy*. London, 1990.

Sprenger, M., and G. Bartoloni. *Etruschi: L'arte*. Milan, 1981.

———. *The Etruscans: Their History, Art, and Architecture*. New York, 1983.

Stanislawski, M. B. "Ethnoarchaeology and Settlement Archaeology." *Ethnohistory* 20.4 (1973): 375–92.

Steiner, A. "Gli etruschi tra noi." *Archeo* 8.12 (December 1993): 54–61.

Steingräber, S. *Etrurien: Städte, Heiligtümer, Nekropolen*. Reise und Studium. Munich, 1981.

———. *Catalogo ragionato della pittura etrusca*. Translated by P. Baglione and D. Rescaldani. Milan, 1984.

————. *Etruscan Painting: Catalogue Raisonné of Etruscan Wall Paintings.* English language ed. Edited by D. Ridgway and F. R. Ridgway. New York, 1986.

Stopponi, S., ed. *Case e palazzi d'Etruria.* Milan, 1985.

Sullivan, J. P. *Propertius: A Critical Discussion.* Cambridge, 1976.

Sumner, G. V. "The Family Connections of L. Aelius Seianus." *Phoenix* 19 (1965): 134–45.

Syme, R. "Caesar, the Senate, and Italy." *PBSR* 14 (1938): 1–31.

————. *The Roman Revolution.* Oxford, 1939.

————. "Personal Names in Annals I–VI." *JRS* 39 (1949): 6–18.

————. "Missing Persons II." *Historia* 7 (1959): 207–12.

————. "Missing Persons III." *Historia* 11 (1962): 146–55.

————. "Ten Tribunes." *JRS* 53 (1963): 55–60.

————. "Senators, Tribes, and Towns." *Historia* 13 (1964): 105–25.

————. "The Consuls of A.D. 13." *JRS* 56 (1966): 55–60.

————. "Pliny the Procurator." *HSCP* 73 (1969): 201–36.

————. "Spaniards at Tivoli." *AncSoc* 13–14 (1982–83): 249–59.

————. "Spanish Pomponii: A Study in Nomenclature." *Gerión* 1 (1983): 255.

Szilágyi, J. G. *Etruzsko-korinthosi Vásafestészet.* Budapest, 1975.

————. *Ceramica etrusco-corinzia figurata.* Translated by E. S. Graziani. Monumenti etruschi, 7. Florence, 1992.

————. *CSE* Hongrie: Budapest, Szépművészeti Múzeum (Musée des Beaux Arts), Debrecen, Déri Múzeum (Musée Déri); Tchécoslovaquie: Prague, Univerzita Karlova (Université Charles IV, Národní Muzeum (Musée Nationale), Brno, Moravské Muzeum (Galerie de Moravie), Liberec, Severočeské Muzeum (Musée de la Bohème du Nord). Rome, 1992.

Tanelli, G. "I depositi metalliferi dell'Etruria e le attività estrattive degli Etruschi." In *Atti: Secondo congresso internazionale etrusco* (supra).

Taylor, L. R. "Caesar's Early Career." *CPh* 36 (1941): 113–32.

————. "The Centuriate Assembly before and after the Reform." *AJPh* 78 (1957): 337–54.

————. *The Voting Districts of the Roman Republic.* Papers and Monographs of the American Academy in Rome, 20. Rome, 1960.

The Etruscan Museum of Poggio Civitate. Florence, 1988.

Thomas, R. F. "From *Recusatio* to Commitment: The Evolution of the Virgilian Programme." *Papers of the Leeds Latin Seminar* 5 (1986): 61–73.

Thomsen, R. *King Servius Tullius: A Historical Synthesis.* Copenhagen, 1980.

Timpe, D. "Fabius Pictor und die Anfänge der römischen Historiographie." *ANRW* I.2 (1972): 928–69.

Torelli, M. "Senatori etruschi della tarda reppublica e dell'impero." *DArch* 3 (1969): 285–363.

————. *Elogia tarquiniensia.* Studi e materiali di etruscologia e antichità italiche, 15. Florence, 1975.

————. *Etruria.* Rome, 1982.

————. *Gli Etruschi: Una nuova immagine.* Florence, 1984.

————. *Lavinio e Roma: Riti iniziatici e matrimonio tra archeologia e storia.* Rome, 1984.

————. "La Storia." In *Rasenna: Storia e civiltà degli Etruschi.* Milan, 1986.

Torelli, M., and R. Peroni. "Interventi." In *La civiltà arcaica di Vulci* (supra).

Toynbee, J. M. C. *Death and Burial in the Roman World.* London, 1971.

Trachtenberg, M. "An Antique Model for Donatello's Marble *David.*" *ABull* 50 (1968): 268–69.

Ucelli Gnesutta, P. "L'abitato delle Sorgenti della Nova." In Istituto italiano di preistoria e protostoria, ed., *Il bronzo finale in Italia* (supra).

Urlichs, L. "Viaggio in Etruria." *Bollettino dell'Istituto di corrispondenza archeologica* 65 (1839): 65–75.

Vagnetti, L. *Il deposito votivo di Campetti a Veio (Materiali degli scavi 1937–1938).* Studi e materiali di etruscologia e antichità italiche, 9. Florence, 1971.

Valtieri, S. "Il 'revival' etrusco nel rinascimento toscano." *L'architettura* 17 (1971): 546–54.

Van Der Meer, L. B. *The Bronze Liver of Piacenza.* Amsterdam, 1987.

Van Essen, C. C. "Elementi etruschi nel rinascimento toscano." *SE* 13 (1939): 497–99.

Vasari, G. *Le vite de' più eccellenti pittori, scultori, ed architettori.* 9 vols. Edited by G. Milanesi. Florence, 1878–85.

Vermeule, E. *Aspects of Death in Early Greek Art and Poetry.* Sather Classical Lectures, 46. Berkeley, Calif., 1979.

Vianello Cordova, A. P. "Una tomba 'protovillanoviana' a Veio." *SE* 35 (1967): 295–306.

Vighi, R. "Il sepolcreto arcaico del Sorbo." *MonAL* 42 (1955): 75.

Virgili, P. "A proposito del mausoleo di Augusto: Baldassare Peruzzi aveva ragione." *Archeologia laziale* 6 (1984): 209–12.

von Freytag gen. Löringhoff, B. *CSE* BRD 3. Munich, 1990.

von Fritz, K. "The Reorganisation of the Roman Government in 366 B.C. and the So-called Licinio-Sextian Laws." *Historia* 1 (1950): 3–44.

von Hesberg, M. R. "Das Mausoleum Augusti." In *Kaiser Augustus und die verlorene Republik: Eine Ausstellung im Martin-Gropius-Bau, Berlin, 7. Juni–14. August 1988.* Edited by M. R. Hofter. Mainz am Rhein, 1988.

————. *Römische Grabbauten.* Darmstadt, 1992.

von Hesberg, M. R., and S. Panciera. *Das Mausoleum des Augustus: Der Bau und seine Inschriften.* Bayerische Akademie der Wissenschaften, Philosophisch-Historische Klasse, 108. Munich, 1994.

Ward-Perkins, J. B. *Roman Imperial Architecture.* Pelican History of Art. Harmondsworth, Engl., 1985.

Watzinger, C. "Mimologen." *MDAI(A)* 26 (1901): 1–8.

Waurick, G. "Untersuchungen zur Lage der römischen Kaisergräber in der Zeit von Augustus bis Constantin." *JRGZ(M)* 20 (1973): 107–46.

Weege, F. *Etruskische Malerei.* Halle, Ger., 1921.

Weinberg, S. S. "Corinthian Relief Ware: Pre-Hellenistic Period." *Hesperia* 23 (1954): 111–37.

Weinman, I. B. *Malstria-Malena: Metals and Motifs in Etruscan Mirror Craft.* Studies in Mediterranean Archeology, 91. Göteborg, Swed., 1990.

Weiss, R. *The Renaissance Discovery of Classical Antiquity.* Oxford, 1969.

Werner, R. *Der Beginn der römischen Republik.* Munich, 1963.

Westendorp Boerma, R. E. H. "L'Enigme de l'appendix Vergiliana." In *Vergiliana.* Edited by H. Bardon and R. Verdière. Leiden, 1971.

Wheeler, R. E. M. *Roman Art and Architecture.* London, 1987.

White, P. "Maecenas' Retirement." *CPh* 86 (1991): 130–38.

———. *Promised Verse: Poets in the Society of Augustan Rome.* Cambridge, Mass., 1994.

Wikander, O. "Ancient Roof Tiles: Use and Function." *OAth* 17.15 (1988): 203–5.

Wilcox, D. J. *The Development of Florentine Humanist Historiography in the Fifteenth Century.* Harvard Historical Studies, 82. Cambridge, Mass., 1969.

Wilk, S. B. *Fifteenth-Century Central Italian Sculpture: An Annotated Bibliography.* Boston, 1986.

Wille, G. *Musica Romana: Die Bedeutung der Musik im Leben der Römer.* Amsterdam, 1967.

Williams, G. "Did Maecenas 'Fall from Favor?' Augustus' Literary Patronage." In *Between Republic and Empire: Interpretations of Augustus and His Principate.* Edited by K. Raaflaub and M. Toher. Berkeley and Los Angeles, 1990.

Winfield-Hansen, H. "Les Couloirs annulaires dans l'architecture funéraire antique." *AAAH* 4 (1965): 35–63.

Wiseman, T. P. "Some Republican Senators and Their Tribes." *CQ* 14 (1964): 122–33.

———. *New Men in the Roman Senate, 139 B.C.–14 A.D.* Oxford, 1971.

Wissowa, G. *Religion und Kultus der Römer.* 2d ed. Munich, 1912.

Wycherly, R. E. "Hippodamus and Rhodos." *Historia* 13 (1964): 135–39.

Yellen, J. E. *Archaeological Approaches to the Present: Models for Reconstructing the Past.* New York, 1977.

Zamarchi Grassi, P. "Cortona: Il II Melone del Sodo in Rassegna degli scavi e delle scoperte." *SE* 57 (1992): 135.

———. *La Cortona dei principes.* Cortona, It., 1992.

Zanker, P. *Il foro di Augusto.* Rome, 1984.

———. *The Power of Images in the Age of Augustus.* Ann Arbor, Mich., 1988.

Zazoff, P. *Etruskische Skarabäen.* Mainz am Rhein, 1968.

Zevi, F. "Il mito di Enea nella documentazione archeologica: Nuove considerazioni." In *L'epos greco in Occidente: Atti del diciannovesimo convegno di studi sulla Magna Grecia, Taranto, 7–12 ottobre 1979.* Taranto, It., 1980.

Zimmer, G. *Spiegel in Antikenmuseum: Bilderheft des Staatlichen Museen Preussischer Kulturbesitz.* Heft 52. Berlin, 1987.

Contributors

STEVEN BULE. Associate Professor of Art History, Brigham Young University; Ph.D., Ohio State University.

ALEXANDRA CARPINO. Assistant Professor of Art History, University of Michigan–Dearborn; Ph.D., University of Iowa.

NANCY THOMSON DE GRUMMOND. Professor and Department Chair of Classics, Florida State University; Ph.D., University of North Carolina.

HELENA FRACCHIA. Professor of Classics, University of Alberta; Ph.D., University of California–Berkeley.

JOHN F. HALL. Associate Professor of Classics and Ancient History and Department Chair of Humanities, Classics, and Comparative Literature, Brigham Young University; Ph.D., University of Pennsylvania.

MARK J. JOHNSON. Assistant Professor of Art History, Brigham Young University; Ph.D., Princeton University.

ROGER T. MACFARLANE. Assistant Professor of Classics, Brigham Young University; Ph.D., University of Michigan–Ann Arbor.

ROBERT L. MAXWELL. Rare Books Librarian, Brigham Young University; Ph.D., University of Toronto.

MARY E. MOSER. Associate Professor of Classical Studies, Dickinson College; Ph.D., University of Pennsylvania.

HELEN NAGY. Associate Professor of Art, University of Puget Sound; Ph.D., University of California–Berkeley.

ROBERT E. A. PALMER. Professor of Classical Studies, University of Pennsylvania; Ph.D., Johns Hopkins University.

LISA PIERACCINI. Instructor of Classical Archaeology, St. Mary's College of California; Ph.D. candidate, University of California–Santa Barbara.

HARRISON POWLEY. Professor of Music, Brigham Young University; Ph.D., University of Rochester.

DOROTHY DVORSKY ROHNER. Adjunct Lecturer in Classics, Metropolitan State College of Denver and Community College of Denver; Ph.D., University of Colorado.

General Index

———

Names of individuals, family groups, and geographic locations are listed in the Index of People and Places. All events (historical or mythical), monuments, artifacts, art objects, literary works, and locations such as plazas and buildings are found in this index, including those named for people or places. Page numbers in *italic type* indicate illustrations.

Actium, battle of, 242, 250, 368
Aeneas: statue of, carrying Anchises, *240*, 241; tomb/heroon of, 231–34, *232*, 238n
Aeneid (Vergil), 217, 248–49, 252, 261n
afterlife, Etruscan beliefs concerning, 70–71, 83, 87n. *See also* architecture, funerary, Etruscan; art, Etruscan; religion, Etruscan
age-specific areas, in domestic architecture. *See* gender-, age-, or class-specific areas, in domestic architecture
Allegory of Good Government (Lorenzetti), *306*, 307, 317
alphabet, 354, 362
annales maximi, 151
Annunciation relief (Pisano), 319, *320*
anthropology, as tool for study of Etruscans, 6, 12, 337–40, 362
Appendix Vergiliana, 263–64n; quoted, 245
Ara Maxima, 250
Ara Pacis Augustae, 218, 234
archaeology: as tool for study of Etruscans, 6–8, 9, 11, 30, 150, 151–52, 153, 172–73nn, 287, 293, 298; settlement, 29–37, 191–211. *See also* ethnoarchaeology; excavations, archaeological
Archaic period, 194, 209, 345, 349; early, architecture of, 119–25, *120*, *122–23*; later, architecture of, 119, 125–33, *125*, *130–31*, *133*, *138*
architecture, domestic: Etruscan, 10, 115, 117, 118–32, *120*, *122–23*, *130–31*, *133*, 134, 139, 141n, 227, 229; Greek, 10, 115, 134, *135*, 144n, 347, 364n; Roman, 10, 115, 137–38, *137*, 345; Tuscan, 341, 343–50, 362. *See also* doors; hut; masonry; pavements; roofs

architecture, funerary, 370, 372; Etruscan, 115, 132, *133*, 139, 145n, 227–29, 320; Greek, 134, *136*, 137, 139, 145n; Roman, 11, 138, 217–18, 222–29, *224–26*, 231. *See also* Augustus, mausoleum of; tombs, Etruscan; tombs, Roman; tumulus tombs
architecture, temple: Etruscan, 115, 132, *133*, *138*, 139; Greek, 134–37, *136*, 139, 144n, 230–31; Roman, 138, 227. *See also* Capitoline Temple
Argo, 74–75, 77
aristocracy, Roman and Etruscan, relations between, 198. *See also* Roman government, Etruscans in
Arringatore ("The Orator"), *xiv*, xv, 9, 18, 198
art, Etruscan, 12, 310–11, 312, 313, 320, 322–30, *325*, *327*, *329*; funerary, 11, 70, 269–71, *270–71*, 275–81, *275*, *277–79*, *281–83*, *286*, 288, 289, 293, 296–98, 300n, 310, 342; sarcophagi and ash urns, *iv–v*, vi, 318, *319*, 337–40, *339*, 343, *344*, *358*, 359; and judgment of Paris, 51–52. *See also* bronze artifacts, Etruscan; dolio (dolii); gems, carved Etruscan; mirrors, Etruscan; women, depiction of, in Etruscan art; *names of individual art pieces*
art, Renaissance, Etruscan influences on. *See* Renaissance, art, Etruscan influences
athletic contests, 274–75, 276, 278, 281, 293, 294, 296
augurs and augury, 155–56, 193, 259n, 294, 365n
Augustan period, 193, 196, 198, 203, 207, 210, 214n, 224, 243

Index of People and Places

Most places named in this index that are located in or near Etruria can be found on the maps on pages 2 and 195. The main index entry for these place names is spelled as commonly found in modern American atlases; where known, Etruscan, Roman, and modern Italian spellings—in that order—appear in parentheses immediately following the main entry. Page numbers in *italic type* indicate an illustration of a person, place, or item found at a place. Entries for names of Etruscan families may also include variants of the name listed in parentheses. With a few exceptions, individuals are indexed by the name by which they are most familiarly known, or by which they are identified in this volume; the full name or some other identifier may be given in parentheses where necessary for clarity.

A NOTE ON THE TYPES

The titles for *Etruscan Italy* were set in Felix Titling, a display face based on the inscriptional letters designed by Felice Feliciano of Verona in 1463. The manuscript is in the Vatican Library and was reproduced in the Italian periodical *La bibliofilia* in 1935 and in an edition by Dr. Giovanni Mardersteig entitled *Alphabetum Romanum*, published in 1960 at Verona.

The text of this book was set in Monotype Fournier, a typeface drawn from the types cut in 1742 by Pierre Simon Fournier (1712–1768), a Parisian type founder, and called "St. Augustin Ordinaire" in Fournier's *Manuel typographique* (2 vols., 1764–66). These types were some of the most influential designs of the eighteenth century, being among the earliest of the transitional style of typefaces, and were a steppingstone to the more severe modern style made popular by Bodoni later in the century. Fournier's types had more vertical stress than the old-style types, greater contrast between thick and thin strokes, and little or no bracketing on the serifs. His italic—a modernized form of the handsomer, more irregular early letter—was an immediate success. In addition to designing a number of typographic ornaments, he also devised, in 1737, the first point system for measuring and naming sizes of type. This adaptation of Fournier was released by the Monotype Drawing Office in 1924.

Typography by Jonathan Saltzman